A Grammar of Lele

STANFORD MONOGRAPHS IN AFRICAN LANGUAGES

William R. Leben and Larry M. Hyman
Series Editors

The aim of the series is to disseminate information about as many African languages as possible, especially about ones that have been to some extent neglected in the past, and to focus on primary materials, such as word lists, paradigms, and grammatical sketches.

A Grammar of Lele

Zygmunt Frajzyngier

CSLI PUBLICATIONS
Center for the Study of
Language and Information
STANFORD, CALIFORNIA

Center for the Study of Language and Information
Leland Stanford Junior University
Printed in the United States
05 04 03 02 01 5 4 3 2 1

Library of Congress Cataloging-In-Publication Data

Frajzyngier, Zygmunt.
A grammar of Lele / Zygmunt Frajzyngier.
p. cm.
ISBN 1-57586-257-3 (alk. paper)
1. Lele language (Chad)--Grammar. I. Title.
PL8453.151 .F73 2001
493'.7--dc21

2001025232
CIP

∞ The acid-free paper used in this book meets the minimum requirements of the American National Standard for Information Sciences — Permanence of Paper for Printed Library Materials, ANSI Z39.48-1984.

Please visit our website at
`http://cslipublications.stanford.edu/`
for comments on this and other titles, as well as for changes and corrections by the author and publisher.

Contents

Acknowledgements		xv
Abbreviations		xvii
1	**Introduction**	**1**
1	Geographical Information	1
2	Sources	2
3	A Brief Outline of Lele Grammar	3
3.1	Phonology	3
3.2	Lexical Categories	3
3.3	Morphology	4
2	**Phonology**	**7**
1	Introduction	7
2	Inventory and Phonotactics of Consonants	7
2.1	Inventory of Consonants	7
2.2	Intervocalic Voicing	11
2.3	Constraints on Consonants in Word-final Position	11
2.4	The *CVCVr/n Constraint	15
2.5	Word-final Devoicing	18
2.6	Velar Stop Palatalization	19
2.7	Consonant Clusters	19
2.8	Clusters with Nasal Consonants and Nasalization of Vowels	20
2.9	Nasal Dissimilation	23
2.10	Liquid --- stop	25
2.11	The Constraint *α lace αplace	26
3	The Vowel System	27
3.1	The Inventory of Vowels	27
3.2	The Vowel Insertion Rule	28
4	Vowel Harmony Rules	29

4.2	High-low Vowel Harmony	31
4.3	Barriers to Front-back Vowel Harmony	32
5	The Tonal System	38
5.1	Tonal Inventory and the Functions of Tone	38
5.2	Tone and Vowel Deletion	39
5.3	Tone Insertion in Syllabification	39
5.4	Tone and Syllabic Structure	40
6	The Morphology of the Verb	43
6.1	The Underlying Form of the Verb	43
6.2	The Formation of the Future and Nominal form	49
6.3	Summary of the Derivation of Verbal Forms	50
7	Conclusions	51
3	**The Structure of the Noun Phrase**	**53**
1	Defining Characteristics of the Noun Phrase	53
2	Phonological structure of nouns	53
3	Major and minor semantic classes	55
4	Gender	55
5	The nominal plural	56
5.1	The Plural Suffix	56
5.2	Plural through Insertion of a	57
5.3	Plural Suffix we	57
5.4	Plural through the Initial Devoicing	58
5.5	Suppletive Plurals	58
6	Nouns without Singular-plural Distinction	59
7	Collective	60
8	Possessive Constructions	60
8.1	Possessive Pronouns for Inalienable Possession	60
8.2	The Tonal Structure of Possessive Pronouns	64
8.3	Inalienable Possessive Constructions and Nominal Possessors	66
8.4	On the Nature of 'Inalienable' Nouns	68
8.5	Pronominal Alienable Possession	69
8.6	Alienable Nominal Possessive	70
8.7	Functions of Alienable and Inalienable Constructions	72
8.8	Coreference and Disjoint Reference in Possessive Constructions	74
9	Modification of One Noun by Another	74
9.1	The Coding of Attributes	75
9.2	Coding the Domain de Dicto of the Head Noun	76
9.3	Coding the Domain de Re of the Head Noun	76
10	Nouns Modified by Verbs	78
11	Nouns Modified by Demonstratives	79
12	Indefinite Modifiers	82
13	Nouns Modified by Quantifiers	83
14	Nouns Modified by Intensifiers	87

15	Nouns Modified by Property Concepts	88
15.1	The Attributive Function through Configuration	88
15.2	Coding the Referentiality of the Head of a Modifying Construction	89
15.3	Referentiality of the Head Coded on a Property Concept Verb	91
16	A Noun Modified by a Numeral	93
17	Attributive Constructions with Numerals	95
18	Conjoined Noun Phrases N and N	96
19	Conclusions	97
4	**Coding Arguments**	**99**
1	Introduction	99
2	The Category 'subject'	99
2.1	Pronominal Subjects	100
2.2	Unspecified Subjects: Human and Locative	101
2.3	Conjoined Nouns in the Subject Function	104
3	The Argument Structure of Verbs of Being and Becoming	104
4	Property Concept Verbs	105
5	Transitive and Intransitive Verbs	107
6	Arguments of Transitive Verbs	109
7	Interaction of Subject and Object Pronouns	111
8	Unspecified Objects: Human, Non-human, and Place	113
9	Argument Structure of Verbs of Fearing and Loving	114
10	The Argument Structure of the Verb jé 'throw'	115
11	Predication of Internal States	116
12	The Argument Structure of the Verb sí 'put, resemble'	117
13	Serial Verb Constructions	118
13.1	Formal Properties of Serial Verb Constructions	118
13.2	The Adverbial Function of Serial Verb Constructions	121
13.3	The Addition of an Argument through Serial Verb Construction	123
13.4	Serial Verb Construction with Different Objects	123
14	Coding the Plurality of Verbs	124
14.1	Forms of Verbal Plurality	124
14.2	The Functions of Verbal Plurality	126
14.3	Verbs without Plural Forms	128
15	Dative and Benefactive Arguments	130
15.1	Double Object Constructions	130
15.2	Coding the Dative through the Preposition	132
16	The Affectedness of the Subject and Reciprocal Coding	136
17	Source	137
18	The Associative Construction	138
19	Coding the Topic of a Mental Verb	140
20	Coding the Affectedness of the Subject:	142
21	Coding the Affectedness of the Subject:	145

22	Locative Argument Marking	147
22.1	Semantic Properties of Verbs of Movement	147
22.2	Inherently Locative Nouns with Directional Verbs	148
22.3	Coding the Locative through Prepositions	149
22.4	Coding the Locative through the Postposition ni	150
22.5	Spatial Orientation with Respect to the Deictic Center	151
22.6	Animate Locatives	153
22.7	The Nominal Object of the Verb è 'go'	154
23	Conclusions	155
5	**Adjuncts**	**157**
1	Introduction	157
2	Locative Adverbs	157
3	Adverbs of Time	159
4	Adverbs of Manner	162
4.1	Inherent adverbs	162
4.2	Adverbial Expressions with a Copula and Negation	164
5	Ideophones	164
6	Adverbs through Reduplication	166
7	Non-inherent Adverbs	166
8	Conclusions	167
6	**Tenses**	**169**
1	Introduction	169
2	The Past Form	169
3	Past and Present Tense through the Nominalized Form	173
4	Future Tenses	174
4.1	Inflectional Future	174
4.2	The Future with the Auxiliary éè 'go'	174
5	Conclusions	176
7	**Aspect and Pragmatically Dependent Causes**	**177**
1	Introduction	177
2	The Telic	177
2.1	Form and Function of Telic	177
2.2.	Grammaticalization of the Telic	180
3	The Inceptive	181
3.1	The Form and Function of Inceptive Aspect	181
3.2	Grammaticalization of the Inceptive Marker	184
4	The Durative	185
5	Pragmatic Dependency	186
6	Conclusions	191
8	**Coding the Deixis of an Event**	**193**
1	Introduction	193
2	The Ventive	193
2.1	The Form and the Function of Ventive	193
2.2	Grammaticalization of the Ventive	196
2.3	Lexicalization of the Ventive Construction	196

3	The Allative	197
4	Conclusions	198
9	**Equational Clauses**	**199**
1	The Scope of the Chapter	199
2	Equational Clauses	199
3	Identificational Clauses	202
4	The Grammaticalization of the Copula	203
5	Tense and Aspect in Equational Clauses	204
6	Equational Clauses with Property Concept Predicates	204
7	Conclusions	206
10	**Possessive, Locative and Existential Clauses**	**207**
1	Introduction	207
2	Possessive Clauses: X has Y	207
3	Tense in Possessive Clauses	210
4	Locative Sentences: X is Located at Y	212
5	Existential Clauses	213
6	Conclusions	214
11	**Reference System**	**217**
1	Introduction	217
2	Deixis	218
3	Definiteness	219
3.1	Form of the Definite Marker	219
3.2	Functions of the Definite Marker	221
3.3	Definiteness and Possessive Constructions	226
4	Referentiality	228
5	Indefiniteness	228
5.1	Coding the Indefiniteness of Arguments and Adjuncts	228
5.2	Coding Indefiniteness in the Background Information	230
6	The Subject Anaphora	232
7	The Role of Subject Pronouns	233
7.1	Third-person Subject Pronouns	234
7.2	Switch-reference in Complex Sentences	243
8	Anaphora for the Object	244
8.1	Overt Coding of Object and Human-non-human Distinction	244
8.2	Nominal Object Versus Unmarked Object	248
9	Coding the Adjunct through an Anaphor	251
10	Locative Deixis	255
11	Locative and Time Anaphoras	256
12	The Propositional Anaphora	259
13	Anaphora to the Verb	259
14	Conclusions	260
12	**Modality**	**261**
1	Introduction	261
2	Indicative Modality	261
3	Dubitative Modality	262

4	Hypothetical Modality	263
5	Imperative and Subjunctive Modalities	269
5.1	Giving Orders	269
5.2	The Subjunctive	270
6	Permission	273
7	Prohibitive Modality	274
8	The Coding of Sufficient Condition	275
9	Conclusions	275
13	**Interrogative Clauses**	**277**
1	Introduction	277
2	Questions about the Truth of the Proposition	277
3	Specific Interrogative Clauses	281
3.1	General Properties of Specific Interrogatives	281
3.2	Questions about the Subject	282
3.3	Questions about the Object	284
3.4	Questions about the Dative and other Prepositional Arguments	288
3.5	Questions about the Associative Argument	288
3.6	Questions about the Locative	289
3.7	Questions about Manner	290
3.8	Questions about the Reason	291
3.9	Questions about the Possessor	292
3.10	Questions about Time	294
4	Conclusions	294
14	**Negation**	**295**
1	Introduction	295
2	Negation of Equational Clauses	295
3	Negation of Possessive Clauses	296
4	Negation of Verbal Clauses	297
5	Negation and Quantification	298
6	Conclusions	300
15	**Focus Constructions**	**301**
1	Introduction	301
2	Contrastive Focus on the Subject	301
3	Non-contrastive Focus on the Subject	305
4	Focus on the Topic	308
5	The Intensifier and Focus	308
6	Focus on the Object and Definiteness	309
7	Focus on an Indirect Object	312
8	The Nominal Dative in Focus	313
9	The Pronominal Dative in Contrastive Focus	315
10	The Focus on Adjuncts	316
11	The Focus on an Associative Phrase	318
12	The Focus on a Propositional Anaphor	319
13	The Focus on a Nominal Predicate	319

14	The Focus on the Predicate	319
15	Conclusions	326
16	**Topicalization**	**327**
1	Introduction	327
2	Topicalization of a Subject	327
3	Topicalization of a Pronominal Subject	330
4	Topicalization of an Object	330
5	Conclusions	332
17	**Backgrounding**	**333**
1	Introduction	333
2	Formal Properties of Backgrounding	333
3	Specific Functions of Backgrounded Material	333
3.1	Adverbial Phrase of Time and Place	333
3.2	Backgrounded Information Introducing an Argument	335
3.3	Backgrounding for Counterexpectation	336
3.4	Backgrounding for Cause-and-effect Relationship	336
3.5	Setting the Circumstances for the Main Clause	338
4	Conclusions	340
18	**Paratactic and Conjoined Clauses**	**341**
1	Introduction	341
2	Paratactic Constructions	341
3	Coding Temporal and Causal Sequences	343
4	Adverb lay 'also' and Clausal Conjunctions	346
5	Coding the Unexpected Cause-and-effect	349
6	Same Subjects in Comment Clauses	354
7	Coding a Counterexpectation	356
8	Coding the Speaker's Contradiction	358
9	Conclusions	359
19	**Complementation**	**361**
1	Introduction	361
2	Complements of Verbs of Saying	361
3	The de Dicto Complementizer	362
4	Omission of the Verb of Saying and the Role of the Complementizer	363
5	Coreference and Disjoint Reference in Complementation	366
5.1	Coding Coreference	366
5.2	Coding Disjoint Reference	367
6	Dubitative Modality in Complementation	370
7	Dubitative Modality from the Point of View	371
8	Coding the Deontic Modality of the Embedded Clause	372
9	Direct Speech	374
10	Embedded Interrogatives	377
11	Specific Questions	378
11.1	Common Features of Embedded Specific Questions	378
11.2	Questions about the Locative	380

12 Causative and Pseudo-causative Constructions 380
13 Complements of the Verb è 'go' 382
14 Conclusions 382

20 Complementation through the Referential Marker 383

1 Introduction 383
2 Complements after Verbs of Knowing 383
3 Complements after Verbs of Perception (see, hear) 386
3.1 Coding of Direct Evidence 386
3.2 Hypothetical Modality with Verbs of Perception 389
4 Complements of Volitional Verbs 390
4.1 Volitional Verbs and their Complementizers 390
4.2 Same-subject Complements of Volitional Verbs 392
4.3 Realistic Wishes: the Complementizer go 392
4.4 Hypothetical Wishes with Respect to Same Subject 394
4.5 Different-subject Complements of Volitional Verbs 395
5 Complement of the Verb ɓàl 'be able to' 397
6 Conclusions 398

21 Complementation through Nominalization 399

1 Introduction 399
2 Nominalized Forms of the Verb and Possessive Constructions 399
3 Nominalization of Transitive Verbs 402
4 Nominalization of Intransitive Verbs 403
5 Conclusions 404

22 Adjunct Clauses 405

1 Introduction 405
2 Purpose 405
3 The Realis Modality of the Reason Clause 405
4 The Hypothetical Modality of the Purpose Clause 406
5 Unrealized Purpose 407
6 Reason Clauses 408
7 Temporal Adverb Clause 409
8 Conclusions 409

23 Temporal Sentences 411

1 Introduction 411
2 Temporal Protasis 411
3 Modality Coding in Temporal Protasis 413
4 Temporal Apodosis Clause 415
5 Conclusions 417

24 Conditional Sentences 419

1 Introduction 419
2 The Conditional Protasis 419
3 The Counterfactual Condition 423
4 The Conditional Apodosis 424

5	Conclusions	425
25	**Comparative Constructions**	**427**
1	Introduction	427
2	Non-predicative Comparisons	427
3	Equal Predicates	427
4	Unequal Comparison	431
5	Conclusions	433
26	**Relative Clauses**	**435**
1	Introduction	435
2	The Forms and Functions of Referential Markers	435
3	The Relativized Subject	438
4	The Relativized Object	439
5	The Relativized Indirect Object	445
6	The Relativized Locative	446
7	Relativized Time Adverbials	447
8	Relativized Associative Arguments	448
9	The Relativized Reason	450
10	Conclusions	450
27	**Elements of Discourse Structure in Lele**	**453**
1	Introduction	453
2	Coding of a New Event	453
3	Coding the (il)logical Consequence of Events	459
28	**A Sample of Lele Texts**	**461**
	A Story of three Wives	461
	Spider and Squirrel	466
	The Woman and the Chicken	471
	Hyena and Goat	473
	Story of a Theft	476
	Story of a Hunt	481
	The Woman who Betrayed her Husband	485
	References	491

Acknowledgements

The initial gathering of the data for this grammar was part of the project "The Complex Sentence in Chadic," supported by the NEH. The work was also supported by grants from the Graduate Committee on the Arts and Humanities, University of Colorado, and from the American Philosophical Society. Subsequent work was supported by the NSF. The ORSTOM station in Maroua served as the base for the project. Henry Tourneux provided invaluable support during my stays in Maroua in both logistics and in intellectual environment. To ORSTOM and its members go my sincere thanks for their hospitality in Maroua and the stimulating intellectual atmosphere there.

I would like to thank language assistants Houmina Pinabeye and Mathias Mupin for working with me on this project. Without their help I would not have been able to complete it.

Simone Ashby has been most attentive and skillful in entering the Lele texts into computer readable form and entering corrections in the grammar. I am most grateful to Marian Safran for her editorial work, without which this grammar would have been even more difficult to read. Mark Werner helped in the final formatting of the book.

Abbreviations

1	First-person
2	Second-person
3	Third-person
ALL	Allative
ANAPH	Anaphor
Ar.	Arabic
ASSC	Associative. Used for associative preposition **ná** and associative pronominal marker **ín-**.
COLL	Collective
COM	Comment clause marker **ba**
COP	Copula
DAT	Dative marker
DEF	Definite
DEM	Demonstrative
DU	Dual
DUB	Dubitative
EP	Epenthetic
EXCL	Exclusive
F	Feminine
Fr.	French
FUT	Future form of the verb
G	Glide
GEN	Genitive marker **kè** (M) or **tè** (F)
GEN:PL	Genitive plural marker **dí**
HUM	Unspecified human subject
HYP	Hypothetical marker and complementizer **na**
IMP	Imperative
IMPF	Imperfective

INCEPT	Inceptive
INCL	Inclusive
LOC	Locative postposition
M	Masculine
NEG	Negative marker
Ng.	Ngambay
NP	Noun Phrase
P	Proximate
PL	Plural
PREP	Preposition
PRO	Pronoun
Q	Interrogative marker
R	Remote
REF	Referential marker **go**, also masculine and plural relative clause marker
S	Sonorant or sentence. The context resolves the potential ambiguity.
SG	Singular
VENT	Ventive
VN	Verbal noun
xxx	Unidentified morpheme

1

Introduction

1 Geographical information

Lele, an East Chadic language (classified as such in Hoffmann 1971, Newman 1977), is spoken in Chad in the town of Kélo and in the canton south of Kélo (Weibegué and Palayer 1982). In 1974 Lele was spoken by some 33.000 people (Garrigues 1974). Its closest relatives are languages spoken to the east of Lele: Nancere, Gabri, and Kaba of Lai, all belonging to the same subgroup within the East Chadic branch. On the northern side Lele borders Marba and Mesme, Chadic languages from the Masa branch, a branch of Chadic different from the East Chadic branch. On the south Lele borders Ngambay, a language from the Adamawa group of the Niger-Congo family.

The information available on Lele consists of a vocabulary included in the dissertation of Garrigues (1974), a dictionary built on that vocabulary by Weibegué and Palayer (1982), a Lele reader by Garrigues-Cresswell with assistance from Weibegué (1981), which includes grammatical notes by Palayer, a collection of texts and conversations by Weibegué (n.d.), and an unpublished Lele-French dictionary by Pamela Simons (n.d.). The dictionary by Weibegué and Palayer (1982) (W & P 1982 hereafter in this work) includes a page on Lele phonology. I have published a study of one type of complementation in Lele (Frajzyngier 1995) and have used Lele data in several comparative studies. My analyses and transcriptions in the present work supersede the analyses and transcriptions used in my previous publications.

Some speakers of Lele claim the existence of dialectal distinctions within the language, with one dialect referred to as **lèlé go kùsíyǫ́ wìlé** 'Lele of the red soil, laterite' and other as **lèlé go kùsíyǫ́ bòré** 'Lele of the white soil, sand' (the absence of tone indicates mid tone). The latter dialect is supposed to be spoken in the triangle whose northern angle is the town of Kélo, whose southwestern corner is the town of Bologo, and whose eastern corner is the village of Mire. The present grammar is based on the variety spoken in Debreng. This dialect differs in phonology from the dialect represented in the texts included in Garrigues 1974. Information on many aspects of Lele culture can be found in the magnificent description in Garrigues 1974.

2 Sources

Data for the present grammar were gathered in summer 1990, spring 1993, and summer 1998. There were two language assistants for the project: Mr. Houmina Pinabeye (born May 15, 1956) and Mr. Mathias Mouping (born in 1971). The ability of Mr. Pinabeye, a high school teacher of French, to indicate very subtle differences in meaning was an extremely helpful factor in the work. Both language assistants belong to the same clan, and they speak the northeastern variety of Lele. Additional natural speech data were drawn from texts published in Garrigues-Cresswell and Weibegué 1981 (cited as G-C & W 1981 hereafter). Lexical entries in W & P 1982 were abundantly used in the illustration of phonological analyses. The material contained in W & P 1982 and other publications represents the southwestern dialect. The differences between the northern and southern varieties of Lele are noted in the present grammar if information is available.

In the spelling convention adopted in the works of Garrigues 1974, G-C & W 1981, W & P 1982, other publications by Weibegué, and New Testament translations, third-person subject and object pronouns are not separated from the verb, and possessive pronouns are not separated from the possessors or the genitive markers, as the case may be. The velar nasal is represented by the digraph **ng**. In my own transcription I decided to separate subject and object pronouns from verbs by a space. Possessive pronouns are separated from possessums by a hyphen. The reason for separating the morphemes is to enable the readers to identify the morphemes involved. The justification for this transcription is based on phonological criteria, mainly on whether the vowel harmony operates across the morphemes. If vowel harmony does operate, that means that the second morpheme is an affix. If vowel harmony does not operate, that means that the second morpheme is not an affix. The present work is based on two sources of data: texts gathered by myself and those gathered by Garrigues-Cresswell. In examples culled from Garrigues-Cresswell, I have inserted hyphens to separate morphemes. The two ways of representing the data should not introduce a difficulty in reading, since all examples coming from Garrigues-Cresswell are identified as such. Whenever my own tonal transcription had more than one variant for the same morpheme in the same function and in the same syntactic environment, I unified the transcription by choosing the variant that agreed with the representation in G-C & W 1981 or W & P 1982.

The present grammar makes no claims with respect to the proper spelling system for Lele. It is desirable, of course, to use characters with which people are familiar from French, and to avoid characters with which people are not familiar. So instead of a velar nasal **ŋ** a digraph **ng** is preferred. The glottalized **ɓ** and **ɗ** can be replaced with **d'** and **b'** in the official orthography, but the glottalized characters are becoming increasingly familiar across West Africa.

3 A brief outline of Lele grammar

3.1 Phonology

The phonological inventory of Lele includes consonants, vowels, and tones. The consonantal inventory includes some interesting asymmetries: It is characterized by just two continuants, **s** and **h**. The vowel system consists of five vowels, some of which may be long. Two constraints on word structure and consonant clusters account for much of the shape of individual words: (1) No consonant clusters are allowed in word-initial and word-final position; (2) the consonants **s**, **d**, **k**, and **j** may not occur word-finally. Whenever a consonant cluster or a disallowed consonant would occur in word-final position, an epenthetic vowel is added to prevent the violation of these conditions. The complex phonetic segments, viz., labiovelars and prenasalized stops, display a dual nature: on the one hand, they behave like single segments in that they can form consonant clusters in intervocalic position, and on the other hand, they cannot occur in word-final position, thus having the property of consonantal clusters. The language does not allow a cluster of consonants produced in the same place. This constraint rules out geminated consonants at the phonetic level. The geminated consonants are, however, allowed at the underlying level. Although the language does not allow consonant clusters in word-final position in the phonetic realization, such clusters do exist in the underlying form and are responsible for the lowering of the preceding high vowel. The different conditions at the phonetic and phonological level explain the form of many morphemes and the presence of mid vowels in verbs. The language has vowel harmony. In Lele vowel harmony is not a result of the operation of phonological, syntactic, or morphological rules, but rather is a means to code the relationship between some morphemes.

3.2 Lexical categories

In the present work the defining characteristic of the lexical category is its role in a larger construction. Thus a verb is a category whose function is to code the predicate, a noun inherently codes an argument, an adjective inherently modifies a noun, and an adverb inherently modifies a verb. The number of adjectives is quite limited, and the language has developed several means of coding modification when the relevant semantic feature has been lexicalized in a category other than verb. Within the class of adverbs there is a subclass of ideophones, characterized by a very limited syntactic distribution, usually confined to one specific verb. Ideophones very often have a phonological structure different from that of other words. There are a limited number of words whose function is simply that of modifier, and they can be used as modifiers of nouns or verbs. Intensifiers are a class of words that relate the whole clause to some other proposition, whether or not actually produced in discourse. The scope of the intensifier is, however, one specific element of the proposition and is different in different clauses.

3.3 Morphology

The vowel harmony rules operating in the language allow a three-way division of the types of morphemes: suffixes, which undergo vowel harmony rules; clitics, which must occur in specified contexts but do not undergo vowel harmony rules; and free morphemes, which also do not undergo vowel harmony rules but have relatively free distribution in the utterance. The inflectional morphology is not very rich: the category verb displays only four subcategories, labeled in the grammar as ‘past’, ‘future’, 'imperative', and ‘verbal noun’. Nouns can have only two categories, singular and plural. There are no inflectional forms for other categories.

3.4 Syntax

Given the relatively limited number of morphological means, it is not surprising to find a very rich system of syntactic constructions in Lele.

The general pattern within the noun phrase is head-modifier. If the modifier is nominal, there are two particles coding the existential status of the head: potential, hypothetical, marked by the hypothetical marker **na**; and actual, specific, marked by the referential marker **go**. Lele has two possessive constructions, one coding alienable possession and the other inalienable possession. The construction coding alienable possession differs from other noun phrases in Lele in that it has the structure modifier-head.

Lele has the categories of subject and object. The nominal subject is coded by position preceding the verb, and the object is coded by position following the verb. First- and second-person pronominal subjects and unspecified human subject forms precede the verb. Third-person singular and plural pronominal subjects follow the verb. If both the subject and the object are third-person pronominal, the subject precedes the object in preverbal position. First- and second-person pronominal objects precede third-person subject pronouns in postverbal position. The locative argument is coded in different ways, depending on the class of the noun that serves as the head of the locative adjunct. Both prepositions and postpositions are deployed for the coding of the locative. Verbs that cannot have three arguments coded by configuration deploy serial verb constructions for the coding of arguments.

There is no particular semantic role associated with the syntactic category subject or object. These categories have different semantic roles associated with different classes of predicates. Of particular interest is a class of predicates that have lexicalized the internal states of humans. These predicates have the human participant as the object, and the internal state as the subject.

Modality is coded by several means. The unmarked clause codes the speaker's belief in the truth of the proposition. The hypothetical modality is coded by clause-initial markers. One of the most fundamental characteristics of Lele is that the hypothetical modality is a distinction made not only at the clausal level but also throughout many functional domains, such as modification of a noun by another noun, clausal complementation, and conditional protasis and apodosis. Doubt in truth is coded by clause-final markers. Negation and interrogative modality are also coded by clause-final markers. Deontic modality is coded by inflectional forms of the verb. Clauses coded by deontic modality have an interesting syntactic property: The order of subject pronouns in the imperative clause is different from the order in the indicative clause. The order of pronouns in the subjunctive is again different from the one in the imperative.

The inflectional tense system is limited to the distinction between future and non-future tenses. There are, however, auxiliary verbs that allow a narrower specification of the time of the event with respect to other events in discourse. Aspectual distinctions are also coded by the system of auxiliary verbs. Of special interest is the existence of the inceptive aspect, coded by the auxiliary **se**, identical with the verb 'rise, get up', and the stative aspect, coded by the auxiliaries **jèn** 'remain' or **ìr̒**'stand'.

There are two types of focus constructions: contrastive focus for the subject, whereby a nominal or pronominal subject is additionally coded by an independent pronoun; and non-contrastive focus, for all arguments and adjuncts where the speaker makes one part of a proposition salient, or newsworthy. There are two means of coding non-contrastive focus: through the fronting of the focused element and through retaining the element in the position it has in a pragmatically neutral clause. If the element is not fronted, it is marked for the focus function by the copula **nè**. Every element of the clause, including the predicate, may be marked for focus by the form **nè**. If the element is fronted, it is separated from the rest of the sentence, i.e. from the comment on the focus construction, by the form **ba**. Since the subject occurs in clause-initial position, whenever the subject is in focus, it is separated from the comment clause by the form **ba.** The focused element in clause-initial position may be preceded by the copula **nè**.

Topicalization involves the fronting of the topicalized element. Topicalization differs from focus construction in that the topicalized element does not have to be part of the ensuing clause, and it is never separated from the ensuing clause by an overt marker of the type of construction.

Complex sentence formation is characterized by the presence of paratactic constructions, i.e. constructions where two or more clauses are not conjoined by a conjunction of any kind. This type of construction codes a sequence of events, usually in the order in which they occurred in reality.

Lele has a backgrounding construction whereby at the beginning of the sentence there is information that provides background to whatever follows. The backgrounded portion of the sentence is coded by the associative marker **ná**. The backgrounded part may be a clause or an adverbial phrase of time, place, or some other circumstance.

Relative clauses are post-nominal, i.e., the head precedes the relative clause. The syntactic function of the head of the relative clause is coded by the presence of other arguments for the roles subject and object, and by anaphoric pronouns for other arguments and adjuncts. The associative argument, however, is coded by the associative preposition **ná** following the verb.

2

Phonology

1 Introduction

The phonetic inventory of Lele and some contrasts between segments are presented in Weibegué 1992. Simons and Burquest 1986 is a study of nasalization in Lele. The present chapter concentrates on phonological rules and other aspects of Lele phonology not covered in those previous works, and it also provides alternative analyses for the discussion of individual segments presented there. More specifically, the chapter describes constraints on syllable structure, functions and mechanisms of vowel harmony, effects of syllable structure on vowel quality, and tonal rules, actually, the interconnection between voicing and tone. The chapter is divided into two parts: a general study of phonology across morphological and lexical categories, and a study of the phonology of the verbal system, providing an opportunity to discover systematic phenomena that otherwise would be difficult to detect.

2 Inventory and phonotactics of consonants

2.1 Inventory of consonants

The following chart presents all consonantal segments. With the exception of the palatal nasal, all of these are underlying consonants as well.

Table 1 Consonants

	Labial	Alveolar	Palatal	Velar	Labio-velar	Glottal
Stops						
Voiceless	p	t		k	kp	
Voiced	b	d		g	gb	
Glottalized	ɓ	ɗ				
Prenasal	mb	nd			ŋb	
Continuants		s				h
Nasals	m	n	ɲ	ŋ		
Liquids		r				
		l				
Glides	w		y			

The consonantal chart presents certain interesting asymmetries. There is a rich series of prenasalized stops occurring with an equally rich series of stops and nasal consonants. There are only two continuants, voiceless alveolar **s** and glottal **h**. There is no voiceless labio-dental **f** or voiced **v** or **z**, all three of which have corresponding stops. All of these segments, with the exception of the palatal nasal, are phonemic in the sense that they are in contrast in at least one position. The following discussion provides evidence of the phonemic status of individual segments and their roles within the word and morpheme structure.

The phonological status of prenasalized stops **mb**, **nd,** and **ŋb**, as monosegmental stops, as opposed to a sequence of nasal and a stop, is provided by their distribution in word-initial and intervocalic position. The monosegmental nature of **mb** is also supported by loan words whose sources have a simple **m**: Arabic **jamal** 'camel' is **jámbàl** in Lele (W & P 1982: 109). In word-initial position the prenasalized stops are in contrast with simple voiced and voiceless stops and also with glottalized stops. Glottalized stops are voiceless. In all examples, verbs if otherwise not marked are quoted in the past form:

(1)	mbòbe	'wait' (VN)	bòlòm	'throwing knife
	mbóyrò	'evening'	bòr	'cut, break'
	ɓòdu	'monkey'	poryi	'lie'
	ɓìsì	'to have diarrhea'	pe	'dig'
(2)	ndoji	'be difficult'	dòjò	'war'
	ndu	'make noise'	du	'3F'
	ɗògì	'keep'	tom	'hit'
	ɗìmsì	'rest'	tùmò	'before'

An argument for the monosegmental status of prenasalized stops is provided by the fact that they can be part of an intervocalic cluster of consonants. Clusters of three consonants are disallowed in Lele, hence the sequence **Cmb** or **Cnd** or **ŋl** is a cluster of two rather than three consonants:

(3)	galmbo	'hunter's bag'	karmba	'half-brother'
	kùrmbàlò	'chief'		

(4)	nìŋlí	'make horizontal movements with the head to indicate negation'
	dòŋlè	'thigh'

The evidence for the monosegmental status of **ŋb** is provided by its distribution, viz. only in word-initial position where no consonant clusters occur (examples drawn from W & P 1982):

(5)	ngbàgàw	'naked, nakedness'
	ngbágsí	'bold'
	ngbéjí	'rat trap'
	ngbìgìw	'very fat'
	ngbìli	'beard, chin'
	ngbògòm	'cold'

The prenasalized stops do not occur, however, in word-final position. That would not be particularly significant for alveolar prenasalized stops, because no alveolar stop can occur in word-final position, but the prenasalized labial is not occurring in word-final position is significant in view of the fact that the simple labial stop, including the labial nasal, can occur in word-final position.

The contrast between velar consonants is illustrated by the following examples:

(6)	kùsá	'fish'	gur	'deceive'
	kìrè	'road'	gìr	'run'
	kpùsì	'level'	gbàdú	'cat'
	kpedili	'make an effort'	gbògló	'old mortar'
	hòb	'wet'		
	hir	'bite'		

The monosegmental rather than bisegmental status of labiovelar stops is supported by the general absence of consonantal clusters in word-initial position (the prenasalized stops are also analyzed as one segment). In addition, some labiovelar stops derive from simple labial stops, as is the case with **gbàdú** 'cat', for which W & P give Arabic **baatu** as the source (1982: 109).

A rather large number of words with initial **kp** are ideophones or onomatopeic. In W & P 1982 these words are categorized as 'descr.', i.e. descriptive. Out of ten entries with initial **kp** in W & P, six either are ideophones or have clearly onomatopoeic meaning:

(7)	kpajag	'about breaking in one hit'
	kpendel	'about breaking at the joint'
	kpo	'about broken things'
	kpujug	'about noise'
	kpung	'in mass'

A non-ideophone in the group of initial **kp** words is **kpá-kpá** 'sandals' (according to W & P 1982: 111 a borrowing from Sango).

Of the twelve entries with the initial **gb**, only one is onomatopoeic, viz. **gpujug** 'onomatopoeic of noise', a variant of **kpujug**. The presence of so many ideophones and onomatopoeia with the voiceless labiovelar and their absence with the voiced labiovelar indicate that the two consonants may actually have a different origin.

The glottal continuant **h** occurs only in word-initial position. It can be followed by all five vowels:

(8)	hab	'find'
	hàm	'search'
	hesí	'slaughter'
	hìb	'pour from one container into another'
	hòb	'wet'
	hun	'grow' (IMP)

Since all vowels can occur in word-initial position, the glottal continuant does not appear to be epenthetic.

Nasal consonants have an underlying contrast between labial, alveolar, and velar place of articulation. All three can occur in word-initial, intervocalic, and word-final position.

(9)	ŋàlàŋ	'trap,	ná	'associative prep.'	ma	'die'
	ŋ	'1SG'	sèn	'know'	ŋem	'keep'

The phonological status of **ŋ** as one segment is supported by the fact that it can occur in word-initial and word-final position, i.e. in positions where no consonant clusters can occur:

(10) ŋéleŋ 'natron'

The intervocalic clusters with **ŋ** as a second segment all involve reduplication. Reduplicated structures behave phonologically as if they consisted of two independent elements:

(11) ŋárŋàr 'prickly heat, a skin illness' (W & P 1982)
ŋòrŋòr 'an insect feeding on the leaves of the gourd'

The palatal nasal is an allophone of the alveolar nasal occurring only before the high front vowel **i**:

(12) [i] 'locative postposition'

Because it is an automatic result of the following high front vowel, the palatalization of the nasal is not further represented in the present work.

2.2 Intervocalic voicing

All stops and affricates in intervocalic position within a word must be voiced. As a result of this constraint, there is no intervocalic **t, k, p** or **c**:

C[-continuant] → [+voice]/ V___V

The evidence for this rule is provided by the distribution of the segments involved and also by the treatment of loan words. If a word has an intervocalic voiceless stop in the original language, this stop becomes voiced once the word is borrowed into Lele, e.g., Arabic **itir** 'aroma' becomes **ídìr** in Lele (W & P 1982: 109).

The only exception to this rule are words that appear to be derived through the process of partial or complete reduplication: **pèpę** 'grass, *Beckeropsis uniseta*', **pépéledí** 'bat, *pipistrel* Fr.'; **toto** 'nevertheless', **tùnòtúnó** 'gecko'. On the basis of the behavior of consonants when reduplication is involved, words formed through reduplication are postulated to behave like a sequence of words rather than like one word. The voiceless continuant **s** does occur in intervocalic position, e.g. **kusu** 'body', **gàsìlà** 'non-initiated boy'. The glottal continuant **h** does not occur in intervocalic position or in word-final position.

2.3 Constraints on consonants in word-final position

Alveolar consonants **j, c, d, s** and velar consonants **g** and **k** cannot occur in word-final position. Different rules operate with respect to the consonant **g** and with respect to **j, d, s,** and **k** in word-final position. Whenever one of these consonants would occur in word-final position, an epenthetic vowel is added at the end of the word. Further on in this work the term *epenthetic vowel* is used for both vowels inserted between consonants and vowels added at the end of words.

Although this latter usage does not constitute epenthesis in the traditional meaning of the word, the insertion and word-final addition are dictated by similar syllable and consonant cluster conditions. The sources of the epenthetic vowels differ, depending on the morphological history of the word. In words that never had a final vowel, the epenthetic vowel is high and has the feature round of the preceding vowel, as per the following rule:

Ø → V[high, αround]/CV[αround] C[j, d, s, c, k]____#

As a result of the constraint on word-final consonants and the rule that accommodates it, there are no word-final uses of **k**, **c**, **j**, **d**, and **s**. As the result of the intervocalic voicing rule, the distinction between **t**, **c**, and **k** and **d**, **j**, and **g** is neutralized in the intervocalic position. The distinction between the underlying word-final velar voiceless and voiced stop is maintained through different rules that apply to these consonants in word-final position.

The voiced stop **g** becomes a palatal glide in word-final position, while the voiceless **k** requires vowel insertion and consequently becomes a voiced velar stop. Here is an illustration of the rules at work. The past form of the verb consists of all consonants and the first vowel. To the nominal form of the verb **bògè** pour, put' corresponds the past form **bòy**. To the nominal form **dògè** 'submerge' corresponds the past form **dògì**. The reason why there is a vowel in the past form of the verb **dògì** is that it has an underlying **k** rather than **g**. The constraint on the non-occurrence of word-final ***k#** is resolved through vowel epenthesis if there is no vowel available, or vowel retention if the vowel deletion would produce word-final velar voiceless stop **k**.

The epenthetic vowel in nouns is not only identical with the vowel of the preceding syllable, but it also carries the tone of the preceding syllable. The constraint has far-reaching consequences for the phonetic realization of nouns and verbs in various syntactic contexts and also enables us to explain these alternations. As an illustration consider the behavior of the noun **kusu** 'body' when followed by possessive pronouns and when occurring without possessive pronouns. The form **kusu** has been recorded in expressions when it is followed by a lexical item rather than a grammatical morpheme:

(13) kusu hámlè kúrà ɗé
body light good NEG
'a light body is not good', e.g. in wrestling

(14) kusu eywá
body pleasant
'desire'

The presence of a word-final vowel when the word is followed by other lexical, rather than grammatical, morphemes would indicate that the vowel is underlying. This impression would be further reinforced by the form of the word when followed by the third-person feminine and the second-person masculine possessive pronouns, the first ending in a back vowel and the second consisting of the labial nasal:

(15) kusu-ro → [kusuro]
body-3F
'her body'

(16) kusu-m
body-2M
'your body'

But when the word is followed by a suffix with a consonant followed by a front vowel, the last vowel of the noun is fronted:

(17) kusi-ge
body-3PL
'their body'

kusi-re
body-2F
'your body'

kusi-ni
body-1PL.EXCL
'our bodies' (when talking to a member of the opposite sex)

The back vowel is also fronted when followed by a palatal glide suffix, again a predictable result:

(18) kus-iy
body-3M
'his body'

But consider the results of the addition of a suffix with the consonant cluster **ŋg**. If the word **kusu** were to have the underlying final **u**, the addition of the first-person dual suffix **nga** would result in the form ***kusu-nga**. But instead the resulting form has a high front vowel at the end of the verb:

(19) kusi-nga
body-1DU.INCL
'our bodies'

The presence of the vowel **i** rather than **u** after the noun **kus** indicates that word-final vowels **i** and **u** are both epenthetic. The epenthesis rules differ depending on the structure of the word. If there is no suffix, the feature round of the epenthetic vowel is determined by the vowel of the stem. If there is a suffix, the feature round is determined by the vowel of the suffix.

The first-person singular possessive form after nouns ending in a vowel is **niŋ**. One would expect therefore that the first-person possessive form for the word 'body' would be ***kusuniŋ**. But the form that actually occurs with the word 'body' is **iŋ**, the form added to nouns ending in a consonant:

(20) kus-in 'my body'

The addition of the first-person singular and the first-person dual inclusive indicates that the underlying form of the noun for body is **kus** and that the last vowel in the form **kusu** is epenthetic. Nevertheless, further on in this work this word will be represented as **kusu** rather than **kus**. One could counter the proposed hypothesis by claiming that the underlying form is indeed **kusu** and that the last vowel is deleted before the addition of the suffix. Such rules have been postulated for several Chadic languages. In Lele this rule cannot be maintained, because there are many examples where the final vowel is preserved before the addition of a suffix:

(21) tamą́-y
wife-3M
'his wife'

Not all CV1sV1 structures are underlyingly CV1s. The way to test whether the final vowel is underlying or epenthetic is to rule out those cases in which the final vowel may be a suffix that happens to have the same vowel as the preceding one, e.g. the verbal nouns of the verbs that have the first vowel **e**. Since all verbal nouns end in **e**, the final and the last vowel are accidentally identical: **ese** 'strength' (VN). The other means of testing is to add an inalienable possessive suffix. Although there are words with **s** and a final vowel identical with the preceding one, these words do not take an inalienable possessive suffix:

(22) **búsú** 'mist', **ɓàsà** 'pottery', **bisí** '*cephalophe* de Grimm'

The final test to be applied is the tonal structure. If the last tone is different from the preceding tone, chances are the last vowel is not epenthetic, as in the case of **bisí** '*cephalophe* de Grimm'. If the last tone is identical with the preceding tone, the question of whether the last vowel is epenthetic or underlying cannot be resolved. This is the case for the words: **búsú** 'mist' and **ɓàsà** 'pottery'.

2.4 The *CVCVr/n constraint

There appears to exist a phonetic structure (not an underlying structure) constraint that does not allow bisyllabic words with an alveolar liquid or alveolar nasal in word-final position. The effects of this constraint allow us to explain a number of phonetic realizations that would otherwise appear to be idiosyncratic. Consider the formation of inalienable possessive constructions for nouns that have the consonant **r** when followed by possessive pronouns but have **r**-less alternations in forms without suffixes. For these nouns the underlying form is CVCVr. The word-final **r** is deleted when the word is in isolation:

r → Ø /CVCV(G)___#
where G stands for glide.

The noun **tumadu** means 'carcass' in inalienable constructions and 'death' in alienable constructions. In inalienable possessive constructions the noun has the suffix **r**:

(23) làmndá tumadur-iy
elephant carcass-3M
'carcass of an elephant'

Cf.:

(24) tumadu làmndá kè-y
death elephant GEN-3M
'death of an elephant'

(25) tumadu go làmndá yé-y kò-rò
death REF elephant mother-3M GEN-3F
'death of the mother of elephant'

The case of the noun **túgú** 'compound' is similar. In alienable constructions it is not followed by **r**:

(26) túgú kò-nòŋ
compound GEN-1SG
'my compound' (may be said only by the head of the family)

túgú kì-nì
compound GEN-1PL.EXCL
'our (EXCL) compound' (may be said by a wife or a child in the family)

In inalienable constructions the word is followed by the suffix **r**:

(27) túgr-íŋ
'my village'

(28) kìn dí túgr-íy (ni)
return 3M village-3M LOC
'he returned to his village'

Before a suffix beginning with **r**, viz. the second- and third-person feminine possessive suffixes, the sequence of two **r**s is reduced:

(29) kìn dú túg-ró (ni)
return 3F village-3F LOC
'she returned to her village'

(30) me kìn túg-ré ɗé gà
2F return village-2F NEG Q
'have you ever returned to your village?'

The deletion of the word-final **r** in structures CVCVr has resulted in some nouns having already been learned as having the structure CVCV. Consider the noun **kudo** 'husband'. The final **r** is preserved in only one variant of its plural forms **kode** and **kodere** (W & P **kodre**). The form with **r** is used before a possessive pronoun beginning with a vowel:

(31) koder-iŋ go súbù
husband:PL-1SG REF three
'my three husbands'

Here is an example of the underlying structure CVCVGr, which becomes in isolation CVCVG. Consider the noun whose quotation form is **dìngàw** 'ferocity':

(32 dìngàw dí-gè
ferocity GEN:PL-3PL
'their ferocity'

(33) dìngàw dú-ngù
ferocity GEN:PL-2PL
'your (PL) ferocity'

In the second- and third-person masculine the consonant **r** makes an appearance:

(34) dìngàwr-ìy
ferocity-3M
'his ferocity' (about wild animals)

(35) dìngàwr-ùm
ferocity-2M
'your (M) ferocity'

The simplest solution is to postulate that the noun ends in the consonant **r**. If there are no affixes to the noun, the word-final **r** is deleted because consonantal clusters are not allowed in word-final position. When a vocalic suffix is added, the consonant is fully realized. Similarly, when the second-person masculine suffix **m** is added, an epenthetic vowel is inserted before the possessive suffix and the final consonant is realized again.

The third- and second-person feminine have the form as if the word ended in a vowel. This must result from the geminate reduction rule r + r → r:

(36) dìngàw-rò
ferocity-3F
'her ferocity'

dìngàw-rè
ferocity-2F
'your (F) ferocity'

The most important element in the deletion of the final **r** is the number of syllables preceding it. If there is only one syllable, the word-final **r** is not deleted:

(37)
sir	'cut'
ír	'stand'
hìr	'clarity, cleanliness'
gùr	'run' IMP
ur	'sin'

Some word-final **r**s are a result of the reduction of a cluster consisting of two **r**s or of **r** and some other consonant produced in the same place of articulation. The evidence for the existence of the root-final (underlying form-final) cluster is provided by the vowel lowering for verbs that have an underlying high vowel (cluster reduction and vowel lowering are described later in this chapter):

(38) lor 'burn' lura 'burn' (IMP)

The existence of the constraint on the word-final nasal in polysyllabic words is provided by the alternations of the noun **tamá** 'woman' as occurring in isolation. When this noun is followed by the third-person masculine singular possessive pronoun **y**, the noun is realized as **tamą́-y**, i.e., it has the nasal vowel **ą**. Simons and Burquest 1986 attribute the nasalization to a retention of the nasal consonant, which they claim must have once been a characteristic of the third-person singular masculine possessive pronoun. Such an explanation cannot be retained, because there are forms with the third-person possessive pronoun that do not have a nasal vowel:

(39) gùbà 'knee' gùbà-y 'his knee'

If we postulate, however, that the underlying structure for the noun 'woman' is **tamán**, the addition of the third-person masculine pronoun **y** would result in a disallowed word-final consonant cluster **ny**. The reduction of this cluster results in the nasalization of the preceding vowel, yielding the form **tamą́-y**. The isolation form **tamá** is simply a result of word-final consonant deletion.

There are word-final alveolar nasals in Lele, but again, as in the case of the alveolar liquids, only in monosyllabic words. Moreover, these words have special characteristics that account for the occurrence of the word-final alveolar nasal.

The verb **jèn** 'remain' is a result of word-final cluster reduction, of which one element, the first one, is the alveolar nasal. Evidence for the presence of the cluster is provided by the vowel lowering in the past tense form. The imperative form has the high vowel **jìnà**. The few nouns that have word-final **n** in their underlying structure are all body parts, i.e. nouns that seldom if ever occur in isolation, and thus in their use do not provide an environment for word-final nasal deletion:

(40) gìn 'forehead'
gàn 'leg'

2.5 Word-final devoicing

There is only one stop allowed in word-final position, the voiceless labial **p**, e.g. [tòp] 'want'. In intervocalic position it is realized as a voiced stop, e.g. the nominalized form [tòbè]. This poses a problem for the choice of the underlying consonant. If one postulates that the underlying form is voiceless, the rule of intervocalic voicing will account for voiced variants. If one postulates underlying voiced segments, then the rule of word-final devoicing will account for the voiceless variants. Given the fact that both rules are valid, the labial stop is represented henceforth as **b**.

The stops are voiceless even if followed by a voiced stop (but not a liquid) in a subsequent morpheme:

(41)	hab gèylè	→	[hapgèylè]
	find health		

2.6 Velar stop palatalization

The velar voiced stop becomes a palatal glide in front of another consonant and in word-final position: g → y /____C,#. Consider the verb /bòg/ 'put'. Evidence for the underlying **g** in this verb is provided by the forms that obtain when the verb is followed by a vowel, e.g. when the verb precedes an object pronoun that begins with a vowel or when it is in the future tense, thus ending in the vowel **e**:

(42)	bòg-ìŋ	dú	sòndró
	put-1SG	3F	fear
	'she frightened me'		

(43)	bòg-ìy	dí	sòndró
	put-3M	3M	fear
	'he frightened him'		

(44)	bóge-ŋ	dú	sòndró
	put:FUT-1SG	3F	fear
	'she will frighten me'		

If the voiced velar stop **g** is followed by another consonant, including a glide, the velar voiced stop becomes palatal glide:

(45)	ŋ	bòy-dù	sòndró
	1SG	put-3M-3F	fear
	'I frightened her'		

(46)	ŋ	bòy-gè	sòndró
	1SG	put-3PL	fear
	'I frightened them'		

The case is similar with the verb **àg** 'take'. In the past tense this verb is realized as [ày]. When the third-person masculine object pronoun is added, the verb has the form [àgìy] 'he took him'. Before another consonant the velar stop also becomes a palatal glide [ą́y-dú] 'he took her'. In the future tense, when the verb is followed by the vowel, the velar voiced stop is fully realized: **ágè.**

2.7 Consonant clusters

There are no phonetic word-initial consonantal clusters. There are no phonetic consonant clusters in word-final position, *CC#. The only examples of intervocalic clusters that do not involve a sonorant are the ones where a velar consonant is followed by an alveolar continuant:

(47) túgsú 'a variety of grass growing on river shores'
ɗògsó 'a basket for sifting' (W & P 1982)

There are also no prenasalized stops in word-final position. The absence of prenasalized stops and labiovelar stops in word-final position indicates that even if in the contemporary language they have the status of single segments, they might have originated from sequences of segments. The prenasalized stops might have originated as a sequence of nasal consonants followed by a stop. The labiovelar consonants might have originated as a velar stop followed by a high and a low vowel, as described in Frajzyngier 1989a. The sequence of events would have the form: **kua** → **kwa** → **kpa**, and similarly for the voiced labiovelar: **gua** → **gwa** → **gba**. Such a derivation of labiovelar consonants is plausible given the fact that there are very few sequences of vowels **u** and **a**, and those that have been attested do not have velar consonants preceding them, e.g.: **ésúá** 'strength'.

The only candidates for consonant clusters in word-initial position, viz. **mb**, **nd**, **nj**, **ŋg**, **ŋb**, have been shown to be prenasalized stops. That is because they can occur as constituents of consonant clusters in intervocalic position and Lele does not have three-consonant clusters.

In intervocalic position the most frequent clusters involve a sonorant as one of its members. In particular the following clusters are attested: V-CR-V, V-RC-V, V-YC-V (verbs in the following examples are represented in the past form, where the word-final vowel **i** must be retained because the verb has a consonant cluster):

(48) hìbrí 'turn'
hirbi 'whistle'
hirwi 'bite'
hòblì 'wet'
hòbrí 'mix'
jólgo 'parasitic plant, *Tapinanthus*'
bàygám 'early'

2.8 Clusters with nasal consonants and nasalization of vowels

The following clusters with a nasal component are attested: V-NC-V, V-CN-V. The characteristic feature of these clusters is that the nasal and the adjacent consonant are produced in different places of articulation. Thus the labial nasal is preceded or followed by an alveolar consonant, or the velar nasal is preceded by an alveolar consonant:

(49)	jemli	'respect'
	jìrmí	'descend'
	jímdúgò	'a variety of big spider'
	kàmyà	'milk, breast'
	ɗugyá	'blind'
	kèmsé	'mosquito'
	tèmle	'maize'

The presence of the velar nasal as the first or second element of a cluster is evidence of its monosegmental nature rather than its being a cluster of consonants **ŋg**:

(50)	hòŋrì	'to become fat'
	kàŋdar	'uvula'
	korŋé	'spirit of the forest'

The presence of prenasalized stops in a consonant cluster is also evidence of their monosegmental nature, because no other three-consonant clusters have been recorded:

(51)	karmba	'halfbrother'

The consonant cluster formation and the rules of epenthesis allow us to determine whether a given sound structure represents a consonant cluster or one segment. This is particularly important for distinguishing between prenasalized stops and consonant clusters consisting of a nasal and a stop. Consonant clusters consisting of three consonants are disallowed. Whenever such a cluster was going to occur, either vowel epenthesis or consonant reduction must apply. The prenasalized stops do not require a vowel epenthesis or a nasal deletion. But how do we know whether a given sound represents a sequence of consonants or a prenasalized stop? Consider the first-person dual pronoun [ŋga]. It could be either a sequence of consonants **ŋga** or a velar nasal. The behavior of the pronoun when added to a verb ending in a consonant indicates that [ŋga] is actually a sequence of consonants. If as a result of morphological processes, a cluster having more than two segments was about to emerge, a segment reduction rather than a vowel insertion occurs:

(52)	tóm-ŋgá	dí	→	[tómgádí]
	hit-1DU.EXCL	3M		
	'he hit the two of us'			

Here is an example of vowel epenthesis. The definite marker has two variants: **ŋ**, occurring after nouns ending in a vowel, and **ŋgòŋ**, after nouns ending in a consonant. If the addition of the definite marker does not create a disallowed cluster, there are no phonological changes after the addition:

(53) bàgày 'flood area' bàgày ŋgòŋ 'the flood area'

But if the suffix is added to a noun ending in **r**, an epenthetic vowel is inserted:

(54) kur 'place' kuru-ŋgoŋ 'the place'

In the list of clusters with nasals there are no clusters consisting of an alveolar nasal followed by a palatal glide or of geminated nasals. A partial answer to this question is provided by Simons and Burquest 1986, who claim that the sequence consisting of a nasal and a glide became a sequence of a nasal glide and the following nasalized vowel. This explanation would account for the form [yǫ] 'intelligent', derived most probably from /nyo/. As it turns out, this explanation is just part of a much more general process of reduction of underlying consonant clusters, which will be described shortly, and the details of this operation are somewhat different.

Clusters of a nasal and a glide are allowed in the underlying structure, and they are phonetically realized as nasalization of the adjacent vowel. If there is a vowel preceding the cluster nasal-glide, this vowel gets nasalized. Texts in G-C & W 1981 and lexical entries in W & P 1982 represent such nasalization by a digraph **ny**. Impressionistically, these entries may be heard as just containing a nasalized vowel or a nasalized vowel and a palatalized nasal followed by the palatal glide. Here are some examples of nasalized vowels:

(55) kį́yé 'collective marker' ← /kínyé/
gų́yé 'spider, story' ← /gúnyé/
ą́ye 'take a spouse' ← /ánye/
tą́y 'slim down' ← /tány/

The presence of a nasalized vowel in the coda of the word indicates that at one time clusters of a nasal followed by another consonant were allowed in word-initial position:

(56) yǫ 'intelligent' ← /nyo/

The presence of such words provides additional evidence that some prenasalized stops originated as clusters of nasals followed by a stop.

There are, however, also instances of the nasalization of vowels when no palatal or labial glide is present:

(57)	ìsą́n	'nothing' (isang in W & P 1982)
	hàhą̀ą̀dí	'Marabout stork'
	ɗǫ = ɗunwa	'smell' (perceive a smell)
	bǫ	'animal, Cobe des roseaux' (W & P 1982)

In order to account for the presence of the nasal vowel in the above words, one can postulate that the nasalization of the vowel is a result of the reduction of the nasal consonant in a cluster consisting of the alveolar nasal and a sonorant: VNS → V̨S. Independent evidence for the presence of this rule is provided by the past tense form of the verb **ɗǫ** 'smell'. The imperative form **ɗunwa** has a high back vowel. The change from high to mid vowel is independently attested in other verbal forms that have a consonantal cluster in the coda of the word. The underlying form of the noun **bǫ** 'animal, *Cobe des roseaux*' would be ***bonw**. The underlying form for **hàhą̀ą̀dí** 'Marabout stork' has to be analyzed as an instance of reduplication of the initial syllable ***nha-nhadi**. Reduction of the cluster with the nasal consonant would account in a systematic way for the nasalization of **a** in syllables following **h**.

Simons and Burquest 1986 provide additional examples of nasalized vowels:

(58)	ndę̀	'(kind of tree)'
	nję̀	'(kind of bird)'

They postulate the following spelling representations for these words: **ndenn** and **njenn**. No explanation of the nasalization of these words is provided other than the statement that these words are 'highly specific' (Simons and Burquest 1986: 35). Yet the explanation of the phonetic form is not exceptional but follows the rules otherwise attested in the language. The phonetic form allows, indeed necessitates, the postulation of the underlying forms as ending in geminated nasal consonants. The vowels, however, could be high front **ndinn** and **njinn**. The first rule would be vowel lowering in an extra-heavy syllable, giving **ndenn** and **njenn.** The next is the rule of nasalization of vowels, which results in the forms **ndęn** and **njęn**. The next rule is the deletion of the nasal consonant after the nasalized vowel, C:

[+nasal] → Ø/ vowel [+nasal]____#,

resulting in phonetic forms **ndę̀** and **nję̀**. The three rules account for all monosyllabic forms consisting of a consonant and the nasal vowel in word-final position.

2.9 Nasal dissimilation

Certain words whose independent form is CVrmV have the form CVrVn in possessive constructions. Consider the two nouns **tormo** 'girl' and **kormo** 'boy'. The forms without possessive pronouns are attested with their final vowel:

(59)	kormo	ná	tím-dí	kál	gé
	boy	ASSC	sister-3M	pass	3PL
	'a boy and his sister have passed by'				

(60)	tormo	ná	ɓón-dó	kál	gé
	girl	ASSC	brother-3F	pass	3PL
	'a girl and her brother have passed by'				

In possessive constructions with pronominal possessors these words display the structure CVrVn:

(61)	teren-niŋ	koren-niŋ	'my daughter'
	toro-m	koro-m	'your (M) . . .'
	teren-de	koren-de	
	teren di	koren di	
	toron-do	koron-do	'her . . .'
	teren dí nì	koren dí nì	'our (EXCL) . . .'

In order to account for the alternation between the forms **kormo** and **tormo** on the one hand and **teren** and **koren** on the other, I propose that the underlying form for 'boy' and 'girl' is **korn** and **torn**. Now, the cluster **rn** is disallowed in word- final position and it is also disallowed in any position by the constraint on consonant clusters produced in the same place of articulation. Therefore, the alveolar nasal **n** dissimilates to **m**, and the forms become **korm** and **torm**. Lele cannot have word-final clusters; therefore an epenthetic vowel identical with the preceding vowel, i.e. the only vowel available in the word, is inserted. Partial evidence for the final vowel being epenthetic is provided by the fact that the tone on the final vowel is the same as on the preceding vowel. Hence the forms **kormo** and **tormo**. The possessive forms involve the addition of suffixes beginning with a consonant. These suffixes are added to the basic, underlying form of the nouns. Hence **korn** and **torn** + Possessive pronoun. If the possessive pronoun begins with a consonant, we have the following sequence: CVrnCV. The syllabification rule inserts a vowel after **r**. This vowel is identical with the preceding vowel, but it undergoes vowel harmony rules, if applicable. Here is an illustration of the complete derivation of the possessive form [terendi] 'his daughter':

Underlying	Epenthesis	Dissimilation
torn	torno	tormo

Possessive forms:

Suffixation	Epenthesis	Fronting
torn + di	toron-di	terendi

A similar process takes place with the plural form **karma** 'children'. The plural form **karma** is derived through the **a** insertion into the form **korn**. This results in the form **karn**. The addition of an epenthetic vowel produces **karna**. Consonant dissimilation produces **karma**. When the word is followed by possessive pronouns, the epenthetic vowel **a** is inserted after **r**. That allows the alveolar nasal to be realized as such, i.e., it does not have to be dissimilated. The addition of possessive pronouns to the form **karan** results in the predictable realization of the alveolar nasal before alveolar consonants, and in the nasal deletion before **m**:

(62)	karan-di	'his children'
	karan-do	'her children'
	karan-iŋ	'my children'
	karan-m → karam	'your (M) children'
	karan-de	'your (F) children'

2.10 Liquid --- stop

An alveolar liquid becomes a voiced alveolar stop following a nasal consonant, as per the rule:

alveolar liquid → voiced stop /nasal ____.

Consider the second- and third-person feminine object and possessive markers, which have the form **-re** and **-ro** respectively. Evidence for the underlying **r** is provided by the forms in intervocalic position and by the forms the possessive markers have after a consonant other than an alveolar nasal:

(63) kùb-re → [kìb-rè]
mouth-2F
'your (F) mouth'

(64) kè-re
GEN-2F
'2F alienable'

When the possessive pronoun occurs after a word ending in an alveolar nasal, the liquid becomes a stop:

(65) ɓén-re → [ɓén-dé]
brother-2F
'your (F) brother'

This rule would appear to be in conflict with the constraint that does not allow a sequence of consonants produced in the same place of articulation, described in the following subsection. But the presence of the sequence here would indicate that what is involved is an underlying **n** and an underlying **r** rather than an underlying **d**.

The consonant **r** never occurs in word-initial position, as already noted by G-C & W 1981. The alveolar **r** does, however, occur in word-medial position between vowels or before another consonant. It also occurs in word-final position.

2.11 The constraint *α place αplace

There is a phonetic structure constraint in Lele that does not allow underlying consonants produced in the same place of articulation to be realized phonetically as a sequence of consonants. If such a sequence were going to occur, the first segment of the sequence would be deleted:

Result: Cα place → Ø /_____ Cαplace

An alveolar liquid is deleted before a nasal: l → Ø/ ____#n. This rule operates only in phrase-internal position. Thus it operates before the locative clitic **ni**. Consider the word **kúl** 'house'. When followed by the locative postposition **ni** the word-final **l** is reduced:

(66) kúl ni → [kúni]
home LOC
'inside the house, room'

(67) kàl nga → [kànga]
go 1DU.INCL
'let's go'

The constraint results in the reduction of all geminated consonants that might emerge as a result of the contact of two morphemes:

(68) kòrù-re → [kòrè]
neck-2F
'your neck'

The constraint also allows for a straightforward explanation of the reduction of **b** before **m**:

(69) kùb-m → [kù-m]
mouth-2M
'your mouth'

The constraint also operates on the cluster of nasal consonants in the same way, viz., the first nasal is deleted. The deletion of the nasal before another nasal indicates that nasality holds the same status as place of articulation:

(70) karan-m → [karam]
children-2M
'your (M) children'

The constraint operates only on the underlying segments. The presence of this constraint is actually the evidence for the existence of underlying segments. If the phonetic segment that shares the feature place with the preceding segment is a derived one, the constraint does not prevent the consonantal sequence from occurring, as is the case with the second-person feminine **-re** and **-ro**, which have the forms **-de** and **-do** respectively after nasal consonants. The sequence **n-d** is allowed in the surface structure:

(71) karan-re → [karan-de]
children-2F
'your (F) children'

It is quite possible that the sequence [nd] is allowed in the surface structure because it is considered a prenasalized stop, an allowed phonetic segment in Lele.

The constraint on two segments' sharing the feature place does not operate at the phrasal boundary:

(72)	kórmò	jè	wèl	ná	bá-y
	child	IMPF	sleep	ASSC	father-3M

'the child sleeps with his father'

3 The vowel system

3.1 The inventory of vowels

There are five underlying vowels:

i		u
e		o
	a	

The mid vowels are lower mid rather than higher mid. All vowels may have long variants. Vowel length is distinctive in open syllables:

(73)	bù-dù	'give her'	bùú	'cloth bag'
	cà	'head'	caá	'put' (IMP)
	sí	'put'	sìí	'meat'
	dè	'eat' (VN)	déè	'eat' (FUT)
	bólí	'drinking pottery'	bóòlí	'unripe fruit'
	sò	'two'	sóòyó	'tamarind tree'

In closed syllables only short vowels may occur. Given the constraint *VVC. (period [.] indicates syllabic boundary), whenever a long vowel occurs before a closed syllable, the vowel is shortened.

3.2 The vowel insertion rule

If a disallowed consonant cluster or syllabic structure was going to occur, vowel epenthesis is one means of overcoming such constraints. The epenthetic vowel is high and the values of the feature round are determined by the consonant that follows the vowel. Consider the word **ɓén** 'brother'. When this word is followed by the second-person masculine possessive pronoun **m** the epenthetic vowel inserted between the noun and the possessive pronoun is **u**, having the same value for the feature round as the labial consonant **m**. The epenthetic vowel copies the tone of the preceding syllable. Since the epenthetic vowel is round, it is also back, and as such causes the backing of the underlying vowel of the word:

(74) ɓén-m → ɓén-ú-m → ɓón-ú-m
brother-2M
'your (M) brother'

The third-person masculine and first-person singular pronouns have two forms: **-ŋ** and **iŋ** for the first singular, and **y** and **iy** for the third-person masculine singular. The forms with the vowel **i** are deployed after verbs ending in a consonant. One can explain the alternative forms of the first-person singular and the third-person masculine pronouns by postulating that the vowel **i** is epenthetic, and that its value for the feature round is determined by the palatal glide **y** and the velar nasal **ŋ**, neither of which is round:

(75) dèr-iŋ dí → [dèr-ìŋ dí]
pull-1SG 3M
'he pulled me out'

(76) dèr-iy dí → [dèr-ìy dí]
pull-3M 3M
'he$_1$ pulled his$_2$ soul out', lit. 'he pulled him out'[1]

Compare the form of these pronouns after a verb ending in a vowel:

(77) ŋ té-y
1SG chase away-3M
'I chased him away'

(78) té-ŋ dí
chase away-1SG 3M
'he chased me away'

The same rule would account for the presence of the vowel **i** before the definite marker when the preceding noun ends in a palatal glide:

(79) wéy kóŋ go ba mé ày-í-ŋ gà
who:M certain REF COM 2F take-EP-DEF Q
'which man did you marry?'

4 Vowel harmony rules

There are two types of vowel harmony in Lele. One relates to the features front-back, and the other to the features high-low. In both vowel harmonies the preceding vowel, V1, receives the relevant characteristics from the following vowel, V2. The vowel harmony operates thus from right to left. The scope of the two vowel harmonies is different, and so is their productivity. The common feature of both vowel harmonies is that whether the harmony applies cannot be predicted from some general rules of morpheme or word formation; rather, the vowel harmony is the marker of certain types of connection that obtain between morphemes.

4.1 Front-back vowel harmony

Front-back vowel harmony is a type of harmony whereby V1 receives the values front or back from V2. Front-back vowel harmony indicates that a word and the following pronoun constitute a possessive construction; that a verb and a following pronoun are not merely a verb object construction but that the verb has a grammatical rather than a lexical function; that the two

[1] This expression is used to describe a serious situation when a sorcerer throws a spell on somebody. In order for the spell to be removed, the victim must lie in the sorcerer's compound on the spot where his soul has been buried.

morphemes constitute one grammatical unit. These functions are amply illustrated and proven in what follows.

First, however, here is a description of the mechanism of vowel harmony. Only the last vowel of the word undergoes the fronting or backing. The rules of vowel harmony are as follows: If the last vowel of the stem is [-low] it acquires the feature [α front] of the vowel from which it is separated by one consonant or a nasal and one consonant. Given the existence of prenasalized stops, it is more than likely that the nasal and following consonant are considered for the purpose of vowel harmony to be one segment. The mechanics of the operation of the vowel harmony is as follows:

V[-low] → [α front] /____(n) + CV[α front]

Consider the word **kùb** 'mouth'. Evidence that it has a high round vowel is provided by the form the word has without possessive pronouns:

(80)	kùb	hámlè	kúrà	ɗé
	mouth	light	good	NEG

'a light mouth is not good,' i.e., 'it is not good to talk fast, without thinking'

When first-person singular pronoun -(i)**ŋ** or second-person feminine pronoun **-re** are added, the word has a high front rather than a high back vowel:

(81) kìb-rè
mouth-2F
'your mouth'

Compare also the forms of the word **ɓén** 'brother' with the third-person masculine and the third-person feminine singular pronouns:

(82) ɓén-dí 'his brother'
ɓón-dó 'her brother'

The vowel of the stem keeps the value of the feature high. The underlying form for the word 'buttocks, bottom' is **to**, as evidenced by possessive constructions with a nominal possessor:

(83) to-re → [tere]
buttocks-2F
'your buttocks'

The mid vowel is also fronted when followed by a palatal glide that belongs to a different morpheme. This is evidence that the features of glides trigger vowel harmony, even if there is no epenthetic vowel:

(84) kudo-y → [kudey]
husband-3M
'his husband' (as of 1998 an insulting term applied to homosexuals)

If a nasal consonant or a glide follows a noun ending in a consonant, such a cluster triggers vowel epenthesis. The epenthetic vowel, in turn, determines the value of the feature front-back of the target vowel in exactly the same way as underlying vowels of possessive pronouns do. The labial nasal assigns the feature round (and automatically back) to the epenthetic vowel. The alveolar nasals assign the features [-round], hence automatically also [-back] to the epenthetic vowel. The epenthetic vowels cause the front-back vowel harmony. Consider the word **ɓén** 'brother'. Before the second-person masculine **m**, the noun has the form **ɓón** and it is followed by an epenthetic vowel:

(85) ɓón-ú-m 'your (M) brother'

Consider the marker **ín-**, which derives the associative form of pronouns. The marker has the vowel **i** or **u** depending on the vowel or the consonant of the pronoun:

(86)

	1SG	ín-ìŋ	1DU.INCL	ín-dí-ngà
			1PL.EXCL	ín-dí-nì
			1PL.INCL	ín-dí-ngà-ngù
	2M	únú-m	2PL	ún-dú-ngù
	2F	ín-dé		
	3M	ín-dí	3PL	ín-dí-gè
	3F	ún-dó		

The associative second-person masculine pronoun is **únú-m**. The explanation of this form is as follows: the underlying form of the second-person possessive pronoun is **m**. Addition of this form to a form ending in a consonant triggers vowel insertion. The inserted vowel is round because of the feature round of the labial nasal **m**. Subsequently, the inserted vowel determines the value of the feature front of the pronominal associative marker **ín**. Similarly with the second-person plural associative pronoun **ún-dú-ngù**. The feature round of the vowel of the plural genitive marker **dí** is determined by the vowel of the following morpheme. In the second-person plural that morpheme is **ngù**, with a high round vowel. Hence the plural genitive marker is **du**, not **di**. The vowel of the plural genitive marker in turn determines the value (round) of the pronominal associative marker, which becomes **ún-**.

4.2 High-low vowel harmony

The values high and low of vowels change under the influence of the mid front vowel. The rule for this vowel harmony is as follows:

V[αhigh] → [-high, -low]/___C-e.

The grammatical status of the vowel **e** is indicated by the hyphen sign -. Under this rule the vowels of the stem undergo the following changes: **u** becomes **o**, and **a** becomes **e**. There are no examples of nouns with high front vowel **i** to test the effects of the suffixation of **e**:

(87)	Singular	Plural	
	kùlbá	kòlb-é	'cow'
	túmàrà	tómèr-è	'duck'
	kùmàngàná	kòmèngèn-è	'gazelle'

It is interesting to note that high-low vowel harmony operates only when the suffix is vocalic and front-back vowel harmony operates only when the suffix begins with a consonant or consists of a consonant only. I have no explanation to offer for this phenomenon.

4.3 Barriers to front-back vowel harmony

Front-back vowel harmony does not always apply when the relevant syntactic and morphological conditions are met. Vowel harmony does not operate when there is a sequence of two underlying liquids between the trigger and the target:

(88) kòr-re → [kòrè] and not *[kèrè]
neck-2F
'your neck'

(89) bòl-re → [bòlrè] and not *[bèlrè]
abundant words-2F
'your abundant words'

(90) túgrí-ré → [túg-ré] and not *[tíg-ré]
village-2F
'your village'

Cf.:

(91) túgrí dí-nì
village GEN:PL-1PL
'our village'

Understanding the barriers to vowel harmony allows us to recover the underlying forms of nouns. Consider the plural form of the word **kódúlò** 'wild cat'. After the addition of the suffix **e**, the vowels of the stem do not undergo any changes. A plausible explanation for this fact may be that the underlying form has in fact a geminated liquid, viz. that it is underlyingly **kódúllò**:

(92) kódúlò kódúlè 'wild cat', 'genet'

The vowel **a** is barrier to vowel harmony. If a noun with word- final **a** has a suffix with a high front vowel, vowel harmony does not affect the vowel **a**, nor does it affect the preceding high round vowel either:

(93) bùgà-niŋ
friend-1SG
'my friend'

(94) bùgà-m
friend-2M
'your friend'

4.4 The function of vowel harmony

Fronting vowel harmony, rather than being an automatic result of a configuration of some consonants and vowels, is a coding means. Evidence for the proposed hypothesis is provided by the following: vowel harmony does not operate throughout the word, but rather is limited only to the last vowel of the stem. Consider the word **kudo** 'husband'. The phonetic realization without possessive pronouns is attested in the following sentence:

(95)	ą́ye	kudo	nè	kanya	sòrè	ɗé
	take a spouse:VN	husband	COP	thing	joking	NEG
	'to take a husband is not a joking matter'					

If the possessive suffix has a front vowel, the last vowel of **kudo** becomes [e], but the first vowel of the word is not affected by vowel harmony:

(96)	kudo-ro	'her husband'
	kude-re	'your husband'
	kude-niŋ	'my husband'

(97) kude-dí-ngà
husband-GEN:PL-1DU.INCL
'our (DU.INCL) husband'

Similarly with other words:

(98) mbódó-re → [mbódéré]
temple-2F
'your temple' (side of forehead)

(99) múglí-y 'his heart'
múglú-ró 'her heart'
múglí-nín 'my heart'
múglú-m 'your heart'

The fundamental function of the vowel harmony is to indicate that a phonological segment or a sequence of segments following the word that has undergone vowel harmony is a grammatical morpheme rather than a lexical item. Consider the fronting of round-back vowels when they are followed by the third-person masculine possessive pronoun **y**. When this is the case, the vowels are fronted:

(100) yó-y → [yéy]
mother-3M
'his mother'

(101) yó-ró
mother-3F
'her mother'

Evidence that the word for 'mother' has a back vowel is provided by its form when it is not followed by a possessive pronoun:

(102) gìdìrè yó
moon mother
'old woman moon' (September-October)

When the round vowels are followed by the palatal glide that is not part of a different grammatical morpheme, the fronting does not take place:

(103)	bùyà	'break':(IMP)	and not	*bìyà
	bóyè	'break':(FUT)	and not	*béyè
(104)	bòy	'pour'	and not	*bèy
Cf.:				
(105)	bùgà	'pour':(IMP)		

Vowel harmony is a phonological means of coding the nature of the morphemes involved in a construction. In particular, it indicates that the morphemes involved constitute one phonological entity.

(106) gùn-re → [gìndè]
front-2F
'your front'
kun-re → [kinde]
eyes-2F
'your eyes'

(107) kùb-rè → [kìb-rè]
'your (F) mouth'

(108) kùb dú-ngù
mouth GEN:PL-2PL
'your mouths'

Compare words with an underlying high front vowel, which does not trigger vowel harmony:

(109) kúrbínyà 'rainy season'
kúlbàdí 'tree, *Securidata longepedunculata*' (W & P 1982)
gúnyé 'spider, story'

There is a genitive plural marker **dí**, which precedes non-singular possessive pronouns. When the marker **dí** is followed by a suffix that has a back vowel, the vowel of the genitive plural marker becomes **u**:

(110) dú-ngù 'yours'
dí-ngà 'ours'

The vowel **a** is not affected by vowel harmony rules:

(111) cà re [càrè] 'your head'
kàb re [kàbrè] 'your hand'
sùmá re [sùmáré] 'your ear'

Vowel harmony does not operate for most verbs when they are followed by subject or object pronouns:

(112) ɗe-du and not *ɗu-du
leave-3F
'he left her'

(113) cib-du kàbú and not *cub-du
pierce:PL-3F hand
'he prohibited her . . . '

(114) cànìgé dèŋglí kolo tumadur-i and not *tumadir-i
Canige hear word death-3SG
'Canige$_1$ heard the news of his$_1$ death'

(115) bòg-ìŋ dú sòndró and not *bèg-ìŋ
put-1SG 3F fear
'she frightened me'

(116) bòg-ìy dí sòndró and not *bèg-ìy
put-3M 3M fear
'he frightened him'

(117) ŋ bòy-gè sòndró and not *bèy-gè
1SG put-3PL fear
'I frightened them'

(118) gìlkíníŋ téy-dú
Gilkinin call-3F
'Gilkinin called her'

Only verbs that have acquired grammatical functions undergo vowel harmony. The verb **bè** 'give' and the dative marker **bé** have their vowels replaced by the vowel of the following object pronoun if the pronoun has a vowel. Evidence that the underlying vowel is front mid is provided by the form of the verb when followed by a noun:

(119) gìlkíníŋ bè làlì kírbì
Gilkinin give money Kirbi
'Gilkinin gave money to Kirbi'

As the marker of dative function the form **bé** has high tone and undergoes vowel harmony when followed by pronouns:

(120) gìlkíníŋ yàá bú-dù kolo
Gilkinin say DAT-3F word
'Gilkinin talked to her'

(121) gìlkíníŋ yàá bí-gì kolo
Gilkinin say DAT-2M word
'Gilkinin talked to you'

The suffix consisting of the palatal glide does not affect the front vowel of the stem:

(122) gìlkíníŋ yàá bé-y na
Gilkinin tell DAT-3M HYP
'Gilkinin told him that . . .'

Once the verb has been grammaticalized, it undergoes vowel harmony even in its lexical function when pronominal objects follow the verb:

(123) gìlkíníŋ bù-dù làlì
Gilkinin give-3F money
'Gilkinin gave her money' (i.e. gave money to her)

(124) gìlkíníŋ bì-gì làlì
Gilkinin give-2M money
'Gilkinin gave you money'

The verb **bè** does not undergo vowel harmony when followed by subject pronouns:

(125) bè dí
give 3M
'he gave'

bè dú
'she gave'

bè gé
'they gave'

The verb **nè** 'make' has acquired the function of copula. When the copula is followed by the referential marker **go**, the copula has a back vowel:

(126) nò go kíndi
COP REF true
'it is true'

The copula also undergoes vowel harmony when it is followed by the property concept word with which it forms a predicative construction. The condition for the vowel harmony to occur is for the property concept word to have a round vowel:

(127) nò mbúlo
COP clumsy
'be clumsy'

Compare the syntactic environment when the verb is followed by a noun with a mid back vowel. In such an environment the verb does not undergo vowel harmony:

(128)	time	nè	gònì	nẹ̀y
	hunger	make	hyena	much
	'Hyena is very hungry'			

Vowel harmony rules must be differentiated from vowel insertion, whose product may overlap with vowel harmony. There are certain morphemes that appear not to have a vowel of their own, or conversely that have a vowel that is assimilated completely to the following vowel. Such is the case with the alienable possessive marker **k** for masculine and plural nouns and **t** for feminine nouns. The vowel of the marker is identical with the vowel of the following morpheme except for the third-person masculine:

(129)	1SG	kò-nòŋ	1DU.INCL	kà-ngà
			1PL.EXCL	kì-nì
			1PL.INCL	kà-ngàngù
	2M	kò-m	2PL	kù-ngù
	2F	kè-rè		
	3M	kè-y	3PL	kè-gè
	3F	kò-rò		

The third-person masculine form is **kè-y**. The form **kè** may be suspected to be the underlying form of the genitive marker. If one accepts this hypothesis, then it would follow that the vowel of the genitive form undergoes complete assimilation for all features of the following vowels.

5 The tonal system

5.1 Tonal inventory and the functions of tone

All syllables in Lele must bear a tone. There are morphemes, both lexical and grammatical, that have an inherent, or underlying, tone. There are also morphemes that do not have an inherent tone and instead receive their tone from the syllable immediately preceding them. This is the case of possessive and object pronouns.

W & P 1982 postulate three level tones: high, mid, and low. They also postulate the existence of falling and rising tones, combinations of the three level tones. Although the three tones have been noted on many lexical items, there are only a few nouns that display the contrast between the three tones (̀ codes low tone, ́ codes high tone, and the mid tone is unmarked throughout the present grammar):

(130 kìrè 'road'
kíré 'compound of a dead person'
kiré 'look' (VN)

(131) ànglè 'torsion'
ànglé 'roundness'
ángle 'fever' (W & P 1982 **angle**)

Some grammatical functions have a tone of their own regardless of what form fulfills this function. Thus all subject pronouns following the verb have high tone in one dialect and mid tone in another. All subject pronouns preceding the verb have mid tone. The tone of a morpheme may undergo a change under the influence of another morpheme, as is the case with the last tone of nouns when followed by the definite marker **ŋ**. Consequently, specific tonal operations are described whenever the appropriate forms and functions are discussed. In what follows I describe only those tonal rules that operate across different classes of morphemes and functions. More specifically, I describe what happens to the tone when the tone-bearing unit, most often the vowel, is deleted, and what happens to a tone when a new syllable is created in order to comply with syllable structure conditions.

5.2 Tone and vowel deletion

If a morpheme, lexical or grammatical, loses a vowel, it also loses its tone. Consider the verb **om̃** 'catch'. The evidence that the verb has two tones is provided by the forms that have two vowels, such as the imperative **umá** and the infinitive **omé**, which have different tones on the first and the second syllable. The inherent tone of the verb is also realized when a vocalic object suffix is added:

(132) kírbì om-íy
Kirbi catch-3M
'Kirbe caught him'

When this verb occurs in the past tense without an object beginning with a vowel, i.e. when its last vowel is omitted, only the first tone of the verb, mid, is realized:

(133) cànìgé om-dú
Canige catch-3F
'Canige caught her'

5.3 Tone insertion in syllabification

If a new syllable is created, it carries a tone identical with that of the preceding syllable. The evidence for this hypothesis is provided by nouns whose last syllable appears to be created by vowel epenthesis, i.e. nouns that without the epenthetic vowel would have ended either in a consonant cluster or in a disallowed consonant, such as **s, j, d, t**. In such nouns, the last syllable bears the same tone as the preceding syllable:

(134)	múglú	'heart'
	kusu	'body'
	moglo	'fast'

If a new syllable is created but one of the morphemes carries its own tone, then the tone of the morpheme is the tone of the new syllable. Consider the definite marker **ŋ**, which carries a low tone and also causes the raising of the preceding tone. The addition of the definite marker to nouns ending in a glide results in a new syllable that has low tone, regardless of the tone of the preceding syllable:

(135) gáw-ŋ̀
hunter-DEF
'the hunter'

(136) jàw-ŋ → [jawŋ̀]
enemy-DEF
'the enemy'

5.4 Tone and syllabic structure

Verbs that have an initial voiced consonant form their plural form through the devoicing of that consonant. If the singular form of the verb has a low tone, the plural form has a mid tone:

(137)	Singular	Plural	Gloss
	bòy	poy	'break'
	bòr	por	'cut'
	dìgrì	tigri	'kill'
	bàá	pa-d-wí	'fall'
	bè	ped-wé	'give/whip'

There are a number of questions that emerge in connection with those plural formations. The first is about the nature of the initial devoicing. One could simply state that initial devoicing is a means of coding the plurality of the verb, as opposed to initial voicing, which codes the singular form of the verb. Such a conclusion cannot be maintained, however, because verbs with initial voiced stops have meanings similar to verbs with initial voiceless stops. Most verbs with initial voiceless or voiced stops do not have punctual, hence clearly singulative, meaning. Here are the lists of all verbs with initial voiceless stops, taken from W & P 1982. Verbs that have singular counterparts with voiced stops have not been included:

(138)	kàb	'whip a little'
	kàdìgí	'sift'
	kàl	'climb'
	kanjirí	'crack'
	kasirí	'crumble'
	kàẃ	'walk'
	kegli	'remain attached'
	kel	'criticize'
	keji	'carry'
	keĺ	'gather'
	kèsì	'share'
	kil	'buy'
	kìn	'return'
	kir	'examine' (no tonal notation)
	kiŕ	'to be gnawed, consumed'
	kirbi	'think'
	kisí	'saw'
	kogi	'to be too large or too small to pass'
	kòglí	'polish'
	kòy	'steal, rob'
	kùjìgìlí	'rinse mouth'
	kuńy	'take a walk' (recall that ny in W & P 1982 codes nasality)

Verbs with initial **p** (verbs that have counterparts with voiced initial stops are excluded):

(139)	padi	'grill'
	pagdí	'shake in a receptacle'
	pàŕ	'open eyes'
	paŕ	'splash, flounder, sin (about women)'
	pàsìní	'disperse'
	pe	'dig'
	pìńy	'blow with mouth, winnow'
	pìl	'wash (tr. or intr.)'
	pòŕ	'detach'
	poryi	'lie'
	posi	'beget many, multiply'

Verbs with initial **t**:

(140)	tab́	'put for communal use'
	tab	'follow'
	tàńy	'become slim'

tar	'stood up'
taŕ	'gather (fees, taxes)'
tasi	'be sour'
tèé	'chase away, follow, remove'
tèl	'sacrifice, offer'
ter	'pull out, uproot'
tib	'tell a story, count'
tìmlì	'oscillate'
tìmlí	'roll in'
tìmsí	'spit'
tòb	'want, love, desire'
tòn	'ask'
tòŕ	'back down, lower the price'

Some of these verbs have the last syllable identical with the verbal plural marking; hence, they certainly code plurality, even if no form without the plural suffix is attested:

(141) kaywí 'split, separate'

With respect to verbs that have voiced/voiceless stop alternation for the unmarked/plural distinction, the relevant question is whether the direction of derivation was from voiced to voiceless or from voiceless to voiced. Given the fact that the variant with the voiceless consonant is semantically more marked, it is likely that the direction of derivation was from the voiced to voiceless.

One could assume a simple devoicing as the means of coding plurality, but no such means have been recorded in other Chadic languages. Comparative evidence from other Chadic languages indicates that gemination of the second consonant is a frequent means of coding verbal plurality (cf. Frajzyngier 1965, 1977, 1997a, Newman 1990). The product of gemination of voiced consonants is a voiceless consonant (cf. Frajzyngier 1989a). If the initial voiceless counterpart in the plural form were to be a result of original gemination, one would have to postulate that the word-initial consonant was geminated, the gemination in word-initial position resulted in a sequence of geminated voiceless consonants, and the geminated consonants were subsequently reduced:

C1[+voice] → C1C1 [-voice] → C1 [-voice].

The consonant remains voiceless in word-initial position (in intervocalic position all stops and affricates in Lele are voiced).

All elements of this scenario are plausible if one assumes the gemination of the first rather than second consonant of the verb as a means of coding plurality. It would then follow that the low tone becomes mid in a syllable with initial heavy coda:

L → M/CCV

Such a solution is also preferred to one that simply postulates tone raising on syllables with voiceless onsets, because there are many syllables with voiceless onsets and with low tone (examples limited to word-initial stops only):

(142)	kàbù	'tree, *Isoberlinia doka*' (W & P 1982)
	kàl	'climb'
	pàjá	'chief's courtier'
	pàŕ	'open'
	tàbàl	'spear'
	tàgà	'kidney, lower back'

The proposed scenario is preferred to one that postulates independent and unmotivated consonant devoicing and tone raising.

6 The morphology of the verb and its implications for phonology

In the present section I describe the formation 'past', 'future', imperative', and the 'nominal' forms of the verb, because they reveal quite interesting properties of the underlying form that have important consequences for the phonetic realization of verbs. I also postulate the existence of the underlying form of the verb. The properties of the underlying form differ significantly from the phonetic realizations. More specifically, the underlying form of the verb may have only three vowels, **a**, **i**, and **u**, and a word syllabic structure that never occurs in the phonetic realization. The underlying form of a word may have an extra-heavy coda, viz. CC#. Postulating such a coda leads to the explanation of the origin of mid vowels in verbal stems: high vowels are lowered to mid when followed by an extra-heavy coda in word-final position. The insights gained in the explanation of these verbal forms make it possible to explain phonological alternations of non-verbal forms as well.

6.1 The underlying form of the verb

There are four forms of the verb, labeled for the sake of reference as: 'past', represented in glosses by the lexical meaning of the verb; 'future', glossed as FUT; 'nominal', glossed as VN (verbal noun); and 'imperative', glossed as IMP. The future and the nominal form share the same final vowel **e** but differ in tone, with future having the first tone high for all verbs. The second tone, if any, is identical with the second tone of the verb.

If one takes the imperative form as representing the underlying tonal structure, the tones of other forms of the verb are quite predictable. The nominal, the imperative, and the past tense forms have identical tone patterns, most fully represented by the form that has a final vowel, e.g. by the nominal form. If one of the forms does not have a final vowel, e.g. the past or the imperative form, the final tone of such a form is not realized. The two-tone representation on monosyllabic verbs carried throughout in W & P 1982 must be an attempt to represent the underlying tones of the verb. The tonal pattern of future forms differs from the other forms in that the first tone in the future is invariably high.

The problems that need to be explained in the verbal paradigm are the vowel variations. More specifically: (1) In the past form some verbs end in the vowel **i** and others end in a consonant. (2) Some verbs in the imperative end in the vowel **a**, others in the vowel **u**, and other verbs end in a consonant. (3) Some verbs that have a high vowel in the imperative have a mid vowel in the past. (4) Some verbs have high back vowel in the imperative and have a high front vowel in the past. In what follows it is shown that all of those variations are governed by the rules of tense formation and by the underlying consonantal structure of the verbs, structure that is only indirectly reflected in the phonetic realization.

An analysis of the imperative form indicates that the verb ends in the vowel **u** if the initial syllable has the vowel **u** and the verb has a consonantal cluster or a consonant that cannot occur in word-final position. Since all of these verbs have identical tones, it is very likely that the word-final vowel is epenthetic, and the features high and round are determined by the first vowel of the verb. The derivation of the past tense form for these verbs consists of adding the vowel **i** to the verbal root, i.e. to the form without the final, epenthetic vowel. The vowel **i** causes the fronting of all preceding high vowels:

Past	Gloss	Future	Nominal	Imperative
ɓìsì	'pass liquid'	ɓísè	ɓìsè	ɓùsù
kirbi	'think'	kírbe	kirbe	kurbu
gìrbì	'forget'	gírbè	gìrbè	gùrbù
kirbi	'think'	kírbe	kirbe	kurbu
dìgrì	'kill'	dígrè	dìgrè	dùgrù

To this class also belong trisyllabic verbs. That would indicate that from the point of view of the structure of the verb, having three syllables is equivalent to having a consonant cluster after the thematic vowel:

Past	Gloss	Future	Nominal	Imperative
kunjili	'learn'	kúnjíle	kunjile	kunjulu
winjiri	'rot'	wínjíre	winjire	wunjuru

The addition of the vowel **i** for the past tense form also explains the variation between the past and the imperative form of monoconsonantal verbs. The vowel **i** is added to the verbal root. But the verbal root includes the final vowel. Since the vowel is **a**, the addition of **a** + **i** results in the vowel **e**, which is the vowel found in the following verbs:

Past	Gloss	Future	Nominal	Imperative
è	'go'	éè	è	à
pe	'dig'	péè	pe	pa
nè	'make'	né	nè	nà

An interesting variation on this theme is presented by the verb to **dì** 'eat soft food'. The derivation of the past tense form indicates that the root of this verb is not composed of a consonant and a vowel, but rather of a consonant alone. The past tense form is added to the root rather than to the vowel **a**, which is an imperative marker:

Past	Gloss	Future	Nominal	Imperative
dì	'eat' (mush)	dé	dè	dà

The evidence that the past form is formed through the addition of the vowel **i** to the verb is provided by the forms that end in a consonant that cannot occur in word-final position or end in a consonant cluster that can not occur in word-final position. Such verbs have the vowel **a** in the imperative and the vowel **i** in the past form in word-final position:

Past	Gloss	Future	Nominal	Imperative
sàgì	'tear'	ságè	sàgè	sàgà
bàsì	'fail, spend'	básè	bàsè	bàsà
dasí	'husk'	dáasé	dasé	dasá
màglí	'repair'	máàglé	màglé	màglá

The formation of the past tense of verbs that end in a consonant in the imperative form on the surface appears to be different: the past tense form does not have the final vowel **i**. But the vowel of the root in the past tense form is front rather than back. This fact is easily explained by the same rule as the one that derives the past tense forms of the preceding verbs: the addition of the vowel **i** to the verb causes fronting of the preceding high vowel. The past tense marker **i**, however, is deleted if the final consonant allows it. All the verbs involved end in consonants **l**, **m**, **n**, **b**, otherwise allowed in word-final position:

Past	Gloss	Future	Nominal	Imperative
gìl	'show'	gílè	gìlè	gùl
ìm	'bury'	ímè	ìmè	ùm
im	'rot'	íme	ime	um
jìb	'stick'	jíbè	jìbè	jùb
wìl	'glean'	wílè	wìlè	wùl
gul	'watch'	gíle	gile	gul
kil	'sell'	kíle	kile	kul
ɓíl	'drag'	ɓîlé	ɓìlé	ɓùl
Past	Gloss	Future	Nominal	Imperative
kìn	'return'	kínè	kìnè	kùn
wìl	'warm up'	wílè	wìlé	wùl
hím	'gather, tr.'	hímé	hìmé	húm

Now we come to the part of derivation that requires postulating underlying forms that never show up in phonetic realization. The verbs involved have a high vowel in the imperative but a mid vowel in the past tense form. Moreover, the imperative form has the final vowel **a**, and its tone may be the same or different from the tone of the preceding syllable. Two verbs in this group provide the necessary clue to what is going on. These verbs have a consonant cluster after the first vowel:

Past	Gloss	Future	Nominal	Imperative
ɗenglí	'hear'	ɗéŋle	ɗenglé	ɗiŋlá
dengri	'be fat'	déngre	dengre	dingra

I propose that the following process is involved. The inherent final vowel of the verb, represented by the imperative form, is **a** or **u**. The vowel **u** occurs when the vowel of the stem is **u**. The vowel **a** occurs when the vowel of the stem is not round, viz. **i** or **a**. The important fact here is that these are underlying vowels of the verb, not suffixes, at least not in the contemporary language. Thus, the underlying form of the verb can have only three vowels: **a**, **u**, or **i**.

The final vowel of the imperative is deleted when the second consonant can constitute the coda of the word. If there is a consonant cluster, such a cluster cannot constitute the coda, and the final vowel of the imperative stem is not deleted. This is the case with the two verbs **ɗiŋlá** 'hear!' and **dingra** 'be fat' (the pragmatics of such expression is beside the point here). The past tense is formed through the addition of the suffix **i** to the underlying form of the verb, hence is **ɗingl** and **dingr**. I propose that the suffix addition occurs after the underlying form of the verb has undergone vowel lowering in the following conditions:

Vowel [+high] → [-high] /___CC#,

i.e., the vowel is lowered when preceding an extra-heavy coda in word-final position. Only after this process has taken place is the past tense form added, resulting in the forms **ɗenglí** 'hear' and **dengri** 'be fat'.

Consider now the following forms, which display the same vowel alternations but apparently without a consonantal cluster to cause vowel lowering:

Past	Gloss	Future	Nominal	Imperative
tèy	'fetch'	tégè	tègè	tìgà
tey	'call'	tége	tege	tiga
jèn	'stay'	jénè	jènè	jìnà
dèsì	'forge'	désè	dèsè	dìsà
wel	'be large'	wéle	wele	wila (W & P 1982)
nèy	'be a lot'	néyè	nèyè	nìyà

I propose that these forms do in fact have the required CC structure after the thematic vowel, but that this structure consists of geminated consonants, which do not show up in the phonetic realization. Both the imperative form and the past tense form provide the evidence for the presence of the geminated consonants. The imperative form retains the vowel **a**; hence there must be the required cluster of consonants or a disallowed consonant to require it. The disallowed consonant explanation cannot be maintained, because palatal slides and nasal consonants are allowed in word-final position. Therefore I propose that the underlying forms for all the verbs in the group above have geminated consonants and that in the past tense form the geminated consonants have caused the lowering of the high vowel of the verb:

IMP	Gloss	Past	Lowering	Reduction	Palatal
tìggà	'fetch'	tìgg	tègg →	tèg	tèy
tigga	'call'	tigg	tegg	teg	tey
jìnnà	'stay'	jìnn	jènn	jèn	
dìssà	'forge'	dìss	dèss	dès	dèsì (-i)
nḭ̀yà	'be a lot'	nìny	nèny	nȩ̀y	

The same rules apply to the high back vowel of the stem when it is followed by geminated consonants. The high vowel becomes mid. The geminated consonant is reduced to a single consonant. If the second consonant of the verb can occupy word-final position, nothing else happens, i.e., although the front vowel is added, it has no effect on the preceding vowel:

Past	Gloss	Future	Nominal	Imperative
bòr	'cut'	bórè	bòrè	bùrà
bòy	'break'	bóyè	bòyè	bùyà
gol	'see'	góle	gole	gúlá (W & P 1982, gulá)

If the word-final consonant is not of the type that can occur in word-final position, after the consonant has been reduced, the past tense form vowel **i** is added:

Past	Gloss	Future	Nominal	Imperative
dògì	'submerge'	dúgè	dùgè	dùgà
òdì	'leave'	ódè	òdè	ùdà
òjì	'help'	ójè	òjè	ùjà
ɗògì	'keep'	ɗógè	ɗògè	ɗùgì (W & P 1982, error?)

If the verb has the root vowel **a**, the vowel is not affected by the suffix **i** when it is separated from that suffix by a consonant. The imperative form of these verbs contains the vowel **a**, which indicates that the preceding consonant is geminated. In the past tense form, the geminated consonant is reduced, and there is no need to retain the vowel **i**, since the consonants involved, **l**, **r**, **b**, are all allowed in word-final position: The past tense form is identical with the imperative form, minus the final vowel **a**:

Past	Gloss	Future	Nominal	Imperative
càl	'go to meet'	cálè	càlè	càlà
dèr	'move'	dérè	dèrè	
kàl	'climb'	kálè	kàlè	kàlà
kày	'finish'	káyè	kàyè	kàyà (W & P 1982, kay)
lèé	'chew'	léè	lè	làá (W & P 1982)
nàr	'forbid'	nárè	nàrè	nàrà
sàb [sàp]	'burn'	sábè	sàbè	sàbà
wàl	'slaughter'	wálè	wàlè	wàlà
ɓàl	'suffice'	ɓálè	ɓàlè	ɓàlà
ɓal	'be colorful'	ɓáalé	ɓalè	ɓalá
al	'sing'	ále	ale	ala
am	'retain'	áme	ame	ama
an	'leave'	áne	ane	ana
gilalí	'tire, tr.'	gílàlé	gilalé	gilalé (W & P 1982)
tab	'follow'	tábe	tabe	taba

There is one class of verbs that W & P quote with an additional tone on the last consonant and a long vowel in the future tense. This additional tone is not heard when the past form is pronounced:

Past	Gloss	Future	Nominal	Imperative
cal	'jump'	cáalé	calé	calá
kál	'pass'	kále	kàlé	kàlá
kab	'whip'	káabé	kabé	kabá
tab	'put together'	táabé	tabé	tabá

The vocalic structure of verbs provides the evidence for the derivation of nasal vowels from a sequence of a clusters consisting of a nasal and another segment. The deletion of a nasal consonant leaves a trace in the nasality of the adjacent vowel:

Past	Gloss	Future	Nominal	Imperative
tą̀y	'slim'	tą́yè	tą̀yè	tą̀yá
węy	'cook'	wę́ye	węye	xxx

The above discussion provides a description of the formation of past and imperative for most verbs in Lele. There are, however, some idiosyncratic properties of individual verbs that must be noted. The verb **è** 'go' has two imperative forms, depending on the syntactic context. When it is followed by the ventive form **jè**, with which it constitutes one predicate, **è** becomes **à** in the imperative, like all other monosyllabic verbs ending in a vowel:

(143) è jè 'come' à-jè

When **è** is not followed by **jè** and means only 'go', the imperative form is suppletive:

(144) è 'go' ìrà

The verb **ege** 'please' does not have an imperative form. The reason for this is that the grammatical subject is the person or thing that triggers the feelings. The grammatical object of this verb is the person that experiences love or pleasure. The verb only partially overlaps with English 'please' in that it cannot have the subject control the event, as evidenced by its unavailability in the imperative modality.

The verb **yà(á)** 'tell' does not have a front vowel in the past form.

6.2 The formation of the future and nominal form

One could provide a very simple rule for the formation of the future and the nominal forms: the vowel **e** is added to the past stem, from which final vowel **i** was removed if there was one. The evidence that the past stem rather than the root is involved in the derivation is provided by the fact that the stems in the nominal form have all undergone high vowel lowering before the consonant clusters (including geminated consonants) and high vowel fronting, which is caused by the high front vowel of the past tense suffix.

The tone on the vowel **e** is identical with the second tone of the verb (if different from the first tone). If the verb is monosyllabic, the tone on the vowel **e** is identical with the tone of the preceding syllable. The future form is derived from the nominal form through the raising of the tone of the first syllable.

Such a simple account is descriptively accurate. It does not explain, however, why the vowel **e** is the marker of the nominal and the future forms. Given the fact that the vowel of the past tense is **i**, it is possible that the nominal form and the future tense are derived through the lowering of the final **i**. The lowering would then be a means of coding rather than a result of the operation of some phonological rules. Such a solution is preferable because it is in harmony with the fact that the nominal form is derived from the past tense form, and instead of postulating a new morpheme, it postulates a new derivational process. Therefore vowel lowering is taken in the present grammar as the means to derive the nominal form.

6.3 Summary of the derivation of verbal forms

The starting element in the derivation is the verbal root, which consists of the initial vowel or consonant followed by the consonant(s). If the root is polysyllabic, it consists of all vowels and consonants up to the last consonant. The vowels of the root can only be **a**, **u**, or **i**. The distribution of consonants in the root follows the rules as described above, viz., if there is a cluster of consonants, both C_1C_2 and C_1C_1 are allowed in the underlying form of the verb. If the consonants are different, only the types listed in the permitted consonant clusters may occur. The large number of postulated underlying C_1C_1 clusters may be explained by assimilation rules, whereby similar consonants produced in the same place of articulation are assimilated with respect to other features, such as voice and manner of articulation.

Root (C)V(C)(C) or (C)VC(C)VC(VC)

The imperative is formed through the addition of the vowel **a** to verbs with the root vowel **a** or **i**, and the vowel **u** to verbs with the root vowel **u**. Addition of the vowels is the first rule that the root undergoes in the formation of the imperative. The vowels **i** and **u** are subsequently deleted from all stems that have a final consonant that is allowed to be also word-final.

Imperative = Root + a/u

The past stem (recall that it represents the non-future tense) has a different path of derivation. The first step is vowel lowering for those verbs that have a root structure (C)V[+high]CC. Subsequently, the sequence CC is reduced to C if the consonants are identical. Only then the past tense suffix **i** is added. If there is a high round vowel in the root, such a vowel is fronted. The past tense form is deleted from all verbs whose roots have a final consonant that may also occur in word-final position.

The nominal form is derived through the lowering of the past stem final vowel **i** to **e**. The future tense form is derived through raising to high the first tone of the nominal form.

7 Conclusions

The consonantal inventory of Lele presents an asymmetrical system with four series of stops, voiceless, voiced, glottalized, and prenasalized, three of which consist of three consonants. There are, however, only two continuants, both voiceless, **s** and **h**. The phonetic inventory includes five vowels, which may be short or long and oral or nasal. The underlying forms of verbs have only three vowels, **a**, **u**, and **i**. The mid vowels **e** and **o** in the verbal system are derived from the corresponding high vowels when occurring in a syllable with a heavy coda in word-final position. It is very likely that mid vowels in other portions of lexical and grammatical morphemes are also historically derived either from high vowels or from a combination of high and low vowels. The nasalized vowels originate from nasal consonants forming a consonantal cluster with a non-nasal consonant. The reduction of the nasal consonants results in the nasalization of the preceding or the following vowel.

The language does not allow word-final consonantal clusters in the phonetic structure, nor does it allow voiced alveolar or velar stops in word-final position. If the underlying structure has any of these segments, an epenthetic vowel must be inserted in word-final position. The language does not allow in the phonetic realization any clusters of consonants produced in the same place of articulation. Hence the geminated consonants are disallowed as well. In the underlying structure there is, however, a very large number of roots that must have geminated consonants. Some of these may have originated as a sequence of consonants produced in the same place of articulation.

Vowel harmony operates from right to left. The function of vowel harmony is to indicate that some components of a word are grammatical affixes, i.e. that they have specific semantic functions. The following grammatical relations are coded by the operation of the vowel harmony: plurality of noun, dative marker for pronouns, predicative constructions with adjectives; associative pronouns; singular and plural possessors.

The language has three tones: low, mid, and high. A loss of a vowel also involves a loss of a tone. An insertion of a vowel also involves an insertion of a tone. Low tone following a voiced consonant becomes mid when following the same consonant that has become voiceless.

3

The Structure of the Noun Phrase

1 Defining characteristics of the noun phrase

A noun phrase is any syntactic construction whose head is a noun. Such a construction can function as an argument of a verb or serve as a head in a modifying construction. The head alone can function as a noun phrase. There are several constructions modifying the nominal head. In all constructions except one, the head is in phrase-initial position and followed by the modifier. In addition to configuration, there are also morphological means of coding the relationship between the head and the modifier. In fact Lele represents an interesting typology of such relationships. In what follows various types of noun phrases are described according to the functions they perform in the language. The following types of noun phrases occur in Lele ('marker' is a morpheme that codes the existential status of the head): (1) Head, (2) Head Modifier, (3) Head Marker Modifier.

In addition to those three constructions, there is one construction where the modifier precedes the head, and the function of the components is coded by a marker following the head: Modifier Head Marker-Pronoun.

2 Phonological structure of nouns

Recall that in the verbal system only three underlying vowels are postulated: **a**, **i**, and **u**. Mid vowels have two sources: Some are derived from high vowels either through the rule of vowel lowering in a syllable with an extra heavy coda, as per the rule:

V [+high] $\rightarrow$ [-high, -low] / ___CC#.

Other mid vowels are derived through the rule of vowel fusion,

a + **i** → **e**, and probably **a** + **u** → **o**.

Given those insights, one could also postulate that nouns that have a mid vowel represent instances of high vowel lowering or vowel fusion. This indeed appears to be the case for some nouns, but it may be quite difficult to prove for others. In the discussion below I analyze only those nouns that are not derived from verbs. Moreover, I have chosen only monosyllabic nouns so as to eliminate instances of vowel harmony, which operates throughout the nouns in the formation of plurals.

First let us consider those cases when one can reasonably postulate vowel lowering: The noun **bǫ** 'animal, Cobe de roseaux, *Redunca*' has a mid nasal vowel. Vowel nasality is a result of the reduction of a cluster of which nasal is the first component. Therefore, the underlying form for this noun is most probably ***bunn**. The next rule to apply is vowel lowering, giving ***bonn**. Nasalization of the vowel produces ***bǫn**. The reduction of nasal consonant after the nasal vowel produces **bǫ**.

In the analyses below I postulate word-final geminated consonants, but in fact these may represent clusters of consonants, usually a sonorant followed by another consonant produced in the same place of articulation.

(1)	cém	←	*címm	'bird, *Soui-Manga*'
	jem	←	*jimm	'caracal'
			Vowel lowering and geminated consonant reduction. Both of those rules are independently motivated in the phonetic structure.	
	gę́y	←	*gíny	'striped rat'
			Nasalization and vowel lowering as per independently established rules.	
	gòl	←	*gùll	'fishing stick'
	kel	←	*kill	'a variety of willow'
	kor	←	*kurr	'forest'

Here is an example that may result from vowel fusion but for which the fusion cannot be proved:

(2)	bò	←	*bàu	'bad smell'

It is thus very likely that the nouns also had only three underlying vowels, **a**, **i**, and **u**, and that the mid vowels are a product of various phonological rules applying to the underlying forms.

3 Major and minor semantic classes

Major semantic classes of nouns are human, non-human, and place and time. The superordinates in each category are **bayndi** 'man' and **kara** 'people' for the class of humans, **kąnya** 'thing' and **isaŋ** 'nothing' for the non-human class, and **kur** 'place, time' for the class of place and time nouns. Note that the distinction between singular and plural superordinates exists only for the class of humans, and the distinction between affirmative and negative superordinates exists only for the class of non-humans.

The three classes represent semantic categories that dictate the deployment of anaphors, a different one for each class, and interrogative pronouns, also a different one for each class. The superordinate words for each class serve as unspecified arguments representing each class. The unspecified arguments can be used as subject, object, possessor, or locative, corresponding to the deployment of 'someone, somebody', 'something', 'some place or somewhere', and 'sometime' in various functions in English.

In addition to the major semantic classes, there are also minor classes, which have distinct syntactic properties. One such class is comprised of toponyms, which unlike other nouns are not marked for the locative function. Another class is comprised of body part names and kinship terms, which in natural discourse seldom appear outside of possessive constructions. These minor classes are discussed when the appropriate functional domains are described.

4 Gender

The reference system, both anaphoric and deictic, codes the distinction of gender. This distinction is used in reference to humans and animals. The gender distinction in humans is purely along the sex distinction, but the distinction among animals is not along the natural sex distinction. Some animals are inherently masculine, others are inherently feminine, and still others have undetermined gender. The gender of the majority of nouns, including animals and humans, is overtly coded only in the deictic and referential system. The majority of nouns are masculine; there are, however, some nouns that are inherently feminine: **gɔ̀ni** 'hyena', **tu** 'goat', **tùwà** 'sun', **ɗigle** 'year', **túgú** 'village', **wáyngulú** 'morning'.

Some nouns appear to have overt markers of feminine. For the class of human nouns there exists a derivational process that creates a feminine form out of the masculine. The masculine nouns with the initial **k** have feminine counterparts derived through the change of **k** to **t**:

(3)	kormo	'boy'	tormo	'girl'
	kurmba	'half brother'	turmba	'half sister'

It is quite possible that the noun **torò** 'hen' also represents the same feminine derivational morpheme **t** at work. The plural of this form is **kórà**. The **k/t** nominal distinction may be based on analogy to the widespread distinction in the system of deictics, where the **t/k** opposition is exploited for the coding of feminine/masculine and plural forms.

5 The nominal plural

Only some nouns have different forms for singular and plural: names for large animals, kinship terms, and few inanimate objects. Whenever a noun has a singular-plural distinction, the singular form is unmarked and the plural is derived from the singular. There exist the following means of forming the plural: suffixation of the front vowel **e**; insertion of the vowel **a**; suffix **we**; devoicing of the first consonant (which may represent a historical gemination); and there are suppletive plurals.

5.1 The plural suffix

The plural form of the nouns that end in a consonant in the singular provides the evidence that in the contemporary language **e** is the underlying form of the plural suffix. The suffix **e** triggers the lowering of root vowel **u** to [o] and the raising of the root vowel **a** to **e**:

(4)	Singular	Plural	
	kumal	komele	'father-in-law'

When suffix **e** is added to nouns ending in a vowel, it replaces the last vowel of the noun. The suffix assumes the tone of the final vowel of the noun.

(5)	lúŋbà	lóŋbè	'horse'
	kùlbá	kòlbé	'cow'
	kùsá	kòsé	'fish'
	kudo	kode	'husband'

(6)	tùmàrà	tòmèrè	'duck'
	dùbàngú	dòbèngé	'sheep' (W & P dòbèngú)

One can summarize the rules operating in the suffixation of **e** as follows:

(7) $V \rightarrow [\,\alpha\text{high}, \beta\text{low}] \;/\_\_\_\; (C)\text{-}V[\,\alpha\text{high}, \beta\text{low}]$

Whether this is part of a more general rule cannot be ascertained, as there are no nouns with the root vowel **i** and a plural formed through the suffixation of **e**.

The behavior of vowels in lowering vowel harmony allows us to establish the status of certain vowels in word-medial position. Consider the vowel **u** following consonant **s** in the noun **kusuba** 'wild animal'. On the face of it one could postulate that all vowels in the word are underlying. But the plural form of this noun is **kosibe** rather than the expected **kosobe**. Hence, one has to postulate that the vowel **u** after **s** is epenthetic because the language does not allow the clusters **sb**. The epenthetic vowel must be high, and its features front or back are determined by the vowel of the following syllable. The vowel **a** has no effect on vowel harmony; hence in **kusuba** it is the preceding vowel that the determines the value of the feature round of the epenthetic vowel. Since in the plural form the penultimate vowel changed to **i** rather than to **o**, it would appear that front-back rather high-low vowel harmony has applied.

5.2 Plural through insertion of a

The formation of the plural through the infix **a** involves the replacement of the first vowel of the noun by the vowel **a**. The evidence that it is a replacement rather than an infixation is provided by the fact that there are no phonological changes that one would expect if the vowel **a** were to interact with the first vowel of the noun. If a noun has feminine and masculine variants, the plural is derived from the masculine form:

(8)	kormo	'boy'	tormo	'girl'
	karma	'children'		
(9)	kurmba	'half brother'	turmba	'half sister'
	karmba (PL)			

The **a** insertion can be combined with the suffix **e**:

(10)	gìrà	gàrè (PL)	'dog'
	kìrgá	kàrgé (PL)	'wild animal'

5.3 Plural suffix we

The suffix **wè** accompanies other changes in the stem. There are only two examples where the suffix **wè** has been recorded with different tones and where it cooccurs with other changes in the stem:

(11)	gìrà	gàrwè (PL)	'dog'
	ba	báŋwé (PL)	'man'

The suffix bears some segmental similarity with the verbal plural suffix **wi**. Given their segmental similarity and the functional similarity, the two suffixes may derive from a common source (cf. Frajzyngier 1997a). At the time of writing this grammar, however, neither the source nor the grammaticalization path has been identified.

5.4 Plural through the initial devoicing

Initial devoicing as a plural coding applies only to nouns with an initial voiced stop. This means of coding plurality is accompanied by the addition of the suffix **e**. The formation of the plural through initial devoicing has been recorded in only one nominal form:

(12)	gìjá	'throwing knife'	(PL kàjé or gàjé)
	kàjé poriŋ	'four throwing knives'	
	kàjé so	'two throwing knives'	

The formation of the plural through the devoicing of the initial consonant is a much more widespread phenomenon in the verbal system.

5.5 Suppletive plurals

Some nouns have only suppletive plurals:

(13)	Singular		Plural	
	tamá	'woman/wife'	kamda	
	torò	'hen'	kórà	
	bayndi	'person'	kara	'people'

Although two examples in this list display the alternation **t/k** in the singular and plural forms, one cannot predict the other consonantal differences between these forms, nor can one predict the vocalic and tonal differences. The lexical characteristic of suppletive plurals is, however, not equivalent to the morphological plurals. If a suppletive plural is modified by a numeral, it must be followed by the word **kusu** 'body' plus a possessive pronoun, which has the function of a classifier, individualizing members of the set:

(14)	dà	túgú	tóŋ	ni	kara	kóndrè[2]
	PREP	village	certain:F	LOC	people	young men
	kusi-ge	sùbù				
	body-3PL	three				

'In a village there were three young men.'

The suppletive plurals of collective constructions cannot be followed directly by numerals.

---

[2] W & P 1982 have **kòndìrè**.

6 Nouns without singular-plural distinction

Several semantic classes of nouns do not have plural forms. These classes include insects and animal and human body parts:

(15)	kòré	'fly'
	kèmsé	'mosquito'
	tùmbó	'bee'
	gúsíŋ	'edible termites'
	mòbló	'house termites'
	ngírsà	'lice' (Ngambay? W & P 1982: 112)

Body parts do not have singular-plural distinction:

(16)	kàb-ìŋ	kàb-ìŋ	go	sò
	hand-1SG	hand-1SG	REF	two
	'my hand'	'my hands'		
	sùmá-níŋ	sùmá-níŋ	go	sò
	ear-1SG	ear-1SG	REF	two
	'my ear'	'my ears'		
	gàn-ìŋ	gàn-ìŋ	go	sò
	leg-1SG	leg-1SG	REF	two
	'my leg'	'my legs'		
		gàn-dú-ngù		
		leg-2SG		
		'your legs'		

Similarly for other body parts:

(17)	kin-iŋ	'my eye/s'	
	kán-íŋ	'my tooth/teeth'	
	hèbé-hèbé-nìŋ	'my lung/s'	
	kìb-ìŋ		
	'my mouth'		
	kùb dú-ngù		
	mouth GEN:PL-2PL		
	'your mouths'		
	hìndà-nìŋ	túg-rò	
	nose-1SG	hole-3F	'my nostrils'

7 Collective

There is a class of nouns that does not have a singular-plural distinction. Instead, these nouns have singular-collective distinction. The singular is unmarked, and the collective is marked by the form **kɨ́nyé** following the noun. This class is composed mainly of wild animals, birds, and insects:

(18)	tídì	tídì	kɨ́nyé	'a flock of birds'
	gòni	gòni	kɨ́nyé	'a group of hyenas'
	simlí	sìmlí	kɨ́nyé	'a flock of guinea fowl'
	kúŋrò	kúŋrò	kɨ́nyé	'a group of wild boars'
	kòsóŋ	kòsóŋ	kɨ́nyé	'pig' (Fr. cochon)

The collective marker **kɨ́nyé** cannot occur with a numeral directly following it. There are two means of adding a numeral to a noun with a collective marker. One means is simply to omit the collective marker and add the numeral to the noun, without a plural marker:

(19) ŋ tìgrì tídì súbù
1SG kill:PL bird three
'I killed three birds'

The other possibility is to add the numeral through the deployment of the referential marker:

(20) Gìdìrè kínyé go gòrò kàrgà-ì sùbù go dà
moon COLL REF ten back-3M three REF PREP
ɗigle kùlèn-dì ni
year belly-3M LOC
'The thirteen months of the year'
(G-C & W 1981: 18-19)

8 Possessive constructions

The description of possessive constructions is organized as follows: I first present the possessive pronouns, which are involved in both pronominal and nominal possessors, and then I describe the forms and functions of inalienable and alienable possessive constructions.

8.1 Possessive pronouns for inalienable possession

The possessive pronouns for inalienable possession are as follows:

1SG	(i)ŋ	1DU.INCL	dí-ngà
		1PL.INCL	dí-ngà-ngù
		1PL.EXCL	dí-nì
2M	m	2PL	dú-ngù
2F	te		
3M	(d)i or iy	3P	dí-gè
3F	do/ro		

The vowel harmony rules apply to the genitive plural marker **dí**, which becomes **dú** when followed by a suffix with a back vowel.

The dual and plural forms constitute independent lexical items in that they have their own tonal structure and their addition does not trigger changes in the preceding noun. Consider the possessive forms of the noun **ɓén** 'brother'. The evidence that the underlying form has a mid front vowel is provided by the plural possessive forms marked by **dí**. No matter what the vowel of the genitive plural marker is, it does not affect the vowel of the preceding noun. Because of this, the plural possessive constructions allow one to discover the underlying vowels of nouns that occur in inalienable possessive constructions:

(21) 1DU.INCL ɓén dí-ngà
1PL.INCL ɓén dí-ngà-ngù
1PL.EXCL ɓén dí-nì
2PL ɓén dú-ngù
3PL ɓén dí-gè

The singular possessive pronouns are suffixes in that they do not have a tonal structure of their own and their addition to a noun triggers front-back vowel harmony when appropriate conditions are met. The alternations in the form of the first-person singular and third-person masculine and feminine require an explanation.

The first-person possessive pronoun has the following alternations: **iŋ** after nouns ending in a consonant other than a labial nasal, and **ŋ** after nouns ending in a vowel and labial nasal:

(22) kàb-ìŋ
hand-1SG
'my hand'

The form **niŋ** occurs after a noun ending in a vowel or in a labial nasal:

(23) cà-nìŋ
head-1SG
'my head'

(24) tím-níŋ
sister-1SG
'my sister'

If one postulates that the underlying form is **niŋ**, then the only rule that is required is the deletion of **n** after another consonant:

n → Ø /C[- labial nasal] ____

This rule is independently motivated in the phonological system and is subsumed by the rule of reduction of consonant clusters that have an identical place of articulation:

(25) gàn-niŋ → [gànìŋ]
leg-1SG
'my leg'

Given these possibilities, the first-person singular inalienable possessive pronoun is postulated as **niŋ**.

The third-person singular has a variant **di** occurring after a noun ending in a consonant:

(26) kám-dí
body hair-3M
'his body hair'

Given the fact that all plural possessive pronouns begin with the marker **dí** and the fact that the third singular has the variant **di**, the two markers may be related. The nature of this relationship, if any, must be left for another study.

The second- and third-person feminine pronouns **re** and **ro** have two phonologically predictable variants: **rV**, occurring after a noun ending in a vowel and a voiced non-nasal stop, and **dV**, occurring after a noun ending in an alveolar or a labial nasal:

(27)	ɓén-dé	'your (F) brother'
	ɓón-dó	'her brother'
	cà-rè	'your head'
	cà-rò	'her head'
	kìb-rè	'your mouth'
	kùb-rò	'her mouth'

If the noun ends in **m**, it selects the variants that occur after an alveolar nasal. Thus the first-person variant selected is **niŋ**, the third-person is **di**, the third-person feminine is **do** rather than **ro**, and the second-person singular is **núm**: **kám** 'body hair' and **lám** 'voice':

(28)	1SG	kám-níŋ
	2M	kám-núm
	2F	kám-dé
	3M	kám-dí
	3F	kám-dó

(29)	1SG	lám-níŋ
	2M	lám-núm
	2F	lám-dé
	3M	lám-dí
	3F	lám-dó

If a noun ends in a consonant other than a labial voiced stop, an epenthetic vowel must be inserted before the second-person singular pronoun **m**:

(30) kan-um
'your tooth'

If the noun ends in a labial stop **b**, the consonant **b** is deleted when the second-person singular suffix **m** is added:

(31) kàb-m → [kàm]
hand-2M
'your hand'

The third-person suffix is **di** when the preceding noun ends in a nasal consonant, **iy** when the noun ends in a consonant other than nasal, and the palatal glide **y** when the noun ends in a vowel:

(32)	kám-dí	'his body hair'
	kàb-ìy	'his hand'
	cà-y	'his head'

(33)	kún	'eye'
	kín-dí	'his eyes'
	kún-dó	'her eyes'
	kín-íŋ	'my eyes'
	kúnú-m	'your eyes'

(34)	hìndá	'nose'
	hìndá-m	'your nose'
	hìndá-y	'his nose'
	hìndá-ró	'her nose'
	hìndá-níŋ	'my nose'

8.2 The tonal structure of possessive pronouns

If the last tone of the noun is low or high, the tone on the syllable that constitutes the singular possessive pronoun is the same as the last tone of the noun. The following paradigm illustrates the addition of suffixes to a high-tone noun. The transcription is phonetic to illustrate the changes that the noun and the suffix are undergoing. The noun undergoes vowel fronting and the second-person feminine suffix undergoes consonant voicing:

(35) já-níŋ
side-1SG
'my side'

If the last tone of the noun is low, the tone on the pronoun is low:

(36	1SG	bùgàn-ìŋ	1DU.INCL	bùgà dí-ngà
			1PL.EXCL	bùgà dí-nì
	2M	bùgà-m	2PL	bùgà dú-ngù
	2F	bùgà-rè		
	3M	bùgą̀-y	3PL	bùgà dí-gè
	3F	bùgà-rò		

(37) gùbàn-ìŋ
knee-1SG
'my knee'

Nouns that W & P 1982 represent as having high-falling tone are treated as high tone for the possessive suffixes:

(38)	kám	'hair'	káàn	'loneliness'
	kám̀-níŋ	'my hair'	káàn-íŋ	'my loneliness'

That indicates that the high-falling tone behaves just like high tone, and that the high-falling tone may be considered a phonological variant of the high tone.

The only variation with respect to the tone of the possessive suffix is linked with the mid-tone nouns. Most mid-tone nouns have mid-tone suffixes:

(39)

kun	'eye'	koro	'child'
kin-iŋ	'my eye'	kore-niŋ	'my child'
kun-um	'your eye'		
kon	'name'	kudo	'husband'
kon-iŋ	'my name'	kude-niŋ	'my husband'
kon-um	'your name'	kudo-ro	'her husband'

There are, however, a few mid-tone nouns that have high-tone suffixes:

(40)

kan	'tooth'	kila	'tongue'
kan-íŋ	'my tooth'	kila-níŋ	'my tongue'
kan-úm	'your tooth'	kila-m	'your tongue'

The pronominal possessor markers are suffixes because they trigger predictable vowel harmony rules. When the noun **ɓén** is followed by the second-person singular pronoun **m**, an epenthetic vowel is inserted. This vowel is high, and it is round because the consonant following is round. The round epenthetic vowel causes rounding of the preceding vowel of the noun:

(41) ɓónú-m 'your (M) brother'

For some body parts I have no information about their underlying structure, because I have no examples containing the noun in isolation. Thus the underlying form for 'thigh' could be either **dòŋlè** or **dòŋlò**.

(42) dòŋlè-nìŋ 'my thigh'
dòŋlò-rò 'her thigh'

The expression 'among X' is a possessive construction consisting of the noun **dùrè** 'center, interior' and 'soft spot on the head of the baby (fontanel)' followed by a plural pronoun:

(43) dùrè dí-gè
center GEN:PL-3PL
'among them'

When **dùrè** is followed by a singular pronoun, it is interpreted as referring to the soft spot:

(44) cà-nìŋ dùrè-rò
head-1SG center-3F
'my soft spot'

8.3 Inalienable possessive constructions and nominal possessors

The inalienable possessive construction has the form: possessor possessum possessive pronoun. The possessive pronoun codes the features of gender, number, and person of the possessor. Although the order of nominal components of the construction would indicate the order modifier-head, the pronominal suffix added to the possessum, i.e. to the head of the construction, allows the interpretation of the construction as consisting of the topicalized possessor followed by the possessum and a pronoun, coding the feature of the possessor:

(45) kírwé dìngàw-rò
leopard ferocity-3F
'the ferocity of the leopard'

(46) gùmnó dìngàwr-ìy
buffalo ferocity-3M
'the buffalo's ferocity'

(47) kùrmbàlo cà-y
chief head-3M
'the head of the chief'

Inalienable possession also includes kinship terms:

(48) kùrmbàlo tamą́-y
chief wife-3M
'the wife of the chief'

(49) kùrmbàlo kamda-y
chief wife.PL-3M
'the wives of the chief'

(50) kùrmbàlo ba-y
chief father-3M
'the father of the chief'

The third-person masculine possessive suffix has two variants, [y] occurring after vowels as in the examples above and **dì** occurring after consonants as in the following examples:

(51) kùrmbàlo koren-di
chief child-3M
'the child of the chief' (cf. **kormo** 'child')

(52) kùrmbàlo gàan-dì
chief leg-3M
'the leg of the chief' (W & P 1982, gàndì)

(53) kùrmbàlo kiin-di
chief eye-3M
'the eye of the chief' (W & P 1982, kindì)

The inalienable possessive construction is deployed for coding spatial and temporal relationships corresponding to 'on the side of', 'in front of', 'behind':

(54) mbóló dà kúní kàrgà-y ni
granary PREP house behind-3M LOC
'the granary is behind the house'

(55) mbóló dà kúní tìmè-y ni
granary PREP house front-3M LOC
'the granary is in front of the house'

(56) mbóló dà kúní já-y ni
granary PREP house side-3M LOC
'the granary is on the side of the house'

(57) teren-iŋ dà tamá-niŋ kàrgà-rò ni
daughter-1SG PREP wife-1SG back-3F LOC
'my daughter is behind my wife'

(58) jòlgùr cà-rò
daybreak head-3F
'the beginning of daybreak'

The inalienable possessive construction is also deployed for the relationship of modification that does not include possession or spatial orientation in any sense of these words. This type of modification involves non-specific head nouns: The following two examples involve potential news, not news that has actually been produced. Such inalienable constructions are functionally in contrast with modification through the referential marker **go** rather than with an alienable possessive construction:

(59) kolo tumadu-ro
news death-3F
'news of her death'

(60) kolo tumadur-um
news death-2M
'news of your death'

The inalienable possessive construction is also used for the part-whole relationships:

(61) wó te-y
mush bottom-3M
'leftovers of mush'

(62) wó kè-y te-y
mush GEN-3M bottom-3M
'his mush from yesterday'

(63) dèglé te-y
jug bottom-3M
'remnant of the food'

(64) dèglé kò-rò te-y
jug GEN-3F bottom-3M
'her remnant of the food'

8.4 On the nature of 'inalienable' nouns

Certain nouns occur mostly in possessive constructions, to the extent that native speakers are often unable to quote such nouns without a possessive form. These are body-part terms and kinship terms. Thus the noun **kudo** 'husband' cannot be used referentially without a possessor:

(65) *kudo je tamą́-y to-ro
husband throw wife-3M buttocks-3M
for 'a husband betrayed his wife'

In the same sentence the word **bayndí** 'man' is perfectly acceptable, and actually the only one allowed if it is the husband who was the betrayer:

(66) bayndí jé tamą́-y to-ro
man throw wife-3M buttocks-3F
'a man betrayed his wife'

An exception is in a type of generic construction:

(67) ą́ye kudo nè kanya sòrè ɗé
take:VN husband COP thing joking NEG
'to take a husband is not a joking matter'

There is no lexical distinction in Lele between 'woman' and 'wife', the term for 'woman' serving both functions. Consequently, the term **tamá** in the function of either 'woman' or 'wife' can be used without a possessive construction:

(68)	tamá	jé	kudo-ro	te-y
	woman	throw	husband-3F	buttocks-3M

'a wife betrayed her husband' lit. 'woman threw away her husband's buttocks'

When body parts occur in alienable possessive constructions, they refer to meat, and the possessor is the person or animal who owns the piece of meat, not the animal from whose body the part has been separated. Body parts occurring in inalienable possessive constructions are part of an animal or a human from whom the body part was separated. The possessor is represented by a possessive pronoun.

8.5 Pronominal alienable possession

Pronominal alienable possession is marked by the genitive masculine demonstrative **k-** or feminine **t-** + possessive pronoun. Whether the masculine or feminine form is used depends on the gender of the head noun, i.e. the possessum. If the possessum has no inherent gender, then the markers **k-** or **t-** code the actual gender of the possessum. The forms **k-** and **t-** are followed by vowels whose articulatory features are determined by the vowel of the following pronoun, and if the pronoun consists of a consonant only, by the characteristics of the consonant. Since the second-person masculine is **m**, the preceding vowel is back. The vowel following **k** or **t** in the third-person singular is **e**, and this indicates that the underlying vowel of the possessive marker is mid:

(69)	1SG	kò-nòŋ	1DU.INCL	kà-ngà
	2M	kò-m	1PL.EXCL	kì-nì
	2F	kè-rè	2PL	kù-ngù
	3M	kè-y	3PL	kè-gè
	3F	kò-rò		

The alienable possessive construction has the form: noun **k/tV**-pronoun. The evidence for the existence of the categories of alienable and inalienable possession comes from constructions where alienable possession is coded by one form and inalienable by another:

(70)

cà-rò	'her head'	*cà kò-rò	for 'her head'
*làlí-y	for 'his money'	làlé kè-y	'his money'
*làlí-rò	for 'her money'	làlé kò-rò	'her money'
kìbì-ŋ	'my mouth'		
kù-m	'your mouth'		
kùb-rò	'her mouth'	kùb kò-rò	'her language'
kìbí-y	'his mouth'	kùb kè-y	'his language'

If the possessum is inherently feminine, the genitive marker is **tV** rather than **kV**:

(71) tídí tò-nòŋ
bird GEN:F-1SG
'my bird' (W & P 1982: 71)

(72) luŋba kò-nòŋ
horse GEN-1SG
'my horse'

(73) jaŋla kò-nòŋ
bench GEN-1SG
'my bench'

8.6 Alienable nominal possessive

An alienable possessum with a nominal possessor is coded by the following construction:

Possessum Possessor kV + Pronoun

The pronoun here codes the features of gender, number, and person of the possessor. The tone on the pronoun is the same as that on the preceding syllable. Since the tone on the genitive marker is low, all possessive pronouns also have low tone.

(74) kúlbá cànìgé kè-y
cow Canige GEN-3M
'cow of Canige'

(75) gìrà cànigé kè-y
dog Canige GEN-3M
'dog of Canige'

(76)

gúrbálò	karma	kè-gè
cloth	children	GEN-3PL

'children's clothes'

(77)

túgú	póì	kúsígè	kè-y
compound	Poi	Kusige	GEN-3M

'compound of Poi Kusige'

The alienable and inalienable constructions can be combined, with one possessive construction embedded in another. When that is the case, the alienable possession marker follows the inalienable marker. The alienable possession marker codes the features gender and number of the possessum of the inalienable construction:

(78)

kolo	ba-y	kè-y
word	father-3M	GEN-3M

'news of his father'

(79)

kolo	yé-y	kò-rò
word	mother-3M	GEN-3F

'news of his mother'

(80)

kolo	yó-ró	kò-rò
word	mother-3F	GEN-3F

'news of her mother'

If there is a sequence of three possessive constructions, three means of coding are deployed, including the referential marker **go**, an inalienable possession marker, and an alienable possession marker:

(81)

gúnyę́	tumadu	go	làmndá	yé-y	kò-rò
story	death	REF	elephant	mother-3M	GEN-3F

'news of the death of the mother of elephant'

(82)

gúnyę́	(go)	làmndá	yé-y	kò-rò
story	REF	elephant	mother-3M	GEN-3F

'news of the mother of elephant'

(83)

tumadu	go	làmndá	ba-y	kè-y
death	REF	elephant	father-3M	GEN-3M

'death of the father of elephant'

The unspecified human possessor is coded by the word **bayndí** 'man', the same word that codes the unspecified human object:

(84) ba se è dà kúso bayndí kè-y
COM INCEPT go PREP field man GEN-3M
ni dà kàrgà túgú ni
LOC PREP behind compound LOC
'there he went into somebody's field behind the compound'

8.7 Functions of alienable and inalienable constructions

There are two types of possessive constructions: One codes alienable possessive and the other inalienable possessive. Each possessive construction is an independent coding means, i.e., its deployment does not depend on the properties of individual lexical items serving as possessums. The evidence for this is provided by the fact that the two constructions can be used with the same noun, and then the resulting meaning is quite different. Here are two examples illustrating the deployment of alienable and inalienable constructions with what is often assumed to be inalienable nouns:

Alienable construction:

(85) kùb kò-nòŋ
mouth GEN-1SG
'my language'

Inalienable construction:

(86) kìb-ìŋ
mouth-1SG
'my mouth'

Alienable construction:

(87) sìlyà kò-nòŋ
liver GEN-1SG
'my piece of liver' (liver is considered the choice piece of meat)

Inalienable construction:

(88) sìlyà-nìŋ
liver-1SG
'my liver'

Here is an example of the deployment of two constructions with what is usually assumed to be an alienable noun:

Inalienable construction:

(89) làlì-y
'money-3M
'its (M) price'

làlì-rò
money-3F
'its (F) price'

Alienable construction:

(90) làlì kè-y
money GEN-3M
'his money'

làlì kò-rò
money GEN-3F
'her money'

Inalienable construction:

(91) kìrè-nìŋ
road-1SG
'access to me'

Alienable construction:

kìrè kò-nòŋ
road GEN-1SG
'my road, my way'

Some nouns may only occur in inalienable possessive constructions:

(92) gúnjùló gúnjùlé-níŋ
'my testicles'

Attributes of objects, such as 'price', are considered inalienable:

(93) kile dí-gè
price GEN:PL-3PL
'their price'

(94) kile-y/ro
price-3M/3F
'its/her price'

8.8 Coreference and disjoint reference in possessive constructions

The distinction between alienable and inalienable possession has been exploited in Lele to convey the difference between coreferentiality and disjoint referentiality with the subject of the main clause. The inalienable form is used to indicate coreferentiality. The alienable form is used to mark disjoint reference through a construction consisting of Noun Pronoun Genitive marker Pronoun:

(95) è dí túgú bùgà-y
go 3M house friend-3M
'he$_1$ went to his$_1$ friend'

(96) è dí túgú bùgà-y kè-y
go 3M house friend-3M GEN-3M
'he$_1$ went to his$_2$ friend'

(97) è dú túgú bùgà-rò
go 3F house friend-3F
'she$_1$ went to her$_1$ friend'

(98) è dú túgú bùgà-rò kò-rò
go 3F house friend-3F GEN-3F
'she$_1$ went to her$_2$ friend'

The same noun can have alienable and inalienable pronominal coding with the third person. The alienable distinction codes disjoint reference; the inalienable distinction codes cross-reference with the subject:

(99) cànìgé dèŋglí kolo tumadur-i
Canige hear word death-3SG
'Canige$_1$ heard the news of his$_1$ death'

(100) cànìgé dèŋglí kolo tumadu kè-y
Canige hear word death GEN-3SG
'Canige$_1$ heard the news of his$_2$ death'

9 Modification of one noun by another

There are three structures deployed in the modification of one noun by another. Each structure has a different semantic function. One structure involves apposition, whereby the first noun is the head and second is the modifier. The remaining structures involve the deployment of grammatical morphemes between the head and the modifier.

9.1 The coding of attributes

Whenever one wants to code an attribute of a noun and the relevant feature has been lexicalized as a noun, the modification is coded through the apposition of the two nouns. The head is followed by the modifier without any morpheme intervening:

(101) ɓodu tamá
monkey woman
'female monkey' (G-C & W 1981: 2-3)

Evidence that **tamá** is a noun:

(102) Tamá, ul ɗé
woman cry:IMP NEG
'woman, do not cry' (G-C & W 1981: 2-3)

(103) gìdìrè ba
moon man
'masculine moon'

(104) kùb lèle
language Lele
'the Lele language'

(105) kàrà túgú
people village
'village people'

The same configuration is also used in the names of the days of the week, which is possibly a recent coinage:

(106) tùwà gùyé pínà
Sun work one
'Monday'

(107) tùwà gùyé sò
Sun work two
'Tuesday'

(108) wèlè kàsùgú
day market
'Sunday'

9.2 Coding the domain de dicto of the head noun

There are two markers that may occur between the head and the modifier: the hypothetical marker (and de dicto complementizer) **na** and the referential (and relative masculine and plural) marker **go**.

The hypothetical **na** is deployed with indefinite heads, in non-possessive constructions. The modifier may be an inherent noun or a noun derived from a verb:

(109) kur na wèl
place HYP day
'morning' (not any specific morning)

(110) kur na índì
place HYP black
'time after darkness set in', 'evening'[3]

The marker **na** also codes hypothetical modality about a possessive construction:

(111) luŋba na kùrmbàlo kè-y
horse HYP chief GEN-3M
'looks like a chief's horse'

9.3 Coding the domain de re of the head noun

The marker **go** can be the only modifier of a noun. When the marker **go** occurs between nouns, it indicates that the modified noun is specific with respect to the potential set of objects. Such is the case with body parts, where there are only two possibilities:

(112) kùb go dàná
mouth REF up
'upper lip'

(113) kùb go kúsínyǫ̀
mouth REF down
'lower lip'

(114) gìdìrè go báỳrá
moon REF good fortune
'month of the good fortune' (one of the thirteen months of Lele calendar) (G-C & W 1981: 20-21)

---

[3] There appear to be no lexicalized expressions for 'noon' and 'midnight'.

In possessive constructions, the marker **go** codes as the specific possessum of the specific possessor:

(115) luŋba go kùrmbàlo kè-y
horse REF chief GEN-3M
'the chief's horse'

as opposed to:

(116) luŋba kùrmbàlo kè-y
horse chief GEN-3M
'a horse of a chief'

The marker **go** is used regardless of the gender of the head noun. Thus the noun **tu** 'goat' is inherently feminine, and yet when it is coded for referentiality, the form **go** is deployed:

(117) tu go kùrmbàlo kè-y
goat REF chief GEN-3M
'the chief's goat'

Nouns that can be either masculine or feminine, such as **kùlbá** 'cow, bull', are also coded for referentiality by the marker **go**:

(118) kùlbá go kùrmbàlo kè-y
cow REF chief GEN-3M
'the chief's cow'

Here are a few examples of the deployment of **go** in natural discourse:

(119) Tùmò go kar-di-nì kínyé
past REF people-GEN:PL-1PL.EXCL COLL
kè-gè
GEN-3PL
'in the time of our ancestors' (G-C & W 1982: 2-3)

(120) kur go kamda ná kùlòngò
time REF women ASSC pregnancy
'time when women were pregnant' (G-C & W 1982: 2-3)

(121) Kara go tumo
people REF past
'people in the old times'

The modifier **ɗàng** 'another' must be preceded by the marker **go**:

(122) tòrò go ɗàng
hen REF another
'another hen' (G-C & W 1982: 38-39)

10 Nouns modified by verbs

Modification through the verb requires the nominalized form of the verb preceded by the referential **go** or the hypothetical **na**, depending on the domain of the head noun. If the reference is to a specific noun, in the domain de re, the marker **go** is used:

(123) kama go isilè
water REF boil:VN
'boiled water'

The omission of the complementizer **go** results in an equational clause:

(124) kama isilè
water boil:VN
'water is boiled'

The evidence that **isilì** is a verb is provided by the following example:

(125) isilì dí kama
boil 3M water
'he boiled water'

(126) kama go bòy
water REF boil
'boiled water'

(127) bòy dí kama
boil 3M water
'he boiled water'

(128) wò go wę̀y
food REF cook
'cooked food'

(129) wę̀y dí wò
cook 3M food
'he cooked food'

(130) Kur go ɓìsè cóòró
place REF pass:VN urine
'place to urinate'

If the head noun is in the domain de dicto, e.g. when one is talking about a potential noun, the modifier is coded by the complementizer **na**:

(131) na-y bóre bé-y kur na jénè
HYP-3M cut DAT-3M place HYP settle:FUT
ná
ASSC
'he would cut him a portion of land to settle in'

11 Nouns modified by demonstratives

Both close and remote demonstratives follow the nouns or pronouns they modify. Demonstratives code the gender of the head they modify. The masculine exponent in demonstrative is **k**- and the feminine is **t**-. To these gender markers are added distance markers for proximate and remote deixis. In addition all demonstratives end in the velar nasal **ŋ**, identical with the definite marker **-ŋ** These elements suggest a possible compositional structure of demonstratives and deictic markers.

The proximate deixis has the vowel **a**:

(132) t-á-ŋ 'this one, feminine'
k-á-ŋ 'this one, masculine'

Further on in the present work the internal structure of demonstratives is not marked, and they are represented monomorphemically, e.g. as **káŋ** and **táŋ**.

The gender of inanimate nouns may vary between dialects. Thus the same noun may be feminine in one dialect and masculine in another. The word **túgú** is feminine in the northern dialect but masculine in the southern dialect (second-hand information coming from the language assistants):

(133) túgú táŋ/káŋ
town DEM:F/DEM:M
'this town'

It is difficult to establish boundaries with respect to gender assignment, because of the interlexical variation within one dialect. The word **kòjò** 'hoe' is masculine in the dialect that has **túgú** as feminine, and it is feminine in the dialect that has **túgú** as masculine:

(134) kòjò káŋ/táŋ
hoe DEM:M/DEM:F
'this hoe'

Demonstratives may be used to modify independent pronouns. This is additional evidence that independent pronouns behave syntactically as nouns:

(135) dàdù táŋ
3F DEM
'this one (F)'

(136) dày káŋ
3M DEM
'this one (M)'

There is no separate plural form of the demonstrative. The masculine demonstrative is used with the plural head:

(137) dàgè káŋ *táŋ
3PL DEM
'these people here'

The proximate demonstrative determines persons and things visible and present in the same space as the speaker, e.g. in the same room. It cannot be used for entities in a different space. Thus speaking about a person behind the window of a room, one has to use a remote demonstrative.

The deixis for an object a little further away, but visible, is coded by the form **koloŋ** for the masculine and the plural and **toloŋ** for the feminine:

(138) bàyŋdí koloŋ
man DEM:R
'the man over there'

(139) tamá toloŋ
woman DEM:R
'that woman over there'

(140) dàgè koloŋ *t-oloŋ
3PL DEM:R:M/DEM:R/F
'these people here'

It is very likely that the masculine remote demonstrative is derived from the word **kolo** 'word' by the addition of the definite marker -**ŋ**. The accidental similarity in the word-initial position of the word **kolo** with the masculine marker made it possible to replace **k** with **t** and obtain the feminine variant. The feminine form is built by analogy to other feminine forms. The word **kolo** also serves in Lele as a subordinator meaning 'because'. The noun **kolo** 'word' may be used with the proximate and remote demonstratives. In the northern dialect it takes the masculine demonstratives **kolo káŋ** 'this word' and **kolo koloŋ** 'that word' (uttered some time ago), and in the southern dialect it takes feminine demonstratives **kolo táŋ** 'this word' and **kolo toloŋ** 'that word' (information reported by the language assistants). There is a language-internal evidence that **kolo** can be used as an anaphor to something that has been said before:

(141)	gi	ɗeŋlí	kib-iŋ	ɗé	gudá	kolo	nè-gì
	2M	listen	mouth-1SG	NEG	today	word	make-2M

'you have not listened to what I said and today you are suffering the consequences' (father educating his son. The noun **kolo** specifically refers to what the father has said.)

The grammaticalization of deictic reference from the anaphor is made more plausible by the fact that the word **kolo** has acquired the meaning of 'matter', 'thing':

(142)	kàlé	kolo	dìgrì	gìrà	yó-ró
	pass:VN	word	kill	dog	mother-3F

'passing the word [that does not concern her], killed the old bitch' (an admonition not to get mixed up with matters that do not concern one)

(143)	gi	sí	kolo	ná	ín-íŋ	gà
	2M	put	word	ASSC	ASSC-1SG	Q

'did you put a word with me?'

For a study of the possible development of deictic markers from anaphors, cf. Frajzyngier 1996.

It is important to note that gender exponents on deixis are independent coding means for gender rather than agreement markers. Their presence does not have to be triggered by the properties of the noun they modify. The evidence for this analysis is provided by the fact that different markers can be used with the same noun:

(144)	kùlbá-ŋ	do	ínjè	toloŋ	ne	kè-y
	cow-DEF	REL:F	over there	DEM:R:F	COP	GEN-3M

'the cow over there is his'

(145) kùlbá-ŋ go ínjè koloŋ ne
cow-DEF REF-M over there DEM:R COP
kè-y
GEN-3M
'the bull over there is his'

The remote demonstrative, just like the proximate demonstrative, can follow deictic personal pronouns:

(146) dày koloŋ
3M DEM
'that one'

The forms where the pronoun is followed by a demonstrative are used in complex sentences as switch reference markers.

12 Indefinite modifiers

The indefinite modifiers are **kóŋ** 'masculine', **tóŋ** 'feminine', and **káŋyé** 'plural':

(147) bayndí kóŋ
man certain

gìrà kóŋ
'certain dog'

tamá tóŋ
woman certain

kara kąnyé
'certain people'

gàrwè kąnyé
'certain dogs'

kàmda kąnyé
'certain women'

The plural form of the indefinite pronoun indicates that it may well be derived from the addition of the nominal plural marker **e** to the masculine indefinite pronoun **kóŋ**. In Lele, as in many Chadic languages, the plural forms of pronouns and demonstratives are derived from the masculine singular forms. If the proposed derivation is correct, then one would have to postulate that at one time two phonological rules operated in Lele, a rule of vowel lowering:

o → a /____CV[-round],

and a rule of glide insertion:

Ø → y/ŋ___e.

The indefinite modifiers can modify independent pronouns:

(148) dàdù tóŋ
3F certain:F
'that one (F)'

13 Nouns modified by quantifiers

In constructions with quantifiers, the head precedes the quantifier. There are two types of quantifiers: unspecific quantifiers, corresponding to 'some', 'all', and specific quantifiers. The latter are drawn from numerals. Let us look at the unspecific quantifiers.

Quantifier **pet** 'all': The quantifier **pet** is represented as **ped** in W & P 1982, but realized as [pet] in my recordings and in G-C & W 1981. Since I do not see a compelling reason to represent it as **ped** in the present work, it is represented as **pet**. It can be used with nouns denoting humans and animals, but not with inanimate objects:

(149) báŋ-wé pet
man-PL all
'all men'

(150) kamda pet
women all
'all women'

(151) loŋbe pet
horse:PL all
'all horses'

(152) *degle pet
clay pot all
for 'all clay pots'

The quantifier **pet** can be used with the noun **kanya** 'thing', whose referent is any noun, whether animate or not, provided it is non-human. The proper scope of this noun is 'unspecified non-human':

(153) kaŋya pet
thing all
'all things/animals'

If the quantifier modifies a possessor, the quantifier occurs after the possessor and before the possessum in the possessive construction:

(154) Kara pet kusi-gè bòr bè kàlo;
people all body-3PL white give cold
'all people become pale because of the cold' (G-C & W 1981: 28-29. The form **bè** 'give' is probably a reduced form of **bè kolo** 'because')

The collective marker **kínyé** is a type of quantifier used with the singular rather than the plural form of the noun:

(155) luŋba kínyé
horse COLL
'horses'

(156) *loŋbe kínyé
horse:PL COLL
for 'horses'

The form **kínyé** cannot be used with names for people or kinship terms, whether singular or plural:

(157) *kara kínyé for 'people'
*bayndí kínyé for 'people'
*tamá kínyé for 'wives'

Quantifier **kóli** 'all': The quantifier **kóli** also follows the noun. It is preceded by the associative marker **ná**. The quantifier **kóli** 'all' may also be followed by the quantifier **pet** for the cumulative meaning 'all'. This quantifier may be used with all types of nouns denoting humans, animals, and inanimates:

(158) báŋ-wé ná kóli pet
man-PL ASSC all all
'all men'

(159) kamda ná kóli pet
women ASSC all all
'all women'

(160) loŋbe ná kóli pet
horse:PL ASSC all all
'all horses'

The ability of the word to occur after the verb is the distinguishing criterion for the category adverb of manner. Thus the form **kóli** 'all, completely' is not an adverb in Lele, because it cannot occur after the verb:

(161) wel dí dùbàngú kóli
skin 3M sheep whole
'he skinned the sheep completely'

(162) *wel dí kóli dùbàngú
skin 3M whole sheep
for 'he skinned the sheep completely'

There is an interesting difference in the deployment of the quantifiers **kóli** and **pet** with animate and inanimate nouns. If the two quantifiers are used, their cumulative meaning is 'all':

(163) degle ná kóli pet
clay pot ASSC all all
'all clay pots'

But if only **kóli** is used, it means 'not even one':

(164) degle ná kóli
clay pot ASSC all
'no more clay pots' (as said by a vendor)

If there is a possessive marker, whether alienable or inalienable, it follows the head and precedes the quantifier. Thus the order of functional components is as follows: Head Possessive Quantifier:

(165) degle kò-nòŋ ná kóli pet
clay pot GEN-1SG ASSC all all
'all my clay pots'

The quantifier **téŋ** 'alone' also follows the head noun with a possessive marker, if any:

(166)	ɓé-ŋ	kòjò	kún-do	téŋ	morngó	téŋ
	give-1SG	hoe	eye-3F	alone	handle of hoe	alone
	'he gave me the blade and the handle of the hoe separately'					

The quantifier **tóme** 'numerous' can be used only with countable nouns.

(167)	báŋ-wé/kamda/loŋbe/degle/temse	tóme
	man-PL/woman/horse/clay pot/mosquito	numerous
	'numerous men/women/horses/clay pots/mosquitos'	

The quantifier **kąnyè** 'some, a few' follows the head noun without any markers intervening. It can be used with all types of nouns:

(168)	báŋ-wé/kamda/loŋbe/degle	kąnyè
	man-PL/woman/horse/clay pot	some
	'some men/women/horses/clay pots'	

The quantifier **ndì** 'a few' (not in W & P 1982) may be followed by an intensifier of quantity **gò** 'only':

(169)	báŋ-wé/kamda/loŋbe/degle	ndì	gò
	man-PL/woman/horse/clay pot	a few	only
	'only a few men/women/horses/clay pots'		

Not every form that functions as a quantifier belongs to the lexical category of quantifier. Thus the form **nę́y** 'many, much' is a verb, as evidenced by the fact that it can have imperative, future, and past tense forms. Which form of the verb is deployed depends on the tense and modality of the clause. If the tense is future, the future form of the verb is deployed:

(170)	Nè	gìdìrè	go	kara	gòmnye,	ná	kara
	COP	moon	REF	people	old:PL	ASSC	people
	kusínyo	nè	jè-gé	gìsè	kolo		
	soil	make	VENT-PL	divination rod	reason		
	hábe-ná	làlì	dà	bàrù	kile-ì		
	find:FUT-ASSC	money	PREP	cotton	sell:VN-3M		
	ni	néènyé	lay				
	LOC	very much:FUT	also				

'during that month, elders and masters of the soil, engage in divination with rods in order to earn much money in the sale of cotton' (G-C & W 1981: 28-29)

This verb can be used with nouns denoting, humans, animals, and inanimate countable and uncountable nouns:

(171) báŋ-wé/kamda/loŋbe/degle/temse   nę́y
man-PL/woman/horse/clay pot/mosquito   many
'many men/women/horses/clay pots/mosquitos'

(172) kama/wo   nę́y
water/mush   many
'much water/mush'

14 Nouns modified by intensifiers

A noun can be modified by the noun **kusu** 'body' followed by pronouns coding the gender and number of the head:

(173) dàŋ   kus-íŋ   ŋ   é   lày
1SG   body-1SG   1SG   go:FUT   also
'I myself will also go'

One of the functions of the intensifier is that of exclusion of other people:

(174) cànígè   kus-iy   túg   ní   gà
Canige   body-3M   compound   LOC   Q
'is Canige at home alone?'

One cannot add to this question an associative phrase implying the presence of other people with Canige:

(175) *cànígè   kus-í   ná   teren-di   túg
Canige   body-3M   ASSC   daughter 3M   compound
ní   gà
LOC   Q
for 'is Canige at home alone with his daughter?'

Another means of intensifying the subject is through the word **pį́yà** 'even':

(176) dàŋ   pį́yà   ŋ   é   lày
1SG   even   1SG   go:FUT   also
'I myself will also go'

(177) dàŋ   pį́yà   ŋ   nè
1SG   even   1SG   do
'I myself did it'

15 Nouns modified by property concepts

There are two types of modifying constructions: one type consists of a modifier following the head and the other consists of a modifier preceded by a referential marker. There is a clear functional distinction between the two constructions.

15.1 The attributive function through configuration

Some property concepts, e.g. color terms, have been lexicalized as verbs. Modification for this category is coded through configuration, whereby the modifier follows the noun without any additional markers for the function of the construction. The verbal form chosen is the one that corresponds to the tense of the event:

(178) ŋ gol kùlbá bòré
1SG see cow white:VN
'I saw a white cow'

(179) tídí wilé/bole
bird red/yellow:VN
'red/yellow bird'

Words that are inherent adjectives, e.g. **kólí** 'whole', also modify nouns through configuration:

(180) dùbàngú kólí
sheep whole
'the whole sheep'

Some property concepts describing size also follow the head they modify. The adjective **tùnya** 'tall, strong' can be used only with respect to women:

(181) tamá tùnya
woman tall:F
'tall/strong woman'

(182) *bay tùnya
man tall:F
for 'tall/strong man'

The property concepts 'true' and 'false' have also been lexicalized as adjectives:

(183) kólò kíndi
word true
'true word'

(184) kolo ságle
word false
'a lie'

15.2 Coding the referentiality of the head of a modifying construction

As in many Chadic languages, modification in Lele may involve a form that otherwise functions as a relative marker, which precedes the modifier. In Lele such a marker is the referential marker **go**, which can be used with all property concept words described in the preceding section. However, the modifying construction with the referential marker and the modifying construction where the modifier simply follows the noun operate in different semantic domains. The form with the referential marker refers to some specific object or event:

(185) kolo go nè ile nàǹg
reason REF make cry:VN DEM
'the reason for crying'

(186) kama go jàl-(wa)
water REF cold-PL
'the cold water'

(187) tamá do lay è jè dú
women REF pretty go VENT 3F
'the pretty woman came'

(188) bá-ŋwè go gòmyé è jè gé
men REF big:PL go VENT 3PL
'the big men came'

(189) ŋ gol kùlbá go/do bòórè
1SG see cow REF:M/REL:F white
'I saw the white bull/cow' (from the set of others that the speaker believes the hearer knows)

The noun **bay** 'man' followed by the referential marker is deployed to nominalize a property concept:

(190) bay go gùmnyá
man REF big
'elder'

The evidence for the functional distinction between the two types of modifying construction is provided by the following variants:

(191) dìgrì dí tu do bòórè kolo téle
kill 3M goat REL:F white reason sacrifice
ná kílà
ASSC ancestral spirits
'he killed the white goat to honor the ancestral spirits' (the speaker believes that the hearer knows the goats of the subject)

Nouns modified through configuration refer to any potential noun with such attributes. They belong to the domain de dicto, i.e. to the domain of things existing in the domain of speech.

(192) dìgrì dí tu bòórè kólò téle ná
kill 3M goat white because sacrifice ASSC
kílà
ancestral spirits
'he killed a white goat to honor the ancestral spirits'

The referential marker is the only means available for the modification of nouns by verbs. Thus the attribute corresponding to 'tall' is realized through the relative form with the predicate corresponding to 'grow':

(193) hìdà go hin
tree REF grow
'a tall tree'

Cf.:

(194) hìdà háŋ hin
tree DEM grow
'that tree has grown'

(195) bay go máyla
man REF old
'an old man'

(196) bayŋdí-ŋ máyla
man-DEF old
'the man has grown old'

The form of the verb chosen in the modifying construction depends on the intended state of the subject. If the event is not ongoing, the past tense form of the verb is used, as in the examples:

(197) hìdà go hin
tree REF grow
'a tall tree'

If the event is ongoing, the nominalized form of the verb is used:

(198) kama go ísíle
water REF boil
'boiling water'

Cf.:

(199) kama ísílí
water boil
'water boiled'

15.3 Referentiality of the head coded on a property concept verb

If a property concept has been lexicalized as a verb, such a verb may have the suffix **wa** added in some constructions. The addition of the suffix **wa** codes the referentiality of the head. In all examples below, the property concept can be used without the comparative suffix, resulting in the simple adjective:

(200) kùlbá ìndù-wa
cow black-REF
'the black cow'

(201) kamda lay-wa è jè gé
women pretty-REF go VENT 3PL
'the pretty women came'

(202) kúlàngà lár-wa
cucumber sweet-REF
'the sweet cucumber'

(203) kúlàngà dą́yn-wa
cucumber bitter-REF
'the bitter cucumber'

The referential form can be used with the negative marker **ɗé**:

(204) kúlàngà lár-wa ɗé
cucumber sweet-REF NEG
'not a sweet cucumber'

The referential marker **wa** cannot be used in the predicative function:

(205) *kúlàngà háŋ lár-wa
cucumber DEM sweet-REF
for 'this cucumber is sweet'

(206) *kúlàngà háŋ dą́yn-wa
cucumber DEM bitter-REF
for 'this cucumber is bitter'

In the predicative construction the referentiality or definiteness of the subject is coded through the appropriate forms following the subject:

(207) kama-ŋ jàl dí
water-DEF be cold 3M
'the water is cold'

(208) kúlàngà háŋ dą́yn sí ɗé
cucumber DEM bitter much NEG
'this cucumber is very bitter'

(209) kama jàl-wa
water cold-REF
'the cold water'

Evidence for the referential function of **wa** is provided by the fact that if a noun is not marked for referentiality, the form **wa** cannot be used:

(210) *ŋ gol kùlbá bòóré-wa
1SG see cow white-REF
for 'I saw a white cow'

Further evidence for the referential function of **wa** is provided by the fact that it can be used with the referential marker **go** but cannot be used with the feminine relative marker **do**, which codes the de dicto domain of the head noun:

(211) ŋ gol luŋba go ìndì-(wa)
1SG see horse REF black-REF
'I saw the black horse'

The horse in the preceding clause can be either male or female. The marker **wa** cannot be used if the feminine relative marker **do** is deployed:

(212) *ŋ gol luŋba do ìndì-wa
1SG see horse REL:F black-REF
for 'I saw the black horse'

Cf.:

(213)	ŋ	gol	luŋba	do	ìndì
	1SG	see	horse	REL:F	black
	'I saw a black female horse'				

Even if the noun is inherently feminine singular, the referential marker is **go**:

(214)	gol	dí	tamá	go	lay-wa
	see	3M	woman	REF	pretty-REF
	'he saw the pretty woman'				

(215)	kamda	go	lay-wa	è	jè-gé
	women	REF	pretty-REF	go	VENT-3PL
	'the pretty women came'				

(216)	gol	di	tamá	do/*go	lay
	see	3M	woman	REF	pretty
	'he saw a woman who was pretty'				

(217)	tamá	go	lay-wa	è	jè
	woman	REF	pretty-REF	go	VENT
	'a prettier woman came'				

(218)	tamá	no	go	lay-wa	è	jè
	woman	COP	REF	pretty-REF	go	VENT
	'it is a pretty woman who came'					

Since the form **do** encodes some unspecified, hypothetical feminine head and the marker **wa** implies referentiality of the head noun, the deployment of the marker with inherently referential properties together with the marker that codes non-referential property results in an internal contradiction, hence the ungrammaticality of clauses with **do** and **-wa**.

16 A noun modified by a numeral

The following is a list of cardinal numerals:

(219) pínà 'one'
sò 'two'
súbù 'three'
pórìn 'four'
bày 'five' cf. bay 'man'
mẹ́néŋ 'six'
mátàlíŋ 'seven'
jurgù 'eight'
célà 'nine'
goro 'ten'

The numeral **goro** 'ten' is a masculine noun. The evidence for this is provided by the formation of the numerals above ten. They are formed through a construction consisting of the word **goro** 'ten' followed by **kárgà-y** 'its (M) back' followed by the appropriate single-digit numeral:

(220) goro kárgà-y pínà 'eleven' (one behind ten)
ten back-3M one
etc.

The multiples of ten consist of **goro** followed by the appropriate single-digit number:

(221) goro sò
ten two
'twenty'

The formation of the numerals between twenty and thirty is the same as the numerals between ten and twenty, viz. 'one behind twenty', etc.:

(222) goro sò kárgà-y pínà
ten two back-3M one
'twenty-one'

The numeral follows the noun:

(223) ìlú pínà
stick one

(224) kàjé sò
knife:PL two

(225) kàjé póriŋ
knife:PL four

The numeral **pínà** 'one' can also serve as a quantifier designating a small quantity. The quantifier-plus-intensifier construction may have in its scope either the subject or object:

(226) kasa kín-dí pìnà pínyà túŋ ni ɗé
guinea corn eye-3M one even home LOC NEG
'there wasn't even one grain of guinea corn at home' (**kasa** is the generic term for guinea corn. Further in this work, it is simply glossed and translated as 'corn'.)

(227) lèé dí kasa kín-dí pìnà pínyà ɗé
eat 3M corn eye-3M one even NEG
'he did not eat even one grain of corn'

The numeral **sò** in the quantifier function means 'both':

(228) Tamá dàgè ná gìrà sò nè kolo kè-gè
woman 3PL ASSC dog two COP word GEN-3P
'it is the words of both the woman and the dog . . . ' (G-C & W 1981: 12-13)

Even if a noun is modified by a numeral, such modification can be coded as approximative rather than exact. This approximative modification is coded by the form **gìna** 'like' preceding the numeral and the propositional anaphor **máànı́** following the numeral. Those are the same forms that are deployed in comparative constructions. In fact the whole construction of approximative numerical quantification is a comparative construction:

(229) Wèlè go gìdìrè wèlè-ì gì mira
remain REF moon remain-3M remain approach
gìna wèlè sùbù máànı́ ná,
like day three ANAPH ASSC
'About three days before the moon comes out . . . ' (G-C & W 1981: 40-41)

17 Attributive constructions with numerals

The attributive construction with numerals as modifiers (ordinal numerals) has the structure: Noun Relative marker numeral Genitive marker-Pronoun. The relative marker is **go** or **do**, depending on the gender and referentiality of the head noun. The possessive pronoun also codes the gender of the numeral, which is always masculine:

(230) gìjá go sò kè-y
throwing knife REF two GEN-3M
'the second throwing knife'

(231) tàmà do sò kè-y
wife REL:F two GEN-3M
'the second wife'

(232) tàmà do súbù kè-y
wife REL:F three GEN-3M
'the third wife'

When one talks about a wife of a specific man, the pronoun coding the numeral is not used. But the head noun is marked by the inalienable possessive pronoun:

(233) tàmà-y do sò
wife-3M REL:F two
'his second wife'

If the head of the nominal construction is a numeral referring to a specific number from the set mentioned earlier in discourse, such a numeral must be preceded by the word **kus** 'body' followed by the plural possessive pronoun:

(234) lèé ge kus-i-ge sùbù
eat 3PL body-EP-3PL three
'there were three who ate'

18 Conjoined noun phrases N and N

Lele makes no distinction between the conjunction of two noun phrases (NPs) and the associative structure. The conjoined noun phrases have the structure NP **ná** NP. Since the marker **ná** also occurs in the structure **ná** NP, with only one NP, it is inherently an associative marker rather than a nominal conjunction. Therefore it is glossed in the present grammar as ASSC for 'associative'.

For nouns that are not human, the structure of the conjoined nouns is N **ná** N:

(235) lùŋbà ná kulbá
horse ASSC cow
'horse and cow'

(236) kama ná sòngó
water ASSC oil
'water and oil'

If the two conjoined nouns are human, the conjoined structure must include the third-person independent pronoun **dàgè** preceding the associative marker, in the structure: NP **dàgè ná** NP.

(237) cànìgé dàgè ná tamą́-y kìn gé cà
Canige 3PL ASSC wife-3M return 3PL head
dí-gè dà Dèbréŋ
GEN:PL-3PL PREP Debreng
'Canige and his wife returned to Debreng'

(238) ŋ gol kire dàgè ná ásúè lìŋdà
1SG see Kire 3PL ASSC Asue yesterday
'I saw Kire and Asue yesterday'

If a noun phrase consists of more than two conjoined noun phrases whose heads are humans, the third-person plural pronoun **dàgè** precedes only the last NP. Thus the syntax of the third-person plural pronoun **dàgè** is similar to the syntax of conjunctions in many languages, in that the conjunction also occurs before the last noun phrase. In Lele the associative marker **ná** occurs, however, before every conjunct:

(239) tíyą̀ *dàgè ná kire dàgè ná ásúè
Tiya 3PL ASSC Kire 3PL ASSC Asue
killi-gé gùjù kè-gè lìŋdà
sell-3M millet GEN-3DU yesterday
'Tiya, Kire, and Asue sold their millet yesterday'

The third-person plural pronoun cannot be used if the conjoined nouns are not human:

(240) kire kil gùjù ná tòngú kè-y lìŋdà
Kire sell millet ASSC beans GEN-3M yesterday
'Kire sold his millet and beans yesterday'

19 Conclusions

The noun phrase in Lele has the structure: Head-Modifier. Even for structures where the nominal head precedes the modifier, the modifier is followed by resumptive possessive pronouns coding the features gender and number of the modifier. In addition to configuration, morphological markers are deployed between two nouns in the coding of modification of one noun by another. The marker **go** codes the referential status of the head noun, and the marker **na** codes the hypothetical status of the head noun.

The language has two possessive constructions: one coding inalienable possession and the other alienable possession. The existence of the two constructions has enabled the language to code cross-reference and disjoint reference between the subject of the clause and the possessor of the object of the clause.

The definite marker in Lele is deployed to code the previous reference for the object and the previous reference and the new topic for the subject.

4

Coding Arguments

1 Introduction

The present chapter describes the coding of arguments of verbal and non-verbal predicates and the coding of adjuncts. The term *argument* refers to categories that either must be obligatorily present with a given predicate or whose presence with a given predicate does not require coding other than through configuration. The term *adjunct* refers to those arguments that may be added to any predicate. The same semantic function may be coded as argument with one verb and as adjunct with another. Although there is a certain correlation between arguments and configurational coding and adjuncts and prepositional coding, this correlation does not fully account for the distinction. The way an argument or an adjunct is coded depends not only on the properties of the predicate but also on the properties of nouns entering into the constructions.

2 The category 'subject'

The existence of the category 'subject' as opposed to the category 'object' in Lele can be argued for by the following criteria: In the coding of affectedness through the form **cà** plus pronoun, the antecedent can only be the subject. In possessive constructions, the coding of cross-reference or disjoint reference has the subject as the antecedent. In paratactic constructions if there is no overt coding of subject, the subject of the preceding clause is also the subject of the following clause.

A nominal argument is coded as a subject by the position preceding the verb. A subject, nominal or pronominal, does not have to be overtly coded in every clause. Imperative clauses may, but do not have to, have second-person singular subjects. Subjects can be either nominal or pronominal. In some constructions, the subject may be both nominal and pronominal at the same time. The nominal subject precedes the verb, but it may be separated from the verb by adverbs of manner:

(1)	gìlkínín	è	kàsùgú	lìŋdà
	Gilkinin	go	market	yesterday
	'Gilkinin went to the market yesterday'			

(2)	gílalé	pínyà	nè-gè
	tiredness	even	make-3PL
	'they are tired'		

2.1 Pronominal subjects

The subject markers for the first- and second-person singular and plural precede the verb, and the subject markers for the third-person singular and plural follow the verb. Pronominal subjects are preceding the verb here, illustrated with the verb **è** 'go':

(3)	1SG	ŋ	ŋ è	1PL.EXCL	ni	ni è
	2M	gi	gi è	2PL	ngu	ngu è
	2F	me	me è			
	Unspecified human **ge**					

The first-person plural inclusive is a special construction consisting of the first-person dual inclusive preceding the verb and the second-person plural following the verb:

(4)	ŋgá	è	ngú	kàsùgú
	1DU.INCL	go	2PL	market
	'we (INCL) went to the market'			

Pronominal subjects following the verb: (with the verb **è** 'go')

(5)	3M	dí	è	dí	3PL	gé	è	gé
	3F	dú	è	dú				

In the dialect with which I have been working, all subject pronouns preceding the verb have mid tone. All subject pronouns following the verb have high tone. In W & P 1982, based on G-C & W 1981, all subject pronouns, whether preceding or following the verb, have mid tones. The differences are probably attributable to dialectal differences.

The third-person masculine singular pronoun **dí** is very often omitted, even if there is no nominal subject present in the clause. If the verb ends in **-di**, the third-person masculine singular must be omitted:

(6) càgdí *dí
'he spread something'

Cf.:

(7) càgdí dú
'she spread something'

Although no material may be inserted between subject pronouns and the following verbs, pronouns are not affixes, because phonologically they constitute separate units. Even the consonantal first-person pronoun **ŋ** followed by the verb **è** 'go' is pronounced as a separate syllable. The reason subject pronouns should not be considered affixes is that they do not trigger vowel harmony in the sense described in the phonology section.

2.2 Unspecified subjects: human and locative

The unspecified human subject is coded by the pronominal marker **ge** preceding the verb or by the nominal **kara** 'people', also preceding the verb. The form **ge**, glossed as HUM, differs from the third-person plural subject in its syntactic position and in tone. It occupies the position of nominal and first- and second-person pronominal subjects, and unlike the third-person plural pronominal subject, the unspecified subject has mid tone:

(8)

ge	yàá	bé-ŋ	na	kìb-rè	hamli
HUM	tell	DAT-1SG	HYP	mouth-2F	light

nę́y
very much
'I was told that you do not keep secrets . . .'

The third-person plural pronoun is coded by the position following the verb and by high tone:

(9)

yàá	gé	bé	kùrmbàlo
say	3PL	DAT	chief

'they told the chief'

The third-person plural subject is used when the speaker knows the referents; the unspecified human subject is used when the speaker does not know the referents. In the present work the unspecified human subject is usually translated by a passive construction, since that is semantically the closest English equivalent:

(10) dày haŋ ba na ge bé-y kùrmbàlò
3M DEM COM HYP HUM give-3M chief
tamą́-y ba na-y wèl ná undo
wife-3M COM HYP-3M sleep COM 3F
hà kur na wèl na ge dìgr-ìy ná
till place HYP day HYP HUM kill-3M COM
kolo tumadu-y ná ɗárí-nìŋ ɗé
reason death-3M COM anger-1SG NEG
'The first one said that if he is given the chief's wife to sleep with till the daybreak, then he can be killed, because death does not worry him.'

An object occurring with an unspecified human subject does not have to be fronted. It may remain in its own position and the sentence may still begin with the subject **ge**:

(11) ge wàl kùlbá-ŋ
HUM cut cow-DEF
'the cow is slaughtered'

(12) ge óm kòyé súg ni
HUM catch thief market LOC
'they caught a thief in the market'

(13) ge yàá bé kùrmbàlò
HUM tell DAT chief
'The chief was informed.'

(14) ge dìgrì-ge sò
HUM kill-3PL two
'Two were killed.'

The unspecified human subject **ge** may include the speaker:

(15) kàyo yàá bé-y na máàní na na
squirrel say DAT-3M HYP ANAPH HYP HYP
à jè na ge é
go:IMP VENT HYP HUM go:FUT
'Squirrel said, if it is like that, then come, one will go' (squirrel is one of the parties that will go)

Compare this sentence with a sentence with a third-person plural subject in the embedded clause:

(16) yàá dú bé-ŋ na hùndù-ge
say 3F DAT-1SG HYP wake up:IMP-3PL
na é gé lèkol
HYP go:FUT 3PL school
'she told me, wake them up so that they will go to school'

There exists also a way of expressing the unspecified human subject through the use of the form **kara** 'people, men'. In natural discourse the forms **kara** and **ge** are used interchangeably. Compare the following fragment, where the first sentence has the unspecified subject coded as **kara** and the second sentence has the unspecified subject coded as **ge**:

(17) Dà gìdìrè sùrmó ni kara wàl sùrmó nèńy
PREP moon hay LOC people cut hay a lot
kolo kúl kè-gè.
reason home GEN-3PL
'During the moon of hay, people cut a lot of hay for their homes.'

(18) Nè gìdìrè gòle sùrmó go Mangse
COP moon collective hunt hay REF Mangse
kè-gè'.[4] Ge kil bàrù go gàrmà sò lay.
GEN-3PL HUM sell cotton REF time two also
'During the moon of hay is the time of collective hunt of people of Mangse. This is also the time of the second selling of cotton' (G-C & W 1981: 36-35).

The unspecified nominal human **kara** is deployed when used as a possessor. The form **ge** cannot be used in this function:

(19) Kara kìb-di-gè kaywí béè kàlo
people lip-GEN.PL-3PL crack:PL DAT reason
nèný lay Ge lèé
cold very much also HUM eat
ngògrò lay.
Ziziphus mauritiana also
'Lips crack a lot because of the cold. One eats fruits of *Ziziphus mauritiana*.'

An unspecified non-human subject (and object) is coded by the noun **kanya** 'thing':

[4] The order **gìdìrè gòlē sùrmó** is probably a typo. It should have been **gìdìrè sùrmó gòlé**.

(20) ką́nya jógé-y tú ke-y
thing bother:VN-3M compound GEN-3M
'something will bother him$_1$ at his$_{1,2}$ place'

kúsí-y jóge-y
body-3M bother:FUT-3M
'his body will bother him'

Unspecified place and time, whether in subject or object function, is coded by the word **kur** 'place, time':

(21) Kur jàl kóli pet.
place be cold all all
'It is cold everywhere' (G-C & W 1981: 54-55)

2.3 Conjoined nouns in the subject function

If the subject consists of conjoined nouns that are [+human], such subjects are identical with the plural noun, and consequently the verb must have the third-person plural subject pronoun **gé**. Moreover, the clause must have the third-person plural independent pronoun **dàgè** following the first noun of the subject. Thus the structure of the clause with a conjoined subject is: NP **dàgè ná** NP verb **gé:**

(22) kiré dàgè ná ásúè è gé kàsúgú
Kire 3PL ASSC Asue go 3PL market
'Kire and Asue went to the market'

The absence of **dàge** results in an ungrammatical clause:

(23) *kire ná ásúè è gé sùk
Kire ASSC Asue go 3PL market (Ar.)
for 'Kire and Asue went to the market'

The third-person plural independent pronoun **dàgè** cannot be used if one or both conjuncts are not human:

(24) kùlbá *dàgè ná lumbà kai-gé
bull 3PL ASSC horse escape
'the bull and the horse escaped'

3 The argument structure of verbs of being and becoming

The verb 'to be, stay, remain' is **jèn**. The verb 'to become' is **wèy**. The verb **jèn** but not the verb **wèy** can be followed by locative arguments. The two verbs share, however, the characteristic of having property concept complements.

(25) tu-ŋ gol go gonì kún-do jèn téŋ
goat-DEF see REF hyena eye-3F remain different
ná se ày dú lúmá na
ASSC INCEPT take 3F trick HYP
'Goat noticed that Hyena had different intentions and tried the following trick'

The verb **jèn** 'remain' cannot be replaced by **wèy** 'become' in the preceding sentence.

(26) hòmyá kè-y áŋ wèy téŋ
sickness GEN-3M DEM become different
'his illness here has changed significantly for the worse'

The noun **kolo** 'word' also means 'anger' and is used with this meaning only as a complement of the verb **wèy** 'become':

(27) wèy dí kolo
become 3M word
'he became angry'

4 Property concept verbs

As we have seen, color terms and some other property concepts have been lexicalized as verbs. The evidence for this lexicalization is provided by the fact that the color terms have past, future, imperative, and verbal noun forms (all forms culled from W & P 1982):

(28)

Past	Gloss	Imperative	Future	Verbal Noun
ìndì	'be black'	ùndù	índè	ìndè
wilé	'be red'	wilé	wíilé	wilé
bol	'be blue'	bula	bóle	bole

These verbs take verbal subject pronouns in the same way as other verbs:

(29) ìndì dí
black 3M
'he is black' (about somebody who is intensely black)

The verb **ìndì** covers a range of colors including black, light blue, and dark blue.

(30) wilé dí
brown 3M
'he is brown' (about somebody whose color is not intensely black)

The verb **wìlé** refers to the range of colors covering red, dark rusty color, pink, light brown, and clay color.

If the subject is nominal, it precedes property concept verbs:

(31) tídí háŋ wilé
bird DEM red
'this bird is red'

(32) tídí háŋ bole
bird DEM blue
'this bird is blue'

The form **bole** refers to the range of colors covering all shades of green, blue, and also light yellow.

(33) me/gi lay
2F/2M pretty
'you are beautiful'

The referential suffix **wa** may occur in the predicative function if the subject has been mentioned before in discourse:

(34) kamda-y sùbù nò go lay wa tú
wives-3M three COP REF pretty very all (Fr.)
'his three wives were all beautiful'

If the subject has not been mentioned in discourse, the referential marker **wa** does not occur. The nominal subject can cooccur with the pronominal subject with the property concept verb:

(35) tamá tolo láy dú
woman DEM pretty 3F
'that woman is pretty'

(36) jè déŋrì dí
IMPF fat 3M
'he becomes fat'

(37) jè tą́yn dí
IMPF slim 3M
'he becomes slim'

(38)	déŋre	dí					
	fat:FUT	3M					
	'he will be fat'						
(39)	tą̃nyè	dí					
	slim:FUT	3M					
	'he will slim down'						
(40)	jè	wílé	dú				
	IMPF	red:FUT	3F				
	'she will become brown' (about a woman who takes medicine to become light skinned, a practice reported to be taking place in the late 1990s)						
(41)	déŋrì	dí	tùmó	kèlèn	káŋ	tą́y	dí
	fat	3M	before	fast	DEM	slim	3M
	'before, he was fat; now he is slim'						

5 Transitive and intransitive verbs

The term *transitive* designates verbs that can be followed by a noun or pronoun without any preposition. An intransitive verb is one that cannot be followed by a noun or pronoun without any preposition:

(42)	ŋ	ómè-y
	1SG	catch:FUT-3M
	'I will catch him'	
(43)	ŋ	òmí-y
	1SG	catch-3M
	'I caught him'	
(44)	ge	dùsí-y
	HUM	put in water-3M
	'he has been put in water' (to get a few mouthfuls as a part of swimming lesson)	

Many verbs can be used as both transitive and intransitive, i.e. with and without an object, without any additional markers of transitivity or intransitivity:

(45)	hay	dí	gùrbòlo	ke-y
	dry	3M	cloth	GEN-3M
	'he spread his clothes' (for drying)			

(46) kìb di -gè hay
mouth GEN:PL dry
'their mouths are also dry', 'they are also thirsty'

Some transitive verbs have non-controlling subjects, although they may have affected objects. In addition to verbs of internal states, consider the verb **ɓàl** 'satisfy, be sufficient'. It is a transitive verb in the sense of its taking two arguments marked by configuration alone, but its subject is not controlling:

(47) gi ɓàl-ìŋ nę́ỳ
2M suffice-1SG be much
'you suffice me a lot' (meaning: 'I had enough of you')

(48) gi ɓálè go òmé-y
2M suffice:FUT REF catch:VN-3M
'you will be able to catch it'

The verb **ɓàl** may participate in a serial verb construction as the second verb, providing a characterization of the main verb:

(49) ŋ dì wo ɓàl-ìŋ
1SG eat mush satisfy-1SG
'I ate mush to my satisfaction'

Of a some interest may be the existence of verbs **dùgì** 'drown' intransitive and **dùsí** 'dip, drown' transitive:

(50) dùgì dí kama ní
drown 3M water LOC
'he drowned in the water'

(51) kòbró dùgì ín-dí-gè kama ní
pirogue drown ASSC-GEN-3PL water LOC
'the pirogue sank with them in the water'

(52) ge dùsí-y
HUM dip-3M
'he has been dipped' (as part of a swimming lesson)

There are, however, no other instances of the potential deployment of **-s** as a causative marker in Lele.

The general characteristic of a verb as 'transitive' or 'intransitive' is not a good predictor of the syntactic properties of verbs in Lele and the semantic functions of their arguments. Instead, a better characterization is to describe the unmarked arguments of the verb, the semantic roles of the arguments, and how additional arguments or adjuncts are added to a given verb.

The language is nominative-accusative, and many transitive verbs have their subjects controlling and their objects affected. This is the case for verbs **dì** 'eat', **sì** 'drink', **sir** 'cut, kill', and many others. This is also the case for all verbs that can have controlling and affected arguments. Nevertheless, there are transitive verbs whose argument structure and semantic properties differ significantly from the properties of corresponding verbs in other nominative-accusative languages. In the following sections I describe first the syntax of transitive verbs and then the argument structures of various classes of verbs.

6 Arguments of transitive verbs

The difference between the subject and the object of a transitive verb is coded by the position of the arguments with respect to the verb. Nominal subjects precede the verb; objects follow the verb.

(53) kire kil gùjù kè-y lìŋdà
Kire sell millet GEN-3M yesterday
'Kire sold his millet yesterday'

If the verb has a third-person subject pronoun, such a pronoun follows the verb, and the object occurs after the pronoun:

(54) kire kil dí gùjù kè-y lìŋdà
Kire sell 3M millet GEN-3M yesterday
'It is Kire that sold his millet yesterday'

(55) wàl dú kùlbá-ŋ
slaughter 3F cow-DEF
'she slaughtered the cow'

Pronominal objects follow the verb. The pronominal object markers are as follows:

1SG	iŋ	1DU.INCL	ŋga	1PL.EXCL	ni
2M	gi			2PL	ŋgu
2F	me				
3 M	iy			3PL	ge
3F	du				

The first-person plural inclusive is formed through the combination of the first-person dual inclusive and the second-person plural: **ŋgaŋgu**.

The tone on the object pronouns replicates the last tone of the verb. If the verb ends in a consonant, the first-person object deployed is **iŋ** and the third-person object is **iy**. The vowel **i** in those two forms may well be epenthetic:

(56)	tóm-ín dí	'he hit me'
	tóm-gí dí	'he hit you (M)'
	tóm-mé	'he hit you (F)'
	tóm-íy dí	'he hit him'
	tóm-dú	'he hit her'
	tóm-gá í	'he hit us (DU.INCL)'
	tóm-gáŋgú dí	'he hit us (PL.INCL)'
	tóm-ní dí	'he hit us (EXCL)'
	tóm-gú dí	'he hit you (PL)'
	tóm-gé dí	'he hit them'

(57)	gìl-ìŋ dí	'he has shown me'
	gìl-gì dí	'he has shown you (M)'
	gìl-mè dí	'he has shown you (F)'
	gìl-ìy dí	'he has shown him'
	gìl-dù	'he has shown her'
	gìl-nì	'he has shown us (EXCL)'
	gìl-ŋgà	'he has shown us (DU.EXCL)'
	gìl-ŋgàŋgù dí	'he has shown the two of us'
	gìl-ŋgù dí	'he has shown you (PL)'
	gìl-gè dí	'he has shown them'

(58)	am-in dí	'he kept me'
	am-gi dí	
	am-me dí	
	am-iy dí	
	am-du	
	am-ni dí	
	am-ga dí (ŋ → Ø /m___C)	
	am-gaŋgu dí	
	am-gu dí (ŋ → Ø /m___C)	
	am-ge dí	

With multisyllabic verbs, the tone on the object pronoun is a copy of the preceding tone:

(59)	jìgrí-ŋ dí	'he scratched me'
	jìgrí-gí dí	'he scratched you (M)'
	jìgrí-mé dí	'he scratched you (F)'
	jìgrí-y dí	'he scratched him'

jìgrí-dú dí	'he scratched her'
jìgrí-ní dí	'he scratched us (EXCL)'
jìgrí-ŋgá dí	'he scratched us (DU.INCL)'
jìgrí-ŋgáŋgú dí	'he scratched us (PL.INCL)'
jìgrí-gé dí	'he scratched them'

If the verb ends in a vowel, the first-person object is **ŋ** and the third-person object is **y**:

(60) co-ŋ dí
take a short cut-1SG 3M
'he took a short cut to meet me'

co-y dí
take a short cut-3M 3M
'he took a short cut to meet him'

7 Interaction of subject and object pronouns

Since all object pronouns follow the verb and the third-person subject pronouns also follow the verb, the distinction between subject and object pronouns for the third person is marked by the morpheme order. The order of morphemes varies, depending on the person. If the subject and object are third-person plural and feminine, the first pronoun following the verb is the subject and the second pronoun is the object. Object pronouns copy the preceding tone, i.e. the tone of the subject pronoun:

(61) gol gé dú
see 3PL 3F
'they saw her'

(62) gol dú gé
see 3F 3PL
'she saw them'

The third-person masculine subject pronoun may be unmarked if there are object pronouns following the verb:

(63) gol-ge
see-3PL
'he saw them'

(64) gol-du
see-3F
'he saw her'

(65) gol-ni
see-1PL.EXCL
'he saw us'

(66) gol-nga
see-1DU.INCL
'he saw the two of us'

If the subject is third-person feminine or plural and the object is first or second person, the object is coded by position after the verb and the subject by position following the object:

(67) gol-nga gé
see-1DU.INCL 3PL
'they saw the two of us'

(68) gol-gi gé
see-2M 3PL
'they saw you'

(69) gol-iŋ dú
see-1SG 3F
'she saw me'

(70) gol-nga dú
see-1DU.INCL 3F
'she saw the two of us'

(71) gol-gi dú
see-2M 3F
'she saw you'

If the subject is first or second person and the object is third person, the subject precedes the verb and the object follows the verb:

(72) ŋ gilalí-dú
1SG tire-3F
'I tired her'

(73) ŋ gol-du dà débrèŋ
1SG see-3F PREP Debreng
'I saw her in Debreng'

(74 ŋ gol-ge dà kuso ni
1SG see-3PL PREP farm LOC
'I saw them on the farm'

(75) ŋ gol-gi dà kuso ni
1SG see-2M PREP farm LOC
'I saw you (M) on the farm'

(76) ŋ gol-me dà kuso ni
1SG see-2F PREP farm LOC
'I saw you (F) on the farm'

(77) gi gol-iŋ dà kuso ni
2SG see-1SG PREP farm LOC
'you saw me on the farm'

8 Unspecified objects: human, non-human, and place

The unspecified human singular object, corresponding to 'somebody', is coded by the word **bayndí** 'man':

(78) yàá bé bayndí ɗé
tell:IMP DAT person NEG
'do not tell anybody'

The unspecified human plural object is coded by the word **kara** 'people, men':

(79) hòmnyá dùglò kérgew
sickness swelling of testicles swelling of testicles
nè kara nèný
make people very much
'people suffer a lot from the swelling of testicles' (G-C & W 1981: 28-29)

The unspecified non-human object is coded by the word **kanya** 'thing':

(80) Kara màglí kanya
people prepare thing
'people arrange things . . . '

The unspecified place marker **kur** is deployed in existential constructions:

(81)	ìyà	nè	kur	nèný	lay
	wound	make	place	very much	also

'wounds are numerous' (G-C & W 1981: 30-31)

(82)	Gìdìrè	gùúgùje	ná	kàlo	nè	kur	ɗèl
	moon	warbling	ASSC	cold	make	place	surpass
	gìdìrè	go	kùb	kàlo.			
	moon	REF	mouth	cold			

'During the moon of warbling, the cold is even greater than during the moon of the beginning of the cold' (G-C & W 1981: 30-31)

9 Argument structure of verbs of fearing and loving

There are two verbs that have lexicalized desire, wish, pleasing. One is **tòb**, whose primary meaning is 'want, love'. This verb takes the object of desire as a syntactic object, and it must be human:

(83)	ŋ	tòb-dù
	1SG	want-3F

'I love/like her'

The other verb is **ege** 'please'. This verb has the object that pleases as the subject, and the person as object:

(84)	kolo	káŋ	ege-ŋ	nògò	go	ɗé
	word	DEM	please-1SG	a little	REF	NEG

'that word pleases me very much', lit. 'pleases me not a little'

(85)	yágé	ko-m	go	gi-né	bé-ŋ
	work	GEN-2M	REF-2M	make	DAT-1SG
	ege-ŋ	síɗé			
	please-1SG	much			

'your work that you did for me pleased me'

Pronominal arguments of the verb **ege** are coded as follows: the person who is loved is coded as the subject, the person who is experiencing the feeling of love is coded as the object:

(86)	dàdù	ege-y
	3F	please-3M

'he loves her'

(87) ege-y dú
please-3M 3F
'he loves her'

(88) ege-ŋ dú
please-1SG 3F
'I like her' or 'she pleases me'

The object of desire can be inanimate, and it is coded as the subject:

(89 kàmyà ege-ŋ
milk please-1SG
'I like milk'

The verb **sòndrí** 'fear' (cf. **sòndró** noun, 'fear') takes the person that fears as subject, and the person that evokes the fear as object:

(90) ŋ sòndrí cánìgé
1SG fear Canige
'I fear Canige'

(91) ŋ sòndrí-dú
1SG fear-3F
'I fear her'

10 The argument structure of the verb jé 'throw'

The verb **jé** 'throw' has a different argument structure from that of other transitive verbs. Its direct object may be the animal or person at which a thing is thrown. Thus, when the throwing involves knives, as in a hunt, the hunted animal is marked in the same way as direct objects are marked, viz. by the position after the verb:

(92) ólkúsìŋ jé bisí-ŋ jé-dú
Olkusin throw antelope-DEF throw-3F
dòŋlo-ro ni
high-3F LOC
'Olkusin threw at the antelope; he threw at her thigh'

11 Predication of internal states

Internal states have an argument structure quite different from that of other verbs. The person or animal experiencing the internal state is coded as the object of the verb **nè** 'make':

(93) kàẃ gé gàg tùwà dùgì-gè gílalé
walk 3PL till sun drown-3PL tiredness
pínyà nè-gè
also make-3PL
'They walked till the sun had drowned them and tiredness overwhelmed them.'

(94) kus-iy ne-y
body-3M make-3M
'he is sick', lit. 'his body makes him'

(95) time nè kara sí ɗé.
hunger make people a lot
'People are very hungry' (G-C & W 1981: 50-51)

(96) kàsìyà nè tamá-ŋ néy
shame make woman-DEF very much
'the woman was very ashamed . . .'

The verb **nè** may also have two objects following it. The first object is the person who suffers, and the second object codes the type of suffering:

(97) tamá kùlòn-dò nè nè-dù hòmnyá
woman belly-3F COP make-3F pain
'the woman's belly ached' (G-C & W 1981: 2-3)

If the internal state has been lexicalized as a noun, the experiencer of the internal state, the object of the verb **nè** 'make', is the topic of the clause. The evidence for the hypothesis that **gònì** 'hyena' is the topic of the first clause in sentence (98) is provided by the obligatory interpretation of clauses of internal states. Consider the following sentence:

(98) time nè gònì àlá gùmyá dú ɗé
hunger make hyena but large 3F NEG
'Hyena is very hungry but she is not large.'

The importance of this example is that both 'hunger' and 'hyena' are feminine nouns in Lele, and if **time** 'hunger' were indeed the topic, one would interpret the sentence as meaning 'hyena is hungry but its hunger is not big'. The evidence that **time** 'hunger' is feminine is provided by the following sentence:

(99) time jogú-ŋ dú
hunger bother-1SG 3F
'hunger, it bothers me'

The reason **time** 'hunger' is the subject of the clause is purely lexical, the notion of being hungry not having been lexicalized as a verb or an adjective.

The notion of 'falling, being in love' is realized through the noun **mìsèú** 'sexual arousal' as subject followed by **nè** and then by a noun or pronoun. The pronouns that follow **nè** are the same as the object pronouns:

(100) mìsèú nè-y
love make-3M
'he is in love'

(101) mìsèú nè-dù
love make-3F
'she is in love'

(102) mìsèú nè cànìgé
love make Canige
'Canige is in love'

12 The argument structure of the verb sí 'put, resemble'

The arguments of the verb **sí** can have quite different roles, depending on which nouns are used. If both subject and object are human, the verb means 'resemble':

(103) sí dí ba-y
resemble 3M father-3M
'he resembles his father'

If the object is not human and there is a locative adjunct, the verb has the meaning 'put':

(104) kùmno sí kàbi-y cà-m ni
God put hand-3M head-2M LOC
'God put his hand on you' (i.e., God blessed you)

13 Serial verb constructions

The term *serial verb construction* in Africanist and general literature refers to constructions where one or more verbs share the same arguments, the same polarity value, as well as the same tense and aspectual systems. Lele has many constructions that meet those criteria. These constructions, however, do differ from each other in many important features. Therefore, in the present discussions, serial verb constructions are described by the formal criteria pertaining chiefly to overt subject coding and to functional criteria, such as the role of the second verb in the construction. The question of why a language has serial verb constructions, the most interesting question from the typological point of view, can best be answered by an explanation of their function. The evidence in Lele clearly points to serial verb constructions' being in complementary distribution with other means of coding. Accordingly, the present description is organized according to the functions of serial verb constructions.

13.1 Formal properties of serial verb constructions

A serial verb construction in Lele has the subject and object marked with the first verb of the construction only. Both verbs have the same tense and modality characteristics. Consider the following clause:

(105)	dìgrì	dú	nȩ̀y
	kill	3F	be numerous
	'she killed a lot'		

That the form **nȩ̀y** in this construction is a verb is shown by the fact that in the future tense it undergoes inflectional changes that only verbs undergo:

(106)	gònì	jè	dígre	dú	nȩ́ye
	hyena	IMPF	kill:FUT	3F	be lot:FUT
	'hyena will kill a lot'				

An additional piece of evidence that **nȩ̀y** is a verb is provided by the fact that it can be used as the only predicate in a clause:

(107)	nȩ̀y	gé
	be numerous	3PL
	'they are numerous'	

The argument that the construction with **nȩ̀y** as the second verb is a serial verb construction is that the subject and object (if any) occur only once, with the first verb of the construction:

(108) dìgrì dú kòrà néỳ
kill 3F chickens be a lot
for 'she killed many chickens'

The subject may not be coded with the second verb:

(109) *dìgrì dú kòrà nẹ̀y dú
kill 3F chickens be a lot NEG
for 'she killed many chickens'

Nor can the object be coded with the second verb:

(110) *dìgrì dú nẹ̀y dú kòrà
kill 3F be a lot NEG chickens
'she killed many chickens'

Negation has been used as one of the testing tools to determine whether a sequence of verbs is a serial verb construction. The assumption usually is that in a serial verb construction, there can be only one polarity value. If a negative marker can be added to a construction, it can follow only the second verb. That follows from the fact that negation occurs in clause-final position. This fact also provides the evidence that the two verbs form one predicate, hence constitute a serial verb construction:

(111) dìgrì dú nẹ̀y ɗé
kill 3F be a lot NEG
'she did not kill many' (but she killed some)

(112) time nè gònì nẹ̀y ɗé
hunger make hyena be much NEG
'Hyena is not very hungry.'

Cf.:

(113) time nè gònì nẹ̀y
hunger make hyena be much
'Hyena is very hungry.'

The verb **kay** 'finish' behaves in a similar way to **nẹ̀y** in that it can follow another verb:

(114) lè tàsí kay ɗé
eat shea fruit NEG
'he did not finish eating the shea fruit'

(115) lè tàsí kay
eat shea fruit
'he ate shea fruit'

(116) kay dí tàsí
finish 3M shea fruit
'he finished the shea fruit'

With other serial verb constructions negation cannot be used:

(117) wá dí tòrò dìgrì ɗé
hit 3F hen kill NEG
'she hit the hen but did not kill it'

Cf.:

(118) wá dí tòrò dìgrì
hit 3F hen kill
'she hit the hen and killed it'

In a non-serial construction the first verb can be negated and the second verb can be in the affirmative. Moreover, if the two verbs have the same referent as object, the object must be coded twice:

(119) wá dí tòrò ɗé àlá dìgrì-y
hit 3F hen NEG but kill-3M
'she did not hit the hen, but she killed it'

There appear to be two variants of serial verb construction: one in which the subject of the first verb is also the subject of the second verb, and one in which the object of the preceding verb is also the object of the following verb:

(120) tamá dèr tíndí ná mụndu se wàdì
woman raise pestle ASSC silence INCEPT hit
ná tòrò-ŋ dìgrì
ASSC hen-DEF kill
'The woman quietly raised the pestle and beat the hen with it to death.'

One cannot add subject or object pronouns to the second verb in serial verb constructions:

(121)

tamá	dèr	tíndí	ná	mųndu	se
woman	raise	pestle	ASSC	silence	INCEPT

wàdì	ná	tòrò-ŋ	dìgrì-*dù	*dú
hit	ASSC	hen-DEF	kill-3F	3F

For 'the woman quietly raised the pestle and beat the hen with it to death.'

A serial verb construction does not represent a sequence of events. If a sequence of events is intended, the subject pronoun can be added to all the verbs in a sentence. This is the case when the inceptive marker separates the two verbs:

(122)

tamá	dèr	tíndí	ná	mųndu	se	wàdì
woman	raise	pestle	ASSC	silence	INCEPT	hit

ná	tòrò-ŋ	se	dìgrì	dú
ASSC	hen-DEF	INCEPT	kill	3F

'The woman quietly raised the pestle, beat the hen, and killed her.'

The difference between the serial verb construction and the coding of a sequence of events is represented by the telic construction where the verb **è** 'go' indicates that the verb that follows it is the completed purpose of the verb that precedes **è**:

(123)

tamá-ŋ	sòndrí	ná	se	ày	tòrò
woman-DEF	fear	ASSC	INCEPT	take	hen

è	ìm
go	bury

'The woman became scared, took the hen, and buried it.'

The approach taken in the present work is that serial verb constructions constitute a linguistic means of coding various functions, more specifically, coding the argument structure and adverbial function, i.e. the function of modifying the verb.

13.2 The adverbial function of serial verb constructions

One of the functions of serial verb constructions is the coding of adverbial function, i.e. the modification of an event or a verb itself. Serial verb construction is deployed when the relevant semantic properties have been lexicalized in a language in a verbal rather than an adverbial category. Here are some other examples of the deployment of a second verb in an adverbial function.

The verb **nę̀y** 'to do a lot, much' has the same tense value as the main verb of the clause. In the examples below, the main verb is **nè** 'make', the predicate of most internal states:

(124) time nè gònì nẹ̀y bé kolo dìgrì
hunger make hyena very much DAT reason kill
dú ìsą́n ɗé
3F nothing NEG
'Hyena is very hungry because it did not kill anything.'

(125) time né gònì néyè
hunger make:FUT hyena be much:FUT
'Hyena will be very hungry.'

One cannot have different values for the tense of the main verb and the second verb in a serial verb construction:

(126) *time nè gònì néye bè kolo
hunger make hyena do much:FUT DAT cause
dìgrì dú ìsą́n ɗé
kill 3F nothing NEG
for 'Hyena is very hungry because it did not kill anything'

The second verb in a serial verb construction also has limited deployment in various modalities. The verb **nẹ̀y** can occur only as the second verb in a serial verb construction, where it has the adverbial function 'do a lot', 'much'. Whether the past, future, or the nominalized form of this verb is used depends on the tense of the first verb. The second verb has the same tense form as the first verb:

(127) dì dí wo nẹ̀y
eat 3M mush be a lot
'he ate a lot'

(128) dé dí wo nẹ́yè
eat:FUT 3M mush be a lot:FUT
'he will eat a lot'

Some serial verb constructions have become fixed lexicalized expressions. The term for rain, clouds, is the same as the term for God, **kumno**. The expression 'it rains' is interesting in that it has a serial verb construction consisting of the verb **bá** (**bàá** [W & P 1982] 'fall' and the verb **ongi** 'push as in childbirth', and 'rain') in association with **bá** 'fall':

(129) kumno se bá ongi
rain INCEPT fall rain
'It started to rain'

The word **kumno** cannot be cross-referenced in the sentence with subject pronouns, whether masculine or feminine:

(130)

kumno	se	bá	*dí/*dú	ongi
rain	INCEPT	fall	3M/3F	rain

'It started to rain'

The distinction between serial verb constructions and verbs in a sequence may rest only in the function of the second verb. In the following sentence, the verb **wàl** 'slaughter' is a second verb in a sequence. Although it has no adverbial function and in fact it is separated from the first verb by an adverb of manner **ná mundu** 'in silence', it does not differ formally from serial verb constructions:

(131)

ɗe-du	jaŋ	jè	wèl	dú	kuná	ná
leave-3F	quietly	IMPF	sleep	3F	sleep	ASSC

an	dí	è	om	dùbàngú	yó-ró	ná
leave	3M	go	catch	sheep	mother-3F	ASSC

mundu	wàl
silence	slaughter

'He left her quietly while she was asleep, left the room, [and] caught an old sheep in silence and slaughtered it.'

13.3 The addition of an argumen through serial verb construction

Another function of serial verb construction is the addition of an argument in clauses involving verbs of saying. If the clause includes an addressee of a verb of saying and an object, the object is coded by the verb **ày** 'take' and the addressee is coded by the verb of saying:

(132)

Tamá	se	jè	ày	kolo	go	nè
woman	INCEPT	IMPF	take	reason	REF	make

ile	ná-ǹg	yàá	bè	ɓòdu.
cry:VN	ASSC-DEF	tell	DAT	monkey

'The woman explains to the monkey the reason for her tears:' (G-C & W 1981: 2-3)

13.4 Serial verb construction with different objects

The second verb in a serial verb construction may have a different object than the first verb, but then the object of the second verb is identical with the subject of the first verb:

(133)

dàdù	tu-ŋ	lèé	kàsùma	ɓàl-dù
3F	goat-DEF	eat	feed (grass, hay)	satisfy-3F

'As for Goat, it ate the feed to its satisfaction'

14 Coding the plurality of verbs

14.1 Forms of verbal plurality

Like many other Chadic languages, Lele has morphological means of adding plural markers to the verb (cf. Frajzyngier 1997a and references there, Newman 1990 and references there). Only some verbs have plural forms. There are only two means of coding plurality, and their distribution depends on the phonological properties of the verb. If the verb ends in a liquid or a glide, the plural suffix is **wi**. If the verb has high or low tone, the tone of the suffix is identical with the tone of the preceding verb. If the verb has mid tone, the tone on the plural suffix is high:

(134) wàl-wì 'cut'
way-wí 'quarrel, launch'
al-wí 'scream, holler'
cal-wí 'jump'
cir-wí 'agitate'

If the third-person subject is added, it occurs after the marker of plurality of the object:

(135) cànìgé wàl-wì dí kòlb-é
canige kill-PL 3M cow-PL
'it is Canige that slaughtered cows'

Another means is devoicing of the initial consonant of the verb. This means is available only for those verbs that have an initial voiced consonant, i.e. **b**, **d**, **g**, or **j**. Recall from the description of phonology that the devoicing of the initial consonant is accompanied by the change of tone from low to mid. Recall also that the initial devoicing can be attributed to the gemination of the initial consonant and the subsequent reduction of the geminated consonant to the simple consonant:

(136)	Singular		Plural
	dèr	'pull out, take out'	ter
	boy	'break'	poy

(With dissyllabic verbs, e.g. verbs that cannot end in a consonant, the second tone becomes high in the plural form:)

(137)	dìgrì	'kill'	tigrí

(138) dìgrì dí gùmá
kill 3M rat
'he killed a rat'

(139) tigrí dí gòm-ɛ́
kill:PL 3M rat-PL
'he killed rats'

The plural form of the verb may be derived through both the devoicing of the initial consonant and the suffix **wi**. This is the case of the form **bàá** 'fall down' and the plural **pad-wí** (W & P 1982 have **padiwí**). The plural form of the verb codes a repetitive event:

(140) ŋ bàá
'I fell'

(141) ŋ pad-wí híré
1SG fall-PL often
'I fell often'

Most likely, the form **pediwi** 'to whip many' is the plural of the verb **bè** 'to give'.

(142) gi pédu-wé gár-wè ɗé
2M whip-PL dog-PL NEG
'you should not whip dogs'

Although W & P 1982 do not indicate this connection, the phonological structure of the verb 'to whip many' is identical with the phonological structure of the verb 'fall'. As far as the semantic connection is concerned, the extension from 'give' to 'hit' is attested in other languages, e.g. in English and Polish. The presence of the consonant **d** in the plural forms of the verbs **pad-wí** and **pediwi** whip' may well indicate that the underlying form of the verb 'to fall' is actually **bàd** rather than **bàá** and that the underlying form of the verb 'to give' is **bèd** rather than **bè**. Recall that the word-final **d** is disallowed. Therefore, it is possible that in these verbs the word-final **d** was deleted. In other words with final **d**, an epenthetic vowel is added.

Another means of deriving a plural verb is through the suffix **m**. The realization of the past form of the verb **tèg** is [tèy]:

(143) tey dí gáŋgù
hit 3SG drum
'he beat a drum'

When the suffix **m** is added, the verb-final velar is deleted and the vowel of the verb becomes round under the influence of the following labial consonant:

(144) tóm dí gáŋgù
beat:PL 3M drum
'he hit many drums at a time'

(145) tóm gé gáŋgù
beat 3PL drum
'they hit many drums at a time'

It may well be that the verb **lam** 'feel by touching' is derived from the verb **ladí** 'touch' through the addition of the suffix **m** to the root **lad**, and the subsequent deletion of **d**. The vowel **a** does not become round, because being low, it is not sensitive to the rounding rule.

14.2 The functions of verbal plurality

The verbal plural codes plurality of action, plurality of intransitive subject, and plurality of the transitive object. If the object is marked for plural, the verb must have a plural suffix:

(146) cànìgé wàl-wì kòlb-é
canige kill-PL cow-PL
'Canige slaughtered cows'

Cf.:

(147) cànìgé wàl kùlbá
canige kill cow
'Canige slaughtered a cow'

But the plural suffix on the verb alone is a means of coding plurality of the object. This is the case for those nouns that do not have a singular-plural distinction:

(148) wal dí hìdà
cut 3M tree
'he cut a tree'

(149) wal-wi dí hìdá
cut-PL 3M tree
'he cut trees'

In the following example the devoicing of the initial consonant is the only means of indicating the plurality of the object, as the noun does not have the singular-plural distinction:

(150) cànìgé bòy dí hídà
canige break 3M stick
'it is Canige that broke a stick'

(151) càǹìgé poy dí hídà
canige break 3M stick
'it is Canige that broke sticks'

The intransitive verbs also code the plurality of participants. Consequently, one cannot use a plural subject with the singular form of the verb:

(152) gìr dí
run 3M
'he ran'

*nga gìr
1DU.INCL run
for 'we ran'

There are two plural forms of the verb **gìr** 'run'. Both forms devoice the initial consonants. Both forms also raise the tone from low to mid. But one form has the plural suffix -**wí** (with the deletion of **r**) and the other has the suffix **ni**:

(153) kiywí gé
run:PL 3PL
'they ran'

kirní gé
run:PL 3PL
'they ran'

nga kirní
'we (INCL) ran'

nga kiywí
'we (INCL) ran'

ni kirní
'we (EXCL) ran'

The plural forms of the verb cannot be used with explicitly singular subjects, even if the intended meaning involves intensive running:

(154) *kiy:wí dí
run:PL 3M
for 'he ran (a lot)'

gìr dí nę̀y
run 3M much
'he ran a lot'

*ŋ kiy:wí for 'I ran'

The plural form of the verb may have a different lexical meaning from its singular form. Thus the plural form **cib** of the verb **jìb** 'pierce' combined with the word **kàbú** 'hand', exceptionally without a possessive marker, means 'prohibit'.

(155) cib-du kàbú nę́y ná yàá bé
pierce:PL-3F hand very much ASSC tell DAT
bayndí ɗé
man NEG
'He prohibited her from telling anybody'

The singular form means 'pierce'. If used with body part, a possessor must accompany the body part:

(156) tàma táŋ jib kùb-rò
woman DEM:P pierce mouth-3F
'this woman pierced her mouth'[5]

14.3 Verbs without plural forms

Not all verbs can have a singular-plural distinction. There are verbs that are inherently plural, viz. that code events that are inherently plural. There is no distinction of number for the verb **wèl** 'sleep':

(157) wèl dí kuná
sleep 3M sleep
'he slept'

ni wèl kuná
1PL.EXCL sleep sleep
'we slept'

wèl gé kuná
'they slept'

There is no singular-plural distinction for the verb **kaw** 'walk':

[5] Refers to currently rare custom of piercing the mouth to insert pieces of straw or other decorative objects.

(158) kaw dí
walk 3M
'he walked'

kaw gé
'they walked'

It is also possible that the verb **om** 'catch' is already marked for plurality by the word-final **m**, and that it happens not to have a corresponding singular counterpart:

(159) om dí tídí
catch 3M bird
'he caught a bird'

(160) om dí tídí kínye
catch 3M bird COLL
'he caught many birds'

(161) óm gé tídí kínye
catch 3PL bird COLL
'they caught many birds'

The verb **am** 'domesticate' does not have a singular-plural distinction:

(162) am dí luŋba
domesticate 3M horse
'he domesticated a horse' (when a young horse is brought to a new household)

(163) am di loŋb-e
domesticate 3M horse-PL
'he domesticated horses'

(164) asi dí luŋmba
raise 3M horse
'he raised a horse'

(165) asi dí loŋb-e
raise 3M horse-PL
'he raised horses'

Similarly the verb **bàsì** 'miss, spend', used metaphorically for 'die', does not have a plural form:

(166) bàsì dí 'he died'
bàsì gé 'they died'

The explanation of why some verbs have a plural form and others do not must be sought in the function of plurality. We can narrow it to the function of coding the plurality of affected arguments. Hence objects of transitive verbs and affected subjects of intransitive verbs can have verbs coded for plurality. The non-affected subjects of intransitive verbs cannot.

15 Dative and benefactive arguments

The semantic function of the recipient of an object or of the beneficiary of an event may be marked by a configuration or by the preposition **bé**. When the dative is marked by configuration alone, it occupies the position after the verb. If there is a direct object, it follows the dative argument without any additional coding. The verb thus has two objects. The coding of two arguments following the verb without any preposition is allowed only if the meaning of the verb involves an activity for the benefit or the detriment of the human argument. The coding of the dative through the preposition is deployed only when the inherent meaning of the verb does not involve the benefit or the detriment of the human argument. There is thus a complementarity between the two means of coding the dative.

15.1 Double object constructions

A verb may be followed by two noun phrases without any additional marking. In such a construction the first noun phrase is the beneficiary of the event and the other is the direct object. The beneficiary is usually a person.

(167) na-y né-y kùryò
HYP-3M make:FUT-3M stranger
'he will make him a stranger', i.e. 'he will be treated as a guest'

If the verb **bè** 'give' has a nominal dative and a nominal direct object, the nominal dative occurs after the direct object:

(168) bè dí làlì cànìgé
gave 3M money Canige
'he gave Canige money'

(169) *bè dí cànìgé làlì
gave 3M Canige money
for 'he gave Canige money'

If the dative argument is a pronoun, it behaves like all other object pronouns, viz., it follows the verb **bè** 'give'. The direct object follows the subject pronoun:

(170) bé-ŋ dí làlì
gave-1SG 3M money
'he gave me money'

(171) ŋ bé-y làlí
1SG give-3M money
'I gave him money'

The verb **bòg** 'put, make' is used with the meaning 'cause' when an emotional state is involved. The experiencer of the verb, whether nominal or pronominal, follows the verb with its pronominal subject, if any, and the noun representing the emotional state follows the experiencer:

(172) bòy dí cànigé sòndró
put 3M Canige fear
'he frightened Canige'

Pronominal experiencers are coded like other object pronouns:

(173) bòg-ìŋ dú sòndró
put-1SG 3F fear
'she frightened me'

(174) ŋ bòy-dù sòndró
1SG put-3F fear
'I frightened her' (for the change g $\rightarrow$ y, cf. phonology)

(175) ŋ bòy-gè sòndró
1SG put-3PL fear
'I frightened them'

The third-person masculine object may be unmarked:

(176) bòy dú sòndró
put 3F fear
'she frightened him'

(177) bòg-ìŋ dú ésúá
put-1SG 3F strength
'she made me strong'

With the verb **ar** 'feed', it is the human argument that is the beneficiary of the predicate, regardless of its position, whether directly after the verb or after another argument:

(178) síndè ar tormo kama
Sinde feed girl water
'Side gave her daughter water'

(179) síndè ar kamá-(ŋ) karma
Sinde feed water-DEF children
'Side fed water to the children'

The verb **tòn** 'ask' behaves differently from other verbs of saying in that it codes the nominal addressee by the position following the verbal complex, without the preposition **bé** preceding it:

(180) tòn dí cànìgé kolo píná
ask 3SG Canige word one
'he asked Canige a question'

The reverse order of arguments after the verb **tòn** is not allowed:

(181) *tòn dí kolo píná cànìgé
ask 3SG word one Canige
for 'he asked Canige a question'

The pronominal addressee is coded by a pronoun following the verb directly rather than by the dative preposition:

(182) tòn-nì gé kolo píná
ask-1PL.EXCL 3PL word one
'they asked us a question'

15.2 Coding the dative through the preposition

If the verb is such that the benefit/detriment is not an inherent part of its meaning, the direct object follows the verb and the dative/benefactive argument is marked by the preposition **bé**[6]:

[6] In G-C & W 1981 the tone on this preposition is sometimes high, sometimes low, and sometimes high-low in the same syntactic environments and in the same tenses. In the present work the preposition is always represented with the high tone except in the material quoted from G-C & W 1981.

(183) síŋdè wę̌y wò bé toron-do
Sinde cook mush DAT daughter-3F
'Sinde cooked mush for her daughter'

The order Direct object Dative is not allowed even if the dative is marked by the preposition **bé**:

(184) *síŋdè wę̌y bé toron-do wò
Sinde cook DAT daughter-3F mush
for 'Sinde cooked mush for her daughter'

If the dative argument is a pronoun, it is marked by the same preposition **bé** preceding the personal pronouns. The mid front vowel of the preposition **be** is raised to **i** or **u** if the following suffix has a high front or a high back vowel respectively. The forms are as follows:

(185)

Singular		Plural	
1	bé-ŋ	1DU.INCL	bé-ngá
2M	bí-gí	1PL.EXCL	bí-ní
2F	bé-mé	2PL	bú-ngú
3M	bé-y	3PL	bé-gé
3F	bú-dú		

If the dative phrase has a pronoun as its head, two orders are possible: Subject Verb Dative Object or Subject Verb Object Dative. Hence the dative phrase with a pronominal head has more freedom of occurrence than the dative phrase with a nominal head. First examples of alternative word orders with semantic datives:

(186) kul bé-ŋ ką̌nya lè
buy:IMP DAT-1SG thing eat
'buy me some food'

(187) kul kañya lè bé-ŋ
buy:IMP thing eat DAT-1SG
'buy me some food'

(188) kul bé-y gùná
buy:IMP DAT-3SG peanuts
'buy him some peanuts'

(189) kul gùná bé-y
buy:IMP peanuts DAT-3SG
'buy him some peanuts'

(190) kul bé-gé tèmlé
buy:IMP DAT-3PL corn
'buy them some corn'

(191) kul tèmlé bé-gé
buy:IMP corn DAT-3PL
'buy them some corn'

Following are examples of alternative word orders with semantic benefactives:

(192) yàgí-dí bí-gí kásà
plant-3M DAT-2M corn
'he planted corn for you'

(193) jè yàgé dí kásà bí-gí
IMPF plant 3M corn DAT-2M
'he will plant corn for you'

(194) tàglí gé bé-ŋ kúní kuléŋ-di
sweep 3PL DAT-1SG room interior-3M
'they swept the room for me'

(195) tàglí gé kúní kuléŋ-di bé-ŋ
sweep 3PL room interior-3M DAT-1SG
'they swept the room for me'

Verbs of saying do not behave like the verb 'to give', and the dative must be marked by the preposition **bé**:

(196) dèr dí bé-ŋ gúnyè
tell 3M DAT-1SG story
'he told me a story'

Because of the lexical meaning of **gúnyè** 'spider, story' and the meaning of the verb **dèr** as 'pick up', the reverse order of arguments produces quite a different meaning:

(197) dèr dí gúnyè bé-ŋ
pick up 3M spider DAT-1SG
'he picked up a spider for me'

If there are no lexical constraints similar to the one illustrated in the preceding example, both orders of arguments are allowed after a verb of saying, even if one of the arguments is a 'heavy noun phrase', e.g. a noun phrase modified by a relative clause:

(198)	yàá	dí	bé-ŋ	kolo-ŋ	go	éywa
	say	3M	DAT-1SG	word-DEF	REF	sweet

'he told me an interesting thing'

(199)	yàá	dí	kolo-ŋ	go	éywa	bé-ŋ
	say	3M	word-DEF	REF	sweet	DAT-1SG

'he told me an interesting thing'

(200)	Ng	yáà	bé	mè	ná	kìrè-ì.
	1SG	tell:FUT	DAT	2F	ASSC	way-3M

'I will tell you the way out of it' (G-C & W 1981: 2-3)

(201)	yàá	béè	bayndi	ɗé
	tell:IMP	DAT	person	NEG

'do not tell anybody!' (G-C & W 1981: 2-3)

If the object of the verb of saying is clausal, only one order is allowed, viz. Dative-Object Complement clause:

(202)	yàá	gé	bé-ŋ	na	ŋ	ìrà
	say	3PL	DAT-1SG	HYP	1SG	go

'they told me to go'

(203)	*yàá	gé	ná	ŋ	ìrà	bé-ŋ
	say	3PL	HYP	1SG	go	DAT-1SG

for 'they told me to go'

The origin of the preposition **bé** as the grammaticalized verb **bè** 'to give' might suggest that it can only be used with respect to arguments for which something is done or given. The behavior of the verb **tòn** 'ask' supports this hypothesis further by not allowing the preposition **bé** with the addressee. Nevertheless, the form **bé** has fully grammaticalized as the dative marker, i.e. the marker of an affected argument, whether positively or adversely:

(204)	lòr	gé	bé-ŋ	kàsà
	burn	3PL	DAT-1SG	corn

'they burned my corn'

(205)	tìgrí	gé	bé-ŋ	gàr-we
	kill:PL	3PL	DAT-1SG	dog-PL

'they killed my dogs'

The dative preposition **bé** can be used for a malefactive as well as a benefactive function:

(206)	ŋ	pádè	cà-y	bórè	bé-y
	1SG	grill:FUT	head-3M	cut:FUT	DAT-3M

'I will get him', lit. 'grill his head, cut it off him'

The object of the clause with the adversely affected dative argument does not have to be a possession of the dative argument:

(207)	ùdrí	gé	bé-ŋ	gajé	karà
	take away	3PL	DAT-1SG	throwing knife	people
	kè-gè				
	GEN-3PL				

'they took away for me the throwing knives of the people'

16 The affectedness of the subject and reciprocal coding

The affectedness of the subject is coded through the use of the word **kusu** 'body' followed by plural pronouns coding the person of the participant. The affectedness of the subject also subsumes the function of the reciprocal, where participants act on each other:

(208)	dà	túgú	tóŋ	ni [pause]		ná	gáw
	PREP	village	certain:F	LOC		ASSC	hunter
	kóŋ	ná	tamą́-y	tòb	gé	kusi-ge	néỳ
	certain	ASSC	wife-3M	like	3PL	body-3PL	a lot

'In a village a certain hunter and his wife loved each other very much.'

(209)	Dàgè	se	ajigi	kusi-gè.
	3PL	INCEPT	greet	body-3PL

'They greeted each other.' (G-C & W 1981: 4-5)

(210)	ngú	hábe	kusu-ngu	wàyán	gà
	2PL	see:FUT	body-2PL	tomorrow	Q

'will you meet tomorrow?'

(211)	òjì	gé	kusi-ge	gà
	help	3PL	body-3PL	Q

'did they help each other?'

The dative reciprocal is coded by the form **kusu** plus pronoun following the verb:

(212)	bé	gé	kusi-ge	sìí
	give	3PL	body-3PL	meat

'they gave each other meat'

The reciprocal form **kusu** plus pronoun may also be marked by the associative preposition, thus functioning in a clause as an adverb of manner:

(213)	dèr	gé	gúnyè	ná	kusi-ge
	pick up	3PL	story	ASSC	body-3PL

'they told each other stories'

The noun **kusu** may be followed by plural pronouns other than the third-person plural:

(214)	ní	dèr	gúnyè	ná	kusi-nì
	1PL	pick up	story	ASSC	body-1PL

'we told each other stories'

(215)	gén	gé	kòlbé	ná	kusi-ge
	change	3PL	cows	ASSC	body-3PL

'they exchanged cows among themselves'

17 Source

Nominal source is coded by the associative preposition **ná** preceding the head noun:

(216)	kil	dí	kùlbá	ná	kiya
	buy	3M	cow	ASSC	Kiya

'he bought a cow from Kiya'

A pronominal source may be coded by two constructions: one involves the associative preposition **ná** 'with' and the associative form of the pronoun, viz. **ín** + Pronoun:

(217)	kil	dí	ná	ín-ìŋ	kùlbá
	buy	3M	ASSC	from-1SG	cow

'he bought a cow from me'

(218)	kil	dí	ná	ín-ìŋ	kùlbá	ɗé
	buy	3M	ASSC	from-1SG	cow	NEG

'he didn't buy a cow from me'

The form **ín** is not used with a nominal argument:

(219)	*kil	dí	kùlbá	ná	ín	kiya
	buy	3M	cow	ASSC	from	Kiya

for 'he bought a cow from Kiya'

The reason one form of the first-person inclusive is postulated is that the marker of the function of the pronoun occurs only once, before the whole complex.

The source may also be coded by the locative particle **ni** occurring after a noun phrase. The noun phrase must be coded as a possessive construction:

(220)	ùdrí	gé	gajé	karà	kè-gè
	take away	3PL	throwing knife	people	GEN-3PL
	kàb-ìŋ	ni			
	hand-1SG	LOC			

'they took away from me the throwing knives of the people'

18 The associative construction

The associative construction consists of the verb plus appropriate subject suffixes (for third person) plus the preposition **ná** 'with'. The associative argument follows the subject. If the subject is an associative construction, the verb must have the plural pronominal marker. After the first component, which must be nominal, there is the plural independent pronoun **dàgè**. The associative marker follows the third-person plural pronoun:

(221)	gìlkínín	dàgè	ná	kiya	kil	gé	kùlbá
	Gilkinin	3PL	ASSC	Kiya	buy	3PL	cow

'Gilkinin and Kiya bought a cow'

A pronoun may be the first component in an associative phrase. But when this is the case, the third-person plural pronoun **dàgè** is not used:

(222)	dày	ná	kiya	kil	gé	kùlbá
	3M	ASSC	Kiya	buy	3PL	cow

'he bought a cow with Kiya'

The pronoun may be the second component in an associative phrase, but the associative form of the pronoun must be used and the third-person plural pronoun **dàgè** must also be deployed:

(223)	kiya	dàgè	ná	ín-dì	kil	gé	kùlbá
	Kiya	3PL	ASSC	ASSC-3M	buy	3PL	cow

'Kiya bought a cow with him'

(224) *kiya dàgè ná dày kil gé kùlbá
Kiya 3PL ASSC 3M buy 3PL cow
for 'Kiya bought a cow with him'

If a source is to be added to a clause that already has an associative construction, then the source may be coded by the associative or by the genitive marker:

(225) gìlkínín dàgè ná kiya kil gé kùlbá
Gilkinin 3PL ASSC Kiya buy 3PL cow
ná pósén
ASSC Posen
'Gilkinin and Kiya bought a cow from Posen'

(226) gìlkínín dàgè ná kiya kil gé kùlbá go
Gilkinin 3PL ASSC Kiya buy 3PL cow REF
pósén kè-y
Posen GEN-3SG
'Gilkinin and Kiya bought a cow of Posen's'

The evidence that the form **ná** is an associative preposition is provided by the fact that it may occur without the first conjunct:

(227) è je dí ná kama
go VENT 3SG ASSC water
'he brought water'

If there is a dative argument marked by the preposition **bé**, then the associative particle **ná** is separated from its object by the preposition. Thus the associative marker behaves very much like a modifier of the verb. It codes the verb for the type of argument it occurs with. The associative preposition resembles a verbal extension of other Chadic languages:

(228) è jè dí ná bé-ngá kama
go VENT 3M ASSC DAT-1DU.INCL water
'he brought us water'

(229) à jè ná bí-ní kama
go:IMP VENT ASSC for-1PL.EXCL water
'fetch us some water'

One cannot use an associative phrase marked by **ná** with a source marked by **ná**:

(230) *à jè ná bé-ŋ kama ná
go:IMP VENT ASSC DAT-1PL.EXCL water ASSC
kùlmá/kiya
well/Kiya
for 'fetch me some water from the well/Kiya'

Instead, a genitive construction with the referential marker is employed, with the source marked for the locative function through the appropriate prepositions and postpositions:

(231) à jè ná bé-ŋ kama
go:IMP VENT ASSC DAT-1PL.EXCL water
go dà kùlmá ni
REF PREP well LOC
'fetch me some water from the well'

The range of specific semantic functions of the associative argument is quite wide. In the following sentence the associative codes the thing for which one barters an object:

(232) jè è jè kèsì jáy bé tamá túg
IMPF go VENT share part DAT wife compound
ni lay jay kóŋ jè ą́y
LOC also part certain:M IMPF take (yes, nasal vowel
ná kasa lay gùnà lay
ASSC corn also peanuts also
'. . . he shared some with his wife at home, and some he
bartered for corn and peanuts.'

19 Coding the topic of a mental verb

The topic of a mental verb, i.e. an object that one thinks about, dreams about, and so on, is coded by the form **cà** plus the possessive pronoun plus the locative marker **ni**. The deployment of the form **cà** plus pronoun is obligatory. The body parts that are supposed to be the seats of the mental activity involved often represent the subjects of such verbs. Thus verbs of 'thinking' and 'worrying' have **kùlò** 'belly' as its subject:

(233) ɗa kùlò-m bùrá cà-nìng ni
leave:IMP belly-2M worry head-1SG LOC
'do not worry about me!' (G-C & W 1981: 4-5)

(234)	kùlèŋ-dì	bor	cà-y/rò	ni
	belly-3M	remember	head-3M/3F	LOC

'he remembers him/her'

(235)	ŋ	jè	kirbi	cà-y	ni
	1SG	IMPF	think	head-3M	LOC

'I think about him'

The form **cà** allows one to distinguish between the locative and the topic-of-conversation function of a phrase:

(236)	kàyo	se	jé	àlé	dà
	squirrel	INCEPT	throw	announcement	PREP
	kùná-y	gų́yé	cà-y	ni	. . .
	uncle-3M	spider	head-3M	LOC	

'Squirrel makes an announcement concerning his uncle Spider . . . '

Cf.:

(237)	kàyo	se	jé	àlé	dà
	squirrel	INCEPT	throw	announcement	PREP
	kùná-y	gų́yé	ni	. . .	
	uncle-3M	spider	LOC		

'Squirrel makes an announcement at the place of his uncle Spider'

(238)	me	ɓàl	go	wesé	cà-nìŋ	ɗé	ná
	2F	able	REF	hide:VN	head-1SG	NEG	ASSC
	ìrá	túgú	ka-re	kè-gè			
	go:IMP	home	parents-2F	GEN-3PL			

'You cannot cover up for me, so go to your parents.'

(239)	sí	gé	kirbe	kè-gè	cànìgé	cà-y	ni
	put	3PL	thought	GEN-3PL	Canige	head-3M	LOC

'they remembered Canige', lit. 'they put their thoughts on Canige's head'

The evidence that the word **cà** represents 'head' is provided by its use as an object of transitive verbs and as a locative argument:

(240)	ŋ	lam	cà-y
	1SG	touch	head-3M

'I felt his head'

(241)	ŋ	ladí	cà-y
	1SG	touch	head-3M

'I touched his head'

(242)

sú	dà	cà-m	ni
put:IMP	PREP	head-2M	LOC

'put [it] on your head'

20 Coding the affectedness of the subject: the punctual aspect

The form **cà** 'head' followed by an inalienable possessive pronoun codes the affectedness of the subject with transitive verbs. One piece of evidence for this function of **cà** plus pronoun is provided by clauses where the same verb takes as its object an ordinary noun and in another clause where it takes the form **cà** + Pronoun as its object. Consider the verb **haba** 'find'. With the form **cà** + pronoun cross-referencing the subject, it is the subject that is affected:

(243)

haba	bé-ŋ	cà-m
find:IMP	DAT-1SG	head-2M

'be successful!', lit. 'find me your head'

Cf.:

(244)

haba	bé-ŋ	wédré
find:IMP	DAT-1SG	car

'find me a car'

The form **cà** is deployed to code the subject in motion, hence the affectedness of the subject. But not every motion requires the deployment of **cà**. An examination of natural and elicited data indicates that **cà** codes only the punctual aspect with verbs of motion:

(245)

Dà	kur	go	kumno	è	dàná	ná	kìn-je
PREP	day	REF	God	go	UP	ASSC	return-VENT
cà-ì	è-je		hab	kara		tòn-gè	na
head-3M	go-VENT		find	people		ask-3PL	HYP

'When the God was going up, he returned, found people, and asked them:' (G-C & W 1981: 7-8)

(246)

yàá	bú-dú		na	ŋ	án	kwánì	
tell	DAT-3F		HYP	1SG	leave	outside	
ba	ŋ	jìb	cà-nìŋ		ná	kòyè	ba
COM	1SG	bump	head-1SG		ASSC	thief	COM
ŋ	dìgr-ìy						
1SG	kill-3M						

'He told her: leaving the house I hit my head against a thief and I killed him.'

(247)

yú	cà-rè	dà	kama	te-y	ni
put:IMP	head-2M	PREP	water	bottom-3M	LOC

ba	me	ágè	ísí-ŋ
COM	2F	take:FUT	bone-DEF

'Plunge to the bottom of the water and you will get the bone.'

With the verb **kàywí** 'divide, split' the addition of **cà** codes the affectedness of the subject:

(248)

kàywí	dí	cà-y
divide	3M	head-3M

'he disappeared'

Cf.:

(249)

kàywí	dí	hída
divide	3M	wood

'he divided wood'

With the verb **jèé** 'throw' the form **cà** codes the information that the subject rather than the object is in movement:

(250)

jèé	dí	cà-y	kìn	ódí
throw	3M	head-3M	return	leave

'he turned around and went back'

Cf.:

(251)

jèé	dí	gìjá
throw	3M	throwing knife

'he launched a throwing knife'

Verbs of movement may have the construction **cà** + Possessive pronoun as their object. The pronoun following **cà** cross-references the subject of the clause. Given the punctual function of **cà** in other constructions, I assume that that such clauses also code punctuality of movement:

(252)

nè	kínè	dí	cà-y	(dà)	dèbréŋ
IMPF	return:FUT	3M	head-3M	PREP	Debreng

'he will return to Debreng'

Cf.:

(253)

nè	kínè	dí	(dà)	dèbréŋ
IMPF	return:FUT	3M	PREP	Debreng

'he will return to Debreng'

Here are examples of the deployment of **cà** plus a possessive pronoun for other persons:

(254)

kìn	dú	cà-rò
return	3F	head-3F

'she returned'

(255)

ŋ	kìn	cà-nìŋ
1SG	return	head-1SG

'she returned'

(256)

kùn	jè	cà-m
return:IMP	VENT	head-2M

'return here!'

(257)

kìn	cà-y
go out again	head-3M

'he went'

(258)

kìn	dí	cà-y	Bongor
return	3M	head-3M	Bongor

'he returned to Bongor'

Cf.:

(259)

kìn	dí	Bongor
return	3M	Bongor

'he returned to Bongor'

The additional piece of evidence that the form **cà** + Pronoun codes the punctual aspect is provided by the fact that this form cannot be used with verbs whose inherent meaning involves punctual movement of the subject, such as **è** 'depart', **ɓá** 'fall', **se** 'get up', **jèn** 'sit down'. The reason why punctual verbs cannot be used with the marker of punctuality is the semantic tautology of lexical and grammatical means:

(260)

ɓá	dí	*cà-y
fall	3M	head-3M

'he fell down'

(261)

è	dí	*cà-y
go	3M	head-3M

'he went'

(262)

se	dí	dà	na
get up	3M	PREP	UP

'he got-up' (**cà-y** may not be inserted after **dí** or anywhere else)

(263) jèn dí kúsìnyǫ́
sit 3M ground
'he sat down'

21 Coding the affectedness of the subject: the non-punctual aspect

The form **kusu** 'body' followed by possessive pronouns coding the number, gender, and person of the subject is also used to code the affectedness of the subject. But unlike the form **cà** plus pronoun, **kusu** codes a non-punctual event.

(264) na-du è go mónge kusu-ro kúsìnyo pinyà
HYP-3F go REF bend body-3F ground even
na-du hab kìrè ɗé lay
HYP-3F find way NEG also
'when she wants to bend forward, she does not find a way to do so' (G-C & W 1981: 10-11)

(265) dàw-gé kusi-gè jèn wàl-gé ɗangá ná
gather-3PL body-3PL stay cut-3PL calabash ASSC
kur wèlè-ì wèlè-ì.
day lie down:VN-3M lie down:VN-3M
'they [women] gather and spend all day lying down and carving calabashes' (G-C & W 1981: 40-41)

(266) ba gi ɗe kusu-m wèl kúní
COM 2M leave body-2M lie down home
'and you lie down at home' (G-C & W 1981: 16-17)

The form **kusu** plus appropriate pronouns can be used as the only argument of the clause:

(267) Gìna tòrò go sol-gé na bàá gùlà na
if hen REF bother-3PL HYP fall left HYP
kusi-gè ná lápínyà pet.
body-3PL ASSC well all
'If the hen falls on her left side, everybody will be well.' (G-C & W 1981: 38-39)

(267) dàdù se è cánmínè ile kusu-ro;
3F INCEPT go bush? weep body-3F
'she went into bush and wept' (G-C & W 1981: 2-3)

The form **kusu** is also used in meanings that in some IE languages involve reflexive markers:

(268)

ŋ	je	wále	kus-iŋ
1SG	IMPF	swear:FUT	body-1SG

'I will swear'

(269)

ɗá	wala	kusu-m	bàb	ɗé
leave:IMP	swear:IMP	body-2M	all	NEG

'do not swear for nothing'

(270)

cànìgé	tèy	kus-iy	ná	ìyá
Canige	hit	body-3M	ASSC	wound

'he hit himself'

(271)

tèy	dí	kus-iy
hit	3M	body-3M

'he hit himself'

(272)

dìgrì	kus-iy
kill	body-3M

'he killed himself'

The form **kusu** is not used, however, if a specific part of the body is an object of the clause:

(273)

bòy	dí	gàn-dì
break	3M	leg-3M

'he broke his leg'

(274)

bòy	dú	gàn-dò
break	3F	leg-3F

'she broke her leg'

One does not use the noun **kusu** with verbs of perception:

(275)

gol	tùnè-y	kama	ni
see	image-3M	water	LOC

'he saw his image in the water'

Therefore, an analysis of **kusu** as a type of reflexive marker is not justified.

22 Locative argument marking

The most important elements determining the form of the locative argument coding are the inherent properties of verbs of movement and the inherent properties of nouns to be deployed as the locative argument. Each verb of movement codes a different aspect of movement. Not all verbs of movement can be followed by locative arguments.

22.1 Semantic properties of verbs of movement

Each verb of movement in Lele has different properties with respect to the parameters it encodes. More specifically, some verbs have lexicalized parameters such as direction away from a deictic center, toward a deictic center, from inside a deictic center; other verbs of movement code just the manner of movement without the direction. As a result of those lexicalizations, if one wants to combine movement, direction, and manner, one has to combine several verbs. The order of the verbs is as follows: manner movement direction. Consider the verb **gìr**, which means 'run away, escape from', as evidenced by clauses where it is the only verb:

(276) gìr go làmndá ba gùmnò ni
run REF elephant fall buffalo LOC
'run from an elephant, fall upon a buffalo' (a proverb)

If one wants to add direction toward a goal rather than away from the source, one has to add verbs coding a different direction, e.g. **è je** 'come' or **è** 'go':

(277) gìr è jè hàŋ
run go VENT here
'he ran in here'

(278) àlá gìr è yàá kolo-ŋ bé kùrmbàlo
but run go tell word-DEF DAT chief
'But instead she ran and informed the chief.'

Without the verb coding directionality, the verb **gìr** cannot be used in the directional sense:

(279) *àlá gìr yàá kolo-ŋ bé kùrmbàlo
but run tell word-DEF DAT chief
for 'But instead she ran and informed the chief' or'But instead she ran to inform the chief.'

The following represents the inherent directional properties of verbs that have them:

(280) è 'go to' jè 'come'
se 'go from'
án 'leave'

In addition some verbs that code manner also code direction, e.g., **gìr** 'to run away, escape from' codes direction away from a deictic center.

22.2 Inherently locative nouns with directional verbs

If the predicate is a directional verb and if the head of the locative expression is inherently locative, such as a locative adverb or a toponym, the locative argument behaves like an object of a transitive verb, i.e., it is marked by configuration alone, occupying the position after the verb of movement. This manner of coding is natural given the fact that the verb inherently codes the direction.

(281) Ng se dàná,
1SG get up UP
'I get up . . .' (G-C & W 1981: 14-15)

The verb **è** codes movement toward a goal; hence there is no need to code in addition the locative argument as a goal:

(282) wìlèn dí è dí Bongor
lack 3M go 3M Bongor
'he is not here, he left for Bongor'

If one wants to code moving away from a source, the verb **se** 'get up, raise' is deployed. If one wants to indicate arrival at a place, the verb **jè** 'come' is deployed, albeit in most cases following the verb **è** 'go to'. In none of these cases is there a need to deploy a locative preposition:

(283) ŋ se bòngór ba ŋ è jè Maroua
1SG leave Bongor COM 1SG go VENT Maroua
ná tùwà gùyé bày
ASSC day work five
'I left Bongor and arrived at Maroua on Friday'

The noun **túgú** 'home, compound, village' functions as either inherently locative or non-locative in that it can occur after a directional verb of movement with or without a locative marker.

(284) ng è-jé ná túgú
1SG go-VENT ASSC village
'I bring them home' (G-C & W 1981: 14-15)

The evidence that the inherently locative complement behaves in the same way as the direct object is provided by the following example, where **túgú** 'home' is not a locative argument:

(285)	Kara	go	tòb-gé	go	ɗòdè	túgú
	people	REL	want-3PL	REF	move:VN	home
	'people who want to move their compound'					

In the following examples the noun **túgú** is marked as an adjunct, i.e., it has a preposition preceding it and the locative postposition following it:

(286)	kà[w]	ngà	túg	kò-m	ni
	go:IMP	1DU.INCL	home	GEN-2SG	LOC
	gólè	kùní	kùlè-ndì		
	see:FUT	home	interior-3M		
	'let's go to your home [and] we will see the interior of the house'				

22.3 Coding the locative through prepositions

There are very few instances in natural discourse where the complement of a directional verb of movement is marked by a preposition. Most often, the coding of an argument as a locative involves those nouns that are not inherently locative and therefore could be interpreted as acting in a number of functions in the clause. Coding them as locatives prevents all other interpretations:

(287)	gìr	ná	ín-dì	hą̀	è	gé	ná
	run	ASSC	ASSC-3M	till (Ar.)	go	3PL	ASSC
	dà	kama	kìb-ìy	ni			
	PREP	river	edge-3M	LOC			
	'She ran with him till they arrived at a bank of the river.'						

(288)	è	dí	dà	dúbù	kòlb-é	kè-gè	ni
	go	3M	PREP	corral	cow-PL	GEN-3PL	LOC
	'he went to the cow enclosure' (elicited)						

The noun **túgú** 'house, village, home' is marked for the locative function when the word means 'house, building' rather than 'home', i.e. the place from which the person comes:

(289)	se	è	gé	dà	túgú	pói	kúsíge-ŋ
	INCEPT	go	3PL	PREP	home	Poi	Kusige-DEF
	kè-y						
	GEN-3M						
	'they went to the house of Poi Kusige'						

(290) è-je-gé ná dà túg ní.
go-VENT-3PL ASSC PREP village LOC
'they take them [harvested plants] to the village'

Cf.:

(291) è-gé túgú sì-gé
go-3PL village drink-3PL
'they return to the village, they drink . . .'

(292) kàyo se om-iy jè se è
squirrel INCEPT catch-3M VENT INCEPT go
ná ín-dí dà kur go tumadu-ŋ ni
ASSC ASSC-3M PREP place REL death-DEF LOC
'Squirrel caught him, [and] brought him to the place of burial.'

Another preposition that can be used with verbs of movement is **gàg** 'until':

(293) càg dí kùbàrò kúsíyòŋ è ná gàg
spread 3M blood ground go ASSC until
sùgyá go kul kàrgà-y ni
grass REF house behind-3M LOC
'he spread the blood on the ground [and] went with it up to the grass behind the house'

22.4 Coding the locative through the postposition ni

If the noun phrase is not inherently locative, the locative phrase is marked by the postposition **ni** (**ní** in W & P 1982), which follows the noun phrase:

(294) na dú è sógú ni
HYP 3F go toilet LOC
'she pretended she was going to the toilet'

(295) dùgì dí kama ni
drown 3M water LOC
'he drowned in the water'

(296) kòbró dùgì ín-dí-gè kama ni
pirogue drown ASSC-GEN:PL-3PL water LOC
'the pirogue sank with them in the water'

The marker **ni** cannot be added if the locative phrase contains a toponym:

(297) *wìlèn dí è dí Bongor ni
lack 3M go 3M Bongor LOC
for 'he is not here, he left for Bongor'

The locative marker **ni** must be added to directional and stative locative expressions with inherently non-locative nouns:

(298)	ŋ	kil-iy	dà	ɓónú-m	ni
	1SG	buy-3M	from	brother-2M	LOC

'I bought it from your brother'

The locative marker is the only marker of the role of the noun when neither the verb nor the properties of the noun imply location:

(299)	ày	bùgú	kàb-ìy	ni	an	ná	kumno
	take	bag	hand-3M	LOC	leave	ASSC	God
	kam-dì						
	water-3M						

'he took a bag into his hands [and] he left in the rain'

When the source is marked by an associative preposition, it is not considered locative. One cannot add the locative marker **ni**:

(300)	ŋ	kil-iy	ná	ɓónú-m	*ni
	1SG	buy-3M	ASSC	brother-2M	LOC

'I bought it from your brother'

Some nouns appear to be lexicalized forms of a noun followed by the locative postposition **ni**. One such noun is **kúní** 'room', a compound of **kúl** 'house' and **ni** (cluster **ln** reduced as per the constraint against sequences of consonants with the same place of articulation); another is **caani** '(in) the field'. In locative expressions these nouns occur without any other postposition:

(301)	na	dú	è	kuni
	HYP	3F	go	room

'she pretended that she was going to her room'

These nouns can also occur as arguments of non-directional verbs.

22.5 Spatial orientation with respect to the deictic center

Spatial orientation with respect to the goal as a deictic center is coded through inalienable possessive constructions where the deictic center is the possessor and various orientations, such as front, back, near, on, under, are the possessums. As in many Chadic and non-Chadic languages of the area, some words that are employed as markers of spatial orientation are names for body parts, but, interestingly, some are not, at least not in contemporary Lele.

Behind:

(302) è ná sùgyá kàrgà-y ni
go ASSC grass behind-3M LOC
'he went with it behind the grass'

In front of:

(303) è ná sùgyá tìmè-y ni
go ASSC grass front-3M LOC
'he went with it in front of the grass'

In, inside:

(304) è ná sùgyá dure-y ni
go ASSC grass middle-3M LOC
'he went with it in the grass'

On, over:

(305) kàw dí sùgyá cà-y ni
walk 3M grass head-3M LOC
'he walked on the grass'

(306) tìdí se gé sùgyá cà-y ni
birds get up 3PL grass head-3M LOC
'birds flew over the grass'

Under:

(307) kalo gìr sùgyá te-y ni
snake run grass bottom-3M LOC
'the snake ran under the grass'

By, near:

(308) gìr dí sùgyá já-y ni
run 3M grass near-3M LOC
'he ran near the grass'

If the locative goal is modified by another construction with respect to a deictic center that is different, then the complement of the directional verb is coded through the inalienable possessive construction:

(309) è ná gàg sùgyá go kul kàrgà-y ni
go ASSC until grass REF house behind-3M LOC
'he went with it [the blood] up to the grass behind the house'

(310)

se	yàá	na-y	jé-y	dà	tòmbòsò
INCEPT	say	HYP-3M	throw-3M	PREP	grass spc.
dùré-y	ni	dà	sóyó	te-y	ni
inside-3M	LOC	PREP	tamarind	bottom-3M	LOC

'He said he threw him in the grass under the tamarind tree.'

The direction may also be coded through the deployment of the word **kìrè** 'road, way, passage' followed by a modifier, which encodes the deictic center:

(311)

è	ná	kìrè	sùgyá
go	ASSC	road	grass

'he went with it toward the grass'

22.6 Animate locatives

If the locative head is [+animate], such a noun must be marked for the locative function by another noun that does contain some locative characteristics. Such nouns serves as possessums of the [+animate] noun. Two nouns are deployed as locative coding means: **já** 'side' in inalienable possessive constructions, and **túgú** 'village, home' in alienable possessive constructions:

(312)

ŋ	se	dà	ɓónú-m	já-y	ni
1SG	leave	PREP	brother-2M	side-3M	LOC

'I come from your brother'

(313)

nè	è	dí	já	go	luŋba	kè-y	(ni)
IMPF	go	3M	side	REF	horse	GEN-3M	LOC

'he is going toward the horse'

If a proper noun serves as a locative goal or source, the lexeme **túgú** 'village, home' precedes such a noun to mark the locative function:

(314)

à	jè	ná	bé-ŋ	kama	
go:IMP	VENT	ASSC	DAT-1PL.EXCL	water	
go	dà	túgú	go	kiya	kè-y
REF	PREP	village	REF	Kiya	GEN-3SG

'fetch me some water from Kiya'

(315)

ŋ	se	dà	túgú	ɓónú-m	kè-y	ni
1SG	leave	PREP	village	brother-2M	GEN-3M	LOC

'I come from your brother'

(316) è dí túgú bùgà-y
go 3M village friend-3M
'he went to his friend'

If the possessor of the form **túgú** is the same as the subject, the locative direction is 'one's place, home' in English, **chez soi** in French:

(317) kìn gé túgú kè-gè
return 3PL home GEN-3PL
'they returned home'

22.7 The nominal object of the verb è 'go'

The verb **è** 'go' can take nominal, non-locative objects. Such objects are selected from a very restricted set of nouns. The nouns that can serve as objects of **è** must denote activities but do not necessarily derive from verbs:

(318) jè é gùyé
IMPF go:FUT work
'he will go to work'

(319) ŋ è gùyé
1 SG go work
'I went to work'

(320) è kuryò
go travel
'he went on a trip'

(321) è gé segré
go 3PL hunt
'they went hunting'

The noun **segré** 'hunt' is not a verbal noun, because there is no cognate verb 'to hunt'.

The definite marker can follow the nominal object if it has been previously mentioned in discourse:

(322) è gé segré-ŋ hàb gé bisí
go 3PL hunt-DEF find 3PL antelope'
'they went for the hunt [and] they found an antelope'

Nouns that do not denote an activity or that are not inherently locative cannot follow the verb **è** 'go' without some additional markers:

(323) *è tamą́-y
go wife-3M
for 'he went to his wife'

Even if a noun denotes an activity, it can be preceded by a directional preposition:

(324)	kíya	dàgè	ná	ólkusíŋ	è	gé	da	segré
	Kiya	3PL	ASSC	Olkusin	go	3PL	PREP	hunt
	'Kiya and Olkusin went on a hunt.'							

23 Conclusions

The arguments of the verb are coded by their configuration with respect to the verb. The subject is the argument preceding the verb; the object is the argument following. The unmarked subject, i.e. the absence of a nominal or pronominal subject in the matrix clause, codes the third-person masculine singular. If the object of the clause is non-human, it is not marked by nominal or pronominal markers if it has been mentioned before in the discourse. There are no semantic roles associated with the categories subject and object. The associated semantic roles depend on the semantic characteristics of the verb. Lele is a nominative-accusative type of language, in that if the verb is such that its arguments can be controlling and affected, the controlling argument is the subject and the affected argument is the object.
There are two means of coding the plurality of the verb: through the suffix **-wi** and through the devoicing of the initial voiced consonant. Verbal plurality codes plurality of the event, plurality of the object of the transitive verb, and plurality of the subject of the intransitive verb.

Verbs of internal states have a special type of coding whereby the person that experiences the internal state is coded as the object, and the cause of the internal state is coded as the subject.

The affectedness of the subject is combined with the aspectual coding: the affected subject and the punctual aspect are marked by the noun **cà** 'head' followed by possessive pronouns; the affectedness of the subject and the non-punctual aspect are coded by the word **kusu** and possessive pronouns.

The dative argument of verbs that have lexicalized action leading to the benefit or the detriment of an object is coded by the position after the verb. If the position after the verb is occupied by another noun, the recipient or beneficiary of the event is coded by the preposition **bé**, derived from the verb 'to give'.

The associative argument is marked by the preposition **nà**. Pronouns have a special associative form used only in associative constructions.

The locative argument of a directional verb is coded as a direct object. If the noun in the locative argument is not inherently locative, it is coded for the locative function by the postposition **ni** and the preposition **dà** (under certain conditions).

5

Adjuncts

1 Introduction

The present chapter describes the expressions that, with very few exceptions, can be added to any clause, regardless of the nature of the verb. These types of expressions have been sometimes called 'adverbs', 'adverbial phrases', and 'adjuncts'. In the present work they are referred to as 'adjuncts'. For each semantic class of adjuncts there are two types of expressions: those that have lexicalized the given semantic notion in the lexical category of adjunct, and those that have lexicalized this notion in other lexical categories. Usually, if a given semantic function has been lexicalized as an adjunct, its addition to a clause does not involve the deployment of prepositions or postpositions. If the given semantic function has been lexicalized in a category other than adjunct, its addition to a clause requires the deployment of prepositions or another coding means.

2 Locative adverbs

Locative adverbs differ from locative complements of directional verbs in that they can be added to any clause. Some of these expressions are inherently adverbial, and consequently they do not require a preposition to code their role in the clause. One of these adverbs is **kúsìyoŋ** 'ground':

(1) càg dí kùbàrò kúsìyoŋ
spread 3M blood ground
'he spread blood on the ground'[7]

The adverb **kwánì** (W & P 1982, **kúwàní**) 'outside' indicates where an event is taking place:

(2) . . . jè yàá bé kàràn-dò kamda kwánì
IMPF tell DAT friends-3F women outside
'[Everything that was going on at home] she would tell to her women friends outside'

The same adverb works similarly with the direct object. If the adverb **kwánì** follows the direct object, it indicates the location of the direct object outside of the deictic center:

(3) kudo-ro-ŋ jè ɗeŋlí kolo kạ́nyé
husband-3F-DEF IMPF hear word certain:PL
kwáni ná [pause] yàá ísaŋ ɗé
outside ASSC say nothing NEG
'Her husband heard certain things outside, but he did not say anything.'

One can put the adverb **kwánì** after the verb and before the direct object. The adverb **kwánì** then acquires the function of manner:

(4) kudo-ro-ŋ jè ɗeŋlí kwáni kolo
husband-3F-DEF IMPF hear outside word
kạ́nyé ná [pause] yàá ísaŋ ɗé
certain:PL ASSC say nothing NEG
'While her husband was inside he heard from outside certain things, but he did not say anything.'

(5) . . . jè yàá kwánì bé kàràn-dò kamda
IMPF tell outside DAT friends-3F women
'[Everything that was going on at home] she would tell outside to her women friends'

Lexical items that are not inherently adverbial even though they are inherently locatives require a preposition to mark their adverbial function:

---

[7] In elicitations, the insertion of the preposition **dà** was allowed before the word **kúsìyōŋ** 'ground,' but in natural discourse no such cases have been recorded.

(6) ŋ gol-iy dà Debreng
1SG see-3M PREP Debreng
'I saw him at Debreng'

(7) ŋ gol Kiya dà Debreng
1SG see Kiya PREP Debreng
'I saw Kiya at Debreng'

If the noun is not inherently locative, the locative preposition **ni** is added at the end of the locative phrase:

(8) ŋ gol kòjò dà kòlb-é dubu
1SG see hoe PREP cow-PL enlosure
dí-gé ni
GEN:PL-PL LOC
'I saw a hoe at the enclosure for the cows'

(9) dèsì dí gèléŋdì dà kúní kè-y-ni
forge 3M bracelet PREP hut GEN-3M-LOC
'he forged a bracelet in his house'

The phrase-final locative **ni** cannot be used with nouns that are inherently locative:

(10) *ŋ gol Kiya dà Debreng ni
1SG see Kiya PREP Debreng LOC
for 'I saw Kiya at Debreng'

3 Adverbs of time

Adverbs of time can occur in clause-initial or clause-final position. Some adverbs of time are marked by the associative marker **ná** and others are unmarked. Those that are unmarked are inherent adverbial expressions, and those that are marked are inherently nouns or belong to other lexical categories.

Among the inherently adverbs of time are **àlè** 'already, as of this time', **anyíŋ** 'recently', **gùdá** 'today'.

The form **àlè** is an adverb indicating that the event has taken place at a time after the lapse of some time presumed known to the hearer. This adverb is glossed as 'already'. The evidence for the function of the adverb is provided by the use of this form in clauses in which it may have no function other than adverbial:

(11) ŋ lèé sì àlé
1SG eat meat already
'I have already eaten meat' (I would prefer another dish)

(12) ŋ nàl àlé
1SG swim already
'I already swam'

(13) Dàdù ɓòdu tòn-dù na kur wèlè kèrè
3F monkey ask-3F HYP time spending GEN-2SG
kay àlè gà.
finish already Q
'Monkey asked her: has the time [of your pregnancy] finished already?' (G-C & W 1981: 4-5)

(14) Wèlè go tamá do ná kùlòngò nè
day REF woman REL:F ASSC pregnancy IMPF
wéè mira àlè ná kamda
give birth:FUT approach already ASSC women
sèn gé go sé tamá kolo wè ɗé.
know 3PL REF put woman reason give birth NEG
'When the time for a pregnant woman to give birth had already approached, other women did not know how to position her for the childbirth.' (G-C & W 1981: 2-3)

In a negative clause, the adverb **àlè** means 'anymore'. The adverb occurs after the negative marker:

(15) Nè máàní ba tamá lèé ɓòdu
COP ANAPH COM woman eat monkey
ɗé àlè
NEG already
'That is why the woman does not eat monkey anymore.' (G-C & W 1981: 4-5)

(16) ge yàá ná kumno ónge ɗé àlè.
HUM say ASSC God rain:FUT NEG already
'one says that it will not rain anymore' (G-C & W 1981: 22-23)

(17) túgú táŋ gè jèn màní ɗé àlè
town this HUM stay ANAPH NEG already
'this town is not inhabited anymore'

The adverb **anyíŋ** 'recently' occurs in clause-final position:

(18) è jè dú anyíŋ
go VENT 3F recently
'she came recently'

The adverb **tùmò** 'before, in the past 'occurring in clause-initial position indicates that the action described in the clause does not happen any longer:

(19) tùmò jèn dí dà dèbréŋ
before stay 3M PREP Debreng
'he used to live in Debreng'

The adverb **tùmò** can be placed after the verb. If the clause also has the allative marker **cáaní**, it occurs after the adverb of time:

(20) kil gé kàmyá tùmò cáaní
trade 3PL milk before away
'they used to sell milk'

An example of an inherently adverbial expression is **gùdá** 'today', categorized as a noun in W & P 1982. It occurs in clause-initial position and is not preceded by the preposition **ná**:

(21) gùdá kil dú kàsà cáaní ná kóli
today sell 3F sorghum away ASSC all
'she sold out sorghum today'

Examples of inherent nouns marked for adverbial function through the preposition **ná**:

(22) ná tóngò jè kil kásà cáaní kírè jáy ni
last year IMPF sell sorghum away road edge in
'last year she was selling sorghum at the side of the road'

(23) ná ɗigle tóŋ pìnà làmndá yé-y
ASSC year certain:F one elephant mother-3M
ne hòmnyá go ma
COP sick REF die
'One year, the mother of elephant was sick, close to her death.'

The adverb **dùkdùk** 'ever' has been recorded only in interrogative clauses:

(24) gi kín túgr-úm dùkdùk ɗé gà
2M return village-2M ever NEG Q
'have you ever returned to your village?'

But it may be the same adverb that is recorded in W & P 1982 as **dug-dug** 'absolutely not'.

4 Adverbs of manner

All adverbs of manner occur in clause-final position. Whether the adverbial phrase is marked by a preposition depends on whether the lexical item is an inherent adverb or not. Some lexical items deployed in an adverbial function are really modifiers without a narrowly defined scope, in the sense that they can be used to modify either a verb or a noun. When this is the case, I illustrate both functions.

4.1 Inherent adverbs

Inherent adverbs are not preceded by any markers indicating their role in the clause. Here is a selection of some of these adverbs:

ndì 'a little bit', which also serves as a quantifier with nouns, e.g. **sfi ndi** 'some meat':

(25) gìr dí ndi
run 3M a bit
'he ran a bit'

(26) gìr dú ndi
run 3F a bit
'she ran a bit'

Some adverbs of manner can occur in affirmative clauses only:

ndi gò 'a bit':

(27) ŋ gìr ndi gò
1SG run a bit only
'I ran a little'

(28) gìr dí ndi gò
run 3M a bit only
'he ran a bit'

Adverb **jaŋ** 'quietly':

(29) ɗe-du jaŋ jè wèl dú kuná
leave-3F quietly IMPF sleep 3F sleep
'he left her quietly while she was asleep . . . '

The adverb **mà** following imperative forms means 'just':

(30) ɗíŋglá mà
listen:IMP just
'just listen!'

(31) úr mà
stop:IMP just
'just stop!'

(32) à jè mà
go:IMP VENT just
'just come'

The modifier **càp** means 'hastily, fast'. It can serve as an adverb or a nominal modifier:

(33) ŋ è jè càp
1SG go VENT fast
'I came fast'

(34) ŋ è jè Maroua ná gan-iŋ càp ɓey
1SG go VENT Maroua ASSC foot-1SG fast only
'I came to Maroua on a fast foot', i.e. for a short period of time

The marker **càr**, possibly related to **càp**, means 'immediately':

(35) goni cál ba kama ni ná ɓàdì nè
hyena jump fall water LOC ASSC go after COP
ísì-ŋ càr
bone-DEF immediately
'The hyena jumped into the water and went immediately after the bone.'

The adverb **pínyà** 'also' cannot be used after the verb, but it can be used before the verb:

(36) kìb dí-gè hay *pínyà
mouth GEN:PL-3PL dry also
'their mouths are also dry', 'they are also thirsty'

(37) kìb dí-gè pínyà hay
mouth GEN:PL-3PL also dry
'their mouths are also dry', 'they are also thirsty'

4.2 Adverbial expressions with a copula and negation

For adverbs expressing quantity, corresponding to 'much', Lele has two expressions formed in a similar way. They consist essentially of the negation of 'little'. One expression can be analyzed as follows:

(38) nò gò go ɗé
COP little REF NEG
'not a little'

It is very likely that the expression is a euphemism for 'a lot, much':

(39) kolo káŋ ege-ŋ nò gò go ɗé
word DEM please-1SG COP a little REF NEG
'that word pleases me very much'

(40) gì lúmá nò gò go ɗé
2M intelligent COP a little REF NEG
'you (M) are intelligent like nobody else'

(41) me lúmá nò gò go ɗé
2F intelligent COP a little REF NEG
'you (F) are intelligent like nobody else'

5 Ideophones

The term ideophone, widely accepted in Africanist literature, designates lexical items that occur in a very limited environments, in most cases with just one other specific lexical item. In Lele all ideophones have the syntactic function of adverbs modifying verbs (rather than modal adverbs).

Some phonological properties, although not exclusive to the class of ideophones, occur nevertheless much more frequently with ideophones than with other lexical items. Very many ideophones are reduplicated. Many ideophones have an initial labiovelar stop, which seldom occurs with other classes of words.

The function of an ideophone depends on what lexical category it occurs with. If an ideophone follows a verb, it has an adverbial function:

mìlmìl 'thick' (about gathering of clouds):

(42) kumno se mìl, mìl, míl
God/cloud raise thick (about the clouds)
'there were thick, dark clouds'

Some ideophones are deployed as if they were onomatopoeic, even if no imitation of a sound is physically possible:

(43) gúló ile kùlúr kùlúr
lizard cry:VN kulur kulur
'Lizard cried, kulur, kulur' (G-C & W 1981: 8-9)

(44) gìr ngóyló ngóyló
run ngoylo ngoylo
'he ran ngoylo ngoylo' (about the running of the chameleon) (G-C & W 1981: 8-9)

pílá pílá 'at the same time':

(45) wíyà ín-dì pílá pílá
turn ASSC-3M at the same time
'turn with him at the same time' i.e. do not lose sight of him

bándà 'here and there'

(46) dày kíyá-ŋ ír tèy bándà
3M Kiya-DEF stay buttock-3M here and there
'Kíya remained here and there'

gàgàgàgà 'for a long time':

(47) da cáaní-ŋ kólòŋ gàgàgàgà
PREP bush-DEF there long time
'in the bush there long time'

Another phonological characteristic of ideophones is the presence of complex consonants in word-initial position. Thus prenasalized stops and labiovelar stops are present in those ideophones that are not reduplicated:

mbùńg 'just':

(48) Wáyngulú go kur wèl mbùńg,
morning REF time remain just then
'In the morning, just at the daybreak' (G-C & W 1981: 18-19)

ndám 'well':

(49) sáar dí je ndám
attach 3M VENT well (packed)
'tied up everything well'

An ideophone may also be onomatopoeic, at least in the speakers' perception of the word. Thus, the form **yùg yùg** 'many [about chicks]' is said to imitate the sound of chicks:

(50) ná tòrò-ŋ tèy karma yùg yùg
ASSC hen-DEF peck children many
'and the hen produced many chicks'

6 Adverbs through reduplication

In many Chadic languages reduplication of any lexical category derives an adverb. In Lele adverbs may also be derived from other lexical categories or from other adverbs. Thus from the adverb **sam** 'a little', reduplication provides the meaning 'slowly':

(51) Láràdí è kàrgà-ni sam sam
chameleon go back-3M a little a little
'chameleon followed him slowly' (G-C & W 1981: 8-9)

The quantifier **téŋ** 'alone' is reduplicated if there are many participants, becoming **téŋtéŋ** 'everyone alone, on his own', i.e. 'separately':

(52) cànìgé ná gìlkíníŋ è gé kàsùgù téŋtéŋ
Canige ASSC Gilkin go 3PL market separately
'Canige and Gilkinin went to the market separately'

7 Non-inherent adverbs

Non-inherent adverbs are marked by the associative preposition **ná**. Thus the notion of being alone is lexicalized through the form **kán** 'loneliness' followed by possessive pronouns. Such a form must be marked for its grammatical role by the associative preposition:

(53) jèn ná kán-dí téŋ
remain ASSC loneliness-3M alone
'he remained alone'

(54) jèn ná kán-dó téŋ
remain ASSC loneliness-3F alone
'she remained alone'

(55)

é	ná	kán-dó
go:FUT	ASSC	loneliness-3F

'she will go alone' (a name given to a girl whose parents have separated)

The form **kán** plus a possessive pronoun can modify a noun:

(56)

ba	kán-dí
father	loneliness-3M

'father alone' (a name given to a boy who has only a father remaining)

Adverbs of manner introduced by the associative preposition **ná** may have a locative function:

(57)

da	ngù	kasa	ná	já	koloŋ
eat	2PL	corn	ASSC	side	DEM:R

'eat at the other side'

But, interestingly, this appears to be a coding of manner rather than of the locative adjunct. The evidence for the status of the phrase marked by **ná** rather than by **dà** is provided by the fact that the phrase marked by **ná** cannot be followed by the locative marker **ni**:

(58)

*da	ngù	kasa	ná	já	koloŋ	ni
eat	2PL	corn	ASSC	side	DEM:R	LOC

for 'eat at the other side'

A locative phrase marked by **dà** may be followed by the locative **ni**:

(59)

da	ngù	kasa	dà	já	koloŋ	(ni)
eat	2PL	corn	PREP	side	DEM:R	LOC

'eat at the other side'

8 Conclusions

The inherent adverbs occur in clause-final position. Ideophones and adverbs derived through reduplication occur after the verb. The non-inherent adverbs are marked for the adverbial function by the associative preposition **ná**.

6

Tenses

1 Introduction

The system of tenses and aspects is built on four verbal forms: (1) past, derived through the addition of the suffix **i** to the root of the verb; the suffix **i** is subsequently dropped in all cases except when the verb ends in a disallowed segment or cluster of segments; (2) the future form, built on the past tense and with the first tone high, the second tone identical with the last tone of the underlying form of the verb, and ending in the vowel **e**; (3) the nominal form, identical with the past tense form and displaying the underlying tone of the verb, but with the word-final vowel **e**; and (4) the imperative form, displaying the underlying segmental and tonal structure of the verb. The last vowel of the imperative is also deleted if the consonantal and syllabic structures allow it. The first three forms, alone or in combination with various auxiliary verbs, produce all the tense distinctions of Lele.

2 The past form

The past tense form is characterized by the form of verb without the final vowel, except for those verbs where the absence of the final vowel would result in a disallowed consonant or consonant cluster in word-final position. Those verbs end in the vowel **i.** Recall that no consonant cluster may occur in word-final position, and that the consonants **s**, **d**, **t**, **k** are not allowed in this position either. The past tense form codes tense rather than an aspectual category. It can be used with bounded and unbounded events. Here is an example of the form occurring with a bounded event:

(1) Tùmò go kar di-nì kínyé
past time REF people GEN.PL-1PL.EXCL COLL
kè-gè ge yàá na nè ɓòdu ba
GEN-3PL HUM say HYP COP monkey COM
gèylì-nì kur go kamda ná kùlòngò.
save-1PL.EXCL time REF women ASSC pregnancy
'At the time of our ancestors, they say, it was the monkey who saved us at the time when women were pregnant.' (G-C & W 1981: 2-3)

(2) kùrmbàlò nè bé-ge kanya máàní tù
chief make DAT-3PL thing ANAPH all (Fr.)
'The chief made all those things for them.'

(3) ge dìgrì-gè sò
HUM kill-3PL two
'Two were killed.'

Here are examples of the deployment of the past tense form in a description of an unbounded event:

(4) Dà tìrnyo kè-gè ni ná, dàgè wàl gé
PREP habit GEN-3PL LOC ASSC 3PL cut 3PL
kamda go ná gé kùlòngò kolo
women REF ASSC 3PL pregnancy because
dérè gé kormo wísìlí.
pull out:FUT 3PL child newborn
'Usually, they cut the pregnant women in order to pull out the baby.' (G-C & W 1981: 2-3)

(5) Kàrgà ni go ge wàl-gè ter
back LOC REF HUM cut-3PL pull out:PL
karma-ǹg ná kamda-ǹg ma gé.
children-DEF ASSC women-DEF die 3PL
'After they were cut, and the babies were pulled out, the women died.' (G-C & W 1981: 2-3)

The unbounded nature of events in which the past tense form occurs argues against its being the perfective aspect:

(6)

Dàdù	jèn	sàm,	ɓòdu-ǹg	se
3F	remain	for a while,	monkey-DEF	INCEPT
yáa	bù-dù	ná		
tell	DAT-3F	ASSC		

'She remained for a while, and monkey tells her . . . ' (G-C & W 1981: 2-3)

Here is an example of the past tense form deployed with the bounded and unbounded event:

(7)

gìr	ná	ín-dì	hą́	è	gé	ná
run	ASSC	ASSC-3M	till (Ar.)	go	3PL	ASSC
dà	kama	kìb-ìy	ni			
PREP	river	edge-3M	LOC			

'She ran with him till they arrived at a bank of the river.'

The past tense form can cooccur with the auxiliary **jè**, which codes an ongoing event:

(8)

tùwà	tóŋ	pìnà	ná	jè	yì	dú	ką́nya
sun	certain:F	one	ASSC	IMPF	pound	3F	thing
tòrò	yó-ró	è	jè	gé	ná	karan-do	
hen	mother-3F	go	VENT	3PL	ASSC	children-3F	
kolo	dé	gé	kasa-ŋ				
reason	eat:FUT	3PL	corn-DEF				

'One day, when she$_1$ was pounding, the old hen$_2$ came with her children to eat the corn.'

Typically transitive verbs with the subject and the object expressed and the verb in the past tense form have only past tense interpretation. The past tense can refer to both remote and recent past, as shown by the fact that one can deploy different adverbial time specifications with this form:

(9)

bòy	dí	kòjò	kò-nòŋ
break	3M	hoe	GEN-1SG

'he broke my hoe'

(10)

bòy	dí	kòjò	kò-nòŋ	kèlèn	káŋ
break	3M	hoe	GEN-1SG	fast	DEM

'he broke my hoe just now'

The past tense may have a durative interpretation:

(11)

píl	dí	gúrbólò	kè-y	ná	wáyŋgùlù	ték
wash	3M	cloth	GEN-3M	ASSC	morning	since

'he washed his clothes from morning till now' (he finished washing)

The past tense form, however, can be and often is used for the coding of time concurrent with the time of speech:

(12)

Ng	tòb	go	bóré	me	gèylè.
1SG	want	REF	save:FUT	2F	cure

'I want to save your life.' (G-C & W 1981: 2-3)

(13)

ngu	gol	gaw	go	kun-do	pìnà	tésí	ɗé-ŋ
2PL	see	well	REF	eye-3F	one	break	NEG-DEF

'you see well that one of her eyes is spoiled already . . .'

The only time reference that is outside of the scope of the past tense form is future. The past tense form of the verb may not be deployed in clauses otherwise marked for the future, e.g. clauses having an adverb clearly marking future time reference:

(14)

*ngá	gol	kùsín-ngá	wàyán	gà
1DU.INCL	see	body-1DU.INCL	tomorrow	Q

for 'will we see each other tomorrow?'

Cf.:

(15)

ngá	góle	kùsín-ngá	wàyáŋ	gà
1DU.INCL	see:FUT	body-1DU.INCL	tomorrow	Q

'will we see each other tomorrow?'

If the verb is inherently durative, such as **jèŋ** 'stay, live', the past tense form has unspecified meaning in the range past-present:

(16)

ŋ	jèn	dèbréŋ
1SG	live	Debreng

'I lived Debreng'

(17)

ŋ	jèn	dèbréŋ	kèlèn	káŋ
1SG	live	Debreng	fast	DEM

'I live in Debreng now'

(18)

ŋ	jèn	tùmò	dà	dèbréŋ
1SG	live	before	PREP	Debreng

'I used to live in Debreng'

The past tense form may be deployed in expressions of repetitive events:

(19)

ŋ	pad-wí	hírè
1SG	fall:PL-PL	often

'I fell often'

(20)

ŋ	bàá
1SG	fall

'I fell'

The evidence for the inherent past tense meaning of the unmarked form of the verb is provided by its use in temporal apodosis, but not protasis, clauses. The unmarked form of the verb in such clauses is interpreted as past tense:

(21)

ná	màyą̀-y	pad-wí	dí	hírè
ASSC	childhood-3M	fall:PL-PL-PL	3M	often

'when he was a child he fell often'

In order to obtain the present tense interpretation of the event of both the protasis and the apodosis clause, one has to use the auxiliary **jè** in the apodosis clause:

(22)

ná	go	kùsi-y	ne-y	jè	pád-wí
ASSC	REF	body-3M	make-3M	IMPF	fall:PL-PL

dí	hírè
3M	often

'when he is sick he falls often'

3 Past and present tense through the nominalized form

The nominal form of the verb alone, i.e. without any auxiliaries, codes past and present tense. But it is deployed only in one type of clause, viz. comment-on-focus clauses. The comment clause is marked by the form **ba**:

(23)

"Tamá,	kolo	me	ba	me	ile	ná	kin-de
woman	reason	what	COM	2F	cry	ASSC	eye-2F

kam-do	máàní	gà?"
water-3F	ANAPH	Q

'Woman, why are you crying so?' (G-C & W 1982: 2-3)

(24)

Nè	máàní	ba	láràdí	dà	kìrè	ni
COP	ANAPH	COM	chameleon	PREP	road	LOC

ɓey	ba
still	COM

'In the meantime, the chameleon was still on the road,

gúló	ile	kùlúr	kùlúr	ba	kara
lizard	cry:VN	kulur	kulur	COM	people

se	yà	gé	na	pùrá-ngú
INCEPT	say	3PL	HYP	detach:IMP-2PL

gúló	àlé.
lizard	already

'Lizard cried kulur, kulur, and people said: release the lizard already' (G-C & W 1981: 8-9)

4 Future tenses

4.1 Inflectional future

There are two means of coding the future tense. One is through the deployment of the future tense form of the verb alone, and the other is through the deployment of the auxiliary **éè** 'go:FUT' preceding the future form of the verb.

The future form of the verb alone, i.e. without the auxiliary, codes an unspecified time in the future when the event will take place:

(25)

Ng	yáà	bé-mè	ná	kìrè-ì.
1SG	tell:FUT	DAT-2F	ASSC	road-3M

'I will tell you how to deal with it' (G-C & W 1981: 2-3)

(26)

Me	góolé	ng	nè	tòb	go	gèylè	mè."
2F	see:FUT	1SG	IMPF	want	REF	save	2F

'You will see that I want to save you' (G-C & W 1981: 2-3)

Since the time is unspecified, the epistemic value of this feature does not include certainty.

4.2 The future with the auxiliary éè 'go'

The future with the auxiliary **éè** 'go' codes a specific time, hence by implication, a more certain future:

(27)

Ng	éè-je	góolé	me	jumar	kàńg.
1SG	go:FUT-VENT	look:FUT	2F	every day	here

'I will come every day to look for you here' (G-C & W 1981: 2-3)

(28)

kur	go	gʉ́nyé	àg-ìy	jè	na-y	é
time	REF	spider	take-3M	VENT	HYP-3M	go:FUT

jé-y	dà	kama
throw-3M	PREP	water

'When Spider took him and was going to throw him into the water,

(29) Kur go gòle màní ná ge
place REF collective hunt ANAPH ASSC HUM
yí tùwà màní ɗé, gì gìna mboɓ ná
put fire there NEG remain like wait ASSC
bay go bòr gòle-ǹg éè tége
man REF cut collective hunt-DEF go:FUT call
dà wèlè go dàì gìsì.
PREP sleep:VN REF 3M concern
'One does not put the fire in the place of collective hunt; one waits till the master of the collective hunts invites [you for the hunt] on the day of his choice.' (G-C & W 1981: 31-32)

(30) Nè day ba è kisí kanya tùmò
COP 3M COM go saw thing fist
kara kángnyé éè kíse-gé ɓey
people some:PL go:FUT sow:FUT-3PL yet
'He is the first to sow; only then other people will be able to sow.' (G-C & W 1981: 48-49)

One could claim that the form **éè** is not an auxiliary but rather the verb 'to go'. Even when a translation would support both the independent verb and the auxiliary hypotheses, the grammatical coding of the subject pronoun with only the second verb provides the evidence for the auxiliary category for the form **éè**:

(31) éè hámè-gé tòrò go ɗàng
go:FUT find:FUT-3PL hen REF another
sólè-gé
strangle-3PL
'they will go to find another hen and strangle it' (G-C & W 1981: 38-39)

(32) ge jè éè wálè-ng . . . ng éè
HUM IMPF go:FUT cut:FUT-1SG 1SG go:FUT
máre
die:FUT
'when they will cut me . . . I will die' (G-C & W 1981: 2-3)

There are two auxiliaries **jè** and **nè** that have been claimed in W & P 1981 as coding future tense, characterizing the forms thus: 'jè = nè prédicatif du futur proche et du duratif' (40). This claim about the proximate future function does not appear to be valid, since the marker **jè** can be used with both proximate and remote future time:

(33) cànìgé jè wálè tù káŋ jòjò
Canige IMPF slaughter:FUT goat DEM immediately
káŋ nò gò kíndì
DEM COP little truth
'Canige will slaughter this goat immediately, for sure.'

(34) cànìgé jè wálè kùlbáŋ káŋ ɗíglè
Canige IMPF slaughter:FUT cow DEM year
goɗàŋ
another
'Canige will slaughter this cow next year.'

An analysis of naturally occurring texts indicates that the form **jè** has one function and **nè** has another, and although both can occur with the future form of the verb, these two auxiliaries can occur with verbal forms other than future and consequently code functions other than the future tense. The function of the form **jè** is described in the next chapter, and the function of the of the form **nè** is described in chapter 15 on Focus.

5 Conclusions

Within the system of tenses in Lele there is a two-way distinction between the non-future tense and future tense. The non-future has as its scope both past and present. The future tense has a two-way distinction, between the potential future in an unspecified time in the future, whose certainty is not asserted, and the specific future, whose certainty is asserted. The future form of the verb codes the potential future. The future whose certainty is asserted is coded by the future form of the auxiliary **è** 'go' and by the future form of the verb.

7

Aspect and Pragmatically Dependent Clauses

1 Introduction

The present chapter deals with the domain of aspect, viz. coding of the state of the event. It has been claimed that many Chadic languages have a distinction between perfective and the imperfective, or in French linguistic literature between *accompli* and *inaccompli.* The aspectual system in Lele does not have those distinctions, at least not in such general terms. The system consists of a telic, an inceptive, and a durative aspect coding the unbounded event.

In the present chapter I also describe the coding of pragmatically dependent clauses. While that does not code the characteristic of the event in a clause, it forces the hearer to interpret the event in connection with other events.

2 The telic

2.1 Form and function of telic

The term *telic* is used in its standard meaning, viz. 'directed or tending toward a goal or purpose, purposeful' (*American Heritage Dictionary*, cf. also Matthews 1997). The category is coded by the past tense form of the verb **è** 'go' combined with the past tense form of the main verb. The verb following **è** is the goal, or purpose, of the event. In addition to coding the purposeful, goal-oriented event, the form also codes the completion of the event. The evidence for this hypothesis is provided by the fact that a clause with telic aspect coding cannot be followed by a clause denying the completion of the event:

(1)

ŋ	è	jè	cìl	kama
1SG	go	VENT	fetch (from a well)	water

*àlá	ŋ	cìl	ɗé
but	1SG	fetch	NEG

'I came and fetched water from a well', *'but did not fetch it'

(2)

ni	è	jè	nè	gùyé	tùm
1PL.EXCL	go	VENT	do	work	together

*àlá	ni	nè	gùyé	ɗé
but	1PL.EXCL	do	work	NEG

'we came and worked together', *'but we did not work'

(3)

tamá-ŋ	sòndrí	ná	se	ày	tòrò
woman-DEF	fear	ASSC	INCEPT	take	hen

è	ìm
go	bury

'The woman became scared, took the hen, and buried it.'

The telic aspect may be deployed with the first verb of the clause:

(4)

dày	go	sùbù	ge	dígrè-y	è	wèl	ná
3M	REF	three	HUM	kill:FUT-3M	go	sleep	ASSC

kùrmbàlò	tamą́-y
chief	wife-3M

'The third one, who was going to be killed, slept with the chief's wife.'

The telicity does not imply subject control:

(5)

Tùwà	wèy	mbórò.	Tùwà	è	mira	go	dòbé.
sun	turn	evening	sun	go	approach	REF	lie:VN

'The sun turned into the evening. The sun has set.' (G-C & W 1981: 8-9)

The telic aspect may be deployed in hypothetical constructions, i.e. in constructions marked by the hypothetical marker **na**:

(6)

Kumno	yàá	na,	na	láràdí	ba
God	say	HYP	HYP	lizard	COM

è	hab-i	tùmò	na
go	find-3M	first	HYP

'The God said: if the lizard finds him first, then . . . '

(7) Kamda go gàrè dèglè isili gé sòngò go gàrè
women REF mold pots boil 3PL oil REF mold
kanya sì gé lay; tamá do tòb go
thing drink 3PL also woman REF want REF
gàrè kanya ná è sì ná ín-dí-gè
mold thing ASSC go drink ASSC ASSC-PL-3PL
sòngò lay.
oil also
'Potters cook oil for successful molding; women who would like to be potters drink oil with them.' (G-C & W 1981: 20-21)

The telic aspect does not have to code the final verb of an event. The requirement is that if there are two predicates, A and B, predicate A is the purpose for the achievement of the goal in predicate B:

(8) Kara yà gé na, láràdí è hab Kumno
people tell 3PL HYP chameleon go find God
yàá bè-ì kolo ɗè.
tell DAT-3M word NEG
'People thought that chameleon had already found God and told him the word.' (G-C & W 1981: 8-9)

(9) ba se è dà kúso bayndí kè-y
COM INCEPT go PREP field man GEN-3M
ni da kàrga túgú ni
LOC PREP behind compound LOC
è póì jè tèmlé wén bùgú
go break:PL VENT corn fill bag
'there he went into somebody's field behind the compound, broke off corn, filled his bag'

The telic aspect may be bounded or not. The following example illustrates an unbounded event, as evidenced by the meaning of the clauses involved and by the adverbial phrase following them:

(10) Tamá è go yéè kanya ná,
woman go REF pound:FUT thing ASSC
ày tìndí toron-do go jíbè ná tìndí
take pestle daughter-3F REF push ASSC pestle
è ladí Kumno kus-i;
go touch God body-3M
nè máàní ná kur wèlè-ì wèlè-ì.
COMP ANAPH ASSC place day-3M day-3M
'While the woman was pounding corn, she took the pestle, raised it, and touched the God with it. And so day after day . . . ' (G-C & W 1981: 10-11)

The following sentence has the telic deployed in the bounded event, as evidenced by the meaning of the clause:

(11) Wèlè pìnà dàdù se yì kanya ày tìndí
day one 3F INCEPT pound thing take pestle
toron-do go na du jíbè ná yè
mortar-3F REL HYP 3F raise:FUT ASSC pound
tìndí è jìb Kumno dà dàná.
pestle go pierce God PREP up
'One day the woman started to pound the corn, and when she was about to raise her pestle she pierced the God up in the sky' (G-C & W 1981: 10-11)

2.2. Grammaticalization of the telic

Given the lexical meaning of the verb **è** 'go', there is little doubt that the verb 'to go' is the source of the telic aspect. In contemporary language there are some clauses where one could still interpret the sequence **è** plus verb as a sequence of verbs signifying 'go and x' rather than as an auxiliary and a verb:

(12) Dàdù è hab ɓòdu dà sóòyó to-roò
3F go find monkey PREP tamarind bottom-3F
ni.
LOC
'She went and found the monkey under the tamarind tree.' (G-C & W 1981: 4-5)

Non-achieved telicity, a domain very close to the purpose clause, is coded by the verb **è** 'go' followed by the referential marker **go**, followed by the hypothetical marker with the subject of the clause, and finally by the verb, with the complements, if any:

(13)

"Bayndí	káǹg	gi	jèn	mira
man	DEM	2M	stay	close

na-du	è	go	yéè	kanya
HYP-3F	go	REF	pound:FUT	thing

na-du	hab	kìrè	ɗé
HYP-3F	find	way	NEG

na-du	è	go	mónge	kusu-ro	kúsìnyo	pinyà
HYP-3F	go	REF	bend:FUT	body-3F	down	even

na-du	hab	kìrè	ɗé	lay."
HYP-3F	find	way	NEG	also

'You, man, who stays close, if she wants to pound, she cannot find her way, even if she wants to bend, she does not find her way either.'

(14)

Dàì	gìrà	lèé	kanya	àsí	nèńy	se	è
3M	dog	eat	thing	sate	very much	INCEPT	go

go	na-i	tée	kasínya	dà	cáaní;
REF	HYP-3M	defecate:FUT	excrement	PREP	field

'The dog had eaten plenty, and wanted to defecate in the field.' (G-C & W 1981: 10-11)

The initial step in the grammaticalization of telicity was a paratactic construction where the first verb was **è** 'go' followed by another verb. The choice of the verb in the paratactic construction was motivated by its semantic features, listed above.

3 The inceptive

3.1 The form and function of inceptive aspect

The category 'inceptive' is coded by the auxiliary verb **se**, identical with the verb 'get up, rise'. The auxiliary may be followed by the main verb in a tensed form or by another auxiliary coding aspect. The fact that it can be coded by an aspectual auxiliary indicates that the form **se** does not code an aspect. The marker codes the beginning of a new event with respect to the preceding event:

(15) Kur wèlè-ì pìnà, tamá do ná
time remain-3M one woman REL:F ASSC
kùlòngò, kur go gì bú-dù wèlè inyew
pregnancy place REF remain DAT-3F remain a little
kolo wéè, dàdù se è cánmínè ile
reason give birth 3F INCEPT go bush(?)[8] weep
kusu-ro; ír sàm
body-3F stand moment
se gol ɓodu tamá.
INCEPT see monkey woman
'One day, a pregnant woman, close to giving birth, went into the bush and wept. Suddenly she stopped and saw a female monkey.' (G-C & W 1981: 2-3)

(16) kùrmbàlò se bòr bé-y kur ba
chief INCEPT cut DAT-3M parcel COM
se jèn mànį́ ná kamda-y go
INCEPT settle ANAPH ASSC wives-3M REF
sùbù
three
'The chief cut him a parcel of land and the man settled there with his three wives.'

The following two clauses illustrate the function of the coding of the new event. The new event may involve a new subject:

(17) Tamá, kolo me ba me ile ná kin-de
woman reason what COM 2F weep ASSC eye-2F
kam-do máànį́ gà?"
water-3F ANAPH Q
'Woman, why are you crying like that?'

(18) Tamá se jè ày kolo go nè ile
woman INCEPT IMPF take reason REF IMPF cry
ná-ǹg yàá bè ɓòdu.
ASSC-DEF tell DAT monkey
'The woman started to tell the monkey the reason for her crying.' (G-C & W 1981: 2-3)

---

[8] The form **cánmínè** (mid tone on n) is not attested in my data nor is it attested in W & P 1982. G-C & W 1981 translate this fragment as 'went into the bush'. The locative form 'in the bush' is **cáaní**, historically consisting of **cáa** and the locative marker **ní**.

(19) Dàdù jèn sàm, ɓòdu-ǹg se
3F remain just monkey-DEF INCEPT
yáa bù-dù ná
say DAT-3F ASSC
'she just remained there. Monkey told her:' (G-C & W 1982: 2-3, instead of the ASSC **ná** it probably should be hypothetical **na**)

(20) kur go gʉ́yé ay tu lèé ɗe ná ne
time REF spider take goat eat THEN ASSC COP
wèlè kab ɗe ná làmndá yé-y
day later then ASSC elephant mother-3M
se ma
INCEPT die
'After Spider took the goat and ate it, a few days later the mother of elephant died.'

It is possible for the subjects of two clauses to be the same, but then the events are new:

(21) tamá-ŋ sòndrí ná se ày tòrò
woman-DEF fear ASSC INCEPT take hen
è ìm
go bury
'The woman became scared, took the hen, and buried it.'

(22) tormo-(ŋ) na dú ódè ná bà-rò ɗè
girl-DEF HYP 3F leave ASSC father-3F NEG
se è ná bayndí-ŋ
INCEPT go COM man-DEF
'She said that she would not go with her father and instead went with the man.' (The original version does not have the definite after **tormo**. The definite marker was added after work with another language assistant.)

Not every verb necessarily represents a new event. In the following sentence, when the news of the death is brought in, the spider's hearing it is not coded as a new event, but the spider's running away is a new event:

(23) ge è jè ná gùyé tumadu go làmndá
HUM go VENT ASSC news death REF mother
yé-y kò-rò ná gų́yé ɗeŋlí se
elephant-3M GEN-3F ASSC spider hear INCEPT
jìb se gìr è cáani
push INCEPT run go bush
'When the news of the death of the mother of elephant was brought in, Spider heard it, got up, and ran away.'

The new event can be represented by the first verb of the clause. The event is new in relationship to the events in preceding sentences. This situation is represented by the following three examples:

(24) àlá se hab jè kùná-y kàyo dà
COM INCEPT find VENT uncle-3M squirrel PREP
kìrè ni
road LOC
'Unexpectedly he encountered his uncle, Squirrel on the road.'
(**kùnà** 'brother of the mother' or 'son of a sister')

(25) se è jè gé dà tálwá ni bé
INCEPT go VENT 3PL PREP pond LOC DAT
kolo na ge sée kam(a)
reason HYP 3PL drink:FUT water
'then they came to a pond in order to drink water'

(26) kùrmbàlò se bòr bé-y kur ba
chief INCEPT cut DAT-3M parcel COM
se jèn màní ná kamda-y go
INCEPT settle ANAPH ASSC wives-3M REF
sùbù
three
'The chief cut him a parcel of land, and the man settled there with his three wives.'

3.2 Grammaticalization of the inceptive marker

Evidence for the lexical meaning of the inceptive marker **se** is provided by clauses where it is the only verb:

(27) se dí ndòjí gùdá
get up 3M late today
'he got up late today'

Evidence for the lexical meaning of **se** is also provided by serial verb constructions where it codes the source from which movement originated:

(28) se gé jè ná kùlbá dà kàsùgù
leave 3PL VENT ASSC cow PREP market
'they returned with a cow from the market'

(29) se-gé jè ná kùlbá dà súk ni
leave-3PL VENT ASSC cow PREP market LOC
'they returned with a cow from the market'

4 The durative

The permanency of an action in the past or present, the durative, is coded by the past tense form of the verb **jèn** 'stay, remain' followed by the main verb of the clause. The durative can be used only in affirmative clauses:

(30) Kara go tumo ná nè gé yage ɗé
people REF past ASSC make 3PL plant:VN NEG
jèn wàl gé nè kasa go an dà cáaní
remain cut 3PL COP corn REF leave PREP bush
ba dì gé.
COM eat 3PL
'In the past people did not plant. They just cut the corn growing in the field and they ate it.' (G-C & W 1981: 10-11)

(31) Kumno pinyà jèn mira ná kusínyo lay.
sky even remain be close ASSC earth also
'The sky was then close to the earth.' (G-C & W 1981: 10-11)

The auxiliary **jèn** has the nominal form if the non-past is involved:

(32) Bayndí hab kìrè go jènè ɗìmsè ɗé
man find way REF remain:VN rest:VN NEG
lay.
also
'Nobody finds a way to rest.' (G-C & W 1981: 28-29)

The verb **jèn** may also occur in the imperative form:

(33) Kúrá jìnà ɗùmsù mbùub wèlè kè-rè.
good remain:IMP rest:IMP wait day GEN-2F
'Good, rest, and await your time.' (G-C & W 1981: 4-5)

The evidence that **jèn** is a verb is provided by clauses when it is the only predicate:

(34) Dàdù jèn sàm,
3F remain moment
'she remained like that for a while' (G-C & W 1981: 2-3)

The sporadic use in the texts of the auxiliary **ír** 'stand' preceding the main verb indicates that it also codes an aspectual distinction, probably also durative:

(35) ng ír nè yage kolo-ǹg gàg,
1SG stand do labor:VN DEM:R-DEF till
tùwà è-je ír dùrò ni jany jany.
sun go-VENT stand center LOC xxx
'I keep working till the sun comes to stand in the middle of the sky.' (G-C & W 1981: 18-19)

(36) ír sàm se gol ɓodu tamá
stand moment INCEPT see monkey female
'after a while she saw a female monkey' (G-C & W 1981: 3)

5 Pragmatic dependency

Lele has grammaticalized the pragmatic dependency of one clause on another. Pragmatic dependency means that a clause has to be interpreted in connection with another clause, whether preceding or following in the discourse. This dependency is coded by the marker **jè**, which can precede a verbal noun, and the past and the future tense forms of the verb. The dependency can be temporal or it can be logical in the sense of being a consequence of some event or proposition. A logical consequence is coded in the following examples:

(37) yé dú-ngù posí-ŋ ɗe ná ŋ
mother GEN:PL-2PL insult-1SG THEN ASSC 1SG
jè léè̀-dú ná kasa go ŋ yì
IMPF eat:FUT-3F ASSC corn ASSC 1SG pound
háŋ
DEM:P
'Your mother has insulted me; therefore I am going to eat her with this corn I pounded.'

(38) na me léè yé dí-nì
HYP 2F eat:FUT mother GEN:PL-1PL.EXCL
ná me jè má lay
ASSC 2F IMPF die:FUT also
'If you eat our mother, you will also die.'

Note that these two examples provide evidence against the claim that **jè** codes a durative aspect. Both of the events marked by **jè** are in fact punctual.

Two clauses in succession may be marked as pragmatically dependent on each other. The following sentence illustrates the temporal dependency of the two clauses, in the sense that while one event was going on, another event was taking place in conjunction with the first-named event:

(39) wèlè go jè yì kḁnya ná tòrò
day REL IMPF pound thing ASSC hen
yó-ró-ŋ dèr kàràn-dò
mother-3F-DEF carry children-3F
è ná tìnɗí tó-ró ni jè dì
go ASSC mortar bottom-3F LOC IMPF peck
gé kasa.
3PL corn
'Each time she$_1$ was pounding, the old hen$_2$ carried her chicks under the mortar and they pecked corn.'

The following example, which in the text occurs after the preceding example, illustrates the deployment of **jè** to code the logical consequence of the preceding event:

(40) tamá-ŋ jè tè-gè hire
woman-DEF IMPF chase away-3PL often
'The woman often chased them away' (because they were eating her corn)

The marker **jè** is deployed in comment-on-focus constructions, where its role is similar to that of the verbal noun:

(41) Nè gìdìrè go simlí jè tèy gé ná
COP month REF guinea fowl IMPF call 3PL ASSC
karma; kanya káǹg pet ná nè gìdìrè
children thing DEM all ASSC COP month
di-gè ɗab.
GEN:PL-3PL right
'It is the month when guinea fowl have their children: everything has its right time' (G-C & W 1981: 20-21)

Here is an example where **jè** follows the contrastive focus construction **dàŋ ŋ** 'as for me':

(42)

láà	gìdìrè	go	dà	kama	te-y	ni
eat:IMP	moon	REF	PREP	water	bottom-3M	LOC
ɓàlà-mè		dàŋ	ŋ	jè	òdì	
suffice:IMP-2F		1SG	1SG	IMPF	go	

'Eat the moon that is at the bottom of the water; it should satisfy you; as for me, I am going away.'

As the marker of a pragmatically dependent clause, **jè** compels a clause to be interpreted in connection with another clause. In the following sentence **jè** codes either the clause that is the premise 'since' or the clause that is the conclusion:

(43)

kur	koloŋ	ba	dày	gṵ́yé	se	yàá	
time	DEM:R	COM	3M	spider	INCEPT	say	
bé-gè	na	na-y	jè	nè	hòmyá	go	
DAT-3PL	HYP	HYP-3M	IMPF	make	sick	REF	
ma	nò	go	tég	lay	na	bé-y	gé
die	COP	REF	long time	also	HYP	give-3M	3PL
na-y	lèé						
HYP-3M	eat						

'At that time Spider said that since he has been sick for a long time, close to dying, they should give [it] to him to eat.'

The marker **jè** codes the imperfective in specific interrogative clauses where the context is underspecified. Without **jè** the clause could be interpreted as referring to a perfective event, an event in the past:

(44)

kùnà-y	kàyo	se	tòn-ìy	na	
uncle-3M	squirrel	INCEPT	ask-3M	HYP	
gi jè	gìrè	mína	mánì	gà	
2M IMPF	run:VN	where	like that	Q	

'His uncle Squirrel asked him: where are you running like that?'

The overt marking of the imperfective is deployed in temporal protasis and apodosis clauses, coding the fact that at the same time one event was taking place, another event was taking place simultaneously:

(45) wèlè go jè yì kḁnya ná tòrò
day REL IMPF pound thing ASSC hen
yó-ró-ŋ dèr kàràn-dò è ná tìnɗí
mother-3F-DEF carry children-3F go ASSC mortar
tó-ró ni jè dì gé kasa.
bottom-3F LOC IMPF peck 3PL corn
'Each time she$_1$ was pounding, the old hen$_2$ carried her chicks under the mortar, and they pecked corn.

(46) Kur go gìdìrè ba an ná, ge ɗe
time REF moon man come out ASSC HUM leave
bùrmò kìb-ì, bàbílìmdí
initiation mouth-3M spouses of the ancestral spirits
jè ile kolo nárè ná karma
IMPF scream reason forbid:FUT ASSC children
go jè lè-gé tòngú.
REF IMPF eat-3PL carrot
'When the male moon comes out, one begins the initiation, and spouses of the ancestral spirits scream to prevent children from eating carrots [in the field].'

(47) Kara gòmnye nè gé ná kere
people big:PL make 3PL ASSC beer
jè bè ba-di-gè kínyé go ma-gé
IMPF give father-GEN:PL-3PL COLL REF die-3PL
tùmò; tom-gé nè mìsé ba bòy-gé
past cut-3PL COP sorghum COM pour-3PL
tìsà ba nè-gé kere sì-gé.
germinated corn COM make-3PL beer drink-3PL
'Elders make beer to offer it to their ancestors. They cut sorghum, pour in germinated corn, cook beer, and drink it.'

The marker **jè** alone indicates that the clause in which it occurs is part of a sequence of events. It may mark the second or the first event in a sequence. Either way of marking assures the same interpretation:

(48) Kara màglí-gé kúní kàrgà-ì jè
people tidy up-3PL house back-3M IMPF
lor-gé wáyngulú ob-gé kolo
light fire-3PL morning warm up-3PL because
kàlo
wind/cold
'People tidy up their backyards and light fires in the morning in order to warm up, because of the cold.' (G-C & W 1981: 30-31)

(49) Kara go yage màbá jè por-gé
people REF plant tobacco IMPF tear off-3PL
kám̀-dí wàl-wì-gé wer tùwà kun-do,
leaf-3M cut-PL-3PL spread sun eye-3F
kur go hay ɗè[9] ná por gé dàì go
place REF dry then (?) ASSC cut 3PL 3M REF
jàl-wá dàb ná tum yì-gé-ná.
fresh-REF mix ASSC together pound-3PL-ASSC
'Those who plant tobacco tear off its leaves, cut them up, and spread them in the sun to dry. Then they cut fresh leaves, mix them with the dry tobacco, and pound it all.' (G-C & W 1981: 24-25)

Finally, consider the following sentence, which contains one instance of the auxiliary **jè** and one instance of the auxiliary **nè**. The marker **jè** indicates that another clause follows. The copula **nè** codes focus on the predicate **jogí** 'bother':

(50) Nè gìdìrè go kara jè nè hòmnyá
COP moon REF people IMPF make sickness
nèný : siré, òsò ná cà anglá,
very much mucus cough ASSC head xxx
kasire nè jogí-gé; ìyà nè kur
medicine COP bother-3PL wound make place
nèný lay.
very much also
'At that time many people are ill: phlegm, cough, rheumatism bother them a lot. Wounds are numerous. (G-C & W 1981: 30-31)

The following title of a narrative does not lend itself to an analysis according to which **jè** marks a pragmatically dependent clause, unless one would consider that **jè** indicates that it is with the material in the narrative that this phrase should be interpreted:

(51) Gùyé Matílè ko-ro go jè nè
work Matilde GEN-3F REF IMPF do
'the work that Matilde does'

Since the marker **jè** codes the temporal dependency of an event on another event, the marker **jè** has acquired an imperfective function. In that function it is deployed, however, only if the unmarked form of the verb could result in a perfective interpretation. Throughout this work the marker **jè** is glossed as IMPF for 'imperfective'. This gloss should, however, be

[9] This may well be a typo for **ɗē** 'then'. The form **dè** means 'already.

taken as a symbolic representation of **jè**. There are many clauses with the past tense form that also have imperfective aspect. Thus the marker **jè** marks the imperfective aspect only if its absence would yield an unintended perfective aspect interpretation.

6 Conclusions

All aspectual forms consist of an auxiliary verb followed by the main verb. The aspectual system consists of the following distinctions: telic, with two variants, completed and non-completed; inceptive; and durative. The telic is coded by the auxiliary **è** 'go'; the inceptive is coded by the auxiliary **se** 'rise, get up, depart'; and the durative is coded by the auxiliary **jèn** 'remain' or **ìr** 'stand'.

8

Coding the Deixis of an Event

1 Introduction

Like many other Chadic languages, Lele codes the spatial location of the event with respect to the place of speech or with respect to some other deictic center. Two deictic categories are encoded: ventive, indicating generally movement toward the deictic center, and allative, indicating, again generally, movement away from the deictic center. Different types of grammatical means code the two categories.

2 The ventive

2.1 The form and the function of ventive

The ventive construction consists of the main verb followed by the verb **jè** (often **je** in G-C & W 1982). If the verb has third-person pronouns, the ventive marker occurs after them. The form **jè** does not have nominal or pronominal subjects of its own.

The sequence of the main verb and ventive marker may be followed by a locative argument, but that argument is not a complement, as it were, of both the main verb and the ventive marker. If the main verb is a directional verb of movement, it codes a different direction from the one coded by the ventive marker (for expository purposes elicited examples are used first):

(1) se dí jè (dà) dèbréŋ lìŋdà nè
leave 3M VENT PREP Debreng yesterday COP
kínè cà-y
return:FUT head-3M
'he came from Debreng yesterday, and he is going to return there'

(2) òdì dí jè dèbréŋ lìŋdá
leave 3M VENT Debreng yesterday
'he came from Debreng'

Cf.:
(3) òdì dí dèbréŋ
leave 3M Debreng
'he left Debreng'

The form **jè** can be deployed with verbs other than verbs of movement, indicating that the event, action, and so on, took place somewhere else and that there was a subsequent movement toward the place of speech:

(4) ŋ lèé jè sìí
1SG eat VENT meat
'I ate the meat [somewhere else and came here]'

An additional piece of evidence for the ventive function of **jè** is a constraint that does not allow **jè** to occur with an adverbial meaning 'here':

(5) *ŋ lèé jè sìí kur kàŋ ni
1SG eat VENT meat place here LOC
for 'I ate the meat here'

Cf.:
(6) ŋ lèé sìí kur kàŋ ni
1SG eat meat place here LOC
'I ate the meat here'

With an adverb of place indicating an indeterminate place, but not the place of speech, the ventive marker can be used:

(7) ŋ lèé jè sì kàŋdi
1SG eat VENT meat in the neighborhood
'I ate the meat there and came here'

Cf.:
(8) ŋ lèé sì kàŋdi
1SG eat meat here
'I ate the meat here'

(9) kìn gé jè ná kùlbá go dà
return 3PL VENT ASSC cow DEM PREP
súk ni
market LOC
'they brought a cow from the market' (the speaker is in the place to which the cow is brought)

(10) kìn gé ná kùlbá go dà súk ni
return 3PL ASSC cow DEM PREP market LOC
túg dí-gé
compound GEN:PL-3PL
'they brought a cow from the market' (the speaker is not in the place to which the cow is brought)

(11) è gé ná kùlbá dà súk ni
go 3PL ASSC cow PREP market LOC
'they took a cow to the market'

The ventive extension is obligatory with the verb **oḿ** 'catch'. If the verb is followed by a pronominal object, the ventive marker comes after the object:

(12) kàyo se om-iy jè se è
squirrel INCEPT catch-3M VENT INCEPT go
ná ín-dí dà kur go tumadu-ŋ ni
ASSC ASSC-3M PREP place REL death-DEF LOC
'Squirrel caught him [and] brought him to the place of the burial.'

The verb **hab** means 'find', but when it is followed by the ventive extension **jè**, it means 'encounter':

(13) àlá se hab jè kùná-y kàyo
COM INCEPT find VENT uncle-3M squirrel
dà kìrè ni
PREP road LOC
'Unexpectedly he encountered his uncle Squirrel on the road.'

A verb with a ventive marker may be followed by another verb:

(14) ná se è jè hìndì tamą́-y
ASSC INCEPT go VENT wake up wife-3M
kuná ni
sleep LOC
'And then he came and woke up his wife.'

(15)

bàyndí-ŋ	jè	è	sègré	ná	tìgrí
man-DEF	IMPF	go	hunt	ASSC	kill:PL:VN

kàrgé	sò	ɗéŋ	sùbù	kura	kɨ́nyé	bísí
wild animals	two	or	three	rabbit	COLL	antelope

kɨ́nyé	nasú	kɨ́nyé	ná [pause]	jè	è
COLL	gnu antelope	COLL	ASSC	IMPF	go

jè	kèsì	jáy	bé	tamá	túg	ni	lay
VENT	share	part	DAT	wife	compound	LOC	also

jay	kóŋ	jè	ɑ́y	ná	kasa	lay
part	certain:M	IMPF	take	ASSC	corn	also

gùnà	lay
peanuts	also

'Each time the man went for a hunt, he killed two or three wild animals, rabbits, small antelopes, gnu antelopes; he shared some with his wife at home, and some he bartered for corn and peanuts.'

(16)

gi	ne	jè	gùyé	bé	wéy	gà
2M	make	VENT	work	DAT	who	Q

'for whom did you work?'

2.2 Grammaticalization of the ventive

As in many Chadic languages (Frajzyngier 1987), the ventive marker is derived from the verb **jè** 'to come'. In the data gathered there are very few sentences where **jè** is the only predicate with the meaning 'come':

(17)

jìb-iŋ	dí	jè	dà	kàŋ
cause-1SG	3M	come	PREP	here

'he made me come here'

The reason why there are so few examples of **jè** being the lexical verb 'to come' is provided by the lexicalization of the ventive marker as described in the next section.

2.3 Lexicalization of the ventive construction

The ventive construction in Lele presents an interesting and still quite rare phenomenon of lexicalization having its source in grammatical construction. When the verb **è** 'go' is followed by the ventive marker **jè**, the two forms constitute a lexical compound. The evidence for the lexicalization from the syntax is provided by the fact that the third-person subject pronouns occur after the verb **jè**, rather than after the verb **è**, as one would expect from other ventive constructions:

(18)

è	je	dí	ná	kama
go	VENT	3M	ASSC	water

'he brought water'

When the lexical form 'come' is deployed in the imperative, only the first verb, **è**, is used in the imperative form:

(19)

à	jè	hàŋ
go	VENT	here

'come here!'

3 The allative

Movement away from the place of speech or from another deictic center is marked by the form **cá(a)ní** 'bush, field', which follows the verb or the object, if any.

(20)

gų́yé	ɗeŋlí	se	jìb	se	gìr	è	cáaní
spider	hear	INCEPT	push	INCEPT	run	go	ALL

'Spider heard it, got up and ran away.'

The noun **cáaní** in the preceding clause behaves like a locative adverb of place. The verb **è** 'go' cannot occur without an adverb of place, and **cáaní** provides the least specific place designation away from the place of speech.

The evidence that **cáaní** has been grammaticalized into the marker of allative deixis is provided by the fact that it is used in clauses where the lexical interpretation 'bush' makes no sense. Thus the notion of selling is coded by the verb **kil** 'buy' followed by the marker **cáaní**, occurring after all the arguments of the clause:

(21)

ŋ	kílè	bé-y	kùlbá	kò-nòŋ	cáaní
1SG	sell:FUT	PREP-3M	cow	GEN-1SG	bush

'I will sell my cow to him'

(22)

kil	dí	kùlbá	kè-y	cáaní	dà	kàsùgù
buy	3M	cow	GEN-3M	away	PREP	market

'he sold his cow at the market'

The notion of allative may have as its scope the object rather than the subject of the clause:

(23)

húm	ką́yà	sóre	kò-m	cáaní	ɗá
gather:IMP	things	play	GEN-2M	ALL	let
bé-ŋ	kírè				
DAT-1SG	road				

'gather your toys away from here and let me go'

(24) kormo káŋ jé cà dí-ngà cáaní
child DEM:P throw head GEN-1DU.INCL ALL
'that child has dishonored us', lit. 'has thrown our head away'

When the marker **cáaní** occurs after a non-movement verb, it has the function of adverbial modification of the verb:

(25) ŋ sáde cáaní
1SG clean:FUT ALL
'I will clean it away'

(26) ŋ sáde kùbàrò cáaní
1SG clean:FUT blood ALL
'I will clean the blood away'

The evidence that **cáaní** means 'bush' is provided by the fact that it can be deployed with the locative preposition **dà**:

(27) ge jé tùwà dà cáaní
HUM throw fire bush ALL
'they put the bush on fire'

The word **cáaní** itself is most probably a complex structure consisting of **cá** and locative marker **ni**. In contemporary Lele there is no noun **cá**. But in the neighboring Chadic language Nancere there is a word **cá** 'field'. An additional argument for the proposed derivation is the fact that **cáaní** cannot be followed by the locative marker **ni**.

4 Conclusions

The ventive form, indicating movement toward a deictic center, is coded by the form **jè** following the main verb. The ventive marker still behaves like the verb 'to come' in that with verbs of movement it has a different locative complement than the main verb. If the locative complement of the ventive marker is not specified in the clause, the deictic center is the place of speech.

Movement away from the deictic center is coded by the locative phrase **cáaní** '[in the] bush', which occupies the place of the locative complement.

9

Equational Clauses

1 The scope of the chapter

This chapter describes two types of clauses: those consisting of a subject and a nominal predicate, called equational clauses; and those that predicate about an object in the environment of speech or discourse, called identificational clauses. (The latter type does not have an overtly marked subject and consists just of the nominal predicate.) These two types are characterized by the presence of a copula. The common characteristic of these clauses is that they cannot be marked for tense or aspect; they can, however, be marked for hypothetical modality.

Although the copula is formally identical with and derived from the verb 'make, do', equational and identificational clauses are not simply clauses that happen to have a different verb. There are important formal and functional differences between clauses with the copula **nè** and clauses with verbal predicates. These differences are pointed out in what follows.

2 Equational clauses

When the subject and the predicate are both nouns, the equational clause has the form Noun **nè** Noun. The copula **nè** is an obligatory component of the construction. If the subject of the equational clause is a first- or second-person pronoun, forms belonging to the verbal subject set are chosen. This fact is explained by the grammaticalization of the copula, viz. by the fact that it originated as the verb 'make':

(1)

ŋ	nò	go	lèlé
1SG	COP	REF	Lele

'I am a Lele'

(2)

ŋ	nè	bay	go	trábà
1SG	COP	one	REF	forging

'I am a blacksmith'

(3)

gi	nè	ɓén-íŋ
2M	COP	brother-1SG

'you are my brother'

The formal difference between the copula and an ordinary verb is in the deployment of the third-person subject pronouns. Third-person singular and plural subjects cannot occur after the copula **nè**, whereas they can, and some must, occur after the ordinary verb. All third-person forms are unmarked, i.e., they do not code the gender or number of the subject:

(4)

nè	ɓén-íŋ
COP	brother-1SG

'he is my brother'

(5)

*nè	dí	ɓén-íŋ
COP	3M	brother-1SG

for 'he is my brother'

(6)

nè	tím-níŋ
COP	sister-1SG

'she is my sister'

(7)

*nè	dú	tím-níŋ
COP	3F	sister-1SG

for 'she is my sister'

Recall that if the subject is plural or consists of a conjoined noun phrase, such a subject must be cross-referenced by the third-person plural pronoun **gé** following an ordinary verb. In copular sentences, the third-person plural pronoun cannot occur after the copula:

(8)

kiya	dàgè	ná	gìlkínín	ne	kósuŋ	go	lèlé
Kiya	3PL	COM	Gilikinin	COP	term	REF	Lele

'Kiya and Gilkinin are Lele names'

(9) nè bąŋyà-nìŋ
COP brothers-1SG
'they are my brothers'

(10) *nè gé bąŋyà-níŋ
COP 3PL brothers-1SG
for 'they are my brothers'

Forms with an unmarked third-person subject can be used both deictically and anaphorically, i.e. when the subject is present in the environment of discourse as well as when the subject has been mentioned in the previous discourse.

One cannot have an equational clause where the subject is a noun and the predicate is a pronoun:

(11) *kiya nè dày
Kiya COP 3M
for 'Kiya is he'

One of the functions of the equational clause is the logical equivalence '=':

(12) Dàng ng nè kìrgá go kúrá gìndé.
1SG 1SG COP animal REF good very
'I am a very good animal' (G-C & W 1981: 2-3)

(13) kiya ne kon-di go lèlé
Kiya COP name-3M REF Lele
'Kiya is his name in Lele'

The construction NP **nè** NP, however, does not carry exclusively the meaning 'X is Y'. Its semantic scope is much wider; it also includes the meaning of 'X belongs to/is associated with Y'. The evidence that the form **nè** is a copula rather than an ordinary transitive verb is provided by the semantic interpretation of the noun following the **nè**. If it were a transitive verb, the noun following **nè** would be an affected object. This, however, is not the case:

(14) láràdí na nè kara go yà-gé
chameleon HYP COP people REF say-3PL
'chameleon would represent people who say . . .'

(15) gúló na nè kara go yà-gé
lizard HYP COP people REF say-3PL
'lizard would represent people who say . . .'

Equational clauses can be marked for hypothetical modality. In addition to the two preceding examples, compare the following:

(16) dày ná na nè tìbré mayna
3M ASSC COMP COP ashes ceiba tree
'he will be like ashes of the ceiba tree'

3 Identificational clauses

Identificational clauses are a type of equational clause without a subject preceding the copula. If the subject is pointed at, the equational clause consists of just to the predicate, regardless of the gender and number of referents pointed to:

(17) nè kíyà
'he is Kiya'

(18) nè kírbì
'she is Kirbi'

(19) nè karma lèléè
COP people Lele
'they are Lele people'

(20) nè gìrà
is dog
'it is a dog'

(21) nè kùlbá
'it is a cow'

(22) nè ámá-niŋ
COP wife-1SG
'she is my wife'

(23) nè tamą́-y
COP wife-3M
'she is his wife'

(24) nè kàmdá-y
COP wife:PL-3M
'these are his wives'

The subject of an identificational clause may be anaphoric and may actually be spelled out in the predicate of the clause:

(25) Kara è-gé kàyrè nèńy, na nè gìdìrè
people go-3PL travel very much HYP COP moon
go báỳrá.
REF good luck
'People travel a lot [during this time] because it is a moon of good luck.' (G-C & W 1981: 18-19)

4 The grammaticalization of the copula

In many languages of the world copulas have grammaticalized from various types of demonstratives or from various types of verbs of existence in place. The interest of the copula **nè** is that it appears to be derived from and identical with the verb **nè** 'do, make'. Evidence for this hypothesis is provided by the fact that the two have an identical form:

(26) kòlbé-ŋ nè kà-ngà.
cows-DEF COP GEN-1DU.INCL
'these cows are ours'

(27) càǹgé nè dí gùyé
Canige do 3M work
'Canige did work'

(28) nè dí tùwà
make 3M fire
'he made fire'

The verb 'do' and the copula behave in the same way with respect to vowel harmony rules. The vowel of the copula **nè** becomes back when followed by a morpheme with a back vowel. Thus if the referential **go** follows **nè**, the resulting sequence is [nò gò]:

(29) jènè kè-y túg díní ni nò go àp
stay GEN-3M house 1PL.EXL in COP REF short
'his stay at our house was short'

(30) ŋ nò go sòndró
1SG COP REF fear
'I am a coward', lit. 'I am [the one] who [is] coward'

(31) ŋ nè bay go sòndró
1SG COP man REF fear
'I am a coward'

5 Tense and aspect in equational clauses

As stated in the chapter introduction, there are no tense aspectual distinctions in equational clauses. Thus no equational clause can have the inceptive **se** or the pragmatical dependency marker **jè** added. Inception into a state is coded by the verb **wèy** 'become':

(32) wèy dú támą̀-y
become 3F wife-3M
'she became his wife'

(33) wèy dí bay go trábà
become 3M man REF blacksmithing
'he has become a blacksmith' (W & P 1982 **tiraba**)

The distinction between present and past for equational clauses is coded only by adverbs of time:

(34) tùmò nè támą̀-y
before COP wife-3M
'she was his wife'

There are no grammatical means to code future tense in an equational clause. Instead, Lele deploys the future form of the verb **wèy** 'become':

(35) wèlè pìná jè wéye kùrmbálò
day one IMPF become:FUT chief
'one day he will be a chief'

Cf.:

(36) wèy dí kùrmbálò
become 3M chief
'he has become a chief'

6 Equational clauses with property concept predicates

Property concept predicates are coded by the copula **nè** followed by the relative clause marker that codes the gender and number of the subject in equational clauses or of the referent in identificational clauses:

(37) tamá-ŋ nò-go sìyą́ bùg
woman-DEF COP-REF bad by nature
'this woman is by nature nasty'

If the property concept has been lexicalized as a verb, the clause is verbal in all respects. That means that there is no copula and the subject coding with property concept words is identical with the subject coding with verbal predicates:

(38) ŋ gùmyá
1SG large
'I am tall'

(39) gùmyá dí
large 3M
'he is large'

(40) mą́yǫ̀ dí
small 3M
'he is small'

Subject pronouns may occur with non-human subjects as a means of coding the gender of the animal:

(41) kùlbá-ŋ mą́yò (dí/dú)
cattle-DEF small (3M/3F)
'the bull/cow is small', cf. **mą́yè** PL

Since the language does not have a non-human pronoun corresponding to 'it', if the subject is non-human and non-nominal, the clause does not have an overt subject:

(42) nò go kíndi
COP REF true
'it is true'

(43) nò go sìyą́
COP REF bad
'it is bad'

(44) nò go kurà
COP REF good
'it is good'

(45) nò go gùmyá
COP REF tall
'it is tall'

(46) nò go máyọ
COP REF short
'it is short'

(47) nò go sàglé
COP REF false
'it is false'

The form **sàglé** 'false', but not **kíndi** 'true', alone may be used in a type of exclamative-equational clause characterized by the high-tone marker **né** in the beginning of the clause. The high tone is the exclamation marker, since the neutral clause has low-tone copula **nè**:

(48) né sàglé
COP false
'it is false!'

7 Conclusions

Equational clauses have the structure Subject Copula Predicate. The copula is **nè**, which is identical with and derived from the verb 'do, make'. Although the copula is derived from a verb, equational clauses have important formal and functional characteristics that make them different from transitive or intransitive clauses. Identificational clauses, predicating about a deictic or an anaphoric referent, do not have a subject preceding the copula.

10

Possessive, Locative and Existential Clauses

1 Introduction

Possessive clauses have the function 'X has Y'. Locative clauses have the function 'X is located at Y'. These two types of clause are characterized by the absence of any verb, not even a copula. Because these clauses have no verb, they cannot be marked for tense.

2 Possessive clauses: X has Y

There are three constructions to code possession. One uses the associative marker **ná**. The structure of a possessive clause with a nominal subject is Subject **ná** Object:

(1) kiya ná luŋba
Kiya ASSC horse
'Kiya has a horse'

If the possessum consists of more than one noun, each noun may be followed by a conjunction **lay** 'also':

(2) kiya ná luŋba lay kùlbá lay
Kiya ASSC horse also cow also
'Kiya has a horse and a cow'

(3) kiya ná luŋba ná kùlbá
Kiya ASSC horse ASSC cow
'Kiya has a horse and a cow'

Negation of a possessive clause is coded by clause-final negative particle **ɗé**:

(4) kiya ná luŋba ɗé
Kiya COM horse NEG
'Kiya does not have a horse'

If the possessor is pronominal, there are different structures for the first and second person on the one hand, and third person on the other. For the first and second person the structure is Pronoun **ná** Object:

(5) ŋ ná luŋba
1SG ASSC horse
'I have a horse'

(6) gi ná luŋba
2SG ASSC horse
'you have a horse'

For the third-person the possessive structure is **ná** Subject **ná** Object. The interesting thing about these constructions is that after **ná** the subject form of the pronoun is used rather than the associative form, i.e. the pronominal form preceded by the associative pronominal marker **ín**:

(7) ná dí ná luŋba
ASSC 3M ASSC horse
'he has a horse'

(8) ná dú ná kàmyá
ASSC 3F ASSC milk
'she has milk'

(9) ná gé ná loŋbé
ASSC 3PL ASSC horse:PL
'they have horses'

The explanation for the difference between first- and second-person possessor coding on the one hand and third-person on the other rests in the manner in which the subject for these persons is marked. For the first and second persons, the subject precedes the verb. For the third person, the subject follows the verb. Since there is no verb in the possessive clause, the conjunction **ná** is put at the beginning of the clause to serve as a morpheme to which the third-person subject is added. We see here at play a purely formal constraint on the expression of a grammatical category. If the third person is used with a gesture, i.e. in deictic rather than anaphoric function, then the third-person independent subject pronoun is used. In such a case there is no need for the formation of a morpheme to suffix the third-person anaphoric pronoun, and the possessive structure for deictic pronouns is Pronoun **ná** Object:

(10) dày ná luŋba
3M ASSC horse
'he (deictic) has a horse'

(11) dàdù ná kàmyá
3F ASSC milk
'she (deictic) has milk'

(12) dàgé ná loŋbé
3PL ASSC horses
'they (deictic) have horses'

The evidence for the anaphoric rather than the deictic function of the third-person pronouns following the associative **ná** is provided by the fact that to a question 'who S?' one cannot answer using the anaphoric form of the pronoun if a deictic answer is intended. Thus the following exchange is not felicitous, because of the violation of the deictic implication of the question:

(13) wé-y ba ná luŋba gà
who-3M COM ASSC horse Q
'who has a horse?'

(14) *ná dú ná
ASSC 3F ASSC
for 'she has it'

The only possible answer is with a deictic pronoun:

(15) dàdù ná
3F ASSC
'she has one'

Note that in the answer the reference is made to the subject mentioned in the preceding sentence; hence the anaphoric form of the subject pronoun is used.

(16) ná dú ná luŋba gà
ASSC 3F ASSC horse Q
'does she have a horse?'

(17) ná dú ná
ASSC 3F ASSC
'she has one'

Even if the object is human but indefinite, it cannot be coded by the object pronoun. Compare the feminine indefinite possessum:

(18) ná dú ná tormo gà
ASSC 3F ASSC daughter Q
'does she have a daughter?'

(19) ná dú ná
ASSC 3F ASSC
'she has one'

Compare plural non-human possessums, which also do not have a corresponding anaphor:

(20) ná dú ná loŋbé gà
COM 3F COM horses Q
'does she have horses?'

(21) ná dú ná
ASSC 3F ASSC
'she has them'

The behavior of pronouns in possessive constructions puts into relief the true nature of pronouns in Lele. The first- and second-person pronouns behave like third-person deictic pronouns. Hence the first-, second-, and third-person pronouns with the prefix **dà** are all deictic. The suffixed third-person pronouns are anaphoric; they refer to a person mentioned earlier in discourse.

3 Tense in possessive clauses

Since no verb is deployed in possessive clauses, there are no inflectional means of coding the time of the event. The past time is coded by the appropriate time adverbs:

(22) tùmò ná luŋba
before ASSC horse
'he used to have a horse'

The future tense is coded by the future form of the verb **háb** 'find':

(23) nè hábe dú luŋba
COP find:FUT 3F horse
'she will have a horse'

(24) hábe dú luŋba
find:FUT 3F horse
'she will have a horse'

(25) na nè gúye kùrá-ŋ hábe dí lálí
HYP make work good-DEF find:FUT 3M money
'if he does good work, he will have money'

If the reference is to a deictic rather than an anaphoric object, then a demonstrative is used. The form of the demonstrative does not code the gender or number of the object:

(26) ná dú ná káŋ
ASSC 3F ASSC DEM
'she has it/her/them'

In the imperative, just as in the future tense, instead of the associative marker, the verb 'to find' is used:

(27) hábà kanya níyà
find:IMP thing many
'find many things' (a wish given somebody going on a trip)

The possessive construction can be used for the coding of existence in place. The construction has the form: Subject Copula Associative marker Locative marker:

(28) Màdú nè ná cáaní lay; tàsí wè cáaní
vitex COP ASSC field also shea give birth field
nèńy lay
very much also
'The fruits of vitex are in the bush. The fruits of shea tree are also abundant' (G-C & W 1981: 42-43)

4 Locative sentences: X is Located at Y

Locative sentences, i.e. expressions corresponding to 'X is at Y' or 'the event X happened at Y', have the subject followed by the locative expression. The locative expression may be coded by the preposition **dà** preceding the locative phrase, regardless of whether the noun is inherently locative. If the noun is inherently locative, it is not followed by the postposition **ni**:

(29)

cànìgé	dà	Debreng
Canige	PREP	Debreng

'Canige is at Debreng'

If the noun is inherently non-locative, it is followed by the postposition **ni**.

(30)

dà	túgú	tóŋ	ni	kara	kóŋdírè
PREP	village	certain	LOC	people	young.PL
kusi-ge	sùbù				
body-3PL	three				

'In a village there were three young men.'

(31)

láà	gìdìrè	go	dà	kama	te-y	ni
eat:IMP	moon	REF	PREP	water	bottom-3M	LOC

'Eat the moon that is at the bottom of the water . . .'

The marker **ni** may also be the only means to code the locative function:

(32)

kasa	kín-dí	pìna	pínyà	túŋ	ni	ɗé
corn	eye-3M	one	even	home	LOC	NEG

'there wasn't even one grain of corn at home'

Non-permanent location for human pronominal arguments is marked by the noun **kusu** 'body' plus a possessive pronoun:

(33)

kusi-y	dà	Debreng
body-3M	PREP	Debreng

'he is in Debreng'

(34)

kusu-ro	dà	Debreng
body-3F	PREP	Debreng

'she is in Debreng'

The interest of this construction rests in the fact that **kusu** in the object position codes non-punctual affectedness of the subject.

Locative sentences, whether affirmative or negative, do not code gender or number of the subject:

(35) luŋba dà cáànì ɗé
horse PREP field NEG
'the horse is not in the field'

(36) kùní sùrmo dà kantón Lele
house hay PREP Canton Lele
'hay houses exist in the Lele district'

(37) wàlàdí dà Debreng
waladi PREP Debreng
'waladi [a datelike tree/fruit] exists in Debreng'

5 Existential clauses

Existential clauses, i.e. clauses that do not necessarily imply existence in a specific place, are marked by the locative anaphor **mànı́** 'there':

(38) kùmnó mànı́
God there
'God exists'

(39) ɗíglè káŋ kàsà mànı́
year DEM corn there
'there is corn this year'

The existential predicate can be negated in two ways. The first is through the negative particle **ɗé** following the anaphor **mànı́**:

(40) kùmnó mànı́ ɗé
God exist NEG
'God does not exist'

The other means is through the negative existential verb **wı́léŋ** 'not to exist':

(41) kùmnó wı́léŋ
God not exist
'God does not exist'

The anaphor **mànı́** can be used with locative constructions:

(42) wàlàdí mànı́ dà Debreng
Doum palm there PREP Debreng
'there are Doum palms in Debreng'

(43)

tìrtíyą	màní	dà	kùsíyọ	cà-y	ni	káŋ
suffering	there	PREP	earth	head-3M	LOC	DEM

'there is suffering on this earth' (an expression of compassion)

The anaphor **màní** can be used with the pragmatically dependent clause marker **jè** and with the copula **nè**:

(44)

tìrtíyą	jè	nè	mani	dà	kùsíyọ
suffering	IMPF	IMPF	exist	PREP	earth
cà-y	ni	káŋ			
head-3M	LOC	DEM			

'there will always be suffering on this earth'

As we have seen, negative existential clauses have the negative predicate **wileŋ** 'not to exist'.

(45)

mìlí	wíléŋ	dà	Debreng
ron palm	lack	PREP	Debreng

'There are no ron palms in Debreng.'

(46)

kama	wileŋ	dà	kùlmá	ni
water	not exist	PREP	well	LOC

'there is no water in the well'

Cf.:

(47)

kama	dà	kùlmá	ni
water	PREP	well	LOC

'there is water in the well'

The verb **wileŋ** does not code gender or number:

(48)

loŋbé	dà	cáànì
horse	PREP	field

'the horses are in the field'

(49)

loŋbé	wileŋ	dà	cáànì
horse	be absent	PREP	field

'the horses are not in the field'

6 Conclusions

Locative sentences have the structure Subject Locative expression. The locative expression must be marked by the locative preposition **dà** or by the locative postposition **ni** or by both markers.

Affirmative existential sentences are marked by the locative anaphor **màní** occurring at the end of the clause. Negative existential clauses are marked by the form **wileŋ** 'not to exist, lack'. Existential expressions may be used in locative clauses as well simply by adding a locative phrase after the existential marker.

11

Reference System

1 Introduction

The purpose of the chapter is to describe the means available for the coding of reference and the functions of these means. The function of each individual means is described through an account of its interaction with other means available for a given domain.

The coding of reference includes the coding of deixis as well as the coding of anaphora. The term *anaphora* is taken here in traditional sense, viz. reference to an antecedent mentioned previously in discourse, whether by the same or a different speaker. The antecedent can be a proposition, a noun phrase, a prepositional phrase, a verb, or even a situation. An anaphor is the element that codes such reference.

The means of coding reference in Lele include lexical items, deictic and anaphoric pronouns, word order, demonstratives, the definite marker, and the absence of overt coding, a zero marking. The multitude of coding means available in Lele makes the interaction among those means particularly interesting. The present chapter will describe the means that have not yet been described here as well as the interaction of various means. The chapter discusses the coding of deixis first, followed by the description of anaphora. The coding of anaphora is organized along the lines of grammatical roles established previously in Chapter 4, on argument structure, viz. subject, object, dative, associative, locative and propositional anaphors. A special section deals with the coding of definiteness, since this coding appears to interact with the coding of all grammatical roles.

The coding of reference is intimately connected in Lele with the coding of the relationship between sentences and clauses in discourse, and of the pragmatic functions of the noun phrases involved. Some of the discussion in the present chapter anticipates the discussion of topicalization presented in Chapter 16.

2 Deixis

Person deixis has the categories of the first- and second-person pronouns. In the second person there is a distinction between masculine and feminine. There is no gender distinction in the plural. There is no third-person deictic marker. One cannot use the form **dày** 'third masculine' or **dàdù** 'third feminine' as deictic markers.

The deictic system for nouns consists of markers that follow nouns. These markers code gender and distance. Each deictic marker ends in the form **ŋ**, identical with the definite marker. The evidence for the proposed compositional structure of deictic markers is provided by the recurring markers of gender and definite across all the forms, and by the recurring distance markers in the proximate and remote deixis:

	Proximate	Remote
Masculine	k-á-ŋ	k-olo-ŋ
Feminine	t-á-ŋ	t-olo-ŋ

The remote deictic markers may actually have a different grammaticalization history. One cannot rule out the remote deictics' having been formed by analogy to the proximate deictics. The remote masculine deictic marker may consist of the noun **kolo** 'word' followed by the definite marker **ŋ**. The feminine form would be formed by analogy, through the replacement of the word-initial **k** by the feminine marker **t**, as in the proximate deictic. Throughout this work the components of the demonstrative pronouns are not separated by hyphens, and the forms are represented as **káŋ**, **táŋ**, **koloŋ**, and **toloŋ**.

(1) tamá táŋ ŋ gol-du lìŋdá
woman DEM:P:F 1SG see-3F yesterday
'this woman I saw yesterday'

(2) tamá toloŋ ŋ gol-du lìŋdá
woman DEM:R:F 1SG see-3F yesterday
'that woman I saw yesterday'

(3) bayŋdí káŋ ŋ gol-iy lìŋdá
man DEM:P:M 1SG see-3M yesterday
'this man I saw yesterday'

(4) bayŋdí kolon ŋ gol-iy lìŋdá
man DEM:R:M 1SG see-3M yesterday
'that man I saw yesterday'

Most inanimate objects have masculine deictic markers. There are, however, a few exceptions. Thus **wèdre** 'car' is feminine, most certainly because it comes from French **voiture**, which is feminine. Another feminine inanimate noun is **tìndí** 'pestle':

(5) tìndí yó-ró
pestle mother-3F
'mortar', lit. 'mother of the pestle' (mortars are used for husking corn)

Since the mortar is called the mother of the pestle, it is also feminine:

(6) gi ą́y tìndí yo-ro ná toron-do túm
2M take pestle mother-3F ASSC daughter-3F also
'you have taken the mortar with its daughter' (about somebody marrying a woman with children)

3 Definiteness

The term *definiteness* covers the forms and function of the marker **ŋ**.[10] The functions of the definite marker are different for subject and object arguments. Moreover, the definite marker is deployed as the coding means for topicalization.

3.1 Form of the definite marker

Addition of the marker **ŋ** to a syllable causes the raising of the tone of that syllable. If the inherent tone of the syllable is mid, it becomes high after the addition of **ŋ**:

(7) kama + ŋ → kamáŋ
water
tamá + ŋ → tamáŋ
wife
tormo + ŋ → tormóŋ
girl

The inherent low tone becomes mid after the addition of the definite marker:

[10] G-C & W 1982 represent the definite article as **ǹg**, i.e. velar nasal and low tone.

(8) làlì + ŋ → làliŋ
money
dòlò + ŋ → dòloŋ
gruel
tòrò + ŋ → tòroŋ
hen

Even the inherent high tone becomes higher when followed by the definite article. In the following examples the second high tone is higher than the first high tone. The available notation system is not rich enough to code the extra high tone; therefore, the syllable with extra high tone is bold:

(9) tìndí + ŋ → tìn**díŋ**
pestle

tèsé + ŋ → tè**séŋ**
star (the syllable **séŋ** has a higher tone than the syllable **sé**)

The tone raising is the idiosyncratic property of the definite marker, rather than a general language rule with respect to word-final heavy syllables. Thus if one adds the second-person masculine marker **m** to nouns ending in mid tone, the tone is not raised:

(10) tamá + m → [tamám]
wife 2M
'your wife'

(11) tormo + m → [torom]
girl 2M
'your daughter'

The definite marker has two segmental realizations: After consonants, the definite marker is **ŋgòŋ**, and after vowels it is **ŋ**:

(12) ɓándaŋ 'bow' ɓándaŋgòŋ

(13) bàgày 'flood area' bàgày ŋgòŋ

If the addition of the form **ŋgòŋ** to a noun ending in a consonant would result in a disallowed syllable structure, a vowel is inserted for syllabification purposes:

(14) kur 'place' kùrùŋgòŋ 'the place'

3.2 Functions of the definite marker

The minimal condition for the deployment of the definite marker is the previous mention of the noun in discourse. The following example has the same noun twice in the same clause: the first mention of the noun, without a definite marker, and the second mention, with the definite marker. Here is an example of the deployment of the definite marker with the subject:

(14)

baydní	è	jè	ná	kòbró	baydní-ŋ	tòb
man	go	VENT	ASSC	boat	man-DEF	want

go	na	hímé-gé	ɗé
REF	HYP	take:FUT-3PL	NEG

'A man came with a boat but he refused to take them.'

Here is an example of the deployment of the definite marker with the object. The noun **kasire** 'medicine' is introduced in the first clause, and when it is repeated in the second clause, it is followed by the definite marker:

(15)

tòn-ìy	na	pa	bé-y	kasire
ask-3M	HYP	dig:IMP	DAT-3M	medicine

baydní-ŋ	na-y	pe	kasire-ŋ	ɗé
man-DEF	HYP-3M	dig	medicine-DEF	NEG

'He$_1$ told him to dig medicine for him$_1$, but the man refused to dig up medicine.'

A previous mention in discourse is, however, not a sufficient condition for the deployment of the definite marker. The additional conditions are different for subject and object. The subject is coded for definiteness only if it is a new topic, but not if it is a continuing topic. Thus, the definite marker when deployed with the subject is the marker of a new topic. The object, in contrast, is always coded for definiteness if it has been previously mentioned. In order to illustrate the operation of this system, let us analyze one story in its entirety. In the first sentence of the story two protagonists are introduced, and neither of them has a definite marker or a demonstrative following it:

(1)

kur	wèlè-y	pìnà	gònì	dàgè	ná	tu	è	gé
place	lie-3M	one	hyena	3PL	ASSC	goat	go	3PL

sègré	dà	cáaní
hunt	PREP	bush

'One day Hyena and Goat went hunting in the bush.'

The first clauses in the following fragment continue with the same two topics. The two participants are represented by the third-person plural pronoun in both subject and object function. The third clause has a new subject, which has not been previously mentioned in discourse and consequently is not marked by a demonstrative or a definite marker:

(2) kàw gé gàg tùwà dùgì-gè gílalé
walk 3PL till Sun drown-3PL tiredness
pínyà nè-gè
also make-3PL
'They walked till the sun had drowned them and tiredness overwhelmed them.'

Sentence (3) has another new subject, although the sentence may well continue with the same topic, viz. the state of the protagonists in the story:

(3) kìb di-gè hay lay
mouth GEN:PL-3PL dry also
'their mouths are also dry', 'they are also thirsty'

The first clause of sentence (4) again has a new subject and a new topic, but the subject and the topic are not the same. The subject is the noun **time** 'hunger', in accordance with the system of coding of internal states, but the topic is **gònì** 'hyena'. The second clause continues the same topic as the first clause, and the topic is represented by the third-person feminine pronoun, since **gònì** 'hyena' is a feminine noun:

(4) time nè gònì nẹ̀y bé kolo dìgrì
hunger make hyena very much DAT reason kill
dú ìsą́n ɗé
3F nothing NEG
'Hyena is very hungry because it did not kill anything.'

Although the hyena is the topic of sentence (4), it is not a new topic, since hyena was one of the two subjects/topics in the preceding clause. Now consider sentence (5). Its subject is **tu** 'goat', a new topic relative to the topic of sentence (4), and it is also a focus of the sentence (5), a contrastive focus, as indicated by the deployment of the independent pronoun. The new topic, representing a noun mentioned previously in discourse, is marked by the independent pronoun followed by the noun. As predicted by the hypothesis, it is marked for definiteness:

(5) dàdù tu-ŋ lèé kàsùma ɓàl-dù
3F goat-DEF eat feed (grass, hay) satisfy-3F
'As for Goat, it has eaten the feed to its satisfaction'

Sentence (6) has both protagonists appearing, and they are coded by the third-person plural pronoun, the standard means for coding known, de re subjects:

(6)

se	è	jè	gé	dà	tálwá	ni	bé
INCEPT	go	VENT	3PL	PREP	pond	LOC	DAT

kolo	na	ge	sée	kam(a)
reason	HYP	3PL	drink:FUT	water

'then they came to a pond in order to drink water'

In sentence (7) both the hyena and the goat are mentioned, but the word **gònì** 'hyena' does not have the definite marker and the word **tu** 'goat' does. The hyena in example (7) continues one of the subjects of the preceding sentence. The word for 'goat', however, is an object that has been mentioned before, and according to the hypothesis, it has to have the definite marker. In addition, 'water' **kama-ŋ** has the definite marker because it was mentioned in sentence (6):

(7)

gònì	dà	kìrbé	kò-rò	ni	ná	gèy
hyena	PREP	thought	GEN-3F	LOC	ASSC	want

go	léè	tu-ŋ	ɓey	ba	sée
REF	eat:FUT	goat-DEF	before	COM	drink:FUT

kama-ŋ
water-DEF

'Hyena in its thoughts wanted to devour the goat before drinking water.'

The definite marker may be added to the subject, making it a new topic:

(7a)

gònì-ŋ	dà	kìrbé	kò-rò	ni	ná
hyena-DEF	PREP	thought	GEN-3F	LOC	ASSC

gèy	go	léè	tu-ŋ
want	REF	eat	goat-DEF

'Hyena in its thoughts wanted to devour the goat . . .'

In actual discourse the definite marker was not added to the subject, because the sentence about the goat is parenthetical to the main line of the narrative. 'Goat' is not a topic of the paragraph.

If the object has been mentioned before in discourse, its mention again in discourse must be accompanied by the definite marker. Thus the omission of **ŋ** from the object of sentence (7b) is grammatical, but it means 'he wanted to eat a goat':

(7b) gòǹì dà kìrbé kò-rò ni gèy
hyena PREP thought GEN-3F LOC want
go léè tu
REF eat goat
'Hyena in its thoughts wanted to devour a goat'

In sentence (8) there is a new subject 'goat', and therefore it has the definite marker. Note that the hyena is not the object of this sentence. The object is a complement clause, whose subject is **gonì kún-do** 'the eye of the hyena':

(8) tu-ŋ gol go gonì kún-do jèn téŋ
goat-DEF see REF hyena eye-3F remain different
ná se ày dú lúmá na
ASSC INCEPT take 3F trick HYP
'Goat noticed that Hyena had different intentions and tried the following trick'

The category definite is not allowed for the nominal modifiers, even if they have been previously mentioned in the clause. Thus in sentence (9) one cannot insert the definite marker after **kama** 'water', because it is the modifier of **dùrè** 'inside'. Notice also that the object of the conjoined clause **ísì go bòré** 'white bone' has no definite marker, because it is introduced for the first time in the narrative:

(9) ìrà-ngà dà kama dùrè-y ni
go:IMP-1DU.INCL PREP water inside-3M LOC
ba nga séè dày go ɗínglé lay
COM 1DU.INCL drink:FUT 3M REF clear also
me ágè ísì go bòré koloŋ
2F take:FUT bone REF white there
'Let us go inside this water; we will drink the one that is clear, and you will take the white bone there'

The next sentence has a new subject, goat. But it follows direct speech in sentence (9) whose subject was first-person dual inclusive; hence the subject included 'hyena', which is also the subject of the sentence (10). The word **ísì** 'bone' has the definite marker because it has been mentioned in the preceding clause. It is also the focus of the clause, as evidenced by the focus marker **nè** preceding it:

(10) goni cál bàá kama ni ná ɓàdì nè
hyena jump fall water LOC ASSC go after COP
ísì-ŋ càr
bone-DEF immediately
'Hyena jumped into the water and went immediately after the bone'

Sentence (11) has a new subject, but subjects of the verb of saying are not topical:

(11)

tu	yàá	bú-dú	na
goat	tell	DAT-3F	HYP

'Goat told her'

In sentence (12) bone is the object. Since it has been mentioned before, it must have the definite marker:

(12)

yú	cà-rè	dà	kama	te-y	ni
put:IMP	head-2M	PREP	water	bottom-3M	LOC

ba	me	ágè	ísí-ŋ
COM	2F	take:FUT	bone-DEF

'plunge to the bottom of the water and you will get the bone'

In sentence (13) the subject, hyena, does not have definite marker because it is followed by a modifier with possessive pronoun coding the gender and number of the subject. Note also that **kama** 'water' in sentence (13) does not have the definite marker in either of its two mentions. In the first mention water is the modifier **kama te-y** 'bottom of the water', and in the second it is part of the lexicalization of the notion 'swim':

(13)

gònì	sùm-rò	se	yí	cà-rò	kama
hyena	be mad:VN-3F	INCEPT	put	head-3F	water

te-y	ni	ná	dusi	kolo	sèn
bottom-3M	LOC	ASSC	sink	because	know

go	nàlè	kama	ɗé
REF	swim:VN	water	NEG

'Foolish hyena put its head at the bottom of the water and it sank because it did not know how to swim.'

The sentence (14) the new subject is not topical, as it is the subject of a verb of saying:

(14)

tu	se	yàá	bú-dù	na
goat	INCEPT	tell	DAT-3F	HYP

'Then Goat told her:'

Given the function of the definite marker as the marker of a new topic for the subject, it is not surprising that the definite marker may follow the possessive construction. Thus, when in a narrative there is a switch of topic, the new topic is followed by the definite marker:

(16) kudo-ro-ŋ jè ɗeŋlí kolo ką́nyé
husband-3F-DEF IMPF hear word certain:PL
kwáni ná [pause] yàá ísaŋ ɗé
outside ASSC tell nothing NEG
'Despite the fact that her husband heard certain things outside, he did not say anything.'

3.3 Definiteness and possessive constructions

Recall that there are two types of possessive constructions: the inalienable, where the possessor precedes the possessum and the possessum has a possessive suffix coding the features of gender and number of the possessor; and the alienable, with the possessum followed by the possessor followed by the genitive marker **kè** and the possessive pronoun coding the features of gender and number of the possessor. The interesting fact about the definiteness coding of these constructions is that the definite marker is added to the possessor only:

(17) se è gé dà túgú pói kúsíge-ŋ
INCEPT go 3PL PREP home Poi Kusige-DEF
kè-y
GEN-3M
'they went to the house of Poi Kusige'

(18) me ba dígrì tòrò kò-noŋ goŋ gà
what COM kill hen GEN-1SG DEF Q
'what killed my hen?' (mentioned before in discourse)

The coding of the definiteness of the possessor remains a somewhat obscure problem. If the possessor is the topic, it is marked for definiteness. In the following example, the subject of the first clause is 'daughter of the man'. But it is the noun **bayndí** 'man' that is the topic, as evidenced by the fact that he is the unmarked subject of the second clause of the sentence:

(19) bayndí-ŋ teren-di yàá na húm-gé
man-DEF daughter-3M say HYP take:IMP-3PL
se hím-gé bòr ná kama
INCEPT take-3PL skim ASSC water
'The daughter of the man told him to take them. He took them and they skimmed across the river.'

If the possessor is not the topic of the clause, it is not coded for definiteness, even if it was mentioned before in the discourse. Consider again sentence (8) from the story of the hyena and the goat. The subject of the embedded clause is 'the eye of hyena', but the hyena, which was mentioned before, is not the topic of the sentence, and it is not marked by the definite marker:

(20) tu-ŋ gol go gonì kún-do jèn téŋ
goat-DEF see REF hyena eye-3F remain different
ná se ày dú lúmá na
ASSC INCEPT take 3F trick HYP
'Goat noticed that Hyena had different intentions and tried the following trick'

Objects of prepositions, if they were mentioned before, are coded by the definite marker:

(21) tormo na du ódè ná ba-ro ɗé
daughter HYP 3F leave:FUT ASSC father-3F NEG
se è ná bayndí-ŋ
INCEPT go ASSC man-DEF
'The girl refused to go with her father and instead went with the man.'

An interesting exception to the rules about the deployment of the definite marker is provided by nouns that have unique reference, i.e. nouns that in given circumstances can have only one referent. Within a village such a noun is **kùrmbàlò** 'chief'. Even if the chief of the village has been mentioned in previous discourse, and even if it is a topic of the clause or a paragraph, an object, or a possessor, it never has the definite marker. Consider the following fragments. In the first sentence the chief is introduced in the narrative:

(22) è gé dà túgú kóŋ ni àlá kùrmbàlò
go 3PL PREP village certain LOC then chief
gol kamda-y sùbù nè go láy wa tú
see wives-3M three COP REF pretty very all (Fr.)
'They arrived at a certain village, [and] the chief saw that the three wives of the man were all beautiful.'

Five sentences later the chief is mentioned again in various roles and is not followed by the definite marker:

(23) donc na-y be kùrmbàlò tamá
therefore (Fr.) HYP-3M give chief wife
ɗé
NEG
'Therefore, he will not give a wife to the chief.'

(24) na-y jénè ná kamda-y go sùbù bas
HYP-3M stay ASSC wives-3M REF three only (Ar.)
'He said that he just wants to stay with his three wives.'

(25) kùrmbàlò se bòr bé-y kur ba
chief INCEPT cut DAT-3M parcel COM
se jèn mànı́ ná kamda-y go sùbù
INCEPT settle ANAPH ASSC wives-3M REF three
'The chief cut him a parcel of land and the man settled there with his three wives.'

4 Referentiality

A noun that has been previously mentioned in discourse and is known, but that is not the argument of a verb, is coded by the referential marker **go** following it:

(26) Nè gìdìrè go simlí jè tèy-gé
COP moon REF guinea fowl IMPF trace-3PL
ná karma;
ASSC children
'It is in this month that guinea fowl have their chicks' (G-C & W 1981: 20-21)

(27) Nè gìdìrè go kara nè jè-gé ná
COP moon REF people COP plant-3PL ASSC
mònò lay.
eleusine also
'It is during this month that they plant eleusine.' (G-C & W 1981: 42-43)

5 Indefiniteness

The term *indefinite* refers to a noun that is specifically marked as unknown. There are two means of coding indefiniteness: one, when it applies to an argument of a clause, and the other, when it applies to the background information.

5.1 Coding the indefiniteness of arguments and adjuncts

Indefiniteness is coded by the word for **bayndí** 'man' for indefinite humans, and by the word **kąnya** 'thing' for indefinite non-human nouns:

(28) ba se è dà kúso bayndí kè-y
COM INCEPT go PREP field man GEN-3M
ni da kàrga túgú ni
LOC PREP behind compound LOC
e póì je tèmlé wén bùgú
go break:PL VENT corn fill bag
'there he went into somebody's field behind the compound, broke off corn, [and] filled his bag'

(29) wèlè go jè yì ką̀nya ná tòrò
day REL IMPF pound thing ASSC hen
yó-ró-ŋ dèr kàràn-dò è ná tìnɗí
mother-3F-DEF carry children-3F go ASSC mortar
tó-ró ni jè dì gé kasa.
bottom-3F LOC IMPF peck 3PL corn
'Each time she$_1$ was pounding, the old hen$_2$ carried her chicks under the mortar and they pecked corn.

The negative equivalent of the indefinite non-human word is **ìsą́n** 'nothing':

(30) time nè gònì nę̀y bé kolo dìgrì
hunger make hyena very much DAT reason kill
dú ìsą́n ɗé
3F nothing NEG
'Hyena is very hungry because it did not kill anything.'

(31) póì kúsíge dàgè ná tamą́-y ná gé ná
Poi Kusige 3PL ASSC wife-3M ASSC 3PL ASSC
ísàn go lèé túŋ ni ɗé
nothing REF eat:VN home LOC NEG
'Poi Kusige and his wife have nothing to eat at home.'

The notion 'everybody' is coded by the form **wéy**, which otherwise codes the interrogative about human participants 'who' followed by the lexeme **pinyà** 'all'. The anaphor for the expression **wéy pinyà** 'everybody' is inherently singular, as evidenced by the singular rather than the plural possessive pronoun that it takes:

(32) Wéy pìnyà kindi ná kòjò kè-ì nè
who all grain ASSC hoe GEN-3M make
kìrè cáaní àlè.
road field
'Everybody goes to the field with his hoe' (G-C & W 1981: 42-43)

The form **wéy** can be reduplicated for the distributive function, i.e. a situation where every participant is individually involved in the event:

(33) Gìnà kur na wèl ɗè ná, wéy wéy
front place COMP turn NEG ASSC who who
pinyà hàm jólgo ná kanya go
even find Tapinanthus ASSC thing REL
yire kindi isili sòngò go kùlèn-dì tòb.
grind:VN grain boil oil REL belly-3M want
'Before the day begins, everybody gets the plant of Tapinanthus and grains for grinding, and cooks the oil of his choice.' (G-C & W 1981: 18-19)

Both affirmative and negative indefinite arguments may be modified by the numeral **pìnà** 'one'. The numeral with indefinite markers appears to function as additional coding of indefiniteness:

(34) pói kúsíge sèn ísàŋ pìnà
Poi Kusige know nothing one
go na-y né go na-y
REL COMP-3M make:FUT REL COMP-3M
lámdè ná dòlo bé karan-di ɗé
cook gruel ASSC gruel DAT children-3M NEG
'Poi Kusige does not know with what he is going to cook gruel for his children.'

A second means of coding indefiniteness of an argument is through the deployment of unspecified pronouns, the same ones that code the scope of specific interrogatives. This means is used for the coding of the emphatic negative:

(35) me pyą è jè ná ɗé
what small go VENT ASSC NEG
'he didn't bring even a small thing'

5.2 Coding indefiniteness in the background information

The term *indefinite noun phrase* refers to noun phrases marked by one of the indefinite pronouns: **kóŋ** 'masculine', **tóŋ** 'feminine', or **káŋyé** 'plural'. In natural discourse these pronouns mark nouns and noun phrases that occur in background information, introducing information about time, place, and participants to be deployed in a conversation or narrative.

(36) dà túgú tóŋ ni kara kóndrè
PREP village certain:F LOC people young men
kusi-ge sùbù
body-3PL three
'In a village there were three young men.'

The indefinite marker may be deployed together with the numeral **pìnà** 'one':

(37) ná ɗigle tóŋ pìnà làmndá yé-y
ASSC year certain:F one elephant mother-3M
ne hòmnyá go ma
COP sick REF die
'One year, the mother of elephant was sick, close to her death.'

(38) tùwà tóŋ pìnà ná jè yì dú
kḁnya
sun certain one ASSC IMPF pound 3F
things
'one day, when she was pounding . . .'

(39) è gé dà túgú kóŋ ni
go 3PL PREP village certain LOC
'They arrived in a certain village . . .'

The indefinite marker may occur when a noun is coded as an unknown member of a group, again in the background information:

(40) tùmò go kara índ'wé ɗeŋlí gé
once REF people humankind:PL understand 3PL
kùb kḁnya ame kè-gè ná tamá
language thing domestic GEN-3PL ASSC woman
tóŋ ɗeŋlí kùb kòrà kè-gè
certain understand language chickens GEN-3PL
'At one time, when humankind understood the language of domestic animals, a certain woman understood the language of chickens.'

The deployment of the indefinite marker in the background information is similar to the deployment of the deictic demonstrative in the same situation. Consider the beginnings of two consecutive sentences in the same narrative:

(41) dày háŋ ba na
3M DEM COM HYP
'The first one said . . .'

(42) dày kóŋ na-y
3M certain HYP-3M
'The other said that if he . . .'

If a noun or a noun phrase does not constitute background information, it is not followed by the indefinite marker. Thus in natural texts a new mention does not have an indefinite pronoun unless it is also part of the background information.

6 The subject anaphora

The problem that the grammar of Lele presents is as follows: given the fact that there are independent pronouns and third-person subject pronouns, and given the fact that the subject may be either nominal or pronominal, or both, and given the fact that there are definite markers marking new but previously mentioned topics, what are the functions of nominal subjects, and what are the functions of pronominal subjects? The following set of hypotheses accounts for the deployment of these means. A nominal subject serves to introduce a new topic of a sentence, not necessarily a new topic of a discourse unit. A pronominal subject is used when the subject is known, and it is the same as the subject of the previous clause. Nominal subjects and pronominal subjects are thus in complementary distribution. The evidence for the proposed hypotheses is as follows: if there is a sequence of complex sentences within which there may be different potential subjects of the next sentence, the nominal subject is repeated whenever it is the sentential topic.

Here is additional evidence that continuing topical subjects are not marked by the definite marker unless they are new topics. In the following sequence both sentences have the same subject, **kàyo** 'squirrel', which is also the topic. It must be repeated because there are two potential third-person masculine subjects, and omission of the nominal subject would lead to ambiguity:

(43) kàyo yàá bé-y na máàní ná [pause]
squirrel say DAT-3M HYP ANAPH ASSC
na à jè na ge é
HYP go:IMP VENT HYP INDEF go:FUT
'Squirrel told him: if it is like that, then come, one will go.'

(44) kàyo se om-iy jè se è
squirrel INCEPT catch-3M VENT INCEPT go
ná ín-dí dà kur go tumadu-ŋ ni
ASSC ASSC-3M PREP place REF death-DEF LOC
'Squirrel took him [and] brought him to the place of burial.'

(45) kàyo se jé àlé dà
squirrel INCEPT throw announcement PREP
kùná-y gų̋yé cà-y ni yàá na . . .
uncle-3M spider head-3M LOC say HYP
'Squirrel makes an announcement concerning his uncle Spider . . .'

When the topic of a sentence is established, it is done with full noun phrases. Thus the beginning of every story has a noun phrase as the subject:

(46) ná ɗigle tóŋ pìnà làmndá yé-y
ASSC year certain:F one elephant mother-3M
ne hòmnyá go ma
COP sick REF die
'One year, the mother of elephant was sick, close to her death.'

In the above sentence one cannot use the third-person feminine subject marker **dú** after the verb **nè** 'make', because the mother of elephant is mentioned for the first time.

7 The role of subject pronouns

First- and second-person subject pronouns must be repeated in sequential and embedded clauses:

(47) yàá bú-dú na ŋ án kwánì ba ŋ
tell DAT-3F HYP 1SG leave outside COM 1SG
jìb cà-nìŋ ná kòyè ba ŋ dìgr-ìy
bump head-1SG ASSC thief COM 1SG kill-3M
'He told her: leaving the house I bumped against a thief and killed him.'

In equational clauses independent pronouns must be deployed:

(48) nè dàŋ ɗé na gí gèy pìyą̀ ná
COP 1SG NEG HYP 2SG want even ASSC
ŋ je wále kus-iŋ
1SG IMPF swear:FUT body-1SG
'It is not me; if you want, I will swear.'

If several clauses in a sequence have a first- or second-person subject, the subject pronoun must be repeated:

(49) gi kése ná kà-m ɗé
2M share:FUT ASSC hand-2M NEG
'you will not share'

(50) gi ládè ná kà-m ɗé
2M touch:FUT ASSC hand-2M NEG
'you will not touch it'

(51) ngu gol gaw go kun-do pìnà tésí ɗé-ŋ
2PL see well REF eye-3F one break already-DEF
ná da ngù kasa ná já koloŋ
ASSC eat:IMP 2PL corn ASSC side DEM:R
'you see well that she is blind in one eye, so go and peck on the other side'

(52) na mé léè yé dí-nì ná
HYP 2F eat:FUT mother GEN-1PL.EXCL HYP
mé jè má lay
2F IMPF die:FUT also
'If you eat our mother, you will also die'

(53) ŋ sèn toto go mé gèy léè-ŋ
1SG know completely REF 2F want eat:FUT-1SG
àlá mé hábe kìrè-níŋ ɗé
but 2F find:FUT way-DEF NEG
'I know very well that you want to devour me, but you will not be able to.'

If the first clause is in the imperative modality and the second clause is in the indicative modality, the second-person singular subject does not have to be overtly marked in the imperative modality, but it must be overtly marked in the indicative modality:

(54) yú cà-rè dà kama te-y ni
put:IMP head-2M PREP water bottom-3M LOC
ba me ágè ísí-ŋ
COM 2F take:FUT bone-DEF
'plunge to the bottom of the water and you will get the bone'

7.1 Third-person subject pronouns

There are different conditions and constraints on the deployment of masculine, feminine, and plural third-person pronouns.

The issue of interest here is the relationship between nominal and pronominal subjects, more specifically, when pronominal subjects are deployed if there is also a nominal subject; when pronominal subjects are deployed if there is no nominal subject; and when pronominal subjects are not deployed.

The minimum condition for the deployment of all pronominal third-person subjects is that the person referred to by the pronoun must be known to the speaker. Compare the two clauses in the following sentence. In the first clause the nominal subject is plural, referring to all humankind, presumably known to the speaker and hearer. Since the nominal subject is plural, the verb is followed by the third-person plural subject marker **gé**. In the second clause, the subject is marked as indefinite, and the verb is not followed by the third-person feminine subject pronoun corresponding to the nominal subject:

(55)

tùmò	go	kara	íncɗwé	ɗeŋlí	gé
once	REF	people	humankind:PL	understand	3PL

kùb	kạnya	ame	kè-gè	ná	tamá
language	thing	domestic	GEN-3PL	ASSC	woman

tóŋ	ɗeŋlí	kùb	kòrà	kè-gè
certain	understand	language	chickens	GEN-3PL

'At one time, when humankind understood the language of domestic animals, a certain woman understood the language of chickens.'

In natural discourse, if the nominal subject is used for the first time, the third-person pronoun cannot be used in indicative, pragmatically neutral clauses. Thus, in none of the following sentences, where the subject has not been mentioned previously, can one insert the third-person subject pronoun:

(56)

kùrmbàlò	nè	bé-gè	kanya	máàní
chief	make	DAT-3PL	thing	ANAPH

tu
all (Fr.)

'The chief made all those things for them' (the chief is mentioned for the first time in the discourse)

(57)

bayŋdí-ŋ	terèn-dì	yà	na
man-DEF	daughter-3M	say	HYP

'the daughter of the man said . . .' (the man is mentioned in the preceding discourse; his daughter is not)

Additional evidence for the function of pronominal subjects is provided by sentences where other means are deployed to code definiteness. If the definite marker is used, the third-person subject pronoun is not used:

(58) bayndí-ŋ se háb gèylè
man-DEF INCEPT find health
'the man recovered his health'

The third-person singular subject pronouns may cooccur with nominal subjects only if the subject is in focus:

(59) à bayŋdí-ŋ yàá dí na na-y gol
but man-DEF tell 3M HYP HYP-3M see
tèmlè màyfò-y na mbùlù-m ní-ŋ
corn hair-3M HYP chin-2M LOC-DEF
'but the man said that he apparently saw corn hair on your chin'

The third-person singular subject pronouns **dí** for masculine and **dú** for feminine as the only subject markers are deployed under rather subtle and interconnected conditions. The minimum condition is for the nominal subject to have been mentioned in the preceding discourse. If there were two potential subjects in the preceding discourse, but in a subsequent clause, one of the potential subjects appears as object, the other subject does not have to be overtly marked by a pronoun:

(60) kudo-ro-ŋ jè ɗeŋlí kolo ką́nyé
husband-3F-DEF IMPF hear word certain:PL
kwáni ná [pause] yàá ísaŋ ɗé
outside ASSC tell nothing NEG
'Despite the fact that her husband heard certain things outside, he did not say anything.'

(61) wèlè pìnà ná gèy na-y gísè-dù
day one ASSC want (Ng.) HYP-3M try:FUT-3F
'One day he wished to test her'

In the next clause, one of the potential subjects is coded as the object; therefore, the other subject does not have to be overtly coded:

(62) ɗe-du jaŋ jè wèl dú kuná ná
leave-3F quietly IMPF sleep 3F sleep ASSC
'He left her quietly while she was asleep,'

But in the next clause only one of the previously mentioned participants appears, and it is overtly coded:

(63)

an	dí	è	om	dùbàngú	yó-ró	ná
leave	3M	go	catch	sheep	mother-3F	ASSC

mundu	wàl
silence	slaughter

'left the room, caught an old ewe in silence, and slaughtered it.'

In the next sentence, the subject is overtly coded because it is a new sentence, a new event, and more important, it is the only participant of the two previously mentioned. But the subject is overtly coded only in the first clause:

(64)

càg	dí	kùbàrò	kúsíyòŋ	è	ná	gàg
spread	3M	blood	ground	go	ASSC	until

sùgyá	go	kul	kàrgà-y	ni
grass	REF	house	behind-3M	LOC

'he spread [the blood] on the ground [and] went with it up to the grass behind the house'

Virtually the same situation obtains in the next sentence: the third-person pronominal subject is overtly coded in the first clause but is unmarked in the remaining five clauses:

(65

wel	dí	dùbàngú	kólí	se	gày
skin	3M	sheep	completely	INCEPT	open

kùlòn-dò	wàl-wì	cà-rò	ná	gàn-dò
belly-3F	cut-PL	head-3F	ASSC	leg-3F

dàw	ná	sí-ró	tum	saar	ná
put together	ASSC	flesh-3F	together	attach	ASSC

kùyò	jé	dà	mbóló	ni
mat	throw	PREP	granary	LOC

'He skinned the sheep, opened its belly, cut its head and limbs, reunited them with its meat, rolled it in a mat, and threw the whole thing into the granary.'

In the next sentence the pronominal subject is not overtly coded, because the second participant is overtly coded as the object, and therefore the subject does not have to be marked:

(66)

ná	se	è	jè	hìndì	tamą́-y
ASSC	INCEPT	go	VENT	wake up	wife-3M

kun	ni
sleep	LOC

'And then he came and woke up his wife.'

Similarly in the next sentence:

(67) yàá bú-dú na . . .
tell DAT-3F HYP
'He told her: . . .'

The third-person pronoun is deployed when within the same sentence there is an attempt at repair or clarification of what has been said in the preceding clause:

(68) dày kíya way-wi bisí-ŋ in mbàtmbàt
3M Kiya launch-PL antelope-DEF xxx miss:PL
kàb-ìy án jé dí bisí kàb-ìy
hand-3M leave throw 3M antelope hand-3M
om-du gàrma tóòmé
catch-3F times many
'Kiya threw at the antelope many times, but missed.'

Another condition for the deployment of the third-person subject pronouns is that a clause has an object preceding the verb, thus creating a potential ambiguity as to the role of the fronted argument. The subject pronoun disambiguates the role of the fronted argument:

(69) òlkùsíŋ wél bìsí-ŋ
Olkusin skin antelope-DEF
'Olkusin skinned the antelope'

(70) ná kóli sáar dí je
ASSC everything attach 3M VENT
ndám
well (packed) Ideophone
'tied up everything well'

(71) kàb-ìy ni
hand-3M LOC
'in his hand'

The few examples given above are all the instances of the deployment of the third-person masculine pronoun in texts taking up twenty-four pages, with many texts having masculine singular protagonists.

The general rule for the coding of coreference of third-person subject pronouns in sequential clauses is as follows: If the third-person singular subject is the same in subsequent clauses, it is not marked unless the conditions listed above have been met. In the following sequence of four clauses the third-person masculine singular subject is not overtly coded even once:

(72) ày bùgú kàb-ìy ni an ná kumno
take bag hand-3M LOC leave ASSC God
kam-dì
water-3M
'he took a [50kg] bag into his hands [and] he left with the rain'

(73) ba se è dà kúso bayndí kè-y
COM INCEPT go PREP field man GEN-3M
ni da kàrgà túgú ni
LOC PREP behind compound LOC
è póì jè tèmlé wén bùgú
go break:PL VENT corn fill bag
'there he went into somebody's field behind the compound, broke off corn, filled his bag'

Similarly in the following sequence, a new subject is mentioned in the first clause and then it is not overtly coded in subsequent clauses:

(74) dày bay go kúsó-ŋ è na-y gólè
3M man REF field-DEF go HYP-3M see:FUT
tèmlé kè-y ná gol bayndí gàŋ-dì dà
corn GEN-3M ASSC see man foot-3M PREP
kúso ni
field LOC
'When the owner of the field went to look at his corn, he saw footsteps in his field'

(75) tab jè gàrma-ŋ gàgàk è jè ná
follow VENT traces-DEF until go VENT ASSC
dà túgú pói kúsígè kè-y
PREP house Poi Kusige GEN-3M
'He followed the footsteps until he arrived at the compound of Poi Kusige.'

(76) tey pôì kúsíge-ŋ tòn-ìy na
call Poi Kusige-DEF asked-3M HYP
'He called Poi Kusige and asked him:'

A similar rule applies to the third-person feminine singular: If there is no intervening subject between the nominal feminine singular subject and its subsequent instantiations, the subject is not coded by the pronoun:

(77) tormo na du ódè ná ba-ro ɗé
daughter HYP 3F leave:FUT ASSC father-3F NEG
se è ná bayndí-ŋ
INCEPT go ASSC man-DEF
'The girl refused to go with her father and instead went with the man.'

(78) [bayndí-ŋ] tormo-ŋ na du ódè
[man-DEF, wrong start] girl-DEF HYP 3F leave:FUT
ná ba-ro ɗé
ASSC father-3F NEG
se kal è gé ná kamda sùbù
INCEPT pass go 3PL ASSC wives three
'The girl said that she would not go with her father, she passed [from the father to the man] and he went with three wives.'

(79) tamá-ŋ ɗeŋlí á jè wèy
woman-DEF understand ASSC IMPF turn
ín-dí-gè pílá pílá
ASSC-GEN:PL-3PL at the same time
'When the woman understood, she was turning around [the mortar] at the same time [as they did]'

The third-person singular pronoun does not have to be used even if its antecedent has been mentioned in a role other than subject. It is enough for the antecedent to be the topic, i.e. to be marked by the definite marker:

(80) bayndí-ŋ teren-di yàá na húm-gé
man-DEF daughter-3M say HYP take:IMP-3PL
se hím-gé bòr ná kama
INCEPT take-3PL skim ASSC water
'The daughter of the man told him to take them. He took them and they crossed the river.'

The third-person plural subject **gé**, in contrast, must always be used, i.e. in the situations in which the third-person singular subject pronouns are not used. The third-person plural pronoun is not omitted, even in sequential clauses, as illustrated by the following fragments:

Fragment 1:
(81) dà túgú tóŋ ni kara kóndrè
PREP village certain:F LOC people young men
kusi-ge sùbù
body-3PL three
'In a village there were three young men.'

(82)

yàá	gé	na
say	3PL	HYP

'They said:'

Fragment 2:

(83)

se	è	gé	dà	túgú	póì	kúsíge-ŋ
INCEPT	go	3PL	PREP	home	Poi	Kusige-DEF

kè-y
GEN-3M

'they went to the house of Poi Kusige'

(84)

dòb	gé	kùní	kùlè-ndì	ni	ná
enter	3PL	house	interior-3M	LOC	ASSC

'They entered the house and'

hàb	gé	tèmlè	wén	bùgú	lay
find	3PL	corn	fill	sack	also

'they found corn filling the sack'

Fragment 3:

(85)

è	gé	segré-ŋ	hàb	gé	bisí
go	3PL	hunt-DEF	find	3PL	antelope'

'they went for a hunt [and] they found an antelope.

Fragment 4:

(86)

hą̀	è	gé	dàwù	gé	ná	kamda	sò
till	go	3PL	gather	3PL	ASSC	women	two

'until they went and joined with two wives'

Fragment 5:

(87)

nè	máàní	ba	kàrà	túgú
COP	ANAPH	COM	people	village

'[it] is like that, that people of the village . . . '

sèn	gé	go	na	póì	kúsíge
know	3PL	REF	HYP	Poi	Kusige

'know that Poi Kusige . . . '

If the subject is not the topic of the preceding sentence, it is deployed as a full noun phrase. Consider the following sequence of sentences: in the first one, the topic is **dày go sùbù** 'the third man'. The sentence also mentions the chief's wife in a prepositional phrase. In the second sentence the chief's wife is the subject and the topic, and she is not coded by the pronominal subject marker:

(88) dày go sùbù ge dígrè-y è wèl ná
3M REF three HUM kill:FUT-3M go sleep COM
kùrmbàlò tamą́-y
chief wife-3M
'The third one, who was going to be killed, went to sleep with the chief's wife.'

(89) kùrmbàlò tamą́-y àn ná wáyngulú
chief wife-3M leave ASSC morning
àgi-y saar-iy dà kàrgà-ro ni
take-3M attach-3M PREP back-3F LOC
'The chief's wife left in the morning, took the fellow, [and] attached him to her back.'

(90) gìr ná ín-dì hàn è-gé ná dà
run ASSC ASSC-3M till go-3PL ASSC PREP
kama kùb-ìy ni
river edge-3M LOC
'She ran with him till they arrived at the bank of the river.'

The same principle is at work in the following two fragments, where a daughter is mentioned in a prepositional phrase in the first sentence, then there is a different topic, and in the third sentence the daughter is a topic, but she is coded by the nominal subject only:

(91) è gé cáanì bayndí-ŋ kalo se yír-íy
go 3PL bush man-DEF snake INCEPT bite-3M
ɗe ná bayndí go segre è jè ná
THEN ASSC man REF hunter go VENT ASSC
teren-ɗì máàní
daughter-3M there
'When they went into the bush, a snake bit the man. Then came a hunter with his daughter to the place.'

(92) tòn-ìy na pa bé-y kasire
ask-3M HYP dig:IMP DAT-3M medicine
bayndí-ŋ na-y pe kasiré-ŋ ɗè
man-DEF HYP-3M dig medicine-DEF NEG
'He told him to dig medicine for him, but the man refused.'

(93) ɗe ná bayndí-ŋ teren-dì se yàá
THEN ASSC man-DEF daughter-3M INCEPT tell
na pa bé-y kasire-ŋ
HYP dig:IMP DAT-3M medicine-DEF
'Then the hunter's daughter told her father to dig up the medicine for the man.'

If the subject, even a new one, is plural, or if it consists of conjoined noun phrases with human or anthropomorphized nouns, the third-person plural subject pronoun **gé** must be used. Its omission would make the sentence uninterpretable. In the following example, relatives of the old elephant are mentioned for the first time:

(94) ɗe ná nòju-ro kínyé se óm gé
THEN ASSC relative-3F COLL INCEPT catch 3PL
tu go bàl nè òb ná kara
goat REF gelded COP invite for work ASSC people
'Then, her relatives caught a large gelded goat and used it to invite people for the purpose of common work:'

(95) kur wèlè-y pìnà gònì dàgè ná tu è
place lie:VN-3M one hyena 3PL ASSC goat go
gé sègré dà cáaní
3PL hunt PREP bush
'One day Hyena and Goat went hunting in the bush.'

7.2 Switch-reference in complex sentences

If the third-person subject of a conjoined clause is different from the third-person subject of the antecedent clause, then the subject of the conjoined clause is preceded by an independent pronoun encoding its gender and number. An independent pronoun is used even if the subject of the conjoined clause is overtly marked. This coding of the subject is identical with the coding of the subject in contrastive focus. The clauses in which switch reference is marked by the pronoun preceding the nominal subject do not involve, however, contrastive focus, as evidenced by the fact that the subject is not followed by the comment clause marker **ba**:

(96)

ge	se	ɗe	gų́yé	ba	dày	gų́yé
HUM	INCEPT	leave	spider	COM	3M	spider

se	yàá	bè	kàyo	na	máàní	na
INCEPT	say	DAT	squirrel	HYP	like that	HYP

à	jè	na	írà	tùu-ŋ	ni
go:IMP	VENT	HYP	go:IMP	home-DEF	LOC

na-y	néè-y	kùryò
HYP-3M	make:FUT-3M	stranger

'Spider was left alone. Spider said to Squirrel: if it is like that, he should come and they will go to his [Spider's] home, and he will make him a stranger' (i.e., he will make him welcome)

(97)

kur	go	tamą́-y	se	sí	kama	go	lerwa
time	REF	wife-3M	INCEPT	put	water	REF	hot

tùwà	ni	dày	kàyo	se	ɗeŋlí	se
fire	LOC	3M	squirrel	INCEPT	hear	INCEPT

yìr	galmbo	kíin-dì
bite	bag	hole-3M

'When the wife put water on the fire, Squirrel heard it, and he chewed a hole in the bag.'

8 Anaphora for the object

8.1 Overt coding of object and human-non-human distinction

Given the fact that the subject and the object can be full nouns, sentences with nominal subjects and objects do occur in Lele natural discourse:

(98)

kùrmbàlò	tòn	póì	kúsíge	na
chief	ask	Poi	Kusige	HYP

'the chief asked P.K.:'

(99)

kùrmbàlò	se	bòr	bé-y	kur . . .
chief	INCEPT	cut	DAT-3M	place

'The chief cut him a parcel of land . . .'

(100)

ɗe	ná	nòju-ro	kínyé	se	óm
THEN	ASSC	relative-3F	COLL	INCEPT	catch

gé	tu	go	bàl
3PL	goat	REF	gelded

'then her relatives caught a large gelded goat . . . '

There is no distinction between third-person anaphors and deictic markers for human objects. The following chart represents the segmental form of these markers. The tone of the object markers is identical with the tone of the preceding verb:

(101)

-iy [after vowels]	3M
-du	3F
-ge	3PL

If a nominal antecedent is human, a reference to it in subsequent verbs within the same sentence requires a pronominal object:

(102) yé dú-ngù posí-ŋ ɗe ná ŋ
mother GEN:PL-2PL insult-1SG THEN ASSC 1SG
jè lée-dú ná kasa go ŋ yì
IMPF eat:FUT-3F ASSC corn ASSC 1SG pound
háŋ
DEM:P
'Your mother has insulted me; therefore I am going to eat her with this corn I pounded.'

(103) tòrò kàràn-dò jé gé dú máàní na
hen children-3F throw 3PL 3F ANAPH HYP
'The chicks answered her thus'[11]

The reference to the same object in subsequent discourse by different participants may be done with a full noun, especially when the preceding clause has a third-person pronoun with a different antecedent:

(104) na me léè yé dí-nì
HYP 2F eat:FUT mother GEN:PL-1PL.EXCL
ná me jè má lay
ASSC 2F IMPF die:FUT also
'If you eat our mother, you will also die'

(105) kùrmbàlò tamą́-y àn ná wáyngulú àg-iy
chief wife-3M leave ASSC morning take-3M
saar-iy dà kàrgà-rò ni
attach-3M PREP back-3F LOC
'The chief's wife left in the morning, took the fellow, [and] attached him to her back . . .'

---

[11] The use of the verb corresponding to 'throw' in the sense 'answer' exists also in French.
—Et si attends, jette Jaume, si tu attends,
'And if wait, replied Jaume, if you wait' (Giono 1929: 175)

If the third-person pronominal object has the same features for gender and number as the preceding object or subject within the same clause, then the pronominal object has the same reference as the preceding object or subject:

(106) kìrbé kè-y jògí-y
thought:PL GEN-3M bother-3M
'his$_1$ thoughts bother him$_1$'

The coding of the same human object is different from the coding of the same human subject in that the object pronoun must always be repeated, be it third-person masculine or feminine singular, or third-person plural:

(107) tumad-iy na gayrį-iy ɗé
death-3M HYP anger-3SG NEG
'his$_1$ death does not worry him$_1$'

(108) na ge dìgr-ìy na ùs-ìy ɗé
HYP HUM kill-3M HYP concern-3M NEG
'if they kill him$_1$, he$_1$ does not care'

(109) dàdù go sùbù dàdù ba bor-iy gèylè
3F REF three 3F COM save-3M health
tą go màgàyndí yír-íy
time (Fr.) REF viper bite-3M
'The third one, it was she who saved his$_1$ life when the viper bit him$_1$.'

(110) kur go gų́nyé àg-ìy jè na-y é
time REF spider take-3M VENT HYP-3M go:FUT
jé-y dà kama-ŋ ni
throw-3M PREP water-DEF LOC
'When Spider took him to throw him into the water,'

The pronominal object may, however, be omitted, as is the case with the last verb of the following example:

(111) tamá-ŋ sòndrí ná se ày tòrò
woman-DEF fear ASSC INCEPT take hen
è ìm
go bury
'The woman became scared, took the hen, and buried her.'

A possible explanation of this fact is that **tòrò** 'hen' as a dead animal in the clause is treated as an inanimate object.

(112) kàw gé gàg tùwà dùgì-gè gílalé
walk 3PL till sun drown-3PL tiredness
pínyà nè-gè
also make-3PL
'They walked till the sun had drowned them and tiredness overwhelmed them.'

If the antecedent is animate, and particularly if it is a large animal, it may be referred to by object pronouns:

(113) bìsí-ŋ gír è da kámá tálúa kíbì ni
antelope-DEF run go PREP water pond mouth LOC
ná bá mànì
ASSC fall there
'The antelope ran away, went to the edge of a pond, and collapsed there'

(114) ólkùsìŋ tab kàrgà-rò ké è hab-du kúsíoŋ
Olkusin follow back-3F till go find-3F ground
tòprí-dú ná tàbàl kè-y
kill-3F ASSC lance GEN-3M
'Olkusin followed behind her till he found her on the ground [and] killed her with his lance.'

(115) tamá dèr tíndí ná mųndu se wàdì
woman raise pestle ASSC silence INCEPT hit
ná tòrò-ŋ se dìgrì dù
ASSC hen-DEF INCEPT kill 3F
'The woman quietly raised the pestle, beat the hen$_1$ with it, and killed her$_1$.'

The non-human previous reference object is not overtly coded:

(116) bayndí go na ay tu káŋ na lèé . . .
person REF HYP take goat DEM HYP eat
'If anybody takes this goat and eats [it] . . .'

(117) na bé-y gé na-y lèé
HYP give-3M 3PL HYP-3M eat
'that they should give him [the goat] so that he would eat [it]'

(118) ŋ késè únù-m ɗé gà
1SG share:FUT ASSC-2M NEG Q
'shouldn't I share [it] with you?'

(119)

gi	láde	ná	kà-m	ɗé
2M	touch:FUT	ASSC	your hand	NEG

'you will not touch [it]'

(120)

dày	kàyo	se	ɗeŋlí	se
3M	squirrel	INCEPT	hear	INCEPT

'Squirrel heard [it] and . . .'

8.2 Nominal object versus unmarked object

The remaining question is when the non-human object is coded by a noun and when it is unmarked. Recall that the language does not have pronominal object markers. The second part of this question is the easier one to answer: If an object has been mentioned with the first verb of a sentence, it is not repeated with subsequent verbs:

(121)

ge	è	jè	ná	gùyé	tumadu	go	làmndá
HUM	go	VENT	ASSC	news	death	REF	elephant
yé-y	kò-rò	ná	gų́yé	ɗeŋlí	se		
mother-3M	GEN-3F	ASSC	spider	hear	INCEPT		
jìb	se	gìr	è	cáani			
push	INCEPT	run	go	bush			

'When the news of the death of the mother of elephant was brought in, Spider heard [it], got up, and ran away.'

In addition, within the same discourse, i.e. a discourse with various participants at the same time and place, if an object has been mentioned by one participant, it is not repeated as an object in the discourse by the same or another participant.

(122)

dày	se	ày	kolo	yàá	bé-y	na-y		
3M	INCEPT	take	word	tell	DAT-3M	HYP-3M		
áyn	tu	go	na	ge	è	jè	ná	go
take	goat	REF	HYP	INDEF	go	VENT	ASSC	REF
ímè	ná	làmndá	yé-y					
bury:FUT	ASSC	elephant	mother-3M					

'He$_1$ told him that he$_1$ took the goat that was brought to be buried together with the mother of elephant.'

(123) na-y áyn na-y lèé ge yàá ɗe
HYP-3M take HYP-3M eat INDEF say THEN
na bayndí go na lèé tu na ge
HYP person REF HYP eat goat HYP HUM
ímè-y ná làmndá yé-y ba
bury:FUT-3M ASSC elephant mother-3M COM
na-y nè gìr
HYP-3M IMPF run
'He took [the goat] and ate [it], and it was said that if a person were to eat the goat, he would be buried together with the mother of elephant, and that is why he was running.'

The repetition of a nominal object is more complicated. The object is repeated in a narrative if it belongs to a different discourse. In the following fragment, **tu** 'goat' is mentioned in the first sentence, which belongs to the discourse of the narrator, and is repeated in the second sentence, which belongs to the discourse of a character in the story.

(124) ɗe ná nòju-ro kínyé se óm
THEN ASSC relative-3F COLL INCEPT catch
gé tu go bàl nè òb ná
3PL goat REF gelded COP invite for work ASSC
kara
people
'Then, her relatives caught a large gelded goat and used it to invite people for the purpose of common work:'

(125) bayndí go na ay tu káŋ na lèé ná
person REF HYP take goat DEM HYP eat ASSC
làmndá yé-y na ma ɗe ná na
elephant mother-3M HYP die THEN ASSC HYP
ge ágè-y ímè-y ná
HUM take:FUT-3M bury:FUT-3M ASSC
làmndá yé-y
elephant mother-3M
'If anybody takes this goat and eats it, and if the mother of elephant dies, then they will bury him together with the mother of elephant'

When the object has been mentioned within the same sentence, it is unmarked, as in the second sentence above: 'if anybody takes the goat and eats [it] . . .'

Within the discourse of the participants, a reference to the same object by a different participant does not require the overt coding of the object:

(126) kur koloŋ ba dày gų́yé se yàá
time DEM:R COM 3M spider INCEPT say
bé-gè na na-y jè nè hòmyá go
DAT-3PL HYP HYP-3M IMPF make sick REF
ma nò go tég lay na bé-y gé
die COP REF long time also HYP give-3M 3PL
na-y lèé
HYP-3M eat
'At that time Spider said that since he was sick for a long time, close to dying, they should give [it] to him to eat.'

The return to the discourse of the narrator requires the mention of the object, even though the reference is to the same object. The object is not, however, repeated with the second verb of the clause:

(127) kur go gų́yé ay tu lèé ɗe ná ne
time REF spider take goat eat THEN ASSC COP
wèlè kab ɗe ná làmndá yé-y
day later then ASSC elephant mother-3M
se ma
INCEPT die
'After Spider took the goat and ate it, a few days later the mother of elephant died.'

Consider also the following fragment where in the first sentence the object, the goat, is not overtly coded, but in the second it appears as a full noun. The case of the omission of the object **tu** 'goat' involves the speech of one of the participants:

(128) kur koloŋ ba dày gų́yé se yàá
time DEM:R COM 3M spider INCEPT say
bé-gè na na-y jè nè hòmyá go
DAT-3PL HYP HYP-3M IMPF make sick REF
ma nò go tég lay na bé-y gé
die COP REF long time also HYP give-3M 3PL
na-y lèé
HYP-3M eat
'At that time Spider said that since he was sick for a long time, close to dying, they should give [it] to him to eat.'

But in the next sentence, the object is already repeated in full with the first verb. This, however, is the speech of the narrator, not one of the participants:

(129) kur go gų̂yé ay tu lèé ɗe ná ne
time REF spider take goat eat THEN ASSC COP
wèlè kab ɗe ná làmndá yé-y
day later then ASSC elephant mother-3M
se ma
INCEPT die
'After Spider took the goat and ate it, a few days later the mother of elephant died.'

9 Coding the adjunct through an anaphor

The anaphora to the non-subject and the non-object is coded by the associative preposition **ná** following the verb. In this function and in this position **ná** does not belong to the category 'preposition' as commonly understood in linguistic literature. The particle behaves like verbal extensions in many Chadic and non-Chadic languages alike.

If the adjunct is human, it is coded by the associative form of the pronoun, which codes the gender, number, and person of the human antecedent:

(130) kàyo se om-iy jè se è
squirrel INCEPT catch-3M VENT INCEPT go
ná ín-dí dà kur go tumadu-ŋ ni
ASSC ASSC-3M PREP place REL death-DEF LOC
'Squirrel caught him [and] brought him to the place of burial.'

If the antecedent is non-human, it is unmarked, and the associative preposition is not followed by a pronoun or a noun:

(131) Kara lè gé ná ùrbòlo wèrì lay,
people eat 3PL ASSC 'urbolo' xxx also
'in addition people also eat fruit of urbolo' (G-C & W 1981: 20-21)

(132 càg dí kùbàrò kúsíyòŋ è ná gàg
spread 3M blood ground go ASSC until
sùgyá go kul kàrgà-y ni
grass REF house behind-3M LOC
'he spread the blood on the ground [and] went with it up to the grass behind the house'

In the following sentence the adjunct anaphor, referring to 'place to settle in', occurs at the end of the sentence:

(133) yàá bé-y na bé-y tamá pìnà
tell DAT-3M HYP give-3M wife one
dà dùrè dì-gè ni na-y bóre
PREP among GEN:PL-3PL LOC HYP-3M cut
bé-y kur na jénè ná
DAT-3M place HYP settle:FUT ASSC
'He$_1$ told him$_2$ that if he$_2$ gives him$_1$ one wife among those [three], he$_1$ will give him$_2$ a place to settle in.'

If the antecedent is a direct object, the anaphor is an instrumental. Moreover, the noun following the preposition **ná** is not its complement:

(134) ŋ bé-y kòjò na nà ná gùyé
1SG give-3M hoe HYP do:IMP ASSC work
'I gave him a hoe to work with'

(135) tamá dèr tíndí ná mʉndu se wàdì
woman raise pestle ASSC silence INCEPT hit
ná tòrò-ŋ dìgrì
ASSC hen-DEF kill
'The woman quietly raised the pestle and beat the hen with it to death'

(136) ɗe ná nòju-ro kínyé se óm
THEN ASSC relative-3F COLL INCEPT catch
gé tu go bàl nè òb ná
3PL goat REF gelded COP invite for work ASSC
kara
people
'Then, her relatives caught a large gelded goat and used it to invite people for the purpose of common work:'

The associative marker is obligatory. The deletion of **ná** in the examples above produces ungrammatical sentences.

In the following sentence the anaphor **ná** refers to the time. The sentence is taken from a narrative describing activities proper for each month of the year:

(137) Kara ɗe-gé ná kanya ame bòy.
people let go-3PL ASSC thing domesticate:VN send
'[In this month] people release domestic animals' (G-C & W 1981: 34-35)

The evidence that the antecedent of **ná** in the preceding example is a time expression is provided by the fact that within the narrative the description of each event includes specification of the time, such as **kur go gìdìrè** 'in this month . . .', **nè gìdìrè go** 'this month'. Compare the deployment of the same verb without the associative preposition following it:

(138) ge lèé dàndáw lay
HUM eat eggplant also
'one eats eggplants' (G-C & W 1981: 20-21)

The associative marker may code an associate argument:

(139) Kumno kùlèn-dì gayri se hím kasa
God belly-3M be angry INCEPT gather corn
pet è ná dàná yom
all go ASSC up be far
'God became very angry, gathered up all the corn, and went with it far up in the sky' (G-C & W 1981: 12-13)

The verb is followed by the marker **ná** when the clause begins with a propositional anaphor in focus. The marker **ná** serves then as an anaphor whose antecedent is the propositional anaphor:

(140) Nè kolo me ba kara índùwé ma
COP reason what COM people human:PL die
gé-ǹg è gé ná kìrè kíndi-gè gà?
3Pl-DEF go 3PL ASSC road truly-3PL Q
'Why do people die and disappear forever?' (G-C & W 1981: 6-7)

(141) Nè tamá dàgè ná gìrà kolo kè-gè
COP woman 3PL ASSC dog word GEN-3PL
ba kara pet nè yagi gé ná kasa ɓey
COM people all make labor 3PL ASSC corn still
ba dì gé ná gùdá.
COM eat 3PL ASSC today
'It is because of the words of a woman and a dog that all people have to plant corn in order to eat today.' (G-C & W 1981: 10-11)

The marker **ná** does not have to refer to a specific argument of the verb. It may refer to any circumstance that has been mentioned before and that is relevant to the predicate. In the following sentence the marker **ná** following the verb codes the reason for the subject's anger:

(142)

Tamá	kùlòn-dò	gayri-du	se	yàá	ná	bè
woman	belly-3F	anger-3F	INCEPT	tell	ASSC	DAT
Kumno	na :					
God	HYP					

'The woman became angry and told God [about it]:' (G-C & W 1981: 10-11)

(143)

Keleng	káǹg	ba	kara	yagi	gé	ɓey	ba
fast	DEM	COM	people	plant	3PL	still	COM
lè	gé	ná	kanya	ɓey.			
eat	3PL	ASSC	thing	still			

'So now the men have to plant in order to eat.' (G-C & W 1981: 12-13)

(144)

Ng	ɗe	te-i,	ng	è	ná	cáaní;
1SG	keep	bottom-3M	1SG	go	ASSC	field

'I keep the rest, to go with it to the field' (G-C & W 1981: 14-15)

Thus the anaphor **ná** codes any circumstance previously mentioned in discourse. The important fact about this marker is that the noun phrase following it is not the complement of the preposition:

(145)

Gi	hím	tòngú	cob;	gi	cob	tòngú	koloǹg,
3M	gather	beans	husk	3M	husk	beans	DEM:R
gi	bòy	kàlo	pìnyí-í,	gi	è-je	pìnyí,	
2M	spread	wind	sift-3M	2M	go-VENT	sift	
gi	ày	táàwá	gi	sí	tùwà	ni,	
2M	take	potsherd	2M	put	fire	LOC	
gi	kuny	ná	tòngú.				
2M	fry	ASSC	beans				

'You gather beans and husk them, you husk them, you spread them in the wind and sift them, you take potsherds and put them in the fire, you fry the beans on it.' (G-C & W 1981: 14-15)

(146)

gi	bòy	kùbrà	màní	se	hindi	ná,
2M	pour	flour	ANAPH	INCEPT	boil	ASSC

'you pour [the remaining] flour there and you boil [the dish] with it' (G-C & W 1981: 14-15)

The associative marker may code an associative object, an object that might have been mentioned several sentences earlier in the discourse:

(147)

Gi	ày	sí	kúsìnyo,	gi	ter :	gi	ày
2M	take	put	ground	2M	extract:PL	2M	take

kàrè	ɓoró,	gi	kèsì	ná	bè	kara
sauce	Grewia	2M	distribute	ASSC	give	people

dì	gé.
eat	3PL

'You pick up [the pottery from the fire] and put it on the ground, you take [the mush] out, you take the sauce of Grewia, give it to the people with the mush, and people eat it.' (G-C & W 1981: 14-15)

10 Locative deixis

The independent locative marker for proximate deixis is **hàŋ** or **kàŋ** 'here'. The two forms appear to be dialectal variants:

(148)

Ng	éè	je	góolé	me	jumar	kàńg.
1SG	go:FUT	VENT	see:FUT	2F	everyday	here

'Everyday I will come to see you here.' (G-C & W 1981: 2-3)

(149)

jà	gùrbàlò	hàŋ
put:IMP	cloth	here

'put the clothes here'

(150)

ŋ	jè	nè	gùyé	hàŋ
1SG	IMPF	do	work	here

'I work here'

The proximate demonstrative that modifies nouns differs from the locative proximate deixis in tone: high for the demonstrative, low for the locative.

(151)

gùrmbàlò	háŋ/káŋ
shirt	DEM:P

'this shirt'

The remote distance independent locative deictic markers are **máŋjè** and **ínjè**. The evidence that they are deictic is provided by the fact that they can be used with gestures. They refer to a place that was mentioned before in discourse but that is at a considerable distance from the place of speech.

(152)

ŋ	jè	é	máŋjè/ínjè	ɗé	àlé
1SG	IMPF	go	there	NEG	anymore

'I do not go there anymore'

The locative deictics **máŋjè** and **ínjè** can be used in reference to places that are not visible, e.g. to other towns. But their meaning is not anaphoric. It is simply an expression of a very remote distance. Even if a sentence has a locative antecedent, the forms **mánjè** and **ínjè** code remote distance, not anaphora:

(153) nàtóngó ŋ jèn Bongor àlá kèléŋ háŋ ŋ
once 1SG stay Bongor but fast DEM:P 1SG
è mánjè ɗé àlé
go there NEG anymore
'I used to live in Bongor but I do not go there anymore'

Evidence that **mánjè** and **ínjè** are deictic expressions is provided by the fact that they cannot be used to refer to proximate locations, e.g. to the neighbor's compound:

(154) *nàtóngó ŋ è túgú bùgàn-ìn kè-y
once 1SG go house friend-1SG GEN-3M
àlá kèléŋ háŋ ŋ é mánjè ɗé
but fast DEM:P 1SG go:FUT there NEG
àlé
anymore
for 'I used to go to a neighbor's house, but I will not go there anymore.'

11 Locative and time anaphoras

There are two means of coding locative anaphora. One is through the definite marker **ŋ**, which may follow any verb of movement:

(155) wéy ba é-ŋ gà
who COM go-DEF Q
'who went there?' (the high tone on the verb **é** caused by the definite marker)

The marker **ŋ** also can be used with the verb 'to come', and then it has a deictic function meaning 'here':

(156) wéy ba è jé-ŋ gà
who COM go VENT-DEF Q
'who came?'

The definite marker **ŋ** cannot be used as a locative anaphor for stative locatives:

(157) nè-dí gùyé mánjè
make-3M work there
'he works there'

(158) nè-dí gùyé-ŋ
make-3M work-DEF
'he does the work', and not 'he works there'

The other means of coding locative anaphora is by the form **màní** 'there'. The natural discourse data provide evidence for this anaphor only for stative locatives. The elicited data indicate that **màní** may be used in directional locatives as well.

Evidence for the anaphoric function of **màní** is provided by clauses with a locative antecedent that may be remote or proximate:

Remote distance:

(159) túwà nóm dóbè í (índì) màní
sun appear set down with him there
'The sun seems to lie down with him there'

(160) è gé cáanì bayndí-ŋ kalo se yír-íy
go 3PL bush man-DEF snake INCEPT bite-3M
ɗe ná bayndí go segre è jè ná
THEN ASSC man REF hunter go VENT ASSC
teren-ɗì máànì
daughter-3M there
'When they went into the bush, a snake bit the man. Then came a hunter with his daughter to the place.'

(161) kùrmbàlò se bòr bé-y kur ba
chief INCEPT cut DAT-3M parcel COM
se jèn màní ná kamda-y go
INCEPT settle ANAPH ASSC wives-3M REF
sùbù
three
'The chief cut him a parcel of land and the man settled there with his three wives.'

The antecedent of the anaphor **màní** may occur in the same sentence. The anaphor may be followed by spatial specifiers, just like any other head of a locative expression:

(162) Kara màglí-gé pàl cáaní gèré dà túgú ní
people build-3PL shed bush if PREP home LOC
kolo bógè kasa màní dà túgú kùlòn-dò
reason put:FUT corn there PREP house belly-3F
ni.
LOC
'People build sheds in the bush or at home to put the corn in.' (G-C & W 1981: 26-27)

The locative anaphor **màní** is deployed if the topicalized, i.e. fronted, noun has a locative function:

(163) túgú káŋ ge jèn màní ɗé àlé
town DEM:P HUM live there NEG anymore
'this town is not inhabited anymore'

(164) túgú koloŋ ge jèn màní ɗé àlé
town DEM:R HUM live there NEG anymore
'that town is not inhabited anymore'

When **màní** is used without an antecedent in the same sentence, it refers to a location mentioned before in discourse. Thus the following sentence cannot be accompanied by a gesture:

(165) ŋ nè gùyé màní ɗé àlé
1SG do work there NEG anymore
'I do not work there anymore'

The interesting thing about the locative anaphora is that if the verb implies movement to a specific place the locative anaphor does not have to be used:

(166) ná go ŋ è Debreng ná díglé téy
ASSC DEM 1SG go Debreng ASCC year holiday
ŋ kìn (màní) ɗé àlé
1SG return there NEG anymore
'since I went to Debreng for the New Year's holiday, I have not returned there'

The anaphor **màní** is also used as a reference to time previously mentioned in discourse.

(167) Nè gìdìrè go gùyé màní nèný sí ɗé.
COP moon REF work then much very NEG
'In this month there is a lot of work.' (G-C & W 1981: 28-29)

12 The propositional anaphora

Anaphora to a previous proposition is coded by several means. If the reference is to events, it is coded by the word **kąyą** 'thing' followed by the form **máàní** 'so'. This latter marker is different from the locative anaphor, **màní**.

(168)

kùrmbàlo	nè	bé	ge	kąyą	máàní	tù
king	do	DAT	3PL	thing	so	all (Fr.)

'the king made things for them so' (i.e. as they asked)

(169)

teren-dì	nè	bé-ge	kąyą	máàní	tù
daughter-3M	do	DAT-3PL	thing	so	all (Fr.)

'his daughter made things for them so' (i.e. as they asked)

(170)

tòrò	kàràn-dò	jé	gé	dú	máàní	na
hen	children-3F	throw	3PL	3F	ANAPH	HYP

'The chicks answered her thus'

(171)

nè	máàní	ba	kàra	túgú
COP	ANAPH	COM	people	village

sèn	gé	go	na	póì	kúsíge
know	3PL	REF	HYP	Poi	Kusige

'[it] is like that, that people of the village know that Poi Kusige . . . '

If reference is made to what somebody has said, the form **kolo** 'word' followed by the definite marker **ŋ** serves as the propositional anaphor:

(172)

àlá	gìr	è	yàá	kolo-ŋ	bé	kùrmbàlo
but	run	go	tell	word-DEF	DAT	chief

'But instead she ran and informed the chief', lit. 'she told the chief the word'

13 Anaphora to the verb

The verb may be repeated in the same sentence in subsequent clauses. If the subject is other than the third-person singular masculine, the subject must also be repeated:

(173)

dìgì	gí	kòy	tèmlé-ŋ	gèsé
2M	2M	steal	corn-DEF	or

gí	kòy	ɗé	gà
2M	steal	NEG	Q

'did you steal the corn or did you not?'

(174) póì kúsíge-ŋ se mąy na-y kòy
Poi Kusige-DEF INCEPT deny HYP-3M steal
tèmlé-ŋ ɗé na-y àn kwáni ná
corn-DEF NEG HYP-3M leave outside ASSC
kúmno kam-di na ɗé
God water-3M HYP NEG
'Poi Kusige denied that he stole the corn. He claimed that he did not leave in the rain.'

14 Conclusions

The reference system of Lele comprises the following means: repetition of a noun, a verb, or of a prepositional phrase; omission of these elements; and deployment of anaphors. The coding of anaphora for different constituents of a clause depends on the means available in the given domain. For the domain of subject, the deployment of the third-person subject pronouns is used to code switch reference.

12

Modality

1 Introduction

The domain of modality in Lele consists of the subdomains of epistemic and deontic modalities. Epistemic modality comprises the following subdomains: indicative modality, dubitative modality, hypothetical modality, interrogative modality, and negative modality. The last two modalities are described in separate chapters following this one. The domain of deontic modality comprises imperative modality, subjunctive modality, permissive modality, and prohibitive modality. The last mood is really a combination of the imperative and the negative.

2 Indicative modality

Indicative modality in Lele, as in many other languages, is the unmarked form of the clause. In verbal clauses the verb ends in the vowel **-i** in the past-present form (deleted in all verbs except those that do not allow vowel deletion) and the vowel **-e** in the future and nominalized form. A clause has indicative modality if it has no modal particles, adverbs, or auxiliary verbs. Indicative modality codes what the speaker wants to convey as his/her belief(s) (cf. Frajzyngier 1985). One could argue, as Palmer 1987 does, that truth is not the unmarked value of the indicative modality, because there are means of overtly coding a speaker's belief in the truth of the proposition. Lele does have such means, e.g. the particle **waŋ** 'really, certainly'.

(1)

kírbì	hab	kùlbá	kò-rò	waŋ
Kirbi	found	cow	GEN-3F	really

'Kirbi has certainly found her cow'

Such expressions are used, however, only if somebody has previously denied the truth of the proposition or expressed doubt about the truth of the proposition (cf. Frajzyngier 1987).

Language-internal evidence for the modal function of the indicative modality is provided by the fact that any other modal function, such as doubt in truth, questions about the truth, negation of truth, and so on, must be overtly coded.

3 Dubitative modality

There are a number of auxiliary verbs to code dubitative modality, i.e. modality whereby the speaker expresses his/her doubts about the truth of the proposition.

One means involves the verb **tòb** 'want' obligatorily followed by the complementizer **go** and then by the main verb with its complements:

(2)

kus-iy	jè	tob	go	né-y
body-3M	IMPF	want	REF	make-3M

'he seems to be sick'

Cf.:

(3)

kus-iy	nè-y
body-3M	make-3M

'he is sick', lit. 'his body makes him'

Another means of hedging about the truth of one's own statement is through the use of the verb **nom** 'to court', which forms a serial verb construction with the following verb, but is limited to a very few expressions:

(4)

kus-íy	nom	né-y
body-3M	court	make-3M

'he seems to be sick'

Cf.:

(5)

cànìgé	nom	kírbí
Canige	court	Kirbi

'Canige courts Kirbi'

(6)

tùwa	nom	dóbe	í (índì)	mànì́
sun	appear	set down	with him	there

'the sun seems to lie down there'

The adverb **brùm** 'hardly' expresses uncertainty in the speaker's perception of the state of affairs:

(7)

kanya	nomí-y	brùm
something	court-3M	hardly

'there is something wrong with him, I believe'

(8)

ŋ	gol	kur	brùm
1SG	see	space	hardly

'I can hardly see'

Doubt in truth of the speaker's perception or evaluation of the state of affairs can also be coded by the modal adverb **waŋ** 'really' followed by the conditional **gèrè** 'if':

(9)

kírbì	hab	kùlbá	kò-rò	waŋ	gèrè
Kirbi	found	cow	GEN-3F	really	if

'Kirbi has apparently found her cow'

4 Hypothetical modality

Hypothetical modality is coded by the hypothetical complementizer **na** preceding the predicate.

(10)

kiya	na	bòy	kòjò	kè-y
Kiya	HYP	break	hoe	GEN-3M

'it appears that Kiya broke his hoe'

If the subject is a third-person pronoun, i.e. the type that follows the verb, the complementizer **na** precedes the verb:

(11)

na	bòy	dí	kòjò	kè-y
HYP	break	3M	hoe	GEN-3M

'it appears that he broke his hoe'

With first- and second-person pronominal subjects, the complementizer precedes the subject pronouns:

(12)

na	ŋ	bòy	kòjò	kò-nòŋ
HYP	1SG	break	hoe	GEN-1SG

'it appears that I broke my hoe'

(13) na gi bòy kòjò kò-m
HYP 2M break hoe GEN-2SG
'it appears that you broke your hoe'

Compare the following fragment from a natural discourse with its counterpart from which the complementizer was removed:

(14) dày ná na nè tìbré mayna
3M ASSC HYP COP ashes ceiba tree
'that person will be like ashes of a ceiba tree'

(15) dày ná nè tìbré mayna
3M ASSC COP ashes ceiba tree
'that person is like ashes of a ceiba tree'

Hypothetical modality can be deployed in matrix and embedded clauses. The verb following the marker of the hypothetical modality can have the future or the imperative form. The imperative form combined with the hypothetical marker codes hypothetical modality and the modality of obligation. The future form of the verb combined with the hypothetical marker codes potential events:

(16) dày kóŋ na-y kálè jénè dà
3M certain HYP-3M climb:FUT sit:FUT PREP
luŋba kùrmbàlò kè-y ni na-y bórè
horse chief GEN-3M LOC HYP-3M cut:FUT
sàríyà na ùs-ìy ɗé
verdict HYP concern:FUT-3M NEG
'The other [said] that if he could climb on the chief's horse and pronounce judgments, [they could kill him], he would not care.'

(17) Ore na wè-gé dà gìdìrè kolòng
goat:PL HYP give birth-3PL PREP moon DEM:R
ni ná ge yàá na karan-do
LOC ASSC HUM tell HYP children:3F
gàn-di-gè na wèy já.
leg-GEN.PL-3PL HYP become side
'It is said that if goats give birth in that month, their kids will have crooked legs.' (G-C & W 1981: 54-55)

All the values of the hypothetical **na** combined with the future and imperative forms of the verb are illustrated in the following fragment:

(18) Kumno se tey láràdí dàgè ná
God INCEPT call lizard 3PL ASSC
gúló yàá bè kara
chameleon tell DAT people
'God called Lizard and Chameleon and he told people'

In the next clause the subject **láràdí** 'lizard' is followed by the hypothetical marker **na**, which precedes the copula **nè**: the statement is that 'the lizard would be the spokesman'

(19) na-i ódè wanyang wáyngulú ná
HYP-3M leave:FUT tomorrow morning ASSC
láràdí na
lizard HYP
'that he would go tomorrow morning and that Lizard'

In the subsequent clause the subject **gìdìrè** 'moon' is followed by the hypothetical marker **na** followed by the verb in the imperative:

(20) nè kara go yà gé na gìdìrè na
make people REF say 3PL HYP moon HYP
ma ìrà ná kìrè kíndi kègè,
die:IMP go:IMP ASSC road truly GEN:3PL
'would be [a spokesman] for people who say that the moon should die and go away forever'

In the next two clauses the same expressions are used with respect to **gúló** 'chameleon' and kara **índùwé** 'humankind':

(21) gúló na nè kara go yà gé na
chameleon HYP make people REF say 3PL HYP
kara índùwé ba na ma gé ìrà
people human:PL COM HYP die 3PL go:IMP
gé ná kìrè kíndiè kè-gè lay.
3PL ASSC road truth GEN-3PL also
'Chameleon would be a spokesman for people who say that humans should die and go away forever.'

The scope of the hypothetical marker **na** depends on its syntactic position. If the hypothetical marker precedes the subject, the whole proposition is in its scope, as illustrated in the next sentence from the same fragment:

(22)

Kumno	yàá	na,	na	láràdí	ba	è
God	said	HYP	HYP	chameleon	COM	go

hab-i	tùmò	na	yàá	bè-ì	kolo	kè-ì
find-3M	first	HYP	tell	DAT-3M	word	GEN-3M

'God said: if it is chameleon who comes first and tells him his word' (G-C & W 1981: 6-7)

Hypothetical modality codes an event as not being real. This may apply to the truth value of the clause:

(23)

kur	wèl	kay	ɗé	ɓey	ná	tamá	na
place	pass	finish	NEG	still	ASSC	woman	HYP

du	è	sógú	ni
3F	go	toilet	LOC

'Before the day ended [while it was still dark] the wife pretended that she was going to the toilet.'

Hypothetical modality may also code the idea that the event was only intended:

(24)

kur	go	gúnyé	ágì-ì	jè	na-ì	è
time	REF	spider	take:FUT-3M	VENT	HYP-3M	go

jéèé-ì	dà	kama-ŋ	ni	dài	kàyo-ŋ
throw-3M	LOC	water-DEF	LOC	3M	squirrel-DEF

se	an	ná	galmbo	kíin-dì	bà
INCEPT	leave	ASSC	bag	hole-3M	COM

se	gìr
INCEPT	run

'When Spider was about to take him to throw him into the water, Squirrel left through the hole in the bag and ran away.'

(25)

bayndí	go	na	ay	tu	káŋ	na	lèé	ná
person	REF	HYP	take	goat	DEM	HYP	eat	ASSC

'The person who would take this goat and would eat it'

(26) kàyo se yàá na na-y sìnà
squirrel INCEPT say HYP HYP-3M know:IMP
máànı́ na-y ɗe gúnyé na ge
ANAPH HYP-3M leave spider HYP HUM
ímè-y ná làmndá yé-y ɗé ba
bury-3M ASSC elephant mother-3M NEG COM
na-y bòr gúnyé gèyl-ìy ba gúnyé na
HYP-3M save spider health-3M COM spider HYP
è jè tòb go dígrè-y gà
go VENT want REF kill:FUT-3M Q
'Squirrel said that if he had known that, he would have left Spider to be buried together with the mother of elephant. Here I saved him, and doesn't he want to kill me?'

(27) póì kúsíge-ŋ se mąy na-y kòy
Poi Kusige-DEF INCEPT deny HYP-3M steal
tèmlé-ŋ ɗé na-y àn kwáni ná
corn-DEF NEG HYP-3M leave outside ASSC
kúmno kam-di na ɗé
God water-3M HYP NEG
'Poi Kusige denied that he stole the corn. He claimed that he did not leave in the rain.'

The evidence that **na** has a hypothetical modality function rather than that of a complementizer is provided by the fact that it can be accompanied by a phrase meaning 'without saying anything':

(28) tamá yàá isaŋ ɗé ba se na du
woman say nothing NEG COM INCEPT HYP 3F
è sógú ni
go toilet LOC
'the wife, without saying anything, made as if she went to the toilet'

After volitional verbs, the deployment of the complementizer **na** (and an obligatorily ensuing subject marker) is a means to code a hypothetical event:

(29) wèlè pìnà ná gèy na-y gísè-dù
day one ASSC want (Ng.) HYP-3M try:FUT-3F
'One day he wished to test her.'

If one omits the complementizer, then the meaning changes to the non-hypothetical:

(30) wèlè pìnà ná gèy gísè-dù
day one ASSC want (Ng.) try:FUT-3F
'One day he wanted to test her.'

Natural texts clearly show that speakers try to avoid categorical statements when an explanation of various phenomena is involved. Instead of producing a straight-forward indicative sentence, the speaker presents a statement as the indirect speech of unspecified human subjects, coded by **ge** 'one' or **kara** 'people'. The matrix clause in such instances has the form **ge yàá** or **kara yàá** 'one says/people say:'. All explanations of the behavior of people, animals, and atmospheric phenomena in the texts gathered by Garrigues-Cresswell have this form.

There exists also a grammatical coding of the speaker's doubt in somebody's claims. This is coded by clause-final particles **sáŋ**, glossed as DUB for 'dubitative', and **gèrè**, which can occur alone or together, in that order. These particles occur with verba dicendi complements (q.v.), but they can also occur with non—verba dicendi. In such cases these markers deny the truth of somebody's claims:

(31) nè dí hómyà sáŋ
make 3M sick DUB
'he claims to be sick'

Cf.:
(32) na-y hómyà sáŋ
HYP-3M sick DUB
'he said that he is sick, but I doubt it'

The evidence for the function of the marker **sáŋ** as a marker of doubt in truth about somebody's claims is provided by the fact that this marker cannot be used with the speaker as subject, i.e., one cannot express doubt in the truth of one's own statement (but one can doubt one's own perception, as illustrated in examples earlier in this chapter) (cf. also Frajzyngier 1985):

(33) *ŋ nè hómyà sáŋ
1SG COP sick DUB
for 'I am sick'

(34) *ŋ yá na ŋ nè hómyà sáŋ
1SG say HYP 1SG make sick DUB
for 'I said that I am sick [but it isn't true]'

Doubt-in-truth markers cannot be used in some equational sentences:

(35) cànìgé nè lele
Canige COP Lele
'Canige is Lele'

But note:

(36) *cànìgé nè lele sáŋ
Canige COP Lele DUB
for 'Canige is Lele, but I doubt it'

If, however, the preceding proposition is presented as a complement of a verb of saying then the doubt-in-truth marker is acceptable:

(37) cànìgé ná-y no go lele sáŋ
Canige HYP-3M COP REF Lele DUB
'Canige said that he is a Lele man, but I have my doubts'

The hypothetical modality is deployed in many types of clauses, including clauses that correspond logically to the conditional protasis and apodosis clauses:

5 Imperative and subjunctive modalities

The imperative and subjunctive modalities are coded by different syntactic constructions, but they deploy the same imperative form of the verb.

5.1 Giving orders

The imperative form of the verb is readily employed among peers but also among people belonging to different age and social groups. Thus one can use the imperative with respect to parents, to a chief, and others, provided that the inherent meaning of the verb will not produce an impolite effect when combined with the imperative. The following imperative construction is considered polite:

(38) da ngù kasa ná já koloŋ
eat:IMP 2PL corn ASSC side DEM:R
'eat the corn at the other side'

The imperative of the verb **ìrà** 'go' in combination with the deictic **mánjè** 'there' is very impolite:

(39) ìrà ngú mánjè
go:IMP 2PL there
'get out of here!'

In the second-person singular, one can deploy a subject pronoun, but it must be the independent form:

(40)

Dàmè	ɗinglá
2F	listen:IMP

'Listen!' (G-C & W 1981: 2-3)

The second-person singular, whether masculine or feminine, does not have to be used. Thus the preceding example is followed by clauses in imperative modality without the subject:

(41)

A-je	ná	bè-ng	gúndù	pìnà	ná
go:IMP-VENT	ASSC	DAT-1SG	gourd	one	ASSC

kama,	ná	gìlàdí	mìsé,	à-je
water	ASSC	stalk	sorghum	go:IMP-VENT

haba-ng	ná	dà	sóòyó	to-roò	ni.
find-1SG	ASSC	PREP	tamarind	bottom-3F	LOC

'Bring me a gourd with water and stalks of sorghum. Come to find me under the tamarind tree.' (G-C & W 1981: 2-3)

The syntax of giving orders differs from the syntax of the indicative modality in that the subject pronoun for the second-person plural follows rather than precedes the verb. If there are any complements, they follow the second-person singular:

(42)

pàmà	ngú
search:IMP	2PL

'search!'

(43)

kùlù	ngú	kùlbá
buy:IMP	2PL	cow

'buy a cow!'

kùl	kùlbá
buy:IMP	cow

'buy (SG) a cow'

5.2 The subjunctive

The term *subjunctive* refers to wishes with respect to the first and third person, and also non-imperative wishes with respect to the second person. Wishes with respect to the first and third person are coded through the imperative form of the verb preceded by a first- or third-person subject:

(44) yàá bèì na gìdìrè na ma ná,
tell DAT-3M HYP moon HYP die:IMP ASSC
ìrà ná kìrè kíndi kara índùwé ma
go:IMP ASSC road truly people human:PL die:IMP
gé ná ana gé jè.
3PL ASSC leave:IMP 3PL VENT
'[he] told him that the moon would die and never return, and the people would die and return' (G-C &W 1981: 8-9)

Wishes with respect to the first-person dual inclusive are coded through the pronoun **ngà** following the verb:

(45) kà[w] ngà túg kò-m ni gólè
go:IMP 1DU.INCL home GEN-2SG LOC see:FUT
kùní kùlè-ndì
home interior-3M
'let's go to your home [and] we will see the interior of the house'

The subjunctive construction for the third person is Pronoun Verb:IMP. Recall that in the indicative modality the third-person pronoun follows the verb:

(46) dí ìrà
3M go:IMP
'let him go'

(47) dú ìrà kàsúgù
3F go:IMP market
'let her go to the market'

(48) dí yàgà bé-ŋ kúsó
3M plow:IMP DAT-1SG field
'let him plow my field for me!'

If the clause has a nominal subject, such a subject is followed by a third-person pronoun agreeing with the nominal subject in gender and number:

(49) kiya dí à jè
Kiya 3M go:IMP VENT
'let Kiya come'

(50) kiya dí ìrà
Kiya 3M go:IMP
'let Kiya go'

(51)	kiya	dí	yàgà	bé-ŋ	kúsó
	Kiya	3M	plow:IMP	DAT-1SG	field

'let Kiya plow my field for me!' (can be said by the father of a bride or by a chief)

Thus the word order in the subjunctive for the third-person is different from the word order in the indicative. It is also different from the word order of the imperative for the second-person plural, where the pronoun follows rather than precedes the verb.

The subjunctive for the first-person plural (and only the first-person inclusive is allowed) is formed by the imperative form of the verb followed by the first-person plural pronoun and complements, if any:

(52)	yà-ngá	kolo	goɗàŋ
	talk:IMP-1DU.INCL	word	another'

'let us talk about something else'

(53) ìrà-ngá
go:IMP-1DU.INCL
'let us go!'

The first-person dual inclusive pronoun followed by the second-person plural pronoun may also be used:

Verb:IMP	ngá	ngú
	1DU.INCL	2PL

(54)	dà	ngá	ngú	wó
	eat:IMP	1DU.INCL	2PL	mush

'let's eat mush!'

(55)	lá	ngá	ngú	sìí
	eat:IMP	1DU.INCL	2PL	meat

'let us eat meat!'

(56)	ìrà	ngá	ngú
	go:IMP	1DU.INCL	2PL

'let us go!'

The first-person and the second-person plural subjunctive are coded by the imperative form of the verb and the reverse word order of the one used in the indicative form. In the indicative form the first- and second-person plural pronouns precede the verb.

6 Permission

Permission is coded by the form **ɗa**, which is the imperative form of the verb **ɗe** 'let, leave', preceding the nominal or pronominal subjects of the main verb. The main verb is in the imperative form.

If there is a nominal subject in the clause, the third-person pronouns may precede or follow the main verb (but not both at the same time). A third-person pronoun should occur in the clause preceding the verb:

(57) ɗa kiya dí à jè
let:IMP Kiya 3M go:IMP VENT
'let Kiya come' (he is trying to see me, so let him come)

Without the third-person pronoun, the clause could mean either: 'leave Kiya and come' or 'let Kiya come'.

(58) ɗa kiya dí ìrà
let:IMP Kiya 3M go:IMP
'let Kiya go'

In natural discourse, because of politeness requirements, the form coding permission may be used to express the speaker's wish with respect to the third person:

(59) (ɗa) (dí) à jè
let 3M go VENT
'let him come'

A wish with respect to the first-person singular requires the auxiliary **ɗá** followed by the first-person subject and the main verb in the imperative form:

(60) ɗa ŋ dá wò
let:IMP 1SG eat:IMP mush
'let me eat'

The imperative form **ɗa** can be followed by a verb in the future tense:

(61) ɗá-ŋ ŋ dé wò
let:IMP-1SG 1SG eat:FUT mush
'let me go, I will eat' (do not bother me, I am going to eat)

The coding of the first-person plural inclusive provides the necessary evidence that the form **ɗa** has not grammaticalized as a subjunctive marker. It cannot be used with the first-person plural inclusive marker **ngá ngú**. The reason it cannot be so used is that the verb **ɗa** still means 'release, let go' and one cannot use this verb with respect to oneself.

(62)

*ɗa	ngá	ŋgú	ìrà
let	1DU.INCL	2PL	go:IMP

for 'let us go'

Unlike the situation for the first-person plural inclusive, the verb **ɗa** 'release' may be used for the first-person singular, but again only in the sense of 'release, allow':

(63)

ɗa	ŋ	ìrà
let	1SG	go:IMP

'let me go', and not 'I have to go'

Given the meaning of the form **ɗe** and its imperative variant **ɗa**, one should not expect to find it used with the verb 'come', because one is already in place. And, indeed, the use of **ɗa** with the verb **è-jè** or its imperative form **à-jè** is disallowed:

(64)

*ɗa	ŋ	à	jè
let	1SG	go:IMP	VENT

for 'I have to come'

7 Prohibitive modality

Prohibitive modality is formed through the placement of the negative particle **ɗé** at the end of a clause containing the imperative form of the verb:

(65)

Tamá,	ul	ɗé.
woman,	cry:IMP	NEG

'Woman, do not cry!' (G-C & W 1981: 2-3)

(66)

ladá	bìsí	kò-nòŋ	ná	kà-m	ɗé
touch:IMP	antelope	GEN-1SG	ASSC	hand-2M	NEG

'Do not touch my antelope with your hands.'

(67)

ìrà	ɗé
go:IMP	NEG

'don't go'

(68)

à	jé-ngú	ɗé
go:IMP	VENT:IMP-2PL	NEG

'don't come'

The prohibitive predicate may have two verbs in a sequence, both of them in the imperative modality:

(69)

ɗá	wala	kusu-m	bàb	ɗé
leave:IMP	swear:IMP	body-2M	all	NEG

'do not swear for nothing'

8 The coding of sufficient condition

The sufficient condition for an event is coded by the verb **ɓàl** 'suffice' in the past tense form followed by the future tense form of the main verb. The function of this auxiliary is to state that given some premise or goal, it is enough to do X to achieve it.

(70)

Me	ɓàl	éè	je	ná	kanya	go	ng
2F	suffice	go:FUT	VENT	ASSC	thing	REF	1SG

jè	yàá	bè-mè	kang.
IMPF	tell	DAT-2F	DEM

'You just come with the things that I tell you to bring.' (G-C & W 1981: 2-3)

9 Conclusions

The modality system of Lele includes indicative, dubitative, and hypothetical in the domain of epistemic modality, and imperative, subjunctive, and a modality expressing permission in the domain of deontic modality.

The imperative and subjunctive modalities are characterized by one morphological and one syntactic characteristic. The morphological characteristic is the use of the imperative form of the stem. The syntactic characteristic is the order of verbs and subject pronouns in the subjunctive modality, which is the reverse of the one in the indicative modality.

13

Interrogative Clauses

1 Introduction

There are two types of interrogative clauses in Lele: questions about the truth of the whole proposition and specific questions, where the truth of the whole proposition is assumed and the speaker asks about individual elements of the proposition, be they arguments, adjuncts, or even predicates. Unlike in many Chadic languages, both types of interrogative clauses can have the same clause-final interrogative particle **gà**. In addition all interrogative clauses have the tone on the penultimate syllable in the clause raised, a phenomenon also found in other Chadic languages (cf. Leben 1989).

2 Questions about the truth of the proposition

Questions about the truth of the proposition (yes/no questions) have only the clause-final interrogative marker **gà**. The clause-final marker cannot be omitted. The raising of the penultimate tone in interrogative clauses is illustrated in the following sentences, where the noun **kàrè** has last tone mid when it occupies the interrogative clause—penultimate position:

(1) dì dí kàre gà
eat 3M sauce Q
'did he eat the sauce?'

Cf.:

(2) dì dí kàrè
eat 3M sauce
'he ate the sauce'

If the tone of the penultimate syllable is inherently high, it stays high in the interrogative clause. But interestingly, the tone preceding the penultimate high tone is raised. Compare the following sentences. In the interrogative, the ventive marker preceding the subject **dí** has mid tone:

(3) kiya è je dí gà
Kiya go VENT 3M Q
'did Kiya come?'

In the affirmative clause, the ventive marker **jè** has low tone, as it does in the position where it precedes the third-person subject **dí**:

(4) kiya è jè dí
Kiya go VENT 3M
'Kiya came'

If the ventive marker is the penultimate syllable in the interrogative clause, its tone is raised to mid (recall that if a nominal subject occurs in a clause, a pronominal subject does not, unless certain conditions are met):

(5) kiya è je gà
Kiya go VENT Q
'did Kiya come?'

Cf.:

(6) kiya è jè
Kiya go VENT
'Kiya came'

The rule about penultimate-tone raising applies to all morphemes that happen to occur in that position:

(7) kiya hàb kùlbá ke-y gà
Kiya find cow GEN-3M Q
'did Kiya find his cow?'

Cf.:

(8) kiya hàb kùlbá kè-y
Kiya find cow GEN-3M
'Kiya found his cow'

(9) kírbì hàb kùlbá kò-ro gà
Kirbi find cow GEN-3F Q
'did Kirbi find his cow?'

Cf.:

(10)	kírbì	hàb	kùlbá	kò-rò
	Kiya	find	cow	GEN-3F

'Kirbi found his cow'

The mid tones are not raised:

(11)	nè	kama	gà
	COP	water	Q

'is it water?'

(12)	nè	kama
	COP	water

'it is water?'

(13)	nè	tormo	gà
	COP	girl	Q

'is it a girl?'

(14)	òò,	nè	tormo
	yes	COP	girl

'yes, it is a girl'

There are low tones before the particle in texts published in G-C & W 1981, but it is not clear whether the tones represent the underlying tones of words or the actual pronunciation in the specific examples:

(15)	Dàdù	ɓòdu	tòn-dù	na	kur	wèlè
	3F	monkey	ask-3F	HYP	time	be heavy:VN
	kè-rè	kay	àlè	gà.		
	GEN-2F	finish	already	Q		

'The monkey asked her: has the time of your heaviness finished already?' (G-C & W 1981: 4-5)

Rhetorical questions do not differ formally from non-rhetorical questions:

(16)	gí	àn	kwáni	ná	kúmno	kam-di	háŋ
	2M	leave	outside	ASSC	God	water-3M	DEM
	ɗé	lay	tèmle	màyfò-y	dà		
	NEG	also	corn	hair-3M	PREP		
	mbùlúm	ni	háŋ	gà			
	chin	LOC	DEM:P	Q			

'If you did not leave in this rain, is there not the hair of corn on your chin?'

Questions about locative predicates are formed with the indicative locative clause with the marker **gà**:

(17)	kus-iy	túg	ní	gà
	body-3M	compound	LOC	Q
	'is he at home?'			
(18)	kusu-ro	túg	ní	gà
	body-3M	compound	LOC	Q
	'is she at home?'			

(19)	cànígè	túg	ní	gà
	Canige	compound	LOC	Q
	'is Canige at home?'			

Questions about possessive equational clauses have different forms for different persons. For the third person the structure is Associative marker Subject Associative marker Object Interrogative marker:

(20)	ná	dí/dú/gé	ná	làli	gà
	ASSC	3M/3F/3PL	ASSC	money	Q
	'does he have money?'				

For the first and second person, the structure is Subject Associative marker Object **gà**:

(21)	gi/mé/ngú	ná	làli	gà
	2M/2F/2PL	ASSC	money	Q
	'do you (M/F/PL) have money?'			

(22)	ŋ́/ŋgá	ná	làli	gà
	1SG/1DU.INCL	ASSC	money	Q
	'do I/we have money?'			

The interrogative marker is added after the negative marker:

(23)	dìgì	gí	kòy	tèmlé-ŋ	gèsé	gí	kòy
	2M	2M	steal	corn-DEF	or	2M	steal
	ɗé	gà					
	NEG	Q					
	'Was it you who stole the corn or wasn't it?'						

(24)	ŋ	kése	únù-m	ɗé	gà
	1SG	share:FUT	ASSC-2M	NEG	Q
	'shouldn't I share it with you?'				

2.1 Doubt in questions about the truth of the proposition

Doubt in questions about the truth of the proposition is coded with the particle **waŋ** 'really, certainly' preceding the clause-final interrogative **gà**. Questions about both equational and verbal clauses may have the particle **waŋ**:

(25)

nè	kírbì	waŋ	gà
COP	Kirbi	really	Q

'is it really Kirbi?'

In verbal clauses, the scope of the doubt is not formally defined. Thus in the following sentence the doubt could be about the subject, the verb, the object, or even about the possessor:

(26)

kírbì	hàb	kùlbá	kò-ro	waŋ	gà
Kirbi	find	cow	GEN-3F	really	Q

'did Kirbi really find his cow?'

(27)

Kara	gòmnye	nè	jègé	gìsè	kolo
people	old:PL	make	put:VN	divining rod	reason

mònò	go	na	ge	néè	dà	cáaní
eleusine	REF	HYP	HUM	make:FUT	PREP	field

na	íré	bé-gè	dà	kuso
HYP	stand:VN	DAT-3PL	PREP	field

kùlèn-dì	ni	néènyé	wang	gà?
belly-3M	LOC	be much:FUT	nevertheless	Q

'The old men practice divination concerning the eleusine that one will plant in the field, whether it will grow for them (G-C &W 1981: 38-39)

3 Specific interrogative clauses

3.1 General properties of specific interrogatives

All specific interrogative clauses in Lele can have the clause-final interrogative marker. In addition, the tone of the penultimate syllable in specific interrogatives is raised, as in questions about the truth of the proposition.

The following semantic classes of nouns have been encoded in interrogative words (wh-words): human, non-human, locative, time.

Specific interrogatives in Lele distinguish between questions in the domain de dicto and questions in the domain de re. Questions in the domain de dicto are the ones that inquire about an unknown participant. Questions in the domain de re inquire about participants that belong to a class known to the speaker. In English the domain de dicto is coded by the forms 'who', 'what', and the domain de re by the forms 'who of . . .' and 'which one'.

The specific interrogative equational clause has the form: **nè** Question Word **gà**. The specific interrogatives in equational clauses make a distinction between masculine, feminine, and plural subjects: **wéy** 'who, masculine singular'; **tóŋgo** 'who, feminine singular'; and **kángé** 'who, plural'. These forms are anaphoric only. They can be deployed in questions about people mentioned in discourse, but not in questions about people present in the speech environment.

(28) nè wéy gà 'who is he?'
nè tóngó gà 'who is she?'
nè kángé gà 'who are they?'

3.2 Questions about the subject

When the question is about the subject, the particle **ba**, the same particle that marks comment-on-focus constructions, follows the question word about a human participant. Questions about the subject without the marker **ba** are ungrammatical. The tone of the penultimate syllable is raised, as in all interrogative clauses:

(29) wéy ba é gà
who COM go Q
'who went away?'

(30) wéy ba è jé gà
who COM go VENT Q
'who came?'

If the question is about a singular subject, the verb cannot have the third-person singular subject marker **dí** or **dú**, as the case may be. The explanation for this fact is to be found in the role of pronominal subject markers. These markers are used only if the subject is known. If the question is about the subject, then the subject is obviously unknown, and therefore it cannot be coded through pronominal markers. If the question is about a plural subject, the third-person plural subject marker **gé** cannot be omitted, again in accordance with the rules about the third-person plural coding. The verb does not have subject suffixes, but rather the interrogative pronoun occurs before the verb:

(31) wéy ba nè *dí bé-y kąnya lèé gà
who COM cook 3M DAT-3M thing eat Q
'who cooked for him?'

The interrogative pronoun for a human participant does not have to be overtly coded if the interrogative clause is the second in a sequence of interrogative clauses, even if the specific question in the preceding clause was about a different grammatical relation. In the following sentence the question in the first interrogative clause is about the possessor, while the question in the second interrogative clause is about the subject. The second interrogative clause does not have an interrogative pronoun:

(32) gàrmà háŋ nè kò-m ɗé ba
footsteps DEM COP GEN-2M NEG COM
ne wèy kè-y ba è jè
COP who GEN-3M COM go VENT
póì tèmle kò-nòŋ háŋ gà
break:PL corn GEN-1SG DEM:P Q
'If those footsteps aren't yours, whose are they then, who came to break off my corn like that?'

In the domain de re, questions about human participants have **wéy** followed by the sequence **kóŋ** 'indefinite masculine' and **go** 'relative masculine and plural marker':

(33) wéy kón go ba ày gálmbò
who INDEF.M REF COM take bag
kò-noŋ gà
GEN-1SG Q
'who [among you] took my bag?'

The plural and feminine interrogative markers differ from the masculine interrogative marker in that they operate only in the domain de re. The deployment of the form **kángé** 'which ones' implies that some participants belong to a group known to the speaker:

(34) kángé ba nè-(gé) bé-y kąya-lèé gà
who:PL COM cook-3PL DAT-3M thing-eat Q
'which ones [among you, or among them] cooked food for him?'

Similarly the interrogative **tóŋ go**, which is the feminine equivalent of the masculine de re marker **kón go**, can be used only with respect to a specific group of women.

(35) tóŋgo ba nè bé-y kąya-lèé gà
who-F COM cook DAT-3M food Q
'who (F) [among you women, or among those women there] cooked for him?'

Questions about non-human participants do not distinguish between the domains de dicto and de re.

(36) me ba dígrì tòrò kò-noŋ gà
what COM kill hen GEN-1SG Q
'what killed my hen?'

The definite marker is deployed to code either the previous mention of the object in discourse or the distance between the speaker and the object:

(37) me ba lèé-gé kòrá kà-ngá-ŋ gà
what COM eat-3PL chickens GEN-1DU.INCL-DEF Q
'what ate our chickens [about which we have talked, or traces of which are visible]?'

(38) me ba lèé-gé kòrá kà-ngá gà
what COM eat-3PL chickens GEN-1DU.INCL Q
'what ate our chickens?'

Questions about the subject of an equational clause may have the copula or may occur without it. The comment clause marker is not deployed if the question is in the domain de dicto, i.e., if the set to which the referent belongs is unknown:

(39) kónù-m nè méè gà
name-2M COP what Q
'what is your name?'

If the question is in the domain de re, i.e., if the set to which the referent belongs is known, the copula is not deployed, and the comment clause marker **ba** is deployed:

(40) kósuŋ go kóngò ba káŋ gà
term REF what COM DEM Q
'what type of term is this?'

3.3 Questions about the object

Questions about the object differ syntactically from questions about the subject in that the contrastive focus construction is just one of the options in the coding of the interrogative. The non-focus option has the object role of the interrogative word coded by its position following the verb. The general interrogative marker **gà** occurs in clause-final position. So the two interrogative markers may occur in the sequence:

(41) mè ą̀y wéy gà
2F marry who Q
'who did you marry?'

(42) mè ə̀yé wéy gà
2F marry:FUT who Q
'who will you marry?'

The distinction between the domain de dicto and the domain de re is coded in questions about human objects. The de re forms are **tóngo** 'who (F)', **kóngo** 'who (M)', and **kánge** 'who (PL)'. These forms are composites of indefinite masculine and feminine forms **kóŋ** and **tóŋ** followed by the referential marker **go**. As in other interrogative clauses, the penultimate syllable in the interrogative clause has a raised tone. Thus the interrogative word **tóŋgo** is realized as [tóŋgó] when occurring in the penultimate position in the clause:

(43) gi ə̀y tóŋgo gà
2M marry who:F Q
'which woman did you marry?'

(44) gi ə̀yé tóŋgó gà
2M marry:FUT who:F Q
'which woman will you marry?'

(45) gi gol wéy gà
2M see who Q
'who did you see?'

(46) gi gol kángé gà
2M see who:PL Q
'which people did you see?'

In questions about non-human objects, **me** behaves like a noun rather than a pronoun. It is not suffixed to the verb but rather occurs after the subject suffix:

(47) lèé dí me gà
eat he what Q
'what did he eat?'

If the interrogative word occurs in clause-initial position because it is in focus, the rest of the clause is the comment, and must be preceded by the comment clause marker **ba**. The object may also be focused in the interrogative clause. The focusing of the interrogative object is coded like other focus constructions, viz. the object is in clause-initial position, and it is followed by the marker **ba** coding the comment clause. The interrogative marker **gà** occurs in clause-final position.

(48)

me	ba	gol	dí	gà
what	COM	see	3M	Q

'what did he see?'

(49)

ná	me	ba	dì	di	ná	wo	háŋ	gà
ASSC	what	COM	eat	3M	ASSC	mush	DEM	Q

'with what did he eat the mush?' (the question could be either about the tool or about the sauce)

(50)

è	jè	di	ná	me	gà
go	VENT	3M	ASSC	what	Q

'what did he bring?'

(51)

jèé	dí	ná	me	gà
throw	3M	ASSC	what	Q

'with what did he launch it?'

(52)

kiya	jèé	ná	me	gà
Kiya	throw	ASSC	what	Q

'with what did Kiya throw it?'

Question words about human and non-human objects can be preceded by the copula **nè**, whether in clause-initial or postverbal position. The copula marks the focus:

(53)

me	ba	gol-dí	ɗé	gà
what	COM	see-3M	NEG	Q

'what didn't he see?' (he has already seen everything)

(54)

nè	me	ba	gi	gol	ɗé	gà
COP	what	COM	2M	see	NEG	Q

'which thing didn't you see?' (when the addressee has seen most things)

If the focused element occupies the post-verbal position, the comment clause precedes the focused element; hence there is no need to deploy the comment clause marker:

(55)

jè	gol-dí	nè	me	gà
IMPF	see-3M	COP	what	Q

'what does he see?'

(56)

gol-dí	nè	me	gà
see-3M	COP	what	Q

'what did he see?'

(57) gol-dí nè wéy gà
see-3M COP what Q
'what did he see?'

The verb of the comment clause may have the definite marker **ŋ**. The function of this marker is to indicate that the questioned object is known to the speaker or proximate to the speaker. Consider the following situation. A son informs his father:

(58) ḿ bóy dèglè
1SG break pot
'I broke a pot'

(59) dèglè kóŋgo ba gi bóy gà
pot which COM 2SG break Q
'which pot did you break?' (when the father is at a distance from the pots)

(60) dèglè kóŋgo ba gi bóyí-ŋ gà
pot which COM 2SG break-DEF Q
'which pots did you break?' (when the father is close to the pots)

(61) tóngo ba gi ą́y-ŋ gà
who:F COM 2M take-DEF Q
'which woman did you marry?'

The coding of the definiteness or distance between the speaker and the questioned object is not available if the questioned object has not been fronted:

(62) gi bóy dèglè kóŋ go gà
2SG break pot certain REF Q
'which pot did you break?'

The function of the focus with questions about the object is to further narrow the set from which potential referents can be selected. The interrogative word **wéy** must be followed by **kóŋgo**, i.e. the marker that codes de re domain in interrogative clauses for masculine referents:

(63) wéy kóŋgo ba mé ą́y-ŋ gà
who:M which:M COM 2F take-DEF Q
'which man did you marry?'

3.4 Questions about the dative and other prepositional arguments

Dative interrogatives and other arguments marked by prepositions have the same prepositions preceding the interrogative markers in the same syntactic position that they occupy in the affirmative clause:

(64) nè dú kàrè bé-wéy gà
cook 3F sauce DAT-who Q
'for whom did she cook the sauce?'

Cf.:
(65) nè dú kàrè bé-ŋ
cook 3F sauce DAT-1SG
'she cooked the sauce for me'

As in several other specific questions, the fronting of the interrogative complex is a means of coding the de re domain of the dative argument. Fronting of the interrogative complex requires the deployment of the comment clause marker **ba**:

(66) nè dú kàrè bé-kángé gà
cook 3F sauce DAT-who Q
'for which people did she cook the sauce?'

(67) gi nè gùyé bé wéy gà
2M make work DAT who Q
'for whom do you work?'

If the definite marker is deployed with the dative interrogative in focus, it is not part of the comment clause, but rather a definite marker for the noun it follows:

(68) bé wéy ba gi nè gùyé-ŋ gà
DAT who COM 2M make work-DEF Q
'for which person do you do the work?'

(69) bé wéy ba gi nè gùyé gà
DAT who COM 2M make work Q
'for which person do you work?'

3.5 Questions about the associative argument

The associative argument is the one that in affirmative clause is marked by the proposition **ná**. Questions about such arguments have the preposition **ná** followed by the interrogative word. Depending on whether the domain de dicto or de re is coded, the interrogative complex follows the verb (domain de dicto) or precedes the verb in a focus construction (domain de re).

(70)

gi	è	ná	wéy	gà
2M	go	ASSC	who	Q

'with whom did you go?'

In contrastive focus construction, however, there is no comment clause-final definite marker **ŋ** as part of the comment clause:

(71)

ná	wéy	ba	gi	e	gà
ASSC	who	COM	2M	go	Q

'with which person did you go?'

The definite marker can be inserted in the above clause, but it will have an anaphoric function, referring to a location mentioned previously in the clause:

(72)

ná	wéy	ba	gi	e-ŋ	gà
ASSC	who	COM	2M	go-DEF	Q

'with which person did you go there?'

3.6 Questions about the locative

Questions about locative adjuncts are marked by the interrogative word **mína** occurring in the position of the locative argument in the indicative clause:

(73)

Me	è	mína	gà?
2F	go	where	Q

'Where are you going? (G-C & W 1981: 4-5)

The imperfective aspect in questions about the locative, as in other specific questions, is marked by the auxiliary **jè**:

(74)

gi	jè	gìrè	mína	máàní	gà
2M	IMPF	run:VN	where	like that	Q

'where are you running like that?'

(75)

cànigé	jè	lé	kànya	mína	gà
Canige	IMPF	eat	thing	where	Q

'where does Canige eat?'

The form **mína** may be preceded by the locative particle **dà**. Notice, however, that unlike in the indicative clauses, there is no clause-final locative marker **ní**. There is no distinction between directional and stative interrogatives about place. The general interrogative **gà** occurs in the clause-final position.

(76)

Kur	go	te	kasínya	mína	gà?
place	REF	defecate	excrements	where	Q
Kur	go	ɓìsè	cóòró	mína	gà?
place	REF	pass liquid	urine	where	Q

'Where is the place to defecate? Where is the place to urinate?' (G-C & W 1981: 10-11)

Whether the locative adjunct is the goal or the source is coded by the lexical verbs. Verb **è** 'go' alone indicates that the question is about the goal:

(77)

è	dí	(dà)	mína	gà
go	3M	PREP	where	Q

'where did he go?'

Questions about the source from which somebody comes provide us with synchronic evidence that the ventive marker **jè** derives from the lexical verb **jè** 'come'. Questions about the source consist of the serial verb construction with the first verb **se** 'get up' followed by the subject and then by the verb **jè** 'come':

(78)

se	dí	jè	(dà)	mína	gà
get up	3M	VENT	PREP	where	Q

'where did he come from?'

The form **mína** is also used to code the non-directional locative:

(79)

jèn	dí	(dà)	mína	gà
remain	3M	PREP	where	Q

'where does he stay?'

(80)

gi	gol-iy	(dà)	mína	gà
2M	see-3M	PREP	where	Q

'where did you see him?'

3.7 Questions about manner

There are two means of asking questions about manner. One is through the interrogative complex in adverbial, i.e. postverbal position, and the other is through the fronting of the interrogative complex. In both types of structures the sentence ends in the interrogative marker **gà**.

If a question about manner is in clause-initial position, it must be followed by the marker **ba**:

(81)

Nè	náa	ba	ɓòdu	gìl	kamda	kìrè	go
COP	make	COM	monkey	show	women	way	REF
wè	gà.						
give birth	Q						

'How has the monkey shown the women how to give birth?' (G-C & W 1981: 2-3)

If the interrogative complex occupies the postverbal position, it consists of the verb **nè** 'make' followed by the referential marker **go** and the associative marker **ná**, in that order. The verb **nè** becomes **nò** in front of the referential marker. The function of the verb **nè** following the main verb and its object, if any, is that of a verbal anaphor in a resumptive clause:

(82)

ge	jè	wę̀y	wo	no	go	ná	gà
HUM	IMPF	prepare	mush	COP	REF	ASSC	Q

'how do they prepare mush?', lit. 'one prepares mush does it with what?'

(83)

ge	jè	nè	ségrè	no	go	ná	gà
HUM	IMPF	do	hunt	COP	REF	ASSC	Q

'how do you hunt?', lit. 'one hunts does it how?'

(84)

gi	kujingili	kùb	go	fùlfùldé	no	go
2M	learn	language	REF	Fulfulde	COP	REF
ná	gà					
ASSC	Q					

'how did you learn Fulfulde?'

3.8 Questions about the reason

There are two means of coding questions about reasons. One means involves the use of the word **kolo** 'reason' followed by the non-human question word **me**. The clause must end with the specific interrogative marker **gà**. The specific interrogative about reason may be in focus, as evidenced by the fact that it is followed by the comment clause marker **ba**:

(85)

Tamá,	kolo	me	ba	me	ile	ná	kin-de
woman	reason	what	COM	2F	cry	ASSC	eye-2F
kam-do	máànі́	gà?					
water-3F	like that	Q					

'Woman, why are you crying like that?' (G-C & W 1981: 2-3)

(86) Nè kolo me ba kara índùwé ma
COP reason what COM people human:PL die
gé-ǹg è gé ná kìrè kíndi-gè gà?
3Pl-DEF go 3PL ASSC road truly-3PL Q
'Why do people die and disappear forever?' (G-C & W 1981: 6-7)

The imperfective aspect in specific interrogatives is coded by the marker **jè**, in accordance with the coding of imperfective in pragmatically dependent clauses:

(87) Nè kolo me ba kara índùwé
COP reason what COM people human:PL
jè yagi-gé ná gùdá káǹg gà?
IMPF labor-3PL ASSC today DEM Q
'Why does mankind have to labor nowadays?' (G-C & W 1981: 10-11)

(88) è jè dí kolo mé gà
go VENT 3M reason what Q
'why did he come?' (high tone on **mé** because it is in interrogative clause-penultimate position)

(89) kíyà è jè kolo mé gà
Kiya go VENT reason what Q
'why did Kiya come?'

(90) sì dí kama ɗé kolo mé gà
drink 3M water NEG reason what Q
'why didn't he drink water?'

The interrogative complex **kolo me** may also be focused. The function of the focus construction is again to narrow the scope of the question to the reasons that the speaker has in mind:

(91) kolo me ba è jè dí gà
reason what COM go VENT 3M Q
'why did he come?'

(92) kolo me ba kiya è jé gà
reason what COM Kiya go VENT Q
'why did Kiya come?'

3.9 Questions about the possessor

Questions about the possessor are formed with the general human interrogative marker **wéy** followed by the appropriate possessive form, alienable or inalienable, with pronouns agreeing with the possessor. With inalienable possession the structure is: **wéy** Noun-Pronoun:

(93) nè wéy tamą̂-y gà
COP who wife-3M Q
'whose wife is she?'

(94) nè tóŋ go kùdò-ró gà
COP certain:F REF husband-3F Q
'whose husband is he?'

For alienable possession the structure must have the genitive marker **kè**. Thus for the third-person masculine possessor with alienable possession, the form is: Noun **wéy kè-y** (the tone on the genitive marker **kè** is high if it occurs in clause-penultimate position):

(95) gàrmà háŋ nè kò-m ɗé ba
footsteps DEM COP GEN-2M NEG COM
nè wèy kè-y ba è jè
COP who GEN-3M COM go VENT
póì tèmle kò-nòŋ háŋ gà
break:PL corn GEN-1SG DEM:P Q
'If those footsteps aren't yours, whose are they then, who came to break off my corn like that?'

(96) jèn dí túgú wéy kè-y gà
stay 3M house who GEN-3M Q
'in whose house did he stay?'

Having this system of coding allows the distinction in Lele between questions about the masculine, the feminine, and the plural possessor in interrogative clauses:

(97) jèn dí túgú wéy kò ró gà
stay 3M house who GEN 3F Q
'in whose (F) house did he stay?'

(98) jèn dí túgú kè-gè gà
stay 3M house GEN-3PL Q
'in whose (PL) house did he stay?'

If a locative question phrase is fronted in a contrastive focus construction, a locative anaphor must follow the verb:

(99) nè túgú wéy kè-y ba jèn dí
COP home who GEN-3M COM stay 3M
mànı́ gà
ANAPH Q
'at whose house is it that he stayed?'

3.10 Questions about time

The question word for time is **míndì** 'when'. If it occurs in clause-penultimate position, it is realized with a high tone on the last syllable.

(100) gi jèn Debreng míndí gà
2M stay Debreng when Q
'when were you in Debreng?'

(101) gi kìsí gùnà míndí gà
2M plant peanuts when Q
'when did you plant peanuts?'

(102) gi ódè míndí gà
2SG leave:FUT when Q
'when will you leave?' (a question asked of a guest, not considered impolite)

4 Conclusions

There are two types of interrogative clauses in Lele: questions about the truth of the whole proposition and specific questions inquiring about one component of the proposition. Both types are characterized by the clause-final interrogative particle **gà** and a raised tone on the penultimate syllable. Questions about the truth of the proposition have only those markers.

Questions about specific arguments may have two structures: one with the question word in the same position as in indicative clauses, and the other with the question word at the beginning of the clause.

There is a general distinction between questions about human and non-human participants. For questions about human participants, there are different question words asking about any potential participant (a participant in the domain de dicto) and participants belonging to a group known to the speaker. Each type of specific question retains the general interrogative characteristics, viz. the clause-final particle **gà** and the raised tone on the penultimate syllable. The function of the fronting of the specific interrogatives is to mark the de re as opposed to the dicto domain for non-human participants.

14

Negation

1 Introduction

Negation of all types of clauses is coded by the clause-final particle **ɗé**. If an interrogative marker **gà** has been added, it follows the negative marker.

2 Negation of equational clauses

Negation of an equational clause has the same form as that of verbal clauses, viz., the negative morpheme **ɗé** is at the end of the clause:

(1)

ŋ	nè	ba-m	ɗé	ŋ	nè
1SG	COP	father-2M	NEG	1SG	COP

kùná-m
uncle-2M

'I am not your father, I am your uncle'

(2)

nò	go	lele	ɗé
COP	REF	Lele	NEG

'he is not a Lele man'

(3)

nò	do	lele	ɗé
COP	REL:F	Lele	NEG

'she is not a Lele woman'

If the subject is referential, the referential marker **go** is deployed regardless of the gender of the subject. The gender is, however, coded by the subject pronoun following the predicate:

(4) nò go lele dú ɗé
COP REF Lele 3F NEG
'she is not a Lele woman'

(5) nò go lele ge ɗé
COP REF:M Lele 3PL NEG
'they are not Lele'

3 Negation of possessive clauses

Negative possessive clauses are simply possessive clauses followed by negation.

(6) kiya ná lúŋbà ɗé
Kiya ASSC horse NEG
'Kiya does not have a horse'

Recall that for third-person pronominal possessors the associative marker must precede both the possessor and the possessum, giving the structure **ná** Possessor **ná** Possessum. In a negative clause, the negative marker **ɗé** is added to this structure:

(7) ná dí ná lúŋbà ɗé
ASSC 3M ASSC horse NEG
'he does not have a horse'

(8) *dí ná lúŋbà ɗé
3M ASSC horse NEG
for 'he does not have a horse'

(9) ŋ ná lúŋbà ɗé
1SG ASSC horse NEG
'I do not have a horse'

The negation of possessive clauses with no overt object has the negative marker **ɗé** following the associative marker:

(10) ná dú ná ɗé
ASSC 3F ASSC NEG
'she doesn't have it/her/them'

The importance of this type of construction is that it indicates that the associative has already acquired the function of the predicate.

4 Negation of verbal clauses

All negative verbal clauses have the clause-final marker **ɗé**. Unlike in many Chadic languages, the tense and aspectual system and coding in negative clauses in Lele are the same as in affirmative clauses.

(11) è dí ɗé
go 3M NEG
'he did not go', 'he does not go'

(12) sì dí kere ɗé
drink 3M beer NEG
'he did not drink beer'

The same markers of the pragmatic status of the clause that are deployed in affirmative clauses can be deployed in negative clauses:

(13) jè sì dí kere ɗé
IMPF drink 3M beer NEG
'he does not drink beer'

(14) nè sì dí kere ɗé
COP drink 3M beer NEG
'he does not drink beer'

The future tense in both the perfective and the past form can be coded in the negative:

(15) jè é dí ɗé
IMPF go:FUT 3M NEG
'he will not go'

(16) lée dí sìí gìrà ɗé
eat:FUT 3M meat dog NEG
'he will not eat dog meat'

As in affirmative clauses, the third-person masculine singular pronoun can be omitted:

(17) è jè ɗé
go VENT NEG
'he does not come'

(18) è jè dú ɗé
go VENT 3M NEG
'she does not come', 'she did not come'

(19) dì dí wo ɗé
eat 3M mush NEG
'he did not eat mush'

(20) jè dì dí wo ɗé
IMPF eat 3M mush NEG
'he does not eat mush'

The negative particle is not clause final if it is embedded in a focus frame with a propositional anaphor in focus. Such a frame must end with the definite marker **ŋ**, which follows the negative marker **ɗé**:

(21) nè máàní ba goni jè ɗe ná
COP ANAPH COM hyena IMPF leave ASSC
tu ɗé-ŋ
goat NEG-DEF
'That is why the hyena does not leave Goat alone'

(22) nè máàní ba kamda go tùmó lèé
COP ANAPH COM women REF before eat
gé tòrò ɗé-ŋ
3PL hen NEG-DEF
'That is why women in the old times did not eat chickens.'

(23) *nè máàní ba kamda go tùmò lèé
COP ANAPH COM women REF before eat
gé tòrò ɗé
3PL hen NEG
for 'That is why women in the old times did not eat chickens.'

5 Negation and quantification

Certain nouns can occur only in negative clauses, and certain nouns can occur only in affirmative clauses:

(24) dìgrì dú ìsą́n ɗé
kill 3F nothing NEG
'she did not kill anything'

The form **ìsą́ŋ** means 'nothing' and can be used only in negative clauses:

(25) *ìsą́ŋ jè jógə́ ŋ
nothing IMPF bother 1SG
for 'nothing bothers me'

(26) *dìgrì dú ìsą́n
kill 3F nothing
for 'she killed something'

The evidence that **ìsą́ŋ** is a noun is provided by the fact that it can also occur as a subject of the clause:

(27) ìsą́ŋ (jè) jógə́-ŋ ɗé
nothing IMPF bother-1SG NEG
'nothing bothers me'

The noun **kanya** 'thing, something' can occur only in affirmative clauses:

(28) kanya jè jógə́-ŋ
thing IMPF bother-1SG
'something bothers me'

(29) dìgrì dú kanya
kill 3F something
'she killed something'

(30) *dìgrì dú kanya ɗé
kill 3F something NEG
for 'she did not kill anything'

The conclusion from the behavior of the two nouns is that although syntactically they belong to the category 'noun', semantically they differ from all other nouns in that they encode quantification.

(31) ní è kùrìyo ba ìsą́n kàl ɗé
1PL.EXCL go trip COM nothing happen NEG
'we went on a trip and nothing happened'

(32) ní è kùrìyo ba kanya kàl
1PL.EXCL go trip COM something happen
'we went on a trip and something happened'

The notion 'not even one' is coded by the use of an object noun followed by the numeral **pìná** 'one':

(33) lè tàsí pìná ɗé
eat shea fruit one NEG
'he did not eat even one shea fruit'

6 Conclusions

Negation in Lele manifests a rather simple system of coding whereby an affirmative clause has the negative marker **ɗé** added at the end. The tense and aspectual system in the negative is the same as in an affirmative clause.

15

Focus Constructions

1 Introduction

The notion 'focus' is taken in the present grammar to mean the speaker's intention to make salient one of the elements of the utterance. 'Focus' includes contrastive focus, where there are two potential participants in the event and the speaker contrasts one participant with the other. Marking one element of the clause as salient marks it as being different from other elements in the discourse or in the clause with respect to expectations that one may have. Some focus-related phenomena in Lele are discussed in Simons 1982. The present chapter presents a fuller discussion of focus in Lele and discusses focus construction in relation to other grammatical categories of the language. For the purpose of analysis, a clause with an element in focus is divided into the focus and the comment. Either or both of these elements can be marked to indicate that they are part of the focus construction.

2 Contrastive focus on the subject

There are several types of focus on the subject. In one type, the focus means that element of the clause on which the speaker wants to concentrate the attention of the hearer. Another type involves contrastive focus, whereby one subject's action, state, or behavior is contrasted with another subject's action, state, or behavior. The coding of the contrastive subject involves the deployment of the independent pronoun preceding the nominal or pronominal subject. The evidence for the contrastive focus function of this construction is provided by narratives with two protagonists whose behaviors are contrasted. In the first sentence of the following narrative the two protagonists are introduced:

(1)

kíyà	dàgè	ná	ólkusíŋ	è	gé	dà
Kiya	3PL	ASSC	Olkusin	go	3PL	PREP
segré						
hunt						

'Kiya and Olkusin went on a hunt.'

In the second sentence, one of the protagonists is the subject of an apodosis clause:

(2)

è	kè-gè	go	se	géŋ	ná
go	GEN-3PL	REF	INCEPT	change?	ASSC
kíyà	hím	kàjé		so	lay
Kiya	gather	throwing knife:PL		two	also
ìlú	pìnà	lay			
stick	one	also			

'when they went, Kiya gathered up two knives and one stick'

In the third sentence, the second protagonist is the subject, and his action is contrasted with that of the first protagonist:

(3)

dày	ólkùsiŋ	ày	tàbál	lay	ná	kàjé
3M	olkusiŋ	took	lance	also	ASSC	knife
poriŋ						
four						

'Olkusin took one lance and four throwing knives

If the subject is not in focus, it is not preceded by the independent pronoun. But if a different subject is in focus again, it is preceded by the independent pronoun, as illustrated by the subsequent sentences in the narrative:

(4)

è	gé	segré-ŋ	hàb	gé	bisí
go	3PL	hunt-DEF	find	3PL	antelope'

'they went for the hunt [and] they found an antelope.'

(5) dày kíya way-wi bisí-ŋ in
3M Kiya launch-PL antelope-DEF xxx
mbàtmbàt kàb-ìy án jé dí bisí
miss:PL hand-3M leave throw 3M antelope
kàb-ìy om-du gàrma tóòmé
hand-3M catch-3F times many
'Kiya threw [a throwing knife] at the antelope many times, but missed.'

The next sentence has a different subject, but it is not preceded by the marker **dày**.

(6) ólkúsìŋ jé bisí-ŋ jé-dú dòŋlo-ro
Olkusin throw antelope-DEF throw-3F thigh-3F
ni
LOC
'Olkusin threw at the antelope; he threw at her thigh'

Here are two clauses in which the focus is changing from one to the other protagonist:

(7) dày kíyà se e jé
3M Kiya INCEPT go VENT
è jé na ge kíse írà
go VENT HYP 3PL share:FUT EXCL
'Kiya started to come; he came in order to share.'

The next sentence also contains a clause with a pronominal subject in focus, once again coded by the independent pronoun followed by the subject pronoun:

(8) dày ólkùsiŋ se yà bé-y na
3M Olkusin INCEPT say DAT-3M HYP
dìgì gí nò mbúlo
2M 2M COP clumsy
'Olkusin told him: you are clumsy'

The subject in focus may also be a topic of the clause and marked as such by the definite marker:

(9) dày kíyá-ŋ ír tè-y bándà
3M Kiya-DEF stay buttock-3M xxx
'Kíya remained here and there'

Contrastive focus on pronominal subjects is marked by the independent pronouns followed by subject pronouns for first- and second-person subjects:

(10)

láà	gìdìrè	go	dà	kama	te-y
eat:IMP	moon	REF	PREP	water	bottom-3M

ni	ɓàlà-mè	dàŋ	ŋ	jè	òdì
LOC	suffice:IMP-2F	1SG	1SG	IMPF	go

'Eat the moon that is at the bottom of the water; it should satisfy you; as for me, I am going away.'

(11)

dìgì	gi	kòy	tèmlé-ŋ	gèsé
2M	2M	steal	corn-DEF	or

gi	kòy	ɗé	gà
2M	steal	NEG	Q

'did you steal the corn, or didn't you?'

The element in contrastive focus does not have to be the subject of the clause. The following example illustrates contrastive focus on the object:

(12)

ŋ	ɓàdì-dù	àlá	ŋ	ɓàdì	dàmè	ɗé
1SG	go for-3F	but	1SG	go for	2F	NEG

'I went after her and not after you'

If the subject is modified by an alienable possessive construction, i.e. a construction in which the possessor precedes the possessum, and both are followed by the genitive marker with a possessive pronoun, the copula occurs not before the possessive noun phrase but rather before the head noun, i.e. before the possessum:

(13)

Tamá	dàgè	ná	gìrà	sò	nè	kolo
woman	3PL	ASSC	dog	two	COP	word

kè-gè	ba	kara	kusi-gè	jè
GEN-3PL	COM	people	body-3PL	IMPF

ɓal-gè	ná	kur	go	yageè	ni.
suffice-3PL	ASSC	place	REF	labor	LOC

'It was the words of both, the woman and the dog, that compelled people to [undertake] the hard agricultural labor.'

The importance of the focus on a possessive construction rests on the fact that the possessor phrase does not behave as one syntactic entity, but rather it is broken. The focus marker is inserted into what appears to be a possessive phrase. Later in this chapter we will see the same phenomenon replicated with respect to all other types of noun phrases.

3 Non-contrastive focus on the subject

In the second type of focus the hearer presents the speaker with unexpected information, which may be the whole proposition or only a part of it. The fundamental and obligatory means for coding this type of focus is through the coding of the comment clause by the form **ba**. The form **ba** is merely a marker of the comment clause. It is deployed whenever the focused element occurs before the comment, e.g. in clause-initial position. Since the subject most often occurs in clause-initial position, the marker **ba** is obligatory in all such cases. This type of coding with its function may be applied to any constituent of the clause, be it subject, object, or adjunct. Here is an example of the focus on a nominal subject:

(14)

yàá	bé-ì	na	gìdìrè	ba	na	ma
say	DAT-3M	HYP	moon	COM	HYP	die
ná	kùn	ana-jè				
ASSC	return:IMP	leave:IMP-VEN				

'he told him that it was the moon that would die and return' (G-C & W1981: 8-9)

If the subject is a third-person pronoun, it is coded by the independent form of the pronoun preceding the comment clause with the marker **ba**:

(15)

kolo	dàdù	go	tùmò	dàdù	ba
because	3F	REF	first	3F	COM
bor-iy	gèylè				
save-3M	health				

'Because the first one, it was she who saved his life.'

Other examples of subject in focus:

(16)

dàdù	go	sò	dàdù	ba	è	jè
3F	REF	two	3F	COM	go	VENT
bor-iy	gèylè	dà	kama	kùb-ìy	ni	
save-3M	health	PREP	river	mouth-3M	LOC	

'The second one, it was she who came and saved his life at the shore of the river.'

(17)

dàdù	go	sùbù	dàdù	ba	bor-iy	gèylè
3F	REF	two	3F	COM	save-3M	health
tą	go	màgàyndí	yìir-ìy			
time (Fr.)	REF	viper	bite-3M			

'The third one, it was she who saved his life when the viper bit him.'

(18)

kumno	yàá	na,	na	láràdí	ba
God	say	HYP	HYP	chameleon	COM

è	hab-i	tùmò	na	yàá	bè-ì	kolo
go	find-3M	first	HYP	say	DAT-3M	word

kè-ì	ná	nè	gìdìrè	ba	ma
GEN-3M	ASSC	COP	moon	COM	die

kínè	áne	ɓey	lay
return:FUT	leave:FUT	still	also

'The God said: if it is the chameleon that finds me first and tells me his word, then it is the moon that would return after it has died' (G-C & W 1981: 6-7)

The element in focus may be preceded by the copula **nè**. This coding of focus may, but does not have to, cooccur with the marker **ba**. The sequence **nè** . . . **ba** may be deployed in contrastive focus constructions, as is the case in the second clause of the following sentence. The subject of this clause is contrasted with the subject of the first clause:

(19)

Gìdìrè	mara	na	ìrà	ná	kìrè
moon	die:IMP	HYP	go:IMP	ASSC	road

'It is you who broke off my corn.'

The focus on a pronominal subject construction in an equational clause deploys the independent form of the pronoun. The contrastive focus marker **ba** follows the subject and precedes the copula. The predicate noun phrase has the definite marker to indicate that the predicate has been mentioned before in discourse. This is the case even if the predicate is a proper noun:

(22)

dày	ba	nè	kíyà-ŋ
3M	COM	COP	Kiya-DEF

'it is he [pointing] who is Kiya' (when one talked about Kiya before)

If the predicate has not been mentioned in discourse, the predicate does not have to have the definite marker:

(23)

dày	ba	nè	kíyà
3M	COM	COP	Kiya

'this one is Kiya'[12]

---

[12] Because of the lexical meaning of the verb nè this clause may also have a different meaning:

dàì	bá	nè	kíyà
3M	COM	make	Kiya

When the subject is in focus, it may also be preceded by the copula **nè**. The structure is: **nè** Subject **ba** Verb Noun Phrase:

(24)

nè	ɓòdu	ba	gèylì-nì	kur
COP	monkey	COM	save-1PL.EXCL	time

go	kamda	ná	kùlòngò
REF	women	ASSC	pregnancy

'it was the monkey who saved us at the time when women were pregnant' (G-C & W 1981: 2-3)

The omission of the copula **nè** does not alter the information function of the clause. The omission of the marker **ba**, on the other hand, eliminates the focus function of the construction:

(25)

(nè)	mìlá-ŋ	ba	dìgrì	bìsí-ŋ	nè
COP	lion-DEF	COM	kill	antelope-DEF	COP

túmnò	ɗé
leopard	NEG

'the lion killed the antelope; it was not the leopard that did it'

(26)

(nè)	cànígè	ba	wal	kùlbá-ŋ̀
COP	cànígè	COM	slaughter	cow-DEF

'it was Canige that slaughtered the cow'

If the copula **nè** is deployed with an argument in clause-initial position, the comment marker **ba** cannot be omitted:

(27)

*nè	cànígè	wal	kùlbá-ŋ̀
COP	cànígè	slaughter	cow-DEF

for 'it was Canige that slaughtered the cow'

If a focused subject is not followed by a comment clause, there is no comment clause marker **ba**. Compare the following sentences in which the focused subject is pronominal and each sentence has different focused subjects in each of its clauses. The second clause in these sentence has no comment clause marker **ba** because there is no comment clause following the second subject:

'it is he who made Kiya' (i.e., it is he who is responsible for the sickness of Kiya. Some i llnesses are believed to have been caused by the ill will of other people.)

(28) (nè) dìgì ba gi nè ɓén-íŋ
COP 2M COM 2M COP brother-1SG
nè dày ɗé
COP 3M:Deictic NEG
'you are my brother, not him'

(29) (nè) dàŋ ba ŋ wal kùlbá nè
COP 1SG COM 1SG slaughter cow COP
dày ɗé
3M.Deictic NEG
'it was me who slaughtered the cow, it was not him'

(30) nè dày ba wàl dí
COP 3SG.Deictic COM slaughter 3M
kùlbá nè dàŋ ɗé
cow COP 1SG NEG
'it was him who slaughtered the cow, it was not me'

The preceding analysis points to two things: That **ne . . . ba** is not a construction in the sense of having unique function different from the functions of other constructions (contrary to Simons 1982) and that each of these markers has a different function.

4 Focus on the topic

The topic of a paragraph, which is not necessarily the subject of the clause, may also be in focus. As a topic, it occurs in clause-initial position. The focus function is indicated by the marker **ba** preceding the comment clause:

(31) tamá̧-ŋ ba kùb-rò hamli síɗé
wife-DEF COM mouth-3F light too much
'The wife had too light a mouth'

The subject of this clause is **kùb-rò** 'her mouth'. The evidence that **tamá** 'wife' is the topic of the paragraph is provided by the fact that she is the subject of the preceding sentence, and in the example in question the word is followed by the definite marker.

5 The intensifier and focus

The word **kusu** 'body' with the appropriate possessive pronouns serves as an intensifier when it follows a noun. The intensifier may be deployed with a focused element. If the noun followed by the intensifier **kusu** is in focus, the marker **ba**, ending the focus phrase, must be deployed. The minimum condition for the coding of focus is the marker **ba**:

(32)	(nè)	dày	kusí-y	ba	(nè)	bé-ŋ̀
	COP	3M	body-3M	COM	COP	give-1SG

'it was he himself who gave it to me'

(33)	(nè)	dàdù	kusu-ro	ba	bé-ŋ
	COP	3F	body-3F	COM	give-1SG

'it was she herself who gave it to me'

(34)	*(nè)	dàdù	kusu-ro	bé-ŋ
	COP	3F	body-3F	give-1SG

for 'it was she herself who gave it to me'

The imperfective aspect in the comment clause is marked by the form **jè**:

(35)	Tamá	dàgè	ná	gìrà	sò	nè	kolo
	woman	3PL	ASSC	dog	two	COP	word

kè-gè	ba	kara	kusi-gè	jè	
GEN-3PL	COM	people	body-3PL	IMPF	
ɓal-gè	ná	kur	go	yageè	ni.
suffice-3PL	ASSC	place	REF	labor	LOC

'It was the words of both, the woman and the dog, that compelled people to [undertake] the hard agricultural labor' (G-C & W 1981:12-13)

6 Focus on the object and definiteness

Focus on the object is also marked by the copula **nè**, optionally when the focused object is fronted, obligatorily when the focused object follows the verb. The fronting of a focused object codes the definiteness of the object. A focused object in the position following the verb is not definite:

(36)	ŋ	léè	nè	sî
	1SG	eat:FUT	COP	meat

'I'd rather eat meat'

(37)	gi	tòb	nè	bà-m	gèré	yó-m
	2M	love	COP	father-2M	or	mother-2M
	gà					
	Q					

'do you love your father or your mother?'

(38)

tígrí-gé	nè	lòŋbé	nè	kolbé	ɗé
slaughter:PL-3PL	COP	horses	COP	cows	NEG

'it is horses that they slaughtered, not cows'

The comment clause marker cannot be used if the argument is not fronted:

(39)

*tígrí-gé	né	lòŋbé	ba	nè	kòlbé	ɗé
slaughter-3PL	COP	horse	COM	COP	cows	NEG

for 'it is horses that they slaughtered, not cows '

That prohibition indicates that the marker **ba** is in fact a marker of the comment on the focus.

(40)

Kara	go	tumo	ná	nè	gé	yage
people	REF	past	ASSC	make	3PL	plant:VN
ɗé	jèn	wàl	gé	nè	kasa	go
NEG	remain	cut	3PL	COP	corn	REF
an	dà	cáaní	ba	dì	gé.	
leave	PREP	bush	COM	eat	3PL	

'In the past people did not plant. They just cut the corn that was growing in the field, and they ate it.' (G-C & W 1981: 10-11)

In the data there is one instance of the object in the postverbal position with the definite marker **ŋ**:

(41)

goni	cál	ba	kama	ni	ná	ɓàdì
hyena	jump	fall	water	LOC	ASSC	go after
nè	ísì-ŋ		càr			
COP	bone-DEF		immediately			

'Hyena jumped into the water and went immediately after the bone.'

The bone had been previously mentioned in the discourse but only between the participants in the event, not as an element of the speaker's own description of the situation. The definite marker here identifies the bone as one mentioned in the conversation among the participants in the event.

When the focused object is fronted, the marker **ba** precedes the comment clause. The copula **nè** preceding an object NP is optional. The form of the construction with the focused object in clause-initial position is as follows: **nè** NP [object] **ba** Subject Verb. The evidence that the fronting of the focused object codes its definiteness is provided by the fact that if the object is human, the verb must have a resumptive pronominal object suffix that codes the features of gender and number of the object in focus:

(42) (nè) canigé ba ŋ gol-iy nè
COP Canige COM 1SG see-3M COP
gìlkíníŋ ɗé
Gilkinin NEG
'it was Canige that I saw; it was not Gilkinin'

(43) nè gìlkíníŋ ba ŋ gol-du nè
COP Gilkinin COM 1SG see-3F COP
canigé ɗé
Canige NEG
'it was Gilkinin that I saw; it was not Canige'

The omission of the resumptive pronoun after the verb results in an ungrammatical sentence:

(44) *nè canigé ba ŋ gol nè
COP Canige COM 1SG see COP
gìlkíníŋ ɗé
Gilkinin NEG
for 'it was Canige that I saw; it was not Gilkinin'

(45) nè gìlkíníŋ dàgè ná canigé ba
COP Gilkinin 3PL ASSC Canige COM
ŋ gol-gé nè kiya ɗé
1SG see-3PL COP Kiya NEG
'it was Gilkinin and Canige that I saw; it was not Kiya'

Focus on first- and second-person objects is marked by using independent forms of the first- and second-person pronouns. Even in such cases the verb may be followed by resumptive pronouns:

(46) nè dàŋ ba cánígé gol-(íŋ) nè dìgì
COP 1SG COM Canige see-(1SG) COP 2M
ɗé
NEG
'it was me that Canige saw; it was not you'

(47) nè dìgì ba cánígé gol-(gi) nè
COP 2M COM Canige see-2M-3M COP
dàŋ ɗé
1SG NEG
'it was you that Canige saw; it was not me'

(48) nè dàmè ba cáńígé gol-me nè
COP 2F COM Canige see-2F COP
dàŋ ɗé
1SG NEG
'it was you that Canige saw; it was not me'

(49) nè dàŋgàngù ba cáńígé gol-ŋga-ngu
COP 1PL.INCL COM Canige see-1PL.INCL
nè dàŋgù ɗé
COP 2PL NEG
'it was us that Canige saw; it was not you'

If the focused object is not human, the resumptive pronoun cannot be used, even if one knows the gender of the animate noun:

(50) nè bìsí ba mìlá-ŋ dìgrì ně
COP antelope COM lion-DEF kill COP
túmnò ɗé
leopard NEG
'it was the antelope that the lion killed; it was not the leopard'

(51) nè gìrà ba ŋ gol nè tù
COP dog COM 1SG see COP goat
ɗé
NEG
'it was the dog that I saw; it was not the goat'

Evidence that the fronting of an object codes its definiteness is provided by the fact that the definite marker cannot be deployed with the fronted object. That is because it would be redundant to have two means to code the same function:

(52) *nè gìrà-ŋ ba ŋ gol-íy/dú nè
COP dog-DEF COM 1SG see-3M/3F COP
tù ɗé
goat NEG
for 'it was the dog that I saw, not a goat'

7 Focus on an indirect object

There are different means for the coding of pronominal and nominal dative arguments. In all constructions the focus-marking copula **nè** immediately precedes the head of the dative phrase, i.e. the recipient of an object or the beneficiary of an event. Having the copula immediately precede the dative argument implies that it is separated from the dative and benefactive marker **bé**. This in itself is an interesting phenomenon in view of the fact that in neutral clauses the dative/benefactive argument is not separated from the marker of its role in the clause. Given the fact that the argument may be separated from the marker of its function in the clause, the coding of the dative and benefactive function in focus constructions has been resolved by different means.

8 The nominal dative in focus

There are two means for coding the focus on a nominal dative. One involves the position of the dative argument at the beginning of the clause followed by the comment clause marked by **ba**. The dative argument is preceded by the copula **nè**. The verb **bè** 'to give' takes two objects: the first is the recipient and the second the thing given. Since the recipient is human, when it is fronted in a focus construction, it behaves like other direct objects in that the verb in the comment clause requires a resumptive pronoun coding the gender and number features of the focused object.

(53) nè canigé ba bè-y dí làlí
COP canige COM give-3M 3M money
bé dí kiya ɗé
give 3M Kiya NEG
'it was to Canige that he gave money; it was not to Kiya'

(54) nè kírbí ba bù-dù dí làlí
COP Kirbi COM give-3F 3M money
bé dí kiya ɗé
give 3M Kiya NEG
'it was to Kirbi that he gave money not to Kiya'

The omission of the focus-marking copula in the above sentences would make the role of the initial noun ambiguous: it could be the dative or the subject argument.

The nominal dative focused argument can also occur after the verb. If the verb has a direct object, the dative may precede or follow the direct object. But in either case, the dative is marked by the copula **nè**. The verb is not followed by a resumptive pronoun if the dative in focus follows it:

(55) bè dí làlí nè canigé bè nè
give 3M money COP canige give COP
kiya ɗé
Kiya NEG
'it was to Canige that he gave money, not to Kiya'

Dative before the object:

(56)

bè	dí	nè	canigé	làlí	bè	nè
give	3M	COP	canige	money	give	COP
kiya	ɗé					
Kiya	NEG					

'it was to Canige that he gave money, not to Kiya'

(57)

gìlkínín	bé	dú	làlí	nè	canigé
Gilkinin	give	3F	money	COP	Canige
bè	nè	kiya	ɗé		
give	COP	Kiya	NEG		

'it was to Canige that Gilkinin gave money, not to Kiya'

(58)

canigé	bé	dí	làlí	nè	gìlkínín
Canige	give	3M	money	COP	Gilkinin
bè	nè	kiya	ɗé		
give	COP	Kiya	NEG		

'it was to Gilkinin that Canige gave money, not to Kiya'

Predictably, if the dative is not in clause-initial position, there is no marker **ba**, because the comment clause precedes rather than follows the argument in focus:

(59)

*canigé	bé-dú-di	làlí	nè	gìlkínín
Canige	give-3F-3M	money	COP	Gilkinin
bè	nè	kiya	ɗé	
give	COP	Kiya	NEG	

for 'it was to Gilkinin that Canige gave money, not to Kiya'

Cf.:

(60)

canigé	bé-dú-di	làlí
Canige	give-3F-3M	money

'Canige gave her money'

If the verb is such that it does not take the dative as the direct object, the dative in focus has the following structure: Dative Copula Pronoun **ba** Comment clause'. Thus the marker of the dative function is separated from the argument it marks by the focus-marking copula **nè**. Again the integrity of the noun phrase is violated:

(61)

bè	nè	dày	ba	ŋwéy	dú	wò
DAT	COP	3M	COM	cook	3F	mush

'it is for him that she prepared the mush'

(62) bè nè dàdù ba làmdì dí dòlò
DAT COP 3F COM cook gruel 3F gruel
'it is for her that he prepared the gruel'

The benefactive may also be coded by the position it has in the pragmatically neutral clause, but in such a case, predictably, there is no comment clause marker **ba**. The independent pronoun is preceded by the copula **nè**:

(63) ŋwéy dú wò bè nè dày
cook 3F mush DAT COP 3M
'it is for him that she prepared the mush'

(64) làmdì dí dòlò bè nè dàdù
cook gruel 3F gruel DAT COP 3F
'it is for her that he prepared the gruel'

Similarly with nominal benefactives:

(65) wóy̧-dú wò bè nè canigé
cook-3F mush DAT COP Canige
'she cooked some mush for Canige'

(66) ŋ è jè go nè yágè bè nè
1SG go VENT REF do plow DAT COP
canigé
Canige
'it is for Canige that I came to plow'

9 The pronominal dative in contrastive focus

There are at least three different types of construction to code focus on a pronominal dative/benefactive argument. When the pronominal dative is an argument of the verb **bè** 'give', the focus on the pronoun is coded by the copula **nè** preceding the independent form of the pronoun. The focused dative may occur after the verb or after the object:

(67) bè dí làlì nè dàŋ bè nè dìgì
give 3M money COP 1SG give is 2M
ɗé
NEG
'he gave money to me, not to you'

If the dative phrase occurs after the verb, the direct object and any other material must be preceded by the marker **ba**:

(68) bè dí nè dàŋ ba làlì bè
give 3M COP 1SG COM money give
nè dìgì ɗé
is 2M NEG
'he gave money to me, not to you'

The dative phrase may also be in clause-initial position, and like all other extra posed arguments in focus, it must be followed by the marker **ba**. The verb, with subject and direct object if any, follows the dative phrase. The main verb may have the pronominal dative marker, which cross-references the pronoun in focus, added:

(69) nè dàŋ ba bé-(ŋ̀) dí lálì
COP 1SG COM give-1SG 3M money
(bè) nè dìgì ɗé
give COP 2M NEG
'he gave money to me, not to you'

10 The focus on adjuncts

The coding of focus for the locative differs from the one used for core arguments. The locative in focus cannot be fronted. It can only follow the verb. The focus function is coded by the copula **nè** preceding the locative phrase. The way a phrase is marked for the locative function depends on the inherent properties of the head of the locative phrase. If the noun is not inherently locative, it is followed by the postposition **ni**:

(70) cànìgé è nè túg ni è cáaní ɗé
Canige go COP home LOC go field NEG
'Canige went home, not to the field'

In a manner similar to that of other prepositional phrases in focus, if the locative argument is marked by the preposition **dà**, the preposition occurs before the copula. What this implies is that it is not the locative phrase itself that is focused, but rather the noun:

(71) cànìgé è dà nè Debreng è cáaní ɗé
Canige go PREP COP Debreng go field NEG
'Canige went to Debreng, not to the field'

Putting the copula before the preposition results in an ungrammatical construction:

(72) *cànìgé è nè dà Debreng è cáaní ɗé
Canige go COP PREP Debreng go field NEG
for 'Canige went home, not to the field'

The locative phrase in focus is the only focused element that cannot be fronted:

(73) *dà nè Debreng ni ba canigé
PREP COP market LOC COM Canige
è-(dí) è-(dí) nè cáaní ɗé
go-3M go-3M COP field NEG
for 'it is to the market that Canige went, and not to the field'

(74) *nè kèló ba
COP Kélo ASSC
for 'it is to Kélo that . . .'

Cf.:

(75) cànìgé è dí nè kèló
Canige go 3M COP Kélo
'it is to Kélo that Canige went'

The focus on the reason why is illustrated by the following sentence, where the reason is coded in the comment clause by the associative preposition **ná** following the verbal complex **yagi-gé** 'they plant':

(76) Nè tamá dàgè ná gìrà kolo
COP woman 3PL ASSC dog word
kè-gè ba kara pet nè yagi-gé
GEN-PL CON people all IMPF plant-3PL
ná kasa ɓey ba dì-gé ná gùdá.
ASSC corn still COM eat-3PL ASSC today
'It is because of the words of a woman and a dog that people have to plant corn in order to eat.' (G-C &W 1981: 12-13)

The focus on a temporal adjunct is coded by the initial position of the adjunct and the marker **ba** preceding the comment phrase. The role of the focused element is coded by the associative preposition **ná** and optionally the anaphor **mànί** in the position following the verb:

(77) Gìdìrè go Lábí ba tìlí ày to
moon REF Labi COM tree take bottom
go wè-gé ná màní nèńy
REF give birth-3PL ASSC ANAPH very much
lay.
also
'It is during the moon of Labi that trees bear much fruit' (G-C & W 1982: 38-39)

The comment clause marker **ba** may be omitted, but then instead, some other marker must appear, a marker that codes the special status of the ensuing clause. In the following examples this special status is marked by the copula **nè**:

(78) Nè gìdìrè go kara nè jè-gé ná
COP moon REF people COP put-3PL ASSC
mònò lay
eleusine also
'It is during this month that people plant eleusine.' (G-C & W 1982: 42-43)

11 The focus on an associative phrase

The coding of focus on an associative phrase has the form **ná nè** NP, i.e., the associative phrase precedes the copula. Hence, as in the case of other adjuncts marked by a preposition, the copula occurs after the marker of the function of the noun within a clause. The associative phrase in focus may occur in the position following the object or in the clause-initial position:

(79) gé jè yì kanya ná nè tìndí
HUM IMPF pound thing ASSC COP pestle
'it is with a pestle that one pounds'

If the associative phrase in focus is in clause-initial position, the remaining material must be preceded by the marker **ba**:

(80) ná nè tìndí ba gé jè yì
ASSC COP pestle COM HUM IMPF pound
kanya
thing
'it is with a pestle that one pounds'

(81) ná nè kírbì ba è jè dí
ASSC COP Kirbi COM go VENT 3M
'it is with Kirbi that he came'

(82) è jè dí ná nè kírbì
go VENT 3M ASSC COP Kirbi
'it is with Kirbi that he came'

12 The focus on a propositional anaphor

The propositional anaphor **máànı́** is preceded by the copula **nè**. Such a complex is followed by the marker **ba**:

(83) nè máàní ba ng nè ile
COP ANAPH COM 1SG COP cry:VN
ná ɓèý.
ASSC only
'That is the reason I am crying.' (G-C & W 1981: 2-3)

(84) nè máàní ba ge tey ná gìdìrè
COP ANAPH COM HUM call ASSC moon
kàmtáàsé.
Nelsonia
'That is the reason why they call it moon Nelsonia.' (G-C & W 1982: 44-45)

13 The focus on a nominal predicate

The nominal predicate follows the subject of an equational clause. The predicate is preceded by the copula **nè**, but it is not followed by the marker **ba**. It may be followed by the marker **ɗéú** 'instead'. The marker **ɗéú** codes counterexpectation on the part of the speaker:

(85) gi nè ɓén-iŋ ɗéú lá
2M COP brother-1SG instead rather than
gi nè kùná-níŋ ɗé
2M COP uncle-1SG NEG
'you are my brother, not my uncle'

14 The focus on the predicate

The focus on the predicate is a seldom-postulated category in language descriptions. In Lele, the same marker that marks focus on the object, the copula **nè**, also marks focus on the predicate. The evidence for the function of this marker is provided by the difference in meaning between the following sentences from natural discourse:

(86)

Me	góolé	ng	nè	tòb	go
2F	see:FUT	1SG	COP	want	REF

gèylè	mè.
save:VN	2F

'You will see that I indeed want to save you.' (G-C & W 1981: 2-3)

Compare this with the non-focused deployment of the same verb:

(87)

Ng	tòb	go	bóré	me	gèylè.
1SG	want	REF	save:FUT	you	save:VN

'I want to save you.' (G-C & W 1981: 2-3)

The notion of focus includes that element of the proposition that the speaker wants to mark as the most salient of the proposition, the one that is the most newsworthy. Partial evidence for the focus function of **nè** is provided by the fact that many clauses with the marker **nè** are followed by the comment-on-focus marker **ba**. Hence, in addition to the meaning of the clauses with **nè**, there is an independent formal argument for its function.

(88)

Nè	máàní	ba	kara	índùwé	nè	ma
COP	ANAPH	COM	people	human:PL	COP	die

gé	ba	è	gé	ná	kìrè	gìdìrè	ma
3PL	COM	go	3PL	ASSC	road	moon	die

ná	kìn	an-jè	káŋ̀g	lay
ASSC	return	leave-VENT	DEM	also

'That is why, when men die, they go away forever, while when the moon dies, it comes out again.' (G-C & W 1981: 8-9)

(89)

Nè	tamá	dàgè	ná	gìrà	kolo
COP	woman	3PL	ASSC	dog	word

kè-gè	ba	kara	pet	nè	yagi-gé
GEN-3PL	COM	people	all	IMPF	plant-3PL

ná	kasa	ɓey	ba	dì-gé	ná	gùdá.
ASSC	corn	still	COM	eat-3PL	ASSC	today

'It is because of the words of a woman and those of a dog that people today have to plant in order to eat.' (G-C & W 1981: 10-11)

The semantic evidence for the focus function of **nè** is provided by the following examples, where the predicate is very much the focus of the sentence:

(90)

Yàá	bú-dù	na :	"ɓòdu	kò-nòng,
tell	DAT-3F	HYP	monkey	GEN-1SG
ng	nè	ile	kolo	
1SG	IMPF	cry:VN	reason	

'she told her thus: my monkey, I am crying because . . .' (G-C & W 1981: 2-3)

(91)

Nè	máàní	ba	ng	nè	ile
COP	ANAPH	COM	1SG	COP	cry:VN
ná	ɓèý.				
ASSC	only				

'That is the reason I am crying.' (G-C & W 1981: 2-3)

The form **nè** can occur before the past form of the verb, as in the preceding examples, and before a future form of the verb, as in the following example:

(92)

Wèlè	go	tamá	do	ná	kùlòngò
day	REF	woman	REF	ASSC	pregnancy
nè	wéè		mira	àlè	ná
IMPF	give birth:FUT		be close	already	ASSC
kamda	sèn	gé	go	sé	tamá
women	know	3PL	REF	put:FUT	woman
kolo	wè		ɗé.		
because	give birth		NEG		

'In the past, when a pregnant woman was about to give birth, other women did not know how to position her for the childbirth.' (G-C & W 1981: 2-3)

If there is a paragraph with several events, the marker **nè** is deployed only once:

(93)

Kara	go	yagi	gé	mònò,	nè	por
people	REF	plant	3PL	eleusine	IMPF	cut
gé	ná	mònò	lay;	dàgè	go	ná
3PL	ASSC	eleusine	also	3PL	REF	ASSC
sìbì	go	pore	mònò	ɗé		
knife	REF	cut:VN	eleusine	NEG		
ná	è gé	hab	gé	kara	tiraba	
ASSC	go 3PL	find	3PL	people	smithing	
dèsì	gé	bé-gè	sìbì	go	pore	ná
smith	3PL	DAT-3PL	knife	REF	cut	ASSC
mònò	lay.					
eleusine	also					

'People who plant eleusine cut eleusine, [and] those who do not have knives to cut eleusine look for a blacksmith to forge them knives to cut eleusine.' (G-C & W 1982: 18-19)

The explanation for such deployment of the marker **nè** is that one does not convey all elements of a narrative in the same way. In particular, the recall of the elements that make up a narrative varies, and some elements whose recall may not be planned are marked by the focus marker **nè**. In the following fragment the form **nè** is deployed only in the penultimate two clauses:

(94)

Kara	kel	gé	ná	kúlànga,	ná
people	gather	3PL	ASSC	cucumber	ASSC
dègé	kángnyé	lay.			
watermelon	certain:PL	also			

'People gather cucumbers and some watermelons.'

(95)

Kara	go	sèn	gé	go	tègè	
people	REF	know	3PL	REF	weave:VN	
kùyò	hìràgà,		tèy	gé	ná	lay.
mat	sleeping mat		weave	3PL	ASSC	also

'Those who know how to weave mats weave them.'

(96)

Dàgè	go	nè	gàr	gé	gumbú	
3PL	REF	IMPF	build	3PL	basket	
karan-di	go	gùsìré	nè	gàr		
child:PL-3M	REF	palm fibers	IMPF	build		
gé	ná	lay,	ge	lèé	maji	wèrò
3PL	ASSC	also	HUM	eat	gardenia	fruit
lay.						
also						

'Those who weave small baskets with palm fibers weave them. One eats gardenia fruits.' (G-C & W 1981: 18-19)

If one postulates that the function of the marker **nè** is to mark focus on the predicate, then it follows that whether the marker is deployed is not predictable from the discourse context or from the sentential context. Compare the first and second sentences in the following fragment, describing the usual events for the given time. The marker **nè** is deployed in the first sentence but not in the second:

(97)

Gàrwè	nè	è	gé	ná	tèé	nèny
dog:PL	IMPF	go	3PL	ASSC	chase	very much
kolo	ánye		gé	ná	kùlòngò	mànı́
reason	take:FUT		3PL	ASSC	pregnancy	ANAPH
lay.						
also						

'Dogs are copulating a lot in order to become pregnant also.'

(98)

Ge	bìŕ	ná	mbóló	
HUM	weed out	ASSC	granary	
te-di-gè	go	sùgì	lay.	
bottom-GEN.PL-3PL	REF	be full of dirt	also	

'One also pulls the weeds from around the granaries' (G-C & W 1981: 20-21)

(99)

Kara	go	Gèbé	nè	sòrè	kè-gè	lay.
people	REF	Gebe	IMPF	feast:VN	GEN-3PL	also

'People of Gebe organize festivities.' (G-C & W 1981: 24-25)

The aspect of the clause preceded by **nè** is always imperfective:

(100)

Dà	kur	wèlè-ì	mira,	tamá
PREP	time	day-3M	approach	woman
kùlòn-dò	nè	nè-dù	hòmnyá,	
belly-3F	IMPF	make-3F	pain	

'When the day approached, and the woman felt pain in her belly . . .' (G-C & W 1981: 2-3)

(101)

Gìdìrè	kùb	kàlo		ná	kara	nè	
moon	mouth	wind		ASSC	people	IMPF	
yí	gé	tùwà,	è	gé	segré	go	omé
put	3PL	fire	go	3PL	hunt	REF	catch
gùmá.							
rat							

'During the moon of the beginning of winds [December] people light fires in order to catch rats' (G-C & W 1981: 26-27)

(102) Kara nèny nè yàgì gé tùwà kúní
people many IMPF light 3PL fire house
ba wèl gé ná ɗálang
COM sleep 3PL ASSC night
'Many people light fires in homes so that they sleep at night.' (G-C & W 1981: 28-29)

(103) Dà gìdìrè kùb kàlo kùlèn-dì ni,
PREP moon mouth wind inside-3M LOC
hòmnyá dùglò kérgew
illness swelling of testicles swelling of testicles
nè kara nèný, dàì go ná
make people very much 3M REF ASSC
dùglò kérgew ná,
swelling of testicles swelling of testicles ASSC
dà gìdìrè kùb kàlo ná, nè jogíí
PREP moon mouth wind ASSC IMPF suffer
síɗé.
a lot
'During the moon of the beginning of winds, many people suffer from the swelling of testicles. Those who have this illness suffer a lot during this month' (G-C & W 1981: 28-29)

The following scheme for the deployment of the focus marker **nè** with the predicate appears to be valid for the natural texts available: A narrative starts with a non-focused predicate. Then, a predicate is marked as the focus in a new addition to the narrative. The new addition is followed by several other sentences, until another new addition is added. Consider the following fragment with four clauses, all part of one paragraph, all describing habitual, unbounded actions. But only the second clause has the imperfective marker **nè**:

(104) Kara dàgí mànybùlò go wàl-gé tùmò sí
people thresh sesame REF cut-3PL before put
cáaní lay.
ALL also
'People thresh the sesame that was harvested the year before and put it away.'

(105)

Kara	nè	poy	gé	gùjù	lay.
people	IMPF	cut:PL	3PL	millet	also

'People also cut the millet.'

Ter-gé	ná	gùnà	Lèle	lay.
pull:PL-3PL	ASSC	peas	Lele	also

'People harvest the ground peas.'

(106)

Kara	ter-gé	bàrù	dà	càaní	lay.
people	pull-3PL	cotton	PREP	field	also

'People harvest cotton.' (G-C & W 1981: 26-27)

In the following fragment all the clauses have the same time reference and the same aspectual value. Yet the first clause has the marker **nè**, and the remaining five clauses do not:

(107)

Kara	tiraba	go	cèé	gèlèngdí	nè
men	smithing	REF	throw:PL	bracelets	IMPF

nè	gé	ná	tiraba	go	gèlèngdí	lay.
do	3PL	ASSC	smithing	REF	bracelets	also

'The blacksmith makes bracelets.'

(108)

Kara	lè	gé	ná	ùrbòlo	wèrì	lay,
people	eat	3PL	ASSC	'urbolo'	xxx	also

'People eat fruits of urbolo,

ge	pe	kùlo	lay,
HUM	dig	tacca	also

one digs up the tubers of tacca,

ge	pe	màblí	dà	cáaní	lay,
HUM	dig	cochlospermum	PREP	field	also

one digs up the tubers of cochlospermum

ge	lèé	dàndáw	lay.
HUM	eat	eggplant	also

one also eats eggplants.' (G-C & W 1981: 20-21)

Within the same sentence different clauses may be marked by **nè** if they have different subjects. Each predicate is separately marked for focus:

(109) Ná ɗigle ná ɗigle kamda nè mar-wi
ASSC year ASSC year women IMPF die-PL
gé kolo ge nè wàl-wì-gè.
3PL because HUM IMPF cut-PL-3PL
'And so, year after year, women were dying because they were cut' (G-C & W 1981: 2-3)

The focus marker **nè** does not occur in negative clauses, even if the event is unbounded:

(110) Nè máànı́ ba tamá lèé ɓòdu
COP ANAPH COM woman eat monkey
ɗé àlè.
NEG already
'That is why women do not eat monkeys anymore.' (G-C & W 1981: 4-5)

(111) Nè tamá dàgè ná gìrà kolo
COP woman 3PL ASSC dog word
kè-gè ba kara pet nè yagi-gé
GEN-3PL COM people all IMPF plant-3PL
ná kasa ɓey ba dì-gé ná gùdá.
ASSC corn still COM eat-3PL ASSC today
'It is because of the words of a woman and the dog that people have to plant in order to eat today.' (G-C & W 1981: 10-11)

15 Conclusions

There are two means of coding focus in Lele. One is through the copula **nè**, which precedes the focused word, and the other is through fronting and the comment clause marked by the comment marker **ba**. If the argument that is usually marked by a preposition is focused, the preposition occurs before rather than after the focus-marking copula **nè**, giving the structure **nè** Noun. The locative phrase in focus cannot be fronted. The predicate may also be focused through the deployment of the copula **nè**.

16

Topicalization

1 Introduction

This chapter, on topicalization, deals with two issues: how different arguments are marked for being the topic of a clause and how a change of topic is marked. Accordingly, the chapter is organized according to the list of different arguments. The change of topic mechanism is the same for all arguments.

2 Topicalization of a subject

The nominal or pronominal subject (except for the third person) always occurs in clause-initial position, and as such it is a topic of its clause:

(1) gìdìrè téy túgú
moon weave house
'the moon has weaved its house' (about the halo surrounding the full moon)[13]

A new topic in the subject function is marked by the definite marker **ŋ** under the condition that it has been previously mentioned in discourse:

[13] A halo around the moon is believed to be the home of the dead chiefs. Hence a full moon with halo means that a chief has died somewhere.

(2) tamá-ŋ jé tòrò túg ní ná
woman-DEF raise hen home LOC ASSC
tòrò-ŋ tèy karma
hen-DEF peck children
yùg yùg
many (about chickens): Ideophone
'The woman raised a hen at home, and the hen produced many chicks.'

(3) tamá-ŋ jè tè-gè hire
woman-DEF IMPF chase away-3PL often
'The woman often chased them away.'

(4) Dàdù jèn sàm, ɓòdu-ǹg se
3F remain a while monkey-DEF INCEPT
yáa bù-dù ná
tell DAT-3F ASSC
'She remained a while, and the monkey told her:' (G-C & W 1981: 2-3)

The change of topic for subject is realized by inserting a new noun as subject of the clause:

(5) tùwà tóŋ pìnà ná [pause] jè yì dú
sun certain:F one ASSC IMPF pound 3F
kąnya tòrò yó-ró è jè gé ná
thing hen mother-3F go VENT 3PL ASSC
karan-do kolo dé gé kasa-ŋ
children-3F reason eat:FUT 3PL corn-DEF
'One day, when she$_1$ was pounding, the old hen$_2$ came with her$_2$ children to eat the corn.'

Once the subject has been established as the topic, it is not repeated until there is a change of the topic:

(6) ná yà bé kàràn-dò na
ASSC tell DAT children-3F HYP
ngu gol gaw go kun-do pìnà tésí
2PL see well REF eye-3F one break
ɗé-ŋ na dà ngù kasa ná
already-DEF HYP eat:IMP 2PL corn ASSC
já koloŋ
side DEM:R
'So she said to her children: you see well that she is blind in one eye, so go and peck at that side [that she does not see]'

The change of topic is again marked by the deployment of the full noun phrase as subject, as shown in the following sentences in sequence:

(7) tamá-ŋ ɗeŋlí ná jè wèy
woman-DEF understand ASSC IMPF turn
ín-dí-gè pílá pílá
ASSC-GEN-3PL at the same time
'The woman understood, and she was turning around [the mortar] at the same time.'

The subject of the verb of saying is not a new topic, because such clauses represent backgrounded information. Hence in the following sentence **tòrò yó-ró** is not followed by the definite marker:

(8) tòrò yó-ró yà bé-gé na
hen mother-3F tell DAT-3PL ASSC
tamá-ŋ nò go sìyą́ bùg ìrà
woman-DEF make REF bad by nature go:IMP
nga dà gùbù cà-y ni
1PL.INCL PREP trash area head-3M LOC
'The old hen told them: this woman is by nature nasty. Let us go on top of the trash pile.'

A noun that is marked for contrastive focus may also be a new topic:

(9) time nè gònì nę̀y bé kolo
hunger make hyena very much DAT reason
dìgrì dú ìsą́n ɗé
kill 3F nothing NEG
'Hyena is very hungry because it did not kill anything.'

(10) dàdù tu-ŋ lèé kàsùma ɓàl-dù
3F goat-DEF eat feed satisfy-3F
'As for Goat, it ate feed to its satisfaction.'

3 Topicalization of a pronominal subject

Topicalization of a pronominal subject is marked by the independent pronoun occurring before the verb. The verb must still have a subject pronoun suffixed or prefixed, as the case may be:

(11)	kolo	dàdù	go	tùmò	dàdù	ba
	because	3F	REF	first	3F	COM
	bor-iy	gèylè				
	save-3M	health				

'Because the first one, it was she who saved his life.'

The independent pronouns may be used with all persons. The topicalization of the pronominal subject occurs in conversations, when the speaker selects a given participant or person mentioned earlier, from the set of potential participants:

(12)	dàŋ	ŋ	è	jè	mbóyrò
	1SG	1SG	go	VENT	evening

'me, I came in the evening'

Cf.:

(13)	ŋ	è	jè	mbóyrò
	1SG	go	VENT	evening

'I came in the evening'

(14)	dàì	kil-dí	gúnà	dà	ɓón-ú-m
	3M	buy-3M	peanuts	PREP	brother-EP-2SG
	ni				
	LOC				

'him, he bought peanuts from your brother'

4 Topicalization of an object

The object can be topicalized in several ways. One way is through position before the verb. If the object is human, the verb has the resumptive object pronoun:

(15)	è	gé	cáaní	bayndí-ŋ	kalo	se
	go	3PL	bush	man-DEF	snake	INCEPT
	yír-íy					
	bite-3M					

'When they went into the bush, a snake bit the man.'

The above clause was, however, preferred by other speakers with the associative preposition **ná** preceding the second clause:

(16) è gé cáanì ná bayndí-ŋ kalo se
go 3PL bush ASSC man-DEF snake INCEPT
yír-íy
bite-3M
'they went into the bush, and the man was bitten by a snake'

Note that in both variants the topicalized object is followed by the definite marker.

Given the frequent claim about the role of passive, including that an unspecified human subject is a means of topicalization of the object, one should consider whether there is a relationship between the unspecified human subject and topicalization of the object in Lele. In clauses with an unspecified human subject the object occupies the position following the verb. The reason why the unspecified human subject **ge** is used to code just this: an unknown agent:

(17) gé è jè ná gùyé tumadu go
HUM go VENT ASSC news death REF
làmndá yé-y kò-rò
elephant mother-3M GEN-3F
'The news of the death of the mother of elephant was brought in.'

(18) dàì haŋ ba na gé bé-y
3M DEM COM HYP HUM give-3M
kùrmbàlò tamą̀-y ba ná-y wèl ná
chief wife-3M COM HYP-3M sleep ASSC
un-do hà kur na wèl na ge
ASSC-3F till place HYP day HYP HUM
dìgr-ìy ná kolo tumadu-y ná ɗárí-nìŋ
kill-3M COM reason death-3M ASSC shock-1SG
ɗè
NEG
'The first one said that if he were given the chief's wife to sleep with till the daybreak, he could be killed, because death did not worry him.'

It appears that the discourse function, if any, of the unspecified human subject is to create the background information for some other information that is going to come. The following sentences, which continue the preceding example, provide the evidence for this hypothesis:

(19) ge yàá bé kùrmbàlò
HUM tell DAT chief
'The chief was informed.'

(20) ge tìgrì-ge sò
HUM kill:PL-3PL two
'Two were killed.'

More evidence for the function of **ge** as marking subjects in the background information is provided by the fact that it can occur as the subject marker in a relative clause modifying the subject in contrastive focus:

(21) dày go sùbù ge dígrè-y è wèl
3M REF three HUM kill:FUT-3M go sleep
ná kùrmbàlò tamą́-y
ASSC chief wife-3M
'The third one, who was going to be killed, went to sleep with the chief's wife.'

5 Conclusions

The nominal subject is the topic of its clause. The change of subject as topic is marked by the introduction of a new nominal subject. The object as topic is marked by fronting and by the definite marker **ŋ**. When a pronominal argument is the topic, it is marked by the independent pronouns, plus an appropriate subject or object pronoun, as the case may be. The unspecified human subject construction pronoun **ge** is not a means of the topicalization of the subject. It codes the unspecified human subject, often deployed in the background information, when it is really not important who the subject is.

17

Backgrounding

1 Introduction

The term *backgrounding* refers to the coding of a portion of an utterance as the background to some other information. Since such a function is not often described as a grammatical category, it is necessary to argue for its existence by the presentation of its formal and functional characteristics.

2 Formal properties of backgrounding

The backgrounded material may consist of a phrase or a clause. The grammatical system of Lele contains formal means of coding the backgrounded information. The formal means is the associative preposition **ná** at the end of the backgrounded phrase or clause. The backgrounded material may also be set off by just a pause. The associative preposition belongs to the backgrounded phrase or clause, as shown by the fact that it must be followed by a pause.

3 Specific functions of backgrounded material

3.1 Adverbial phrase of time and place

The backgrounded information can be an adverbial phrase coding time or place. Sentences of this type provide the necessary evidence that the associative marker is not a clausal or phrasal conjunction but, as postulated, the marker of the backgrounded information:

(1) tùwà tóŋ pìnà ná [pause] jè yì dú
sun certain:F one ASSC IMPF pound 3F
ką̀nya tòrò yó-ró è jè gé ná
thing hen mother-3F go VENT 3PL ASSC
karan-do kolo dé gé kasa-ŋ
children-3F reason eat:FUT 3PL corn-DEF
'One day, when she$_1$ was pounding, the old hen$_2$ came with her children to eat the corn.'

Here is an example of backgrounded information marked by a pause:

(2) ná ɗigle tóŋ pìnà làmndá yé-y
ASSC year certain:F one elephant mother-3M
ne hòmnyá go ma
COP sick REF die
'One year, the mother of elephant was sick, close to her death.'

The fundamental condition for the backgrounding is for the backgrounded information to be non-specific, indefinite:

(3) wáŋgulú tóŋ pìnà ná kumno e
morning certain:F one ASSC cloud raise
mìl, mìl, míl
thick, dark
'one morning there were thick clouds'

It is enough to omit the indefinite marker, and the associative marker may not be used:

(4) wáŋgulú *ná kumno se mìl, mìl, míl
morning ASSC cloud raise thick, dark
'that morning there were thick clouds'

Example of backgrounded information involving an adverb of place:

(5) dà túgú tóŋ ni ná [pause]
PREP village certain:F LOC ASSC
gáw kóŋ ná tamą́-y t òb gé
hunter certain:M ASSC wife-3M like 3PL
kusi-gè néỳ
body-3PL very much
'In a village a certain hunter sorcerer and wife loved each other very much.'

Note that the pause occurs in the above example only after the backgrounded portion. It does not occur after the second deployment of the preposition **ná** when it is a part of the associative phrase.

The backgrounded information may consist of a clause. Some clausal backgrounds also determine the time of the event:

(6)

kur	go	gúnyé	è	ná	kàyo	tu-ŋ
time	REF	spider	go	ASSC	squirrel	home-DEF

ni	ná	se	yàá	bé	tamą́-y
LOC	ASSC	INCEPT	tell	DAT	wife-3M

na	sú	kama	go	lèr	wá	tùwà
HYP	put:IMP	water	REF	hot	very	fire

ni
LOC

'When Spider came home with him, he told his wife to put some water on the fire.'

(7)

tùmò	go	kara	índ'wé	ɗeŋlí	gé
once	REF	people	human:PL	understand	3PL

kùb	ką̀nya	ame	kè-gè	ná	tamá
language	thing	domestic	GEN-3PL	ASSC	woman

tóŋ	ɗeŋlí	kùb	kòrà	kè-gè
certain	understand	language	chickens	GEN-3PL

'At one time, when humankind understood the language of domestic animals, a certain woman understood the language of chickens.'

3.2 Backgrounded information introducing an argument

The backgrounded information may also serve as a means to introduce an argument of the sentence. In the following example the backgrounded information introduces the subject:

(8)

tamá-ŋ	jé	tòrò	túg	ní
woman-DEF	raise	hen	home	LOC

ná	tòrò-ŋ	tèy	karma	yùg yùg
ASSC	hen-DEF	peck	children	many:Ideophone

'The woman raised a hen at home, and the hen produced many chicks'[14]

[14] **yùg yùg** 'ideophone, many young ones' only about uncountable but individualized entities, e.g., chicklings, ducklings, guineafowl. Cannot be used for pigs, sheep, cows, men. The use of **yùg yùg** with respect to human offspring is considered insulting.

The preceding example is ungrammatical if the associative marker **ná** is omitted. The reason for the ungrammaticality is that the two clauses without the associative marker could be interpreted as sequential events or events coding a cause-and-effect relationship, neither of which is the intended meaning:

(9)	*tamá-ŋ	jé	tòrò	túg	ní
	woman-DEF	raise	hen	home	LOC
	tòrò-ŋ	tèy	karma	yùg yùg	
	hen-DEF	peck	children	many:Ideophone	

for 'The woman raised a hen at home, and the hen produced many chicks'

In the following example the backgrounded information constitutes the topic of the sentence and the object of the ensuing clause:

(10)	kaŋya	pet	go	jè	kàl	túg
	thing	all	REF	IMPF	pass	compound
	ni	ná [pause]	jè	yàá	kwánì	bé
	LOC	ASSC	IMPF	tell	outside	DAT
	karan-do	kamda				
	friends-3F	women				

'Everything that was going on at home she would tell to her women friends'

3.3 Backgrounding for counterexpectation

The backgrounded information does not have to have an argument or adjunct relation to the clause that follows it. But it must have some logical relation. One of the logical relationships is counterexpectation. Thus in the following sentence the husband heard what his wife was doing (background) but did not say anything:

(11)	kudo-ró-ŋ	jè	ɗeŋlí	kolo	ką́nyé
	husband-3F-DEF	IMPF	hear	word	certain:PL
	kwáni ná [pause]	yàá	ísaŋ	ɗé	
	outside ASSC	tell	nothing	NEG	

'Despite the fact that husband heard certain things outside, he did not say anything.'

3.4 Backgrounding for cause-and-effect relationship

The backgrounded information may provide the necessary justification, premise, or cause for ensuing events. Here are several examples in which the backgrounded information provides the reason for the ensuing clauses:

(12)

kàsìyà	nè	tamá-ŋ	néy	ná	
shame	make	woman-DEF	very much	ASSC	
se	sar-wí	kąya	kò-rò	òdì	è
INCEPT	attach-PL	thing	GEN-3F	leave	go
túgú	ka-ro				
home	parents-3F				

'Since the woman was very much ashamed, she tied up her stuff, left, and went to her parents.'

(13)

yé	dú-ngù		posí-ŋ	ɗe	
mother	GEN:PL-2PL		insult-1SG	THEN	
ná	ŋ	jè	lée-dú	ná	kasa
ASSC	1SG	IMPF	eat:FUT-3F	ASSC	corn
go	ŋ	yì	háŋ		
ASSC	1SG	pound	DEM:P		

'Your mother has insulted me; therefore I am going to eat her with this corn I pounded.'

(14)

me	ɓàl	go	wesé	cà-nìŋ	ɗé
2F	able	REF	hide:VN	head-1SG	NEG
ná	[pause]	ìrá	túgú	ka-re	
ASSC		go:IMP	home	parents-2F	
kè-gè					
GEN-3PL					

'You cannot cover up for me, so go to your parents.'

(15)

tu-ŋ	gol	go	gonì	kún-do	jèn	
goat-DEF	see	REF	hyena	eye-3F	remain	
téŋ	ná	se	ày	dú	lúmá	na
different	ASSC	INCEPT	take	3F	trick	HYP

'Goat noticed that Hyena had different intentions and tried the following trick'

In the following sentence the backgrounded information contains the premise for the ensuing clause:

(16) ge se ɗe gʉ́yé ba dày gʉ́yé
HUM INCEPT leave spider COM 3M spider
se yàá bè kàyo na máàní
INCEPT say DAT squirrel HYP like that
na à jè na írà tùu-ŋ
HYP go:IMP VENT HYP go:IMP home-DEF
ni na-y néè-y kùryò
LOC HYP-3M make:FUT-3M stranger
'Spider was left alone. Spider said to Squirrel: if this is like that, he should come and they will go to his [Spider's] home, and he will make him a stranger [i.e., he will make him welcome]'

(17) tamá-ŋ ɗeŋlí ná jè wèy
woman-DEF understand ASSC IMPF turn
ín-dí-gè pílá pílá
ASSC-GEN-3PL at the same time
'The woman understood, and she was turning around [the mortar] at the same time.'

The omission of the associative marker **ná** renders the sentence ungrammatical:

(18) *tamá-ŋ ɗeŋlí jè wèy
woman-DEF understand IMPF turn
ín-dí-gè pílá pílá
ASSC-GEN-3PL at the same time
for 'The woman understood, and she was turning around [the mortar] at the same time.'

3.5 Setting the circumstances for the main clause

The backgrounded information may also include the circumstances necessary for the interpretation of the second clause:

(19) gònì dà kìrbé kò-rò ni ná
hyena PREP thought GEN-3F LOC ASSC
gèy go léè tu-ŋ ɓey ba
want REF eat:FUT goat-DEF before COM
sée kama-ŋ
drink:FUT water-DEF
'Hyena in its thoughts wanted to devour Goat before drinking water.'

If the associative is deleted, the truth value of the sentence does not change, but the sentence has a different pragmatic function, viz., instead of establishing the information as a background, it is presented as in a straightforward indicative sentence:

(20) gònì dà kìrbé kò-rò ni gèy
hyena PREP thought GEN-3F LOC want
go léè tu-ŋ . . .
REF eat goat-DEF
'Hyena in its thoughts wanted to devour Goat'

(21) wèlè go jè yì kąnya ná tòrò
day REL IMPF pound thing ASSC hen
yó-ró-ŋ dèr kàràn-dò
mother-3F-DEF carry children-3F
è ná tìnɗí tó-ró ni jè dì
go ASSC mortar bottom-3F LOC IMPF peck
gé kasa.
3PL corn
'Each time she$_1$ was pounding, the old hen$_2$ carried her chicks under the mortar and they pecked corn.

The omission of the associative marker **ná** produces a grammatical sentence, but the subjects of the first and the second clause are coreferential! It is the hen that pounds corn and brings her children to the mortar:

(22) wèlè go jè yì kąnya tòrò
day REF IMPF pound thing hen
yó-ró-ŋ dèr kàràn-dò è ná
mother-3F-DEF carry children-3F go ASSC
tìnɗí to-ro ni jè dì-gé kasa
mortar bottom-3F LOC IMPF peck-3PL corn
'Each time she$_1$ was pounding, the old hen$_1$ carried her children under the mortar and they pecked corn.

The associative marker may occur at the beginning of a sentence. The background in such cases may be implied, as the knowledge shared by a participant, and not necessarily spelled out in the preceding discourse:

(23) ná yàá bé kàràn-dò na ngu gol
ASSC tell DAT children-3F HYP 2PL see
gaw go kun-do pìnà tésí ɗé-ŋ
well REF eye-3F one break already-DEF
ná da ngù kasa ná já koloŋ
ASSC eat:IMP 2PL corn ASSC side DEM:R
'So she said to her children: you see well that she is blind in one eye, so go and peck at the other side [that she does not see]'

The backgrounded information may also constitute a condition for the second clause. Conditional sentences are described later in the present work, so here is just an example:

(24)	na	me	léè		yé	dí-nì
	HYP	2F	eat:FUT		mother	GEN:PL-1PL.EXCL
	ná	me	jè	má		lay
	ASSC	2F	IMPF	die:FUT		also

'If you eat our mother, you will also die.'

4 Conclusions

The associative marker **ná** deployed after a phrase or a clause marks the preceding element as background necessary for the interpretation of the clause following it. The nature of the specific semantic relationship between the backgrounded material and the material following it is not specified. The backgrounding simply instructs the hearer to interpret the clause in connection with its preceding background. The backgrounded element may be a time or place adverb, or a clause providing the reason, justification, logical premise, or condition for the following clause.

18

Paratactic and Conjoined Clauses

1 Introduction

The present chapter describes four types of connections between clauses forming a complex sentence. The first type comprises paratactic constructions, where clauses occur in a sequence without any conjunction between them. These clauses share the same subject, whether repeated or not. The second type comprises clauses conjoined by the comment clause marker **ba**. The third type comprises clauses conjoined by the counter-expectation conjunction **àlá**. And the fourth type comprises clauses conjoined by conjunction **ɗéú** or **lá**. For each type I provide argumentation why it should be considered a type of complex sentence, and I describe its form and function.

2 Paratactic constructions

Paratactic constructions are characterized by several clauses without any conjunction between them. Paratactic constructions represent the unmarked means of complex sentence construction. Subjects in paratactic constructions must be the same. The reason paratactic clauses are considered part of a complex sentence is that the third-person singular subject does not usually occur in the second and subsequent clauses of the construction. Separate sentences within a discourse may have different subjects, and their subjects are always overtly marked. If they have identical objects, objects may also be overtly coded. Both of these cases are illustrated in the following fragment consisting of two sentences:

(1) tòn-ìy na pa bé-y kasire
ask-3M HYP dig:IMP DAT-3M medicine
bayndí-ŋ na-y pe kasiré-ŋ ɗé
man-DEF HYP-3M dig medicine-DEF NEG
'He$_1$ told him$_2$ to dig medicine for him$_1$, but the man$_2$ refused.'

Paratactic constructions represent a sequence of events, usually in the order in which they occurred in reality. Clauses in paratactic constructions have the same subject. The paratactic constructions do not, however, explicitly code the temporal sequence of events or the causal dependency of events. That function is coded by another construction. In natural discourse data the subject in paratactic construction is coded only once, with the first verb:

(2) ng hím tìbrè go kùyéè ni bòy
1SG find ashes REF hearth LOC throw
cáaní
ALL
'I gather ashes from the hearth and throw them away' (G-C & W 1981: 14-15)

(3) kùrmbàlò tamą́-y àn ná wáyngulú
chief wife-3M leave ASSC morning
àg-iy saar-iy dà kàrgà-rò ni gìr
take-3M attach-3M PREP back-3F LOC run
ná ín-dì hą́ è gé ná
ASSC ASSC-3M till (Ar.) go 3PL ASSC
dà kama kìb-ìy ni
PREP river edge-3M LOC
'The chief's wife left in the morning, took the fellow, attached him to her back, ran with him till they arrived at a bank of the river.'

(4) ɗe ná nòju-ro kínyé se
THEN ASSC relative-3F COLL INCEPT
óm gé tu go bàl nè
catch 3PL goat REF geld COP
òb ná kara
invite for work ASSC people
'Then, her relatives caught a large gelded goat and used it to invite people for the purpose of common work:'

Clauses in paratactic constructions must have the same polarity values. Thus one cannot have the first clause in the affirmative and the second clause in the negative:

(5)

ŋ	hàb	tèndèlú	wènỳ-ná	wò
1SG	find	turning stick	prepare-ASSC	mush
*ɗé				
NEG				

'I found a turning stick [and] prepared mush'

Different tenses in the two clauses require the overt coding of the subject of the second clause. The two clauses are still paratactic, as evidenced by the fact that the object of the first clause is coded as an instrument of the second clause with the associative marker **ná**:

(6)

ŋ	hàb	tèndèlú	ŋ	wéènyè-ná
1SG	find	turning stick	1SG	prepare:FUT-ASSC
wò				
mush				

'I found a turning stick [and] will use it to prepare mush'

Paratactic constructions can be used in the imperative modality, with both verbs being in the imperative. Such constructions do not imply that the purpose was actually accomplished:

(7)

ìrà	làá	sìí
go:IMP	eat:IMP	meat

'go eat meat!'

3 Coding temporal and causal sequences

The temporal sequence of events is coded by the sequence **ɗe ná**. The two forms are pronounced without any pause between them. One reason I analyze them as a sequence of two morphemes rather than one is that the second component is identical with the associative marker **ná**. The second, and more important, reason is that the form **ɗe** can be separated from **ná** by the definite marker **ŋ**. The origin of the form **ɗe** is not obvious. Most likely it is derived from the verb **ɗe** 'leave, let go'. At least one other grammatical marker indicating a relationship between clauses is derived from a verb (**se** inceptive, from the verb **se** 'get up'). In addition to the phonological identity of the temporal **ɗe** and the verb **ɗe** 'leave, let go', there exists also independent semantic evidence. The verb **ɗe** combined with the word **kusu** 'body' followed by appropriate pronouns has acquired the temporal function 'after':

(8) Gi   ɗe   kusu-m, . . .
2M   leave   body-2M
'Afterwards, you . . .', lit. 'you leave your body' (G-C & W 1981: 16-17)

The sequence **ɗe ná** is glossed as 'THEN ASSC'. There are two related functions of **ɗe ná**. One is to indicate temporal and the other cause-and-effect relationships between two events. The verb in the clause following **ɗe ná** may be in the past or future tense form, depending on whether the events to be described are in the past or the future:

(9) è   gé   cáaní   bayndí-ŋ   kalo   se
go   3PL   bush   man-DEF   snake   INCEPT
yír-íy   ɗe   ná   bayndí   go   segre
bite-3M   THEN   ASSC   man   REF   hunter
è   jè   ná   teren-di   màní
go   VENT   ASSC   daughter-3M   there
'When they went into the bush, a snake bit the man. Then came a hunter with his daughter to the place.'

The form **ɗe ná** may occur at the beginning of the sentence, indicating the temporal sequence of the events:

(10) tòn-ìy   na   pa   bé-y   kasire
ask-3M   HYP   dig:IMP   DAT-3M   medicine
bayndí-ŋ   na-y   pe   kasire-ŋ   ɗé
man-DEF   HYP-3M   dig   medicine-DEF   NEG
'He told him to dig medicine for him, but the man refused.'

(11) ɗe   ná   bayndí-ŋ   teren-di   se
THEN   ASSÇ   man-DEF   daughter-3M   INCEPT
yàá   na   pa   bé-y   kasire-ŋ
tell   HYP   dig:IMP   DAT-3M   medicine-DEF
'Then the hunter's daughter told her father to dig up the medicine for him.'

(12) pe   bé-y   kasire-ŋ   ɗe   ná
dig   DAT-3M   medicine-DEF   THEN   ASSC
bayndí-ŋ   se   hab   gèylè
man-DEF   INCEPT   find   health
'When he had dug up the medicine, then the man recovered his health.'

(13) ná ɗigle tóŋ pìnà làmndá yé-y
ASSC year certain:F one elephant mother-3M
ne hòmnyá go ma
COP sick REF die
'One year, the mother of elephant was sick, close to her death.'

(14) ɗe ná nòju-ro kínyé se
THEN ASSC relative-3F COLL INCEPT
óm gé tu go bàl
catch 3PL goat REF geld
'Then, her relatives caught a large gelded goat . . . '

If the events are hypothetical, the temporal **ɗe ná** may be followed by a clause with hypothetical modality. The verb in the hypothetical clause is in the future tense:

(15) bayndí go na ay tu káŋ na
person REF HYP take goat DEM HYP
lèé ná làmndá yé-y na ma
eat ASSC elephant mother-3M HYP die
ɗe ná na ge ágè-y
THEN ASSC HYP HUM take:FUT-3M
ímè-y ná làmndá yé-y
bury:FUT-3M ASSC elephant mother-3M
'If anybody takes this goat and eats it, and if the mother of elephant dies, then they will bury him together with the mother of elephant'

The evidence that the form **ɗe ná** is not a clausal conjunction is provided by the fact that it may precede an adverbial expression. The clause that follows the adverbial expression may again be preceded by the form **ɗe ná**, giving the structure: Clause **ɗe ná** Adverb **ɗe ná** Clause:

(16) kur go gų́yé ay tu lèé ɗe
time REF spider take goat eat THEN
ná ne wèlè kab ɗe ná làmndá
ASSC COP day later then ASSC elephant
yé-y se ma
mother-3M INCEPT die
'After Spider took the goat and ate it, a few days later the mother of elephant died.'

The form **ɗe ná** also indicates a cause-and-effect relationship between the clause and a logical conclusion from the premise stated in the preceding clause:

(17)

yé	dú-ngù		posí-ŋ	ɗe	
mother	GEN:PL-2PL		insult-1SG	THEN	
ná	ŋ	jè	lée-dú	ná	kasa
ASSC	1SG	IMPF	eat:FUT-3F	ASSC	corn
go	ŋ	yì	háŋ		
ASSC	1SG	pound	DEM:P		

'Your mother has insulted me; therefore I am going to eat her with this corn I pounded.'

(18)

ngu	gol	gaw	go	kun-do	pìnà	tésí
2PL	see	well	REF	eye-3F	one	break
ɗé-ŋ	ná	da		ngù	kasa	ná
THEN-DEF	ASSC	eat:IMP		2PL	corn	ASSC
já	koloŋ					
side	DEM:R					

'you see well that she is blind in one eye, so go and peck at the other side'

4 Adverb lay 'also' and clausal conjunctions

The adverb **lay** 'also' occurs at the end of a clause. If there is a sequence of clauses, the adverb may occur at the end of every clause in the sequence. The functional domain of this adverb is the coding of propositional relations. Its function is to indicate that a proposition X is true at the same time or under the same conditions as another proposition is true:

(19)

na	me		léè	yé	dí-nì
HYP	2F		eat:FUT	mother	GEN:PL-1PL.EXCL
ná	me	jè	má	lay	
ASSC	2F	IMPF	die:FUT	also	

'If you eat our mother, you will also die.'

This adverb codes the speaker's point of view in the evaluation of the relationship between propositions, as opposed to a participant's point of view.

(20)

kàw	gé	gàg	tùwà	dùgì-gè	gílalé
walk	3PL	till	sun	drown-3PL	tiredness
pínyà	nè-gè				
also	make-3PL				

'They walked till the sun had drowned them and tiredness overwhelmed them.'

(21) kìb di-gè hay lay
mouth GEN:PL-3PL dry also
'their mouths are also dry', 'they are also thirsty'

From the adverb coding the truth of a proposition in the same conditions in which another proposition holds, there is but one step to the function of the clausal coordinated conjunction:

(22) kur koloŋ ba dày gų́yé se yàá
time DEM:R COM 3M spider INCEPT say
bé-gè na na-y jè nè hòmyá
DAT-3PL HYP HYP-3M IMPF make sick
go ma nò go tég lay na
REF die COP REF long time also HYP
bé-y gé na-y lèé
give-3M 3PL HYP-3M eat
'At that time Spider said that since he was sick for a long time, close to dying, they should give [it] to him to eat.'

(23) Kara kángnyé yà gé na:
people INDEF:PL say 3PL HYP
"Gìdìrè ma ìrà ná kìrè kíndi."
moon die:IMP go:IMP ASSC way truly
'Some people said: moon should die and be gone forever.'

Kara kángnyé yà bè-ì na :
people INDEF:PL say DAT-3M HYP
Kara índùwé na ma gé ná
people human:PL HYP die 3PL ASSC
ìrà gé ná kìrè kíndí-gè lay."
go:IMP 3PL ASSC road truly-3PL also
'Some people also said that humans should die and be gone forever'

(24) ìrà-ngà dà kama dùrè-y ni
go:IMP-1DU.INCL PREP water inside-3M LOC
ba nga séè dày go
COM 1DU.INCL drink:FUT 3M REF
ɗínglé lay me ágè ísì go bòré
clear also 2F take:FUT bone REF white
koloŋ
there
'Let us go inside this water; we will drink the one that is clear, and you will take the white bone there'

The adverb **lay** can occur after the negative marker **ɗé**. Thus the property of **lay** differs significantly from 'also' in English in that one proposition may be negative and the other affirmative:

(25)

gí	àn	kwáni	ná	kúmno	kam-di
2M	leave	outside	ASSC	God	water-3M

háŋ	ɗé	lay	tèmle	màyfò-y	dà
DEM	NEG	also	corn	hair-3M	PREP

mbùlúm	ni	háŋ	gà
chin	LOC	DEM:P	Q

'If you did not leave in this rain, is that not the hair of corn on your chin?'

(26)

Nè	gìdìrè	go	gùyé	màní
COP	moon	REF	work	ANAPH

nèny	síɗé.	Bayndí	hab	kìrè	go
very much	very much	man	find	way	REF

jènè	ɗìmsè	ɗé	lay.
remain	rest:VN	NEG	also

'During this month there is a lot of work. Nobody can find time to rest.' (G-C & W 1981: 28-29)

The function of the marker **lay** partially overlaps with the function of the coordinated conjunctions in Romance, Germanic, and Slavic languages:

(27)

dòb	gé	kùní	kùlè-ndì	ni	ná
enter	3PL	house	interior-3M	LOC	ASSC

'They entered the house and'

hàb	gé	tèmlè	wén	bùgú	lay
find	3PL	corn	fill	sack	also

'they found corn filling the sack'

gàrbá	póì	kúsíge	kè-y
shoes	Poi	Kusige	GEN-3M

'and the shoes of Poi Kusige'

ná	kama	njòbnjòb	lay
ASSC	water	dripping	also

'with water dripping'

The adverb **lay** is deployed with each proposition that is involved in the relationship of holding the truth at the same time:

(28)

bàyndí-ŋ	jè	è	sègré	ná	tìgrí
man-DEF	IMPF	go	hunt	ASSC	kill:PL:VN

kàrgé	sò	ɗéŋ	sùbù	kura	kį̀nyé
wild animals	two	or	three	rabbit	COLL

bísí	kį̀nyé	nasú	bísí	kį̀nyé	ná [pause]
antelope	COLL	gnu	antelope	COLL	ASSC

jè	è	jè	kèsì	jáy	bé	tamá
IMPF	go	VENT	share	part	DAT	wife

túg	ni	lay	jay	kóŋ
compound	LOC	also	part	certain:M

jè	ą́y	ná	kasa	lay	gùnà	lay
IMPF	take	ASSC	corn	also	peanuts	also

'Each time the man went for a hunt, he killed two or three wild animals, rabbits, small antelopes, gnu antelopes; he shared some with his wife at home, and some he bartered for corn and peanuts.'

(29)

kàjé	kè-y	go
throwing knife:PL	GEN-3M	REF

bòy	cáaní-ŋ	hàb	hábe[15]	ɗé	tùm
throw	ALL-DEF	find	find:FUT	NEG	together

lay	me	pyą	è	jè	ná	ɗé
also	what	small	go	VENT	ASSC	NEG

tùm	lay	bìsa	pínà	pį́ą
together	also	dead	game	one small

kàb-íy	ni	ɗé	tùm	lay
hand-3M	LOC	NEG	together	also

'his throwing knives that he had thrown in the bush he did not find; he didn't bring even a small thing, not even one animal killed, there was nothing in his hands'

5 Coding the unexpected cause-and-effect relationship between propositions

The form **ba**, which is glossed as COM for comment clause marker, indicates that the clause following it represents the non-predictable consequence of what preceded it. Since the consequence is not an automatic result of the events in the preceding clause, there is a need for overt coding. This function of the morpheme **ba** is therefore similar to its function as the comment

[15] I analyze the expression **hàb hábè** as a cognate object construction. I recorded it, however, with a high-low tone pattern, which corresponds to the future rather than to the verbal noun form.

marker after an element in focus. One cannot predict from the focus information what the comment is about.

One of the characteristics of the unpredictable effect clause is that its subject is different from that of the preceding clause:

(30) Nè máàní ba láràdí dà kìrè
COP ANAPH COM chameleon PREP road
ni ɓey ba gúló ile kùlúr kùlúr
LOC still COM lizard cry kulur kulur
ba kara se yà-gé na
COM people INCEPT say-3PL HYP
pùrá-ngú gúló àlè.
release:IMP-2PL lizard already
'The chameleon, however, was still on the road, and the lizard cried, kulur kulur. And the people said: release the lizard.' (G-C & W 1981: 8-9)

(31) na-y áyn na-y lèé ge yàá ɗé
HYP-3M take HYP-3M eat HUM say THEN
na bayndí go na lèé tu na
HYP person REF HYP eat goat HYP
ge ímè-y ná làmndá yé-y
HUM bury:FUT ASSC elephant mother-3M
ba na-y nè gìr
COM HYP-3M COP run
'He took the goat and ate it, and it was said that if a person eats the goat, he will be buried together with the mother of elephant, and that is why he ran.'

A different subject, is not, however, a required condition for the effect clause. In the following examples the subjects of the cause-and-effect clauses are the same, but in each case the effect is unexpected:

(32) yú cà-rè dà kama te-y
put:IMP head-2M PREP water bottom-3M
ní ba me ágè ísí-ŋ
LOC COM 2F take:FUT bone-DEF
'put your head at the bottom of the water and you will get the bone'

(33) yàá bú-dú na ŋ án kwánì
tell DAT-3F HYP 1SG leave outside
ba ŋ jìb cà-nìŋ ná kòyè ba
COM 1SG bump head-1SG ASSC thief COM
ŋ dìgr-ìy
1SG kill-3M
'He told her: leaving the house I bumped against a thief and killed him.'

(34) ge yàá bé-ŋ na kìb-rè hamli
HUM tell DAT-1SG HYP mouth-2F light
nę́y ba ŋ gìsì-mè gùdá káŋ
very much COM 1SG test-2F today DEM
'I was told that you do not keep secrets, so I have tested you today.'

The comment marker **ba** together with clause-final marker **ɓéy** 'still, yet' is also deployed in temporal sentences of the type 'do X before Y':

(35) à jè gulá kùbàrò go bòy
go:IMP VENT look:IMP blood REF pour
dà kúsìnyoŋ ba ŋ sáde cáaní
PREP ground COM 1SG clean:FUT ALL
ɓéy
still/yet
'Come and see the blood spread on the ground before I clean it.'

Without the clause-final marker **ɓéy**, the sentence has a quite different meaning:

(36) à jè gulá kùbàrò go bòy
go:IMP VENT look:IMP blood REF pour
dà kúsìnyoŋ ba ŋ sáde cáaní
PREP ground COM 1SG clean:FUT ALL
'come and see the blood [that was] spread on the ground and then I will clean it'

(37) ge se ɗe gų́yé ba dày gų́yé
HUM INCEPT leave spider COM 3M spider
se yàá bé kàyo
INCEPT say DAT squirrel
'They left Spider [in peace], and Spider told Squirrel . . .'

(38) dày háŋ ba na ge bé-y
3M DEM COM HYP HUM give-3M
kùrmbàlò tamą́-y ba na-y wèl ná
chief wife-3M COM HYP-3M sleep ASSC
undo hà kur na wèl na
3F till place HYP day HYP
ge dìgr-ìy ná kolo tumadu-y ná
HUM kill-3M ASSC reason death-3M ASSC
ɗárí-nìŋ ɗè
shock-3M NEG
'The first one said that if he were given the chief's wife to sleep with the daybreak, then he could be killed, because death did not worry him.'

The marker **ba** cannot be omitted from the string **dày h-aŋ ba na ge bé-y** 'he said that if they give'. The subject of the second clause is different from the subject of the next clause, hence the presence of the marker. In the next sentence, the subject of the first clause is the same as the subject of the next clause, and the marker **ba** cannot be inserted between the two clauses: One cannot have the string ***dàì k-óŋ ba na-y kálè:**

(39) dày kóŋ na-y kálè jénè
3M INDEF HYP-3M climb:FUT sit:FUT
dà jaŋla kùrmbàlò ke-y ni na-y
PREP bench chief GEN-3M LOC HYP-3M
bórè sàríyà na ge dìgr-ìy na
cut judgment HYP HUM kill-3M HYP
ùs-ìy ɗè
concern-3M NEG
'The other said that if he could climb on the chief's bench and pronounce judgments, they could kill him, he did not care.'

The two markers **ba** cannot be omitted from the following sentence, because in each of the clauses with **ba** the subject is different from that in the immediately preceding clause:

(40)

kàyo	se	yàá	na	na-y	sìnà
squirrel	INCEPT	say	HYP	HYP-3M	know

máànì́	na-y	ɗe	gų́yé	na	ge
ANAPH	HYP-3M	leave	spider	HYP	HUM

ímè-y	ná	làmndá	yè-y	ɗé
bury-3M	ASSC	elephant	mother-3M	NEG

ba	na-y	bòr	gúnyé	geìl-y	ba
COM	COP-3M	save	spider	health-3M	COM

gų́yé	na	è	jè	tòb	go	dígrè-y	gà
spider	HYP	go	VENT	want	REF	kill-3M	Q

'Squirrel said that had he known that, he would have left Spider to be buried together with the mother of elephant. Here he saved Spider, and Spider wants to kill him.'

The marker **ba** by itself indicates a change of subject. The evidence for this is provided by the fact that when **ba** precedes a clause with no overt coding of the subject, the subject of that clause is interpreted as different from the subject of the preceding clause:

(41)

kùrmbàlò	se	bòr	bé-y	kur	ba
chief	get up	cut	DAT-3M	parcel	COM

se	jèn	mànì́	ná	kamda-y	go
INCEPT	settle	ANAPH	COM	wives-3M	REF

sùbù
three

'The chief cut him a parcel of land and the man settled there with his three wives.'

If the marker **ba** were omitted from the above sentence, the second clause would be interpreted as having the same subject as the first clause:

(42)

kùrmbàlò	se	bòr	bé-y	kur
chief	get up	cut	DAT-3M	parcel

se	jèn	mànì́	ná	kamda-y	go
INCEPT	settle	ANAPH	COM	wives-3M	REF

sùbù
three

'The chief cut him a parcel of land and [he, the chief] settled there with his three wives.'

(43)

Nè	máàní	ba	láràdí	dà	kìrè
COP	ANAPH	COM	chameleon	PREP	road

ni	ɓey	ba	gúló	ile	kùlúr kùlúr
LOC	still	COM	lizard	cry:VN	kulur kulur

ba	kara	se	yà	gé	na
COM	people	INCEPT	say	3PL	HYP

pùrá	ngú	gúló	àlè.
detach:IMP	2PL	lizard	already

'The chameleon, however, was still on the road, and the lizard cried, kulur kulur. And the people said: release the lizard.' (G-C & W 1981: 8-9)

(44)

Kasínya	tòb	go	ane	te-ì	ni
feces	want	REF	leave	anus-3M	LOC

ba	se	ile	yàá	na:
COM	INCEPT	cry	say	HYP

'He urgently needed to go, he cried thus:' (G-C & W 1981: 10-11)

6 Same subjects in comment clauses

The cases where the clauses marked by **ba** have the same subject as the preceding clause do not contradict the fundamental function of **ba** as that of marking the unexpected consequences of the preceding clause. If the subjects are the same, then some other element of the proposition is different. In the first sentence of the following fragment, the first clause states 'when people die' and the comment clause is unexpected (in the context of the story) 'they are gone forever'

(45)

Nè	máàní	ba	kara	índùwé	nè
COP	ANAPH	COM	people	human:PL	IMPF

ma-gé	ba	è-gé	ná	kìrè	kíndi-gè,
die-3PL	COM	go-3PL	ASSC	road	true-3PL

gìdìrè	ma	ná	kìn	an-jè	káŋ̀g	lay.
moon	die	ASSC	return	leave-VENT	DEM	also

'That is why when people die they are gone forever, but when the moon dies it returns.' (G-C & W 1981: 8-9)

The comment clause marker **ba** may occur in the sentence-initial position, thus having the function of a discourse conjunction. The function of the marker **ba** in the sentence-initial position is the same as in the sentence-internal position. The sentence marked by **ba** represents the unexpected consequence of the preceding sentence in discourse:

(46)

àу	bùgú	kàb-ìy	ni	an	ná	kumno
take	bag	hand-3M	LOC	leave	ASSC	God

kam-dì
water-3M

'he took a [50kg] bag into his hands [and] he left with the rain'

(47)

ba	se	è	dà	kúso	bayndí
COM	INCEPT	go	PREP	field	man

kè-y	ni	da	kàrga	túgú	ni
GEN-3M	LOC	PREP	behind	compound	LOC

e	pói	je	tèmlé	wén	bùgú
go	break:PL	VENT	corn	fill	bag

'And he went into somebody's field behind the compound, broke off corn, [and] filled his bag.'

Elicited evidence that the clauses conjoined by **ba** contain unexpected information shows that an ordinary, expected sequence of events coded by **ba** is ungrammatical:

(48)

*è-dí	túgú	kè-y	ba	se	píl	kama
go-3M	home	GEN-3M	COM	PERF	wash	water

for 'he returned home and washed'

(49)

è-dí	túgú	píl	kama
go-3M	home	wash	water

'he returned home and washed'

It is enough to have the second clause with a new subject, thus assuring unexpected information, for the marker **ba** to be used:

(50)

cànìgé	wàl	kulbá	ba	gìlkínín	é	kil-dú
canige	killed	cow	COM	Gilkinin	go	sell-3F

cáaní	kàsùgú-ni
ALL	market-at

'Canige slaughtered a cow, and Gilkinin sold it [cow] at the market'

Similarly, different subjects coded by pronouns can readily occur in clauses conjoined by **ba**:

(51)

bé-ŋ	dí	láalì	ba	ŋ	se
give-1SG	3M	money	COM	1SG	INCEPT

gír
ran away

'he gave me money and I ran away'

(52) *bé-ŋ dí láalì ba se gír
give-1SG 3M money COM INCEPT ran away
for 'he gave me money and ran away'

The marker **ba** can be used with the same subject only when it clearly codes a temporal clause. The clause marked by the conjunction **ba** does not have to be the second in a temporal sequence of events: It can be the first, provided it is preceded by the appropriate temporal markers:

(53) gònì dà kìrbé kò-rò ni ná
hyena PREP thought GEN-3F LOC ASSC
gèy go léè tu-ŋ ɓey ba
want REF eat:FUT goat-DEF before COM
sée kama-ŋ
drink:FUT water-DEF
'Hyena in its thoughts wanted to devour Goat before drinking water.'

7 Coding a counterexpectation

The marker **àlá**, glossed as 'lo' (as in 'lo and behold'), codes that the clause following it is not a logical consequence of the preceding clause and moreover that it is somewhat unexpected. It can be used with same-subject clauses. In the following fragment the subject kills the mother in the first sentence and then addresses the children of the victim in the next. The second sentence is not an expected consequence of the first sentence, and the marker **àlá** cannot be omitted in the second sentence:

(54) tamá dèr tíndí ná mu̥ndu se
woman raise pestle ASSC silence INCEPT
wàdì ná tòrò-ŋ dìgrì
hit ASSC then-DEF kill
'The woman quietly raised the pestle and beat the hen with it to death'

(55) àlá se yà bé kàràn-do na
lo INCEPT tell DAT children-3F HYP
'Then she_1 told her_2 children . . . '

The marker **àlá** is even used as a discourse conjunction when it is at the beginning of a sentence. As proposed it is used in situations that describe an unexpected event:

(56) àlá se hab jè kùná-y kàyo
COM INCEPT find VENT uncle-3M squirrel
dà kìrè ni
PREP road LOC
'Unexpectedly he encountered his uncle Squirrel on the road.' (**kùnà** 'brother of the mother' or 'son of a sister')

(57) gi nè kùrmbàlò wáŋ àlá ŋ sòndrí-gi
2M COP chief even lo 1SG fear-2SG
ɗé
NEG
'even though you are a chief, I do not fear you'

The counterexpectation may involve two propositions:

(58) kur wèl kay ɗé ɓey ná tamá
place pass finish NEG still ASSC woman
na du è sógú ni
HYP 3F go toilet LOC
'Before the day ended [while it was still dark] the wife pretended that she was going to the toilet.'

(59) àlá gìr è yàá kolo-ŋ bé kùrmbàlo
lo run go tell word-DEF DAT chief
'But instead she ran and informed the chief.'

The origin of **àlá**, which is not in W & P 1982, is an interesting story of grammaticalization. It probably comes from the Arabic interjection **alla**, used in West Africa and possibly other areas as an interjection of surprise. This interjection no doubt comes from the Arabic name for God. It has begun to function in the same range as the marker **ba**, viz. in different-subject clauses:

(60) è gé dà túgú kóŋ ni àlá
go 3PL PREP village certain LOC then
kùrmbàlò gol kamda-y sùbù nè go
chief see wives-3M three COP REF
láy wa tú
pretty very all (Fr.)
'They arrived at a certain village, [and] the chief saw that the three wives of the man were all beautiful.'

8 Coding the speaker's contradiction

The speaker's contradiction or denial of the expectations of somebody else is coded by the particle **ɗéú** occurring between two clauses. The particle, glossed as 'instead', may be followed by the particle **lá** 'rather':

(61)

gi	nè	ɓén-iŋ		ɗéú	(lá)
2M	COP	brother-1SG		instead	rather than
gi	nè	kùnán-íŋ	ɗé		
2M	COP	uncle-1SG	NEG		

'you are my brother, not my uncle'

If the form **lá** is used, the form **ɗéú** can be omitted:

(62)

gi	nè	ɓén-iŋ	lá	gi
2M	COP	brother-1SG	rather than	2M
nè	kùnán-íŋ	ɗé		
COP	uncle-1SG	NEG		

'you are my brother rather than my uncle'

The following sentence can be produced only if the addressee has previously said that he would farm with a daba:[16]

(63)

gi	yáge	ná	pàŋlí	ɗéú	lá
2M	plough:FUT	ASSC	daba	instead	rather
gi	yágì	ná	kòjò	gà	
2M	plough	ASSC	hoe	Q	

'you were expected to farm with a daba, and instead you farmed with a hoe, didn't you?'

The particles **ɗéú**, **ɗéú lá**, and **lá** cannot be replaced by the conjunction **àlá**:

(64)

*gi	yáge	ná	pàŋlí	kòjò	àlá
2M	plow:FUT	ASSC	daba	hoe	COM
gi	yágì	ná	kòjò	gà	
2M	plow	ASSC	hoe	Q	

for 'you were expected to farm with a daba, and instead you farmed with a hoe, didn't you?'

---

[16] A type of hoe.

9 Conclusions

Four types of complex sentences have been described. Paratactic constructions have identical subjects. The subjects of the second and ensuing clauses are not overtly marked. There is no conjunction between the clauses. The adverb **lay** 'also' is deployed to code a clause as being true under the same conditions or at the same time that a preceding or following clause is true. An unexpected consequence is coded by the comment clause marker **ba**. Counterexpectation is coded by the borrowed conjunction **àlá**.

19

Complementation

1 Introduction

The term *complementation* refers to the realization of an argument of a verb by a clause. This chapter deals with complements of verbs of saying, verbs of perception, volitional verbs, and cognitive verbs. Complementation in Lele is interesting because there are several complementizers that interact with inherent properties of verbs and with various modalities. The fundamental issues involved in complementation are the coding of modality, epistemic or deontic, for several types of verbs. Within epistemic modality there is a distinction between the de dicto and re domains (cf. Frajzyngier 1995). The structural elements involved with complementation in Lele are complement-taking verbs, complementizers, the form of the verb in the complement clause, and the word order in the complement clause.

2 Complements of verbs of saying

The fundamental verb of saying is **yàá**. The argument range of this verb includes the object of what has been said. The addressee, if any, must be preceded by the dative marker **bé** (**bè** in G-C & W 1981). Depending on the syntactic frame in which it occurs, the verb **yàá** corresponds to English 'tell', 'say', and 'speak'. In the present grammar this verb is glossed by one of these three glosses. This verb must occur when it is the only verb of the sentence, e.g. in interrogative clauses:

(1) yàá dí na mè
say 3M HYP what
'what did he say?'

(2) jè yàá dí na mè
IMPF say 3M HYP what
'what does he say?'

In the future the verb **yáá** has all tones high:

(3) jè yáá dí na mè
IMPF say:FUT 3M HYP what
'what will he be saying?' (during the meeting)

(4) yáa dí na mè
say:FUT 3M HYP what
'what will he say?' (perfective)

Other verbs may be deployed as verbs of saying through metaphorical usage. Thus the verb **jé** 'throw' is used as meaning 'answer'.

3 The de dicto complementizer

The de dicto complementizer is **na**, glossed in the present work as HYP for hypothetical, in order to distinguish it from the complementizer **go**, which codes referential complementation. The hypothetical function and the de dicto complementizer function belong to the same grammaticalization chain (cf. Frajzyngier 1991). If there is a verb of saying in the clause, the complementizer follows the verb with its subject pronouns, if any:

(5) ni yàá na
1PL.EXCL say HYP
'we said that . . .'

(6) ngù yàá na
2PL say HYP
'you (PL) said that . . .'

If there is no verb in the matrix clause, the complementizer follows the subject. The complementizer must be followed by a proposition, direct or indirect speech. The subject followed by the complementizer cannot be used alone:

(7) ni na . . .
1PL.EXCL HYP
'we said that . . .'

(8) ngù na . . .
2PL HYP
'you said that . . .'

The complementizer **na** is deployed after the verb of saying in constructions corresponding to 'they call X Y'. The third-person pronouns in complements of the verb of saying follow the complementizer rather than the verb, as is the case in matrix clauses:

(9) Nè máàní ba ge tey ná gìdìrè
COP ANAPH COM HUM call ASSC moon
kon-di na "Bàn-sà".
name-3M HYP Ban-sa (friend-drink:IMP)
'That is why one calls this moon by the name "Ban-sa" [drink my friend!]' (G-C & W 1981: 52-53)

(10) ge tey-ge na hìr kolo se-gé
HUM call-3PL HYP hir reason get up-3PL
nèny hìr.
a lot hir
'they call them [birds] hir, because they rise with the noise hir' (G-C & W 1981: 54-55)

The addressee of the verb of saying is coded by the dative preposition **bé**, which may precede a noun or a pronoun:

(11) kàyo yàá bé-y na máàní na
squirrel say DAT-3M HYP like that HYP
na
HYP
'Squirrel told him, if it is like that, then . . . '

4 Omission of the verb of saying and the role of the complementizer

In narratives and conversations, the verb of saying is usually omitted if there is no addressee in the matrix clause. The complementizer alone indicates what the predicate of the matrix clause is:

(12)

na-y	jene	ná	kamda-y	go	sùbù
HYP-3M	stay	COM	wives-3M	REF	three

bàs
only (Ar.)

'He said that he just wants to stay with his three wives.'

(13)

tormo	na	dú	ódè	ná	bà-rò	ɗé
girl	HYP	3F	leave	ASSC	father-3F	NEG

se	è	ná	bayndí-ŋ
INCEPT	go	ASSC	man-DEF

'The girl said that she will not go with her father and instead went with the man.'

(14)

donc	na-y	bé	kùrmbàlò	tamá
therefore (Fr.)	HYP-3M	give:FUT	chief	wife

ɗé
NEG

'Therefore, he said, he will not give a wife to the chief. '

The complementizer can also be omitted after the subject, provided that the preceding clause contains a verb of saying. In the following fragment of a narrative, the first sentence has a verb of saying and the complementizer:

(15)

yàá-gé	na
say-3PL	HYP

'They said:'

In the subsequent clause in the narrative there is no complementizer after the subject. The complementizer **na** following the comment clause marker **ba** is the marker of hypothetical modality:

(16)

dàì	hàŋ	ba	na	ge	bé-y
3M	here	COM	HYP	HUM	give-3M

kùrmbàlò	tamą́-y	ba	na-y	wèl	ná
chief	wife-3M	COM	HYP-3M	sleep	ASSC

un-do
ASSC-3F

'The first one said that if he is given the chief's wife to sleep with. '

In the subsequent sentence the verb of saying is omitted and the complementizer **na** indicates the nature of the predicate of the matrix clause and also of the hypothetical modality:

(17) dày kóŋ na-y kále jénè
3M certain HYP-3M climb:FUT sit:FUT
dà jaŋla kùrmbàlò kè-y ni na-y
PREP bench chief GEN-3M LOC HYP-3M
bórè sàríyà na ge dìgr-ìy
cut judgment (Ar.) HYP HUM kill-3M
na ùs-ìy ɗé
HYP concern-3M NEG
'The other said that if he could climb on the chief's bench and pronounce judgments, they could kill him, he did not care.'

Given the fact that the verb of saying can be omitted, the complementizer takes on the role of the independent coding of what follows as being in the domain of speech. Look at the following fragment. The first sentence ends with a clause '[goat] undertook the following trick'. This sentence ends with the complementizer **na**. The next sentence is the speech that the goat made:

(18) tu-ŋ gol go gonì kún-do jèn
goat-DEF see REF hyena eye-3F remain
téŋ ná se ày dú lúmá na
different ASSC INCEPT take 3F trick HYP
'Goat noticed that Hyena had different intentions and tried the following trick'

(19) ìrà-ngà dà kama dùrè-y ni
go:IMP-1DU.INCL PREP water inside-3M LOC
ba nga séè dày go
COM 1DU.INCL drink:FUT 3M REF
ɗínglé lay me ágè ísì go bòré
clear also 2F take:FUT bone REF white
koloŋ
there
'Let us go inside this water; we will drink the one that is clear, and you will take the white bone there'

The complement clause may precede the matrix clause. When this is the case, the matrix clause verb is followed by the propositional anaphor **máànɪ́**. The antecedent of the anaphor is the complement of the verb of saying:

(20) gi kése ná kà-m ɗé
2M share:FUT ASSC hand-2M NEG
'you will not share'

gi 2M | láde touch:FUT | ná ASSC | kà-m hand-2M | ɗé NEG

gi	láde	ná	kà-m	ɗé
2M	touch:FUT	ASSC	hand-2M	NEG

'you will not touch it'

òlkúsíŋ	yá	bè-y	máàní
Olkusin	tell	DAT-3M	ANAPH

'Olkusin told him like that'

The de dicto complementizer **na** can also be used after other verbs, as described later in the present chapter.

The de dicto complementizer does not have to be deployed.

(21)

Tamá	ng	kirbi	kùlèn-dè	nè-mè	hòmnyá.
woman,	1SG	think	belly-2F	make-2F	sickness

'Woman, I think your belly aches you.' (G-C & W 1981: 4-5)

5 Coreference and disjoint reference in complementation

Complements of verbs of saying are typical environments where confusion might arise between reference to participants in the ongoing discourse and reference to participants in the reported discourse, and between participants of the matrix clause and participants of the embedded clause. If a language has grammaticalized means of coding cross-reference and disjoint reference, such means are deployed first of all in the complements of verbs of saying.

5.1 Coding coreference

The coreference of the third-person subject pronoun of the embedded clause with the third-person subject pronoun of the matrix clause is coded by the subject pronoun of the embedded clause following the complementizer. For the third-person masculine, the pronoun is a suffix, identical with the object suffix:

(22)

kumno	se	tey	láràdí	dàgè	ná
God	INCEPT	call	lizard	3PL	ASSC

gúló	yàá	bè	kara	na-i
chameleon	tell	DAT	people	HYP-3M

ódè	wanyang	wáyngulú
depart:FUT	tomorrow	morning

'God$_1$ called the lizard and chameleon and told people that he$_1$ would go tomorrow morning . . . ' (G-C & W 1981: 6-7)

(23) càǹìgé na-y nè bay go ségrè
canige HYP-3M COP person REF hunt
'Canige$_1$ said that he$_1$ is a hunter'

Similarly with the verb **kirbi** 'think':

(24) kirbi-dí na-y nè bay go ségrè
think-3M HYP-3M COP person REF hunt
'he$_1$ thinks that he$_1$ is a hunter'

(25) na-y bòy kójò kè-y
HYP-3M break hoe GEN-3M
'[he$_1$ said] that he$_1$ broke his hoe' (the hoe does not have to belong to the speaker)

For the third-person feminine, the pronoun following the complementizer is also the object form, i.e., it has mid rather than high tone:

(26) yàá dú na du bòy kójò kò-rò
say 3F HYP 3F break hoe GEN-3F
'she$_1$ said that she$_1$ broke her hoe'

5.2 Coding disjoint reference

If the third-person subject of the embedded clause is different from the subject of the matrix clause, the subject of the embedded clause is realized by a full noun:

(27) yàá bé-ì na gìdìrè ba na
tell DAT-3M HYP moon COM HYP
ma ná kùn ana jè
die:IMP ASSC return:IMP go out:IMP VENT
'He told him that it is the moon that, if it dies, would return and come out' (G-C & W 1981: 8-9)

(28) Kara yà-gé na nè gìdìrè go kumno
people say-3PL HYP COP moon REF sky
hilbí ná màní
swell ASSC there
'people say that it is during this month that the sky swells' (G-C & W 1981: 38-39)

(29) Ge yàá ná[17] kur na jèr
HUM say HYP place HYP be humid
'One says that the place is humid' (G-C & W 1981: 8-9)

Disjoint reference between the third-person object and the dative pronoun is coded through the deployment of pronouns:

(30) tòn-ìy na pa bé-y kasire
ask-3M HYP dig:IMP DAT-3M medicine
'he told him_1 to dig him_2 medicine . . .'

(31) ɗe ná bayndí-ŋ teren-di se
THEN ASSC man-DEF daughter-3M INCEPT
yàá na pa bé-y kasire-ŋ
tell HYP dig:IMP DAT-3M medicine-DEF
'Then the hunter's daughter told her $father_1$ to dig up the medicine for him_2'

The natural discourse data with respect to the coding of disjoint reference for the third-person clearly indicate that Lele avoids the deployment of pronouns in the embedded clause. Pronouns are used when deixis rather than anaphora is involved. If the subject of the embedded clause is different from the subject of the main clause, then the independent form of the third-person pronoun followed by a demonstrative proximate or remote follows the complementizer:

(32) cánígè ná dày kólòŋ nè bay go
canige HYP 3M there COP person REF
ségrè
hunt
'Canige said that he [one over there] is a hunter'

I took a sentence from a natural discourse where coreference was coded and asked speakers to provide a disjoint reference variant. This exercise should not be taken as reflecting natural discourse data, nor should it be rejected outright, because it reflects a native speaker's manipulation of the structure of his own language. I asked the speakers to convert the following sentence with a coreferential third-person subject into one with a disjoint reference subject:

---

17 Probably should be **na** rather than **ná**.

(33) dày kóŋ na-y kále jénè
3M certain HYP-3M climb:FUT sit:FUT
dà luŋba kùrmbàlò kè-y ni na-y
PREP horse chief GEN-3M LOC HYP-3M
bórè sàríyà na ùs-ìy ɗé
cut judgment HYP concern-3M NEG
'The other said that if he could climb on the chief's horse and pronounce judgments, [they could kill him], he did not care.'

The coding of disjoint reference is realized through the position of the subject pronoun after the verb of the embedded clause rather than after the complementizer:

(34) dày kóŋ na kále dí jénè
3M certain HYP climb:FUT 3M sit:FUT
dà luŋba kùrmbàlò kè-y ni na
PREP horse chief GEN-3M LOC HYP
bórè dí sàríyà na ùs-ìy
cut:FUT 3M judgment HYP concern-3M
ɗé
NEG
'The other$_1$ said that if he$_2$ could climb on the chief's horse and pronounce judgments, [they could kill him$_2$], he did not care.'

In elicited sentences, the coding of disjoint reference as opposed to coreference is achieved through the deployment of independent pronouns. If the embedded clause does not have a subject pronoun, its subject is coreferential with the subject of the matrix clause. If the embedded clause has a pronoun, its subject is different from the subject of the matrix clause:

(35) kìrbí dí na-y nè bay go
think 3M HYP-3M COP person REF
sègré
hunter
'he$_1$ thinks that he$_1$ is a hunter'

(36) cànìgé kirbi na dày koloŋ nè
Canige think HYP 3M DEM:R COP
bay go sègré
person REF hunter
'Canige$_1$ thinks that he$_2$ is a hunter'

6 Dubitative modality in complementation

All data for this subsection have been obtained through elicitation. Doubt in truth of the complement clause, from the point of view of the person who reports a speech, is marked by the marker **sáŋ** occurring in clause-final position:

(37)

na-y	nè	bay	go	ségrè	sáŋ
HYP-3M	COP	person	REF	hunt	DUB

'he said that he is a hunter, but I doubt that it is true'

Cf.:

(38)

cánígè	na-y	nè	bay	go	ségrè
Canige	HYP-3M	COP	person	REF	hunt

'Canige said that he is a hunter'

The marker **gèrè** 'or, if' can follow the marker **sáŋ** to further reinforce the doubt:

(39)

ge	yàá	bé-ŋ	na	cànìgé	dàgè
HUM	tell	DAT-1SG	HYP	Canige	3PL
wàì	gé	sáŋ	gèrè		
fight	3PL	DUB	IF		

for 'I was told that Canige and some people with him fought [against each other], but I am not sure'

The marker **gèrè** 'doubt' alone cannot be used as a marker of doubt in the complement clause:

(40)

*ge	yàá	bé-ŋ	na	cànìgé	dàge
HUM	tell	DAT-1SG	HYP	Canige	3PL
wàì	gé	gèrè			
fight	3PL	IF			

for 'I was told that Canige and some people with him fought but I am not sure [that they did]'

Recall, however, that the marker **gèrè** can be used as a marker of doubt in the matrix clause:

(41)

cànìgé	dàgè	wàì-gé	gèrè
Canige	3PL	fight-3PL	IF

'I am not sure that Canige and some people with him fought [against each other]'

7 Dubitative modality from the point of view of the subject of the matrix clause

Dubitative modality from the point of view of the subject of the matrix clause is coded by the hypothetical marker **na** following the subject of the embedded clause. Recall that the marker **na** follows the nominal subject and precedes the pronominal subjects in matrix clauses to code doubt in truth on the part of the speaker. The deployment of the complementizer **na** within the complement clause is thus the same as within the matrix clause. Since the complement clause must be preceded by the de dicto complementizer, when the complement clause has a nominal subject, the complementizer precedes and follows the nominal subject:

(42)

canigé	yàá-di	na	kiya	na	bòy
Canige	say-3M	HYP	Kiya	HYP	break
kòjò	kè-y				
hoe	GEN-3M				

'Canige said that perhaps Kiya broke his hoe'

If the subject of the embedded clause is first -or second-person pronominal, the independent form of the pronoun is deployed, followed by the complementizer, followed by the subject pronoun of the embedded clause. It is more than likely that one of the motivations for the deployment of the independent form of the pronoun is to avoid the sequence of two de dicto complementizers:

(43)

canigé	na	dàŋ	na	ŋ	bòy	kòjò
Canige	HYP	1SG	HYP	1SG	break	hoe
kè-y						
GEN-3M						

'Canige said that perhaps I broke his hoe'

(44)

canigé	na	dìgì	na	gí	bòy	kòjò
Canige	HYP	2M	HYP	2M	break	hoe
kè-y						
GEN-3M						

'Canige said that perhaps you broke his hoe'

(45)

canigé	na	dàmè	na	mé	bòy	kòjò
Canige	HYP	2F	HYP	2F	break	hoe
kè-y						
GEN-3M						

'Canige said that perhaps you (F) broke his hoe'

If the subject of the embedded clause is third-person feminine, the subject pronoun follows the verb of the embedded clause, as it does in the matrix clause. The independent form of the pronoun must still be deployed:

(46)

canigé	na	dàdù	na	bòy	dú	kòjò
Canige	HYP	3F	HYP	break	3F	hoe

kè-ì
GEN-3M

'Canige said that perhaps she broke his hoe'

8 Coding the deontic modality of the embedded clause

Deontic modality can be marked for any number of matrix clause verbs, not necessarily verbs of saying. In the present section most clauses with deontic modality follow verbs of saying (even omitted ones). At the end of the section, deontic complements of other verbs are illustrated as well.

The deontic complements have the same de dicto complementizer **na** as the non-deontic complements. In deontic complements, however, the verb has the imperative form, while in non-deontic complements it has the indicative form:

(47)

bayndí-ŋ	teren-di	yàá	na	húm-gé
man-DEF	daughter-3M	say	HYP	take:IMP-3PL

se	hím-gé	bòr	ná	kama
INCEPT	take-3PL	skim	ASSC	water

'The daughter of the man told him to take them. He took them and they skimmed across the river.'

Like the complements in the indicative modality, but unlike the complements in the imperative modality of the matrix clause, all pronominal subjects, including the first- and second-person pronouns, must follow the complementizer and precede the verb of the complement clause. All pronouns following the complementizer have mid tone:

(48)

ni	yàá	bú-ngù	na	ngù	ìrà
1PL.EXCL	say	DAT-2PL	HYP	2PL	go:IMP

'we told you to go'

(49)

na	ŋgù	ìrà
HYP	2PL	go:IMP

'they say that you should go'

(50)

na	nì	ìrà
HYP	1PL.EXCL	go:IMP

'they say that we should go'

(51)

ŋ	yàá	bé-gè	na	ge	ìrà
1SG	say	DAT-3PL	HYP	3PL	go:IMP

'I told them to go'

(52)

ŋ	yàá	bú-dù	na	dù	ìrà
1SG	say	DAT-3PL	HYP	3F	go:IMP

'I told them to go'

The third-person singular subject pronoun can be omitted in the embedded clause whether it is coded as addressee of the matrix clause or not:

(53)

yàá-dí	bú-dù	na	ìrà
say-3M	DAT-3F	HYP	go:IMP

'he told her to go'

In the following example the subject is not overtly marked in the embedded clause, and in the matrix clause it is not even an argument, but rather a possessor of another argument:

(54)

ɗee	ná	bayndí-ŋ	teren-dì	se
THEN	ASSC	man-DEF	daughter-3M	INCEPT

yá	na	pa	bé-y	kasire-ŋ
tell	HYP	dig:IMP	DAT-3M	medicine-DEF

'Then the hunter's daughter told her father to dig up the medicine for the man.'

The imperative form of the verb can cooccur with the hypothetical modality:

(55)

kàyo	yàá	bé-y	na	máàní	na
squirrel	say	DAT-3M	HYP	like that	HYP

na	à	jè
HYP	go:IMP	VENT

'Squirrel said, if it is like that, come . . .'

The verb **tòn** 'ask' may also have a deontic complement, also formed with the imperative form of the verb in the embedded clause:

(56)

tòn-ngá	gé	na	ngá	ìrà-(ngú)
ask-1DU.INCL	3PL	HYP	1DU.INCL	go-(2PL)

'they asked us to go'

Verbs other than verbs of saying can have deontic complements as well. Here the verb **bòg** [bòy] 'send' is followed by a deontic complement:

(57) kùrmbàlò se bòg [bòy] kara kè-y
chief INCEPT send people GEN-3M
ná wáyngulu na ìrà gé hàbà
ASSC morning HYP go:IMP 3PL find:IMP
gáw-ŋ́
hunter-DEF
'The chief sent his people in the morning to go and find the hunter.'

9 Direct speech

Both direct and indirect speech must have the same complementizer **na**. The fundamental difference between direct and indirect speech in Lele is the deployment of pronouns coding the subject and the addressee. In direct speech the first-person pronoun refers to the speaker of the quoted speech and the second-person pronoun refers to the addressee of the quoted speech:

(58) yàá bú-dú na ŋ án kwánì
tell DAT-3F HYP 1SG leave outside
ba ŋ jìb cà-nìŋ ná kòyè ba
COM 1SG bump head-1SG ASSC thief COM
ŋ dìgr-ìy
1SG kill-3M
'He told her: leaving the house I bumped against a thief and killed him.'

(59) tu yàá bé-y na
goat tell DAT-3N HYP
'the goat told him . . .'

(60) yú cà-rè dà kama te-y
put:IMP head-2M PREP water bottom-3M
ní ba me ágè ísí-ŋ
LOC COM 2F take:FUT bone-DEF
'put your head at the bottom of the water and you will get the bone'

(61) kùnà-y kàyo se tòn-ìy na
uncle-3M squirrel INCEPT ask-3M HYP
gi jè gìrè mína mánì gà
2M IMPF run:VN where like that Q
'His uncle Squirrel asked him, where are you running like that?'

Compare indirect speech with a third-person addressee:

(62) kùná-y kàyo se tòn-ìy na
uncle-3M squirrel INCEPT ask-3M HYP
jè gìr dí mína máàní gà
IMPF run 3M where like that Q
'His uncle Squirrel asked him where he was running like that.'

The choice between direct speech and indirect speech is an issue not merely of style but rather of resolving the potential ambiguity between the participants of the reported speech and the participants of the ongoing speech.

Indirect speech has third-person pronouns throughout and the identity of the subject is ambiguous. The subject could be the addressee of the matrix clause or some other third person:

(63) dí yú cà-y dà kama te-y
3M put:IMP head-3M PREP water bottom-3M
ni ba dí ágè ísí-ŋ
LOC COM 3M take:FUT bone-DEF
'he should put his head at the bottom of the water and he would get the bone'

In narratives, direct speech is the prevalent way of reporting what somebody has said. Direct speech must, however, be preceded by a verb of saying with its subject and complementizer, or at least a complementizer. Here is an example of the direct speech preceded by a full clause with the verb of saying:

(64) tu se yàá bú-dù na
goat INCEPT tell DAT-3F HYP
'Then the goat told her:'

(65) ŋ sèn toto go mé gèy
1SG know completely REF 2F want
léè-ŋ àlá mé hábe kìrè-níŋ ɗé
eat:FUT-1SG but 2F find:FUT way-DEF NEG
'I know very well that you want to devour me, but you will not be able to.'

(66)

láà	gìdìrè	go	dà	kama	te-y
eat:IMP	moon	REF	PREP	water	bottom-3M

ni	ɓàlà-mè	dàŋ	ŋ	jè	òdì
LOC	suffice:IMP-2F	1SG	1SG	IMPF	go

'Eat the moon that is at the bottom of the water; it should satisfy you; as for me, I am going away.'

Here is an example of direct speech introduced just by the complementizer, without even the coding of the addressee:

(67)

tu-ŋ	gol	go	gonì	kún-do	jèn
goat-DEF	see	REF	hyena	eye-3F	remain

téŋ	ná	se	ày	dú	lúmá	na
different	ASSC	INCEPT	take	3F	trick	HYP

'Goat noticed that Hyena had different intentions and tried the following trick'

(68)

ìrà-ngà	dà	kama	dùrè-y	ni
go:IMP-1DU.INCL	PREP	water	inside-3M	LOC

ba	nga	séè	dày	go
COM	1DU.INCL	drink:FUT	3M	REF

ɗínglé	lay	me	ágè	ísì	go	bòré
clear	also	2F	take:FUT	bone	REF	white

koloŋ
there

'Let us go inside this water; we will drink the one that is clear, and you will take the white bone there'

The difference between direct and indirect speech is most clearly seen in the deontic complements of verbs of saying. In direct discourse the pronouns of the embedded clause follow the verb, i.e. behave as in matrix clauses:

(69)

ná	yàá	bé	kàràn-dò	na	ngu	gol
ASSC	tell	DAT	children-3F	HYP	2PL	see

gaw	go	kun-do	pìnà	tésí	ɗé-ŋ
well	REF	eye-3F	one	break	already-DEF

ná	da	ngù	kasa	ná	já	koloŋ
ASSC	eat:IMP	2PL	corn	ASSC	side	DEM:R

'So she said to her children: you see well that she is blind in one eye, so go and peck at the other side [that she does not see]'

(70)

kur	koloŋ	ba	dày	gṵ́yé	se	yàá
time	DEM:R	COM	3M	spider	INCEPT	say

bé-gè	na	na-y	jè	nè	hòmyá
DAT-3PL	HYP	HYP-3M	IMPF	make	sick

go	ma	nò	go	tég	lay	na
REF	die	COP	REF	long time	also	HYP

bé-y	gé	na-y	lèé
give-3M	3PL	HYP-3M	eat

'At that time Spider said that since he was sick for a long time, close to dying, they should give [it] to him to eat.'

10 Embedded interrogatives

The basic verb 'to ask' is **tòn**. This verb can take interrogative as well as deontic complements, as has been illustrated earlier. Unlike in some other Chadic languages, the verb **yàá** 'say, tell, speak' cannot have interrogative complements.

If the verb **tòn** is followed not by a clause but rather by a noun phrase, there is no complementizer **na**:

(71)

tòn-iŋ	dí	dà	kanya	go	ŋ	lèé
ask-1SG	3M	PREP	thing	REF	1SG	eat

jè	ni
PERF	in

'he asked me about the thing I ate'

The interrogative complement of the verb **tòn** may be direct or indirect speech. In both cases the complement may be preceded by the dicto complementizer **na**. But with indirect speech the deployment of the complementizer is obligatory, and with direct speech it is optional. Whether the speech of the interrogative complement is direct or indirect, the form of the interrogative complement is the same as that of the interrogative matrix clause, save for the deployment of pronouns, as described earlier in the section on direct speech. Since these forms are the same, the present section is limited to the illustration of the deployment of various types of interrogative clauses as complements.

Direct speech:

(72)

kùnà-y	kàyo	se	tòn-ìy	na
uncle-3M	squirrel	INCEPT	ask-3M	HYP

gi	jè	gìrè	mína	mánì	gà
2M	IMPF	run:VN	where	like that	Q

'His uncle Squirrel asked him, where are you running like that?'

(73)

gi	jè	gìr	è	mína	máàní	gà
2M	IMPF	run	go	where	like that	Q

'where are you running like that?'

(74)

tey	póì	kúsíge-ŋ	tòn-ìy	na
call	Poi	Kusige-DEF	asked-3M	HYP

'He called Poi Kusige and asked him:'

(75)

gàrmà	háŋ	nè	kò-m	ɗé	ba
footsteps	DEM	COP	GEN-2M	NEG	COM
ne	wèy	kè-y	ba	è	jè
COP	who	GEN-3M	COM	go	VENT
póì	tèmle	kò-nòŋ	háŋ	gà	
break:PL	corn	GEN-1SG	DEM:P	Q	

'If those footsteps aren't yours, whose are they, then? Who came to break off my corn like that?'

(76)

kùrmbàlò	tòn	póì	kúsíge	na
chief	ask	Poi	Kusige	HYP

'the chief asked Poi Kusige:'

(77)

dìgì	gí	kòy	tèmlé-ŋ	gèsé
2M	2M	steal	corn-DEF	or
gí	kòy	ɗé	gà	
2M	steal	NEG	Q	

'was it you who stole the corn or wasn't it?'

11 Specific questions

11.1 Common features of embedded specific questions

Specific embedded interrogatives have exactly the same form as main clause specific interrogatives. They end in clause-final **gà**. If the speech is direct, the complementizer is not obligatory:

(78)

Kudo-ro	tòn-dù:	"Me	è	mína	gà?
husband-3F	ask-3F	2F	go	where	Q

'Her husband asked her: where are you going?' (G-C & W 1981: 4-5)

Here are a few examples of various specific questions, mainly to illustrate the identity of the forms of the embedded interrogative and the matrix clause interrogative.

Questions about a human subject:

(79) tòn-iŋ di na wéy ba è jè
ask-1SG 3M HYP who COM go VENT
gol-gì gà
see-2M Q
'he asked me who visited you'

If the question is about an argument other than the subject, the word **wéy** must be preceded by the copula **ne**, which otherwise marks focus:

(80) ŋ tòn-ìy na dàdù nè wéy gà
1SG ask-3M HYP 3F COP who Q
'I asked him who she is'

(81) ŋ tòn-ìy na gol-di nè wéì gà
1SG ask-3M HYP see-3M COP who Q
'I asked him who he saw'

(82) ŋ tòn-ìy nè wéy ba gi
1SG ask-3M COP who COM 2M
bé-y làlí gà
give-3M money Q
'I asked him who you gave the money to'

Questions about an inanimate subject have the marker **ba** following the question word **me**:

(83) tòn-iŋ dí na me ba jìb-iŋ
ask-1SG 3M HYP what COM sting-1SG
máàní gà
ANAPH Q
'he asked me what stung me there'

An embedded question about a non-human object can have various forms of the interrogative clause added after the complementizer **na**:

(84) ŋ tòn-ìy na me ba gol-di gà
1SG ask-3M HYP what COM see-3M Q
'I asked him what he saw'

(85) ŋ tòn-ìy na gol dí nè me gà
1SG ask-3M HYP see 3M COP what Q
'I asked him what he saw'

11.2 Questions about the locative

A question about the locative is marked by **mínà** 'where' preceding the embedded clause-final **gà**. The embedded clause is preceded by the complementizer **na**:

(86)	tòn-iŋ	dú	na	ŋ	wél	jè	mínà	gà
	ask-1SG	3F	HYP	1SG	sleep	VENT	where	Q

'she asked where I slept'

(87)	ŋ	je	tòn	na	jèé-dí	kòjò-ŋ
	1SG	IMPF	ask	HYP	throw-3M	hoe-DEF
	dà	mínà	gà			
	PREP	where	Q			

'I ask where he threw the hoe'

12 Causative and pseudo-causative constructions and the evidence for the de dicto function of na

The verb **jìb** 'push, cause' may be followed by nominal or clausal complements. When it is followed by nominal complements, it means 'push, provoke':

(88)	jìb-iŋ	dí	ná	ŋ	bà	kama	ni
	push-1SG	3M	ASSC	1SG	fall	water	LOC

'he pushed me and I fell into the water'

When the verb **jìb** takes clausal complements, it has a causative-like function, viz., 'make somebody do x'. There are two ways in which the complement clause may be added to the verb **jìb**.

In one construction, the subject of the embedded clause is coded as the object of the verb **jìb** and does not occur elsewhere in the embedded clause. Moreover, there is no complementizer between the main and the embedded clause.

(89)	jìb-iŋ	dí	jè	è	jè	ná
	cause-1SG	3M	come	go	VENT	ASSC

'he made me come there with him'

The number of types of complement clauses that the verb **jìb** can take is very limited. One cannot use it with the verb **wèl kùná** 'sleep':

(90)	*jìb-iŋ	dí	wèl	kùná
	cause-1SG	3M	lie	sleep

for 'he made me sleep'

(91)

*jìb-iŋ	dí	wèl
cause-1SG	3M	lie

for 'he made me lie'

In the other construction, the verb **jìb** is also followed by the object, nominal or pronominal, but it also has the complementizer **na** preceding the embedded clause with an overt subject coreferential with the object of the main clause. The verb in the embedded clause is in the imperative form. This construction does not have a causative meaning, in the sense of 'make X do Y', but rather has the same function as complements of verbs of saying: the event of the complement clause has not been completed. This is a pseudo-causative construction. The meaning of the construction is no doubt due to the deployment of the complementizer **na**:

(92)

ŋ	jìb-dú	na	nà	kạnya	lèé
1SG	push-3F	HYP	cook:IMP	thing	eating

'I told her to cook some food'

(93)

dàdù	jìb-gè	na	kùjà-gé	kúní
3F	push-3PL	HYP	clean:IMP-3PL	house
kùlèn-dì				
belly-3M				

'she told them to clean the inside of the house'

(94)

jìb-ìŋ	dí	na	ŋ	údà
push-1SG	3M	HYP	1SG	go:IMP

'he told me to go'

(95)

ŋ	jìb-ìy	na	dí	údà
1SG	make-3M	HYP	3M	go:IMP

'I told him to go'

Evidence that the **na** complements of the verb **jìb** do not entail the completion of the event is provided by the fact that they can be followed by clauses denying the completion:

(96)

jìb-ìŋ	dí	na	ŋ	údà	ba
push-1SG	3M	HYP	1SG	go:IMP	COM
ŋ	è	ɗé	bèi		
1SG	go	NEG	yet		

'he told me to go, but I didn't go yet'

Hence the function of the complementizer **na** is to change the inherent de re domain of the verb **jìb** 'push' into the de dicto domain.

13 Complements of the verb è 'go'

The verb **è** may be followed directly by a verb in the past tense form and then it has the function of the telic aspect. But this verb may also be followed by the complementizer **na** and the verb form in the future. Such a construction codes unrealized purpose:

(97)

dày	bay	go	kúsó-ŋ	è	na-y
3M	man	REF	field-DEF	go	HYP-3M

gólè	tèmlé	kè-y
see:FUT	corn	GEN-3M

'When the owner of the field went to see his corn . . .'

14 Conclusions

The complementizer **na** codes the de dicto domain. With verbs of saying, including the verbs 'to say', 'to ask', it is the only means of introducing a complement clause. It is deployed with both direct and indirect speech. With other verbs, such as the verb **jìb** 'push', **è** 'go', the complementizer **na** is just one of several means of introducing a complement clause. For those verbs the complementizer **na** codes the domain de dicto, hypothetical, of the complement clause. In natural discourse, the verb of saying is most often deleted if there is no addressee in the matrix clause. The de dicto complementizer is the only indicator that the clause has a predicate that is a verb of saying.

20

Complementation through the Referential Marker

1 Introduction

In the present section I describe a number of complement clause constructions that involve the referential marker **go**, which serves as the de re complementizer. In order to better illustrate its function, I contrast it with the complementizer **na** when both complementizers can be used. The fundamental function of the referential marker **go** is to indicate that the proposition of the complement clause deals with real events in the universe, with physical events affecting specific participants.

2 Complements after verbs of knowing

The verb **sèn** 'to know' can have either of the complementizers alone or the complementizer **go** followed by the complementizer **na**. The reverse order of complementizers is not allowed.

The structure with the verb **sèn** followed only by the complementizer **go** indicates that the knowledge is through the subject's own experience. Thus the embedded clause after the complementizer **go** may be followed by a clause indicating direct evidence:

(1)

ŋ	sèn	go	gi	gírbí	jè	kòjò
1SG	know	REF	2M	forget	VENT	hoe

kò-m	bé	kolo	ŋ	gol
GEN-2M	DAT	reason	1SG	see

'I know that you forgot your hoe, because I saw [that you forgot your hoe]'.

(2)

gònì	sùm-rò	se	yí	cà-rò
hyena	be mad:VN-3F	INCEPT	put	head-3F

kama	te-y	ni	ná	dusi	kolo
water	bottom-3M	LOC	ASSC	sink	because

sèn	go	nàlè	kama	ɗé
know	REF	swim:VN	water	NEG

'Foolish Hyena put its head at the bottom of the water, and it sank because it did not know how to swim.'

A sentence with the complementizer **go** alone is ungrammatical if followed by a clause indicating hearsay as the source of information:

(3)

ŋ	sèn	go	mé	gírbí	kòjò	kè-rè
1SG	know	REF	2F	forget	hoe	GEN-2F

*bé	kóló	ge	yàá-ŋ
DAT	reason	HUM	tell-1SG

for 'I know that you (F) forgot your hoe, because I was told so.'

(4)

ŋ	sèn	toto	go	mé
1SG	know	completely	REF	2F

gèy	léè-ŋ	àlá	mé	hábe
want	eat:FUT-1SG	but	2F	find:FUT

kìrè-níŋ	ɗé
way-DEF	NEG

'I know very well that you want to devour me, but you will not be able to.'

When the two complementizers occur together, then the clause indicates that the knowledge of the speaker does not derive from personal experience, e.g. perception, but rather from some other source, such as hearsay information. Evidence for this meaning comes from the following facts. One can have a sentence containing both **go** and **na** and followed by a clause indicating hearsay as a source of information:

(5) ŋ sèn go na gì gírbí jè
1SG know REF HYP 2M forget VENT
kòjò kò-m bé kóló ge yàá-ŋ
hoe GEN-2M DAT reason HUM tell-1SG
'I know that you (M) forgot your hoe, because I was told so'

If the complementizer **go** is followed by the complementizer **na** and the embedded clause is followed by a clause indicating personal experience, the sentence is ungrammatical:

(6) *ŋ sèn go na gi gírbí jè
1SG know REF HYP 2M forget VENT
kòjò kò-m bé kolo ŋ gol
hoe GEN-2M DAT reason 1SG see
for 'I know that you forgot your hoe, because I saw [that you forgot your hoe].'

The following sentence, which contains the propositional anaphor **máàní**, is a conclusion from the story in the narrative. The verb **sèn** is followed by both the referential marker **go** and the complementizer **na**:

(7) ne máàní ba kàra túgú
COP ANAPH COM people village
sèn gé go na pói kúsíge
know 3PL REF HYP Poi Kusige
na jè kóy tèmlè kè-gè
HYP IMPF steal corn GEN-3PL
'And that is how people of the village know that it is Poi Kusige who steals their corn.'

The verb **sèn** may be followed by the complementizer **na** alone, but that does not code knowledge through personal perception:

(8) ŋ sèn na gi nè kùrmbàlò bé
1SG know HYP 2M COP chief DAT
kolo ge yàá-ŋ *bé kolo ŋ gol
reason HUM tell-1SG DAT reason 1SG see
'I know that you are a chief, because I was told so'

The hypothesis about the function of the two complementizers is further supported by the imperative forms, corresponding to English 'know that'. In such constructions either the complementizer **na** or **go** can be deployed. The complementizer **go** is used when the speaker has personal knowledge of the facts described in the embedded clause:

(9) sìnà go gi ánè
know:IMP REF 2M come out:FUT
kùrmbàlo wèlè pìná
chief day one
'know that one day you will be a chief' (a chief admonishing his son)

Hearsay knowledge of the proposition of the embedded clause is coded by the complementizer **na**:

(10) sìnà na gi ná nòjù-m
know:IMP HYP 2M ASSC relatives-2M
dà màní
PREP there
'know that you have relatives there' (I was told so)

Cf.:

(11) sìnà go gi ná nòjù-m
know:IMP REF 2M ASSC relatives-2M
dà màní
PREP there
'know that you have relatives there' (I know them)

3 Complements after verbs of perception (see, hear)

There are two main semantic domains with respect to complementation after verbs of perception. One domain is direct evidence, when the subject of the main verb has seen or heard the event described in the embedded clause. The other is indirect evidence, when the subject of the main clause only concludes about the event described in the embedded clause.

3.1 Coding of direct evidence

Direct perception on the part of the subject is coded either by the absence of a complementizer or by the complementizer **go**. When there is no complementizer, the verb of the complement clause may be in the past tense form. The subject of the embedded clause is coded as the object of the matrix clause. At the same time it functions as the subject of the embedded clause:

(12) Dàdù ɓòdu ɗenglí tamá nè ile,
3F monkey hear woman IMPF cry
'The monkey heard the woman cry . . . '

(13) kùrmbàlò gol kamda-y sùbù nè go
chief see wives-3M three COP REF
láy-wà tú
beautiful-REF all (Fr.)
'the chief$_1$ saw that his$_2$ wives were all beautiful'

(14) dàì le gol kamda-y sùbù tú nè
3M also see wives-3M three all COP
go láy-wà
REF beautiful-REF
'the man$_1$ also saw that his$_1$ wives were beautiful'

Additional evidence for the syntactic object status of the subject of the embedded clause is provided by the behavior of pronominal subjects in the same position. The third-person plural subject has mid rather than high tone, and more important, it occurs before rather than after the predicate of the embedded clause:

(15) kùrmbàlò gol ge nè go láy-wà
chief see 3PL COP REF beautiful-REF
tú
all (Fr.)
'the chief saw$_1$ that they were all beautiful'

The third-person singular and masculine subject pronouns of the embedded clause are coded as direct objects of the main clause. Even if the subject of the embedded clause is coded as the object of the matrix clause, it can also be overtly coded in the embedded clause:

(16) ŋ gol-iy go jè è (dí)
1SG see-3M REF IMPF go 3M
'I saw him going'

(17) ŋ gol-iy go è (dí)
1SG see-3M REF go 3M
'I saw him depart'

(18) ŋ gol-du è (dú)
1SG see-3F go 3F
'I saw her go'

For the remaining persons, i.e. the third-person plural and the first- and second-person singular, dual, or plural, the subject of the embedded clause remains suffixed or prefixed to the verb of the embedded clause, and at the same time the verb of the main clause has an object pronoun coding the gender, number, and person of the subject of the embedded clause:

(19)	ŋ	gol-ge	è	gé
	1SG	see-3PL	go	3PL
	'I saw them go'			

(20)	ŋ	gol-iŋ	(dí)	ŋ	è
	1SG	see-1SG	3M	1SG	go
	'he saw me go'				

(21)	gol-gi	(dí)	gi	è
	see-2M	3M	2M	go
	'he saw you go'			

(22)	gol-me	dí	me	è
	see-2F	3M	2F	go
	'he saw you go'			

The complementation of transitive verbs is similar:

(23)	ŋ	gol-i	wàl	tù
	1SG	see-3M	slaughter	goat
	'I saw him slaughter a goat'			

(24)	ŋ	gol-du	gàr	déglè
	1SG	see-3F	mold	pot
	'I saw her mold a pot'			

(25)	gol-iŋ-dí	ŋ	wal	tù
	see-1SG-3M	1SG	slaughter	goat
	'he saw me slaughter a goat'			

The nominal subject of an embedded clause remains in its position preceding the verb of the embedded clause. The verb of the matrix clause does not have an object pronoun coding the gender and number of the subject of the embedded clause. The pronominal subject suffix coding the gender and number of the nominal subject of the embedded clause may follow the verb of the embedded clause:

(26)	ŋ	gol-*iy	canigé	è	(dí)
	1SG	see-3M	Canige	go	3M
	'I saw Canige go'				

(27)

ŋ	gol-*du	gìlkínín	è-(dú)
1SG	see-3F	Gilkinin	go-3F

'I saw Gilkinin go'

(28)

ŋ	gol-*ge	gìlkínín	dàgè	ná	canigé	è-gé
1SG	see-3PL	Gilkinin	3PL	ASSC	Canige	go-3PL

'I saw Gilkinin and Canige go'

The complementizer **go** indicates conclusions drawn from a perception of the subject:

(29)

tu-ŋ	gol	go	gonì	kún-do	jèn	téŋ
goat-DEF	see	REF	hyena	eye-3F	remain	different

'Goat noticed that Hyena had different intentions . . .' (the goat did not see the onset of new intentions)

(30)

ngu	gol	gaw	go	kun-do	pìnà	tésí	ɗé-ŋ
2PL	see	well	REF	eye-3F	one	break	already-DEF

'you see well that one of her eyes is already spoiled . . .' (the participants did not see the eye becoming spoiled)

With the verb **ɗeŋlí** 'to hear' the preferred structure is to have the word **lám** 'noise' as the object, followed by the possessive form of the subject of the embedded clause: Subject Verb [hear] **lám** ['noise'] Possessive **go** Verb:

(31)

ŋ	ɗeŋlí	lám-dì	go	jè	è	jè
1SG	hear	noise-3M	REF	IMPF	go	VENT

'I heard him coming'

3.2 Hypothetical modality with verbs of perception

Hypothetical modality with verbs of perception is marked by the complementizer **na** or by the combination **gi na** 'as if'. The structure of such a sentence is Subject Verb (**gi**) **na** Clause. The complementizer **na** can occur alone, but the complementizer **gi** cannot and must always be accompanied by **na**. The meaning of sentences with hypothetical modality is that the subject perceived something but is not sure of his perception:

(33)

ŋ	gol	na	wàl	(dí)	kúlbà
1SG	see	HYP	slaughter	3M	cow

'I saw that he slaughtered a cow' (but maybe it is not true)

With a verb of hearing the complementizer **na** codes a hearsay source:

(34) càǹìgé ɗeŋlí na gírbí dú jè kòjò
Canige hear HYP forget 3F PERF hoe
kò-rò
GEN-3F
'Canige heard that she forgot her hoe'

(35) ŋ gol gi na gírbì-dú jè kòjò
1SG see HYP HYP forget-3F PERF hoe
kò-rò
GEN-3F
'I saw that it looked as if she forgot her hoe'

Sentences containing a verb of perception followed by the complementizer **na** or **gi na** indicate, not that the action was perceived, but rather some traces of the action.

One cannot combine the complementizers **go na** with a verb of perception. Thus the following sentences are ungrammatical:

(36) *ŋ gol-íy go ná wàl dí
1SG see-3M REF HYP slaughter 3M
kúlbà
cow
for 'I saw him slaughter a cow'

(37) *ŋ gol-íy ná go wàl-dí kúlbà
1SG see-3M HYP REF slaughter-3M cow
for 'I saw him slaughter a cow'

4 Complements of volitional verbs

4.1 Volitional verbs and their complementizers

There are at least two volitional verbs that can take clausal complements: **tòb** 'like, love, want' and a word borrowed from Ngambay, **gèy** 'want'. The form **gèy** occurs often in natural spoken data, hence its inclusion in the present discussion. Evidence for the lexical meaning 'love, like, want' of the verb **tòb** is provided by the following examples:

(38)

dà	túgú	tóŋ	ni	ná [pause]	gáw
PREP	village	INDEF:F	LOC	ASSC	hunter

kóŋ	ná	tamą́-y	tòb	gé	kusi-gè
certain:M	ASSC	wife-3M	like	3PL	body-3PL

néỳ
very much

'In a village a certain hunter sorcerer and his wife loved each other very much.'

(39)

mùlù-níŋ	tòb-mè
heart-1SG	love-2F

'I love you'

(40)

gi	tòb	nè	bà-m	gèrè	yó-m
2M	love	COP	father-2M	or	mother-2M

gà
Q

'do you love your father or your mother?'

The two verbs can occur in the speech of the same speakers and appear to have different meanings:

(41)

ŋ	tòb-mè	àlá	kà-rè	gèy	ɗé
1SG	love-2F	but	parents-2F	want	NEG

'I love you but your parents do not approve'

The ensuing analysis deals with the verb **tòb**. The verb **tòb** can take the complementizer **na** alone, **go** alone, or a combination of **go** and **na** in that order. Natural discourse and elicited data point to a clear functional differentiation between the two complementizers. The complementizer **go** is deployed when the matrix and the embedded clause have the same subjects and not when the subjects are different. The complementizer **na** must be deployed when the matrix and the embedded clause have different subjects and may be deployed when they have the same subjects but only following the complementizer **go**.

This functional distinction is consistent with the function of the two complementizers in other syntactic environments. The complementizer **go** is the de re complementizer. All things being equal, a subject's wishes with respect to her/his own actions are more realistic, have more chance of being fulfilled, than the subject's wishes with respect to somebody else. Wishes with respect to somebody else are marked by the de dicto complementizer **na**.

In what follows I first describe the system occurring in natural discourse and some elicitations, the clear-cut system, and then the system as it emerges from other elicitations.

4.2 Same-subject complements of volitional verbs

There are two forms of same-subject complements of volitional verbs: one with the complementizer **go** alone, and the other with the complementizer **go** followed by the complementizer **na**. The complementizer **go** alone codes realistic wishes, wishes that have no reason to be considered conditioned by anything else. The sequence **go na** codes hypothetical wishes, wishes that can be fulfilled only if something else happens, or even wishes that are unrealistic under any conditions.

4.3 Realistic wishes: the complementizer go

For first- and second-person pronominal subjects of matrix and embedded clauses only the complementizer **go** can be used to code realistic wishes. The subject of the complement clause is not overtly marked. The verb of the complement clause may have different tense forms. In the following example the verb is in the future tense form:

(42) Ng tòb go bóré me gèylè.
1SG want REF save:FUT 2F life
'I want to save your life' (G-C & W 1981: 4-5)

In the following example the verb is nominalized:

(43) Me góolé ng nè tòb go
2F see:FUT 1SG COP want REF
gèylè mè.
save:VN 2F
'You will see that I want to save you.' (G-C & W 1981: 4-5)

In elicitation data the complementizer is optional:

(44) ŋ jè tòb (go) é
1SG IMPF want REF go:FUT
'I want to go'

(45) gi jè tòb (go) é gà
2M IMPF want REF go:FUT Q
'do you want to go?'

(46) ni jè tòb (go) é
1PL.EXCL IMPF want REF go:FUT
'we would like to go'

In natural speech data, however, the complementizer is never omitted.

The third-person singular masculine subject of the verb **tòb** does not have to be overtly marked, as it does not have to be marked with other verbs:

(47) tòb go é
want REF go:FUT
'he wants to go'

(48) . . . na-y bòr gúnyé geìl-ì ba gų́yé
. . . HYP-3M save spider health-3M COM spider
na è jè tòb go dígrè-y gà
HYP go VENT want REF kill:FUT-3M Q
'he said that he saved Spider, and Spider wants to kill him?'

Unlike with first- and second-person subjects, the complementizer **go** cannot be omitted with third-person subjects, regardless of whether the subject is overtly marked:

(49) *tòb dí é
want 3M go:FUT
for 'he wants to go'

Third-person feminine and plural pronominal subjects must be overtly marked:

(50) tòb dú/gé go é
want 3F/3PL REF go:FUT
'she/they want to go'

The unspecified human subject can also be used with the verb **tòb**:

(51) ge tòb go é
HUM want REF go:FUT
'they want to go' (does not include the speaker)

The subject of the verb **tòb** does not have to be controlling. Clauses with non-controlling subjects point to the grammaticalization of the verb **tòb** as the marker of the proximate future:

(52) Kasínya tòb go ane te-ì
feces want REF leave:VN buttocks-3M
ni . . .
LOC
'He was about to go . . .' (G-C & W 1981: 10-11)

4.4 Hypothetical wishes with respect to same subject

Hypothetical wishes with respect to the same subject are coded by the sequence **go na** or by the marker **na** alone. The use of the complementizer **na** requires the overt coding of the subject of the complement clause, even if the subject of the matrix and the embedded clauses are the same.

The sequence of complementizers **go na** follows the volitional verb in the negative clause, i.e. when the wish is not realized:

(53)

bayndí	è	jè	ná	kòbró	bayndí-ŋ	tòb
man	go	VENT	ASSC	boat	man-DEF	want

go	na	hímé-gé	ɗé
REF	HYP	take:FUT-3PL	NEG

'A man came with a boat but he refused to take them.'

Another speaker preferred omitting the complementizer **go** altogether for the relevant portion of this sentence and instead offered:

(54)

bayndí-ŋ	tòb	na-y	hímé-gé	ɗé
man-DEF	want	HYP-3M	take:FUT-3PL	NEG

'the man refused to take them'

As is always the case with the complementizer **na**, the third-person pronominal subject follows the complementizer and precedes the verb:

(55)

tòb	dú	go	na	du	hábe	karma
want	3F	REF	HYP	3F	find:FUT	children

súbù
three

'she would like to have three children'

(56)

ŋ	tòb	go	na	ŋ	hábe
1SG	want	REF	HYP	1SG	find:FUT

karma	súbù
children	three

'I would like to have three children'

(57)

tòb	dí	go	na-y	é
want	3M	REF	HYP-3M	go:FUT

'he would like to go'

Here is an example where the borrowed volitional verb **gèy** is followed by the complementizer **na** alone, i.e. without the complementizer **go**. The third-person subject is coded as the object of the complementizer:

(58)

wèlè	pìnà	ná	gèy	na-y
day	one	ASSC	want (Ng)	HYP-3M
gísè-dù				
try:FUT-3F				

'One day he wished to test her.'

4.5 Different-subject complements of volitional verbs

Different-subject complements of volitional verbs must be overtly coded regardless of the person. The complement clause with different subjects is always marked by the complementizer **na**. The verb in the complement clause must always be in the imperative modality:

(59)

ŋ	tòb	na	canigé	ìrà
1SG	want	HYP	Canige	go:IMP

'I want Canige to go'

Deployment of the complementizer **go** even when followed by the complementizer **na** with different subjects yields an ungrammatical sentence:

(60)

*ŋ	tòb	go	(na)	canigé	ìrà
1SG	want	REF	HYP	Canige	go:IMP

for 'I want Canige to go'

As the consequence of the imperative modality of the complement clause, the second-person plural and third-person singular pronominal subjects of the embedded clause follow the verb:

(61)

ŋ	tòb	na	à	jè	dí
1SG	want	HYP	go:IMP	VENT	3M

'I wanted him to come'

The first-person inclusive subject is coded by the first-person dual form **ngà** preceding the verb, and the second-person plural form **ngù** following the verb:

(62)

jè	tóbè	gé	na	ngà	ìrà
IMPF	want:FUT	3PL	HYP	1DU.INCL	go:IMP
ngù					
2PL					

'they will want us (INCL) to go'

(63)

jè	tòb	gé	na	ngà	ìrà	ngù
IMPF	want	3PL	HYP	1PL	go:IMP	2PL

'they want us to go'

Doubt in truth after volitional verbs is expressed by the morpheme **sáŋ** or **gèrè** or the combination of the two in the clause-final position:

(64)

tòb	dí	na	gi	à	je
want	3M	HYP	2M	go:IMP	VENT
sáŋ	gèrè				
DUB	IF				

'he wanted you to come' (but I am not sure that he really did)

A special case is presented by sentences with the third-person singular subject in the matrix clause and the third-person plural subject in the embedded clause. The third-person singular subject can, but does not have to be, a member of the subject group of the embedded clause. Whether the matrix subject is part of the embedded clause subject or not, the complement clause is coded as having different subjects, i.e., it has the complementizer **na** rather than **go**. Moreover, the verb in both types of clauses occurs in the imperative form.

The membership of the third-person singular subject in the group of the third-person plural subject of the embedded clause is coded through the position of the third-person plural subject between the complementizer and the verb:

(65)

tòb	dú	na	ge	ìrà
want	3F	HYP	HUM	go:IMP

'she wanted them to go' (she is a part of 'them')

If one wants to indicate that the third-person subject of the singular is not a part of the third-person plural subject of the embedded clause, this is coded by the position of the third-person plural subject after the verb of the embedded clause:

(66)

tòb	dí	na	ìrà	gé
want	3M	HYP	go:IMP	3PL

'he wanted them to go' (he is not a part of 'them')

This order, viz. having the third-person subject following the verb in a clause beginning with the complementizer **na** is a special feature of the complements of volitional verbs. In complements of other verbs, the third-person subject, whether singular or plural, must follow the complementizer:

(67)

yàá	dí	na	ge	è
want	3M	HYP	3PL	go

'he said that they went'

(68) *yàá dí na è ge
want 3M HYP go 3PL
for 'he said that they went'

5 Complement of the verb ɓàl 'be able to'

The verb **ɓàl** 'be able to' can have only the de re complementizer because of the inherent properties of the matrix clause verb. All complement clauses must have the complementizer **go**. The verb in the embedded clause can have the nominalized or the future tense form depending on the intended tense. If the present tense form is intended, the nominalized form of the verb is used:

(69) ɓàl dí go òjé-ŋ
be able 3M REF help:VN-1SG
'he can help me'

(70) gi ɓàl go òmé-y ɗé
2M be able REF catch:VN-3M NEG
'you are not able to catch it'

(71) me ɓàl go wesé cà-nìŋ ɗé
2F be able REF hide:VN head-1SG NEG
'you cannot cover up for me'

(72) ŋ tòn na wéì ba ɓàl go
1SG ask REF who COM be able REF
òjé-ŋ gà
help-1SG Q
'I asked who could help me'

If the future time in the embedded clause is intended, the future tense of the verb is deployed:

(73) ŋ tòn-ìy na ɓále dí go
1SG ask-3M HYP be able:FUT 3M REF
ójè-ŋgà gà
help:FUT-1DU.INCL Q
'I asked whether he would be able to help us'

(74)

ŋ	tòn-gì	ná	gi	ɓàl	go
1SG	ask-2M	HYP	2M	be able	REF
ójé-ŋ		gà			
help:FUT-1SG		Q			

'I asked you whether you could help me'

6 Conclusions

The referential marker **go** is deployed as the de re complementizer with verbs of perception. It can also occur after cognitive verbs to code knowledge derived from personal experience. With volitional verbs the complementizer **go** codes realistic wishes with respect to the subject of the embedded clause. Such wishes are realistic only if the subject of the embedded clause is coreferential with the subject of the matrix clause. If the subject of the embedded clause is different from the subject of the matrix clause, the de dicto complementizer **na** is deployed, coding a hypothetical wish.

21

Complementation through Nominalization

1 Introduction

Complementation through nominalization in Lele presents an interesting phenomenon given the fact that there are two possessive constructions, one for alienable and one for inalienable possession. Because there are two constructions, the distinction between nominalization from the point of view of the agent-controller and that from the point of view of the affected, or non-controlling, argument can be coded.

2 Nominalized forms of the verb and possessive constructions

Nominalized forms of the verb can take either alienable or inalienable possessive forms. For transitive verbs, there is a clear functional distinction between the two forms. The inalienable possessive form codes nominalization from the point of view of the object. The alienable possessive form codes the event from the point of the agent. As an illustration, consider the verbs **dasì** 'husk' and **dàgí** 'filter'. The nominalized forms can take both possessive forms. With the inalienable possessive, the meaning is 'the way it can be husked', 'the way it filters'. With the alienable possessive form, it means 'her way of husking something' or 'her way of filtering':

(1)	dase	kò-rò	kurà	ɗé
	husk:VN	GEN-3F	good	NEG
	'her way of husking is not good'			

(2)	dase	kò-y	kurà	ɗé
	husk:VN	GEN-3M	good	NEG
	'her way of husking is not good'			

(3)	dase-y	kurà	ɗé
	husk:VN-3M	good	NEG
	'it cannot be husked well'		

(4)	dage	kò-rò	kurà	ɗé
	filter:VN	GEN-3F	good	NEG
	'her way of filtering is not good'			

(5)	dage	kò-y	kurà	ɗé
	filter:VN	GEN-3M	good	NEG
	'her way of filtering is not good'			

(6)	dage-y	kurà	ɗé
	filter-3M	good	NEG
	'it does not filter well'		

Thus the alienable and inalienable possessive forms have different functions with respect to the nominalized forms of the verb. The list below shows what possessive constructions a given verb can take. As expected, transitive verbs can take either the alienable or the inalienable possessive form. Some intransitive verbs can take only one form, the alienable possessive marker. But some intransitive verbs can take both alienable and inalienable possessive markers. The verbs that can take both forms are those where the subject is also affected, e.g. undergoing change, moving. With such verbs, the alienable form codes the event from the point of view of the subject's control, and the inalienable form codes the event from the point of view of the subject's affectedness.

(7)	dere-y	ndóji̇̀
	move-3M	difficult
	'it is difficult to move'	

(8)	dere	kè-y	ndóji̇̀
	move	GEN-3M	difficult
	'his moving was difficult'		

In the list below, + means that the construction is allowed, - means that the construction is not allowed. In some cases, the nominalized form of the verb has acquired a narrow lexical meaning. In such cases, instead of the sign +, the lexicalized meaning alone is given:

Past		VN	Inalienable	Alienable
an	'leave'	ane	'release'	+
al	'sing'	ale	-	+
bàsì	'fail, spend'	base	-	+
dèr	'move'	dere	+	+
sàgì	'tear'	sage	'a tear'	+
tàb	'follow'	tabe	'massage'	+
càl	'go to meet'	cale	-	+
dùgì	'submerge'	duge	+	+
gòl	'see'	gole	+	+
tey	'call'	tege	'invitation'	+
dì	'eat'	de	+	+
kìl	'sell'	kile	+	+
wèy	'become'	weye	-	+
wȩy	'cook'	wȩye	+	+
Past		VN	Inalienable	Alienable
kab	'whip'	kabé	+	+
ɓíl	'drag'	ɓilé	+	+
cál	'jump'	càlé	+[18]	+
kál	'pass'	kàlé	+	+
ɗeŋlí	'hear'	ɗèŋlé	+	+
sàb	'burn'	sàbè	+	+
gìl	'show'	gìlè	+	+
wìl	'glean'	wìlè	+	+
wàl	'slaughter'	wàlè	+	+
lèé	'chew'	lè	+	+
pèé	'dig'	pè	+	+
bòy	'break'	bòyè	+	+
kìn	'return'	kìnè	+	+
òdì	'leave'	òdè	+	+
òjì	'help'	òjè	+	+
dìgrì	'kill'	dìgrè	+	+
nè	'make'	nè	-	+
è	'go'	è	-	+
tèy	'fetch'	tègè	+	+
kày	'finish'	kàyè	+	+
wèl	'pass time'	wèlè	+	+
ìm	'bury'	ìmè	+	+
kàl	'climb'	kàlè	+	+
bòr	'cut'	bòrè	+	+

18
búrgú	háŋ	càlé-y	ndòjì
wall	DEM:P	jump-3M	difficult

'this wall cannot be jumped over'

ɓàl	'suffice'	ɓàlè	-	+
jìb	'stick'	jìbè	+	+
nàr	'forbid'	nàrè	(interdiction)	+
tą̀ñ	'slim'	tą̀nyé	+	+
wíl	'warm up'	wìlé	+	+
jèn	'stay'	jèné	(position)	+
hím	'gather'	hìmé	+	+
kál	'pass'	kàlé	+	+

3 Nominalization of transitive verbs

The alienable possessive structure is used for nominalizations with the point of view of agent of the transitive verbs. The construction has the form Verb:VN Object GEN-Pronoun:

(9) węye wò kò-rò mòglí kèlèŋ
cook:VN food GEN-3F fast fast
'her cooking of food was fast'

(10) gàrè kúní kè-gè kurà sìɗé
build:VN house GEN-3P good very
'their building of the house was good'

The nominalization from the point of view of the object has the inalienable possessive construction, and the whole structure has the form: Noun Verb:VN-Pronoun, where the pronoun encodes the features of gender and number of the noun:

(11) wò węye-y mòglí kèlèŋ
food cook:VN-3M fast fast
'the cooking of mush was fast'

(12) kúní gàrè-y kurà sìɗé
house build:VN-3M good very
'the buiding of the house was good'

The role of the possessive construction is best illustrated where the noun involved could be a potential agent or patient. In such cases, inalienable possession codes nominalization from the point of view of the patient, and alienable construction from the point of view of the agent:

(13) ɗìgrè kìrwè kò-rò kurà sìɗé
kill:VN leopard GEN-3F good very
'her killing of the leopard was very good'

(14)	kìrwè	ɗìgrè-rò	kurà	sìɗé
	leopard	kill:VN-3F	good	very

'the killing of the leopard was very good' (the leopard **kìrwè** is killed; leopard is feminine)

If the transitive verb has an object and the nominalization is from the point of view of the agent, the object keeps its place after the verb, and the nominal agent occurs after the object, followed by the inalienable possessive construction:

(15)	ɗìgrè	tu	kìrwè	kò-rò	kurà	sìɗé
	kill:VN	goat	leopard	GEN-3F	good	very

'the way the leopard killed the goat was very good'

One can also nominalize the clause from the point of the object and preserve the agent in the clause at the same time. Such a clause has the inalienable possessive construction for the object followed by the alienable possessive construction for the agent: Object Verb:VN-Pronoun Agent GEN-Pronoun:

(16)	tu	ɗìgrè-rò	kìrwè	kò-rò	kurà	sìɗé
	goat	kill:VN-3F	leopard	GEN-3F	good	very

'the killing of the goat by the leopard was very good'

Thus, there exists considerable freedom in nominalizations, which may include both arguments of the transitive verb:

(17)	kúní	gàrè-y	kò-nòŋ	kurà	sìɗé
	house	construction-3M	GEN-1SG	good	very

'my construction of the house was good' (the house does not have to belong to the builder)

(18)	gàrè	kúní	kò-nòŋ	kurà	sìɗé
	construction	house	GEN-1SG	good	very

'my construction of the house was good' or 'the construction of my house was good'

4 Nominalization of intransitive verbs

Recall that some intransitive verbs can occur with both alienable and inalienable constructions, and others can occur only with the inalienable possessive construction. The inalienable construction codes the point of view of the affectedness of the subject, and the alienable construction codes the point of view of control, or to be more precise, of the non-affectedness of the subject. Compare the two expressions with the same verb, inalienable **jènè-y** and alienable **jènè kè-y**:

(19) jènè kè-y dà màrùá èsì sìɗé
stay:VN GEN-3M PREP Maroua difficult very
'his stay in Maroua is very difficult'

(20) jènè-y dà màrùá èsì sìɗé
stay:VN-3M PREP Maroua difficult very
'the place he lives in Maroua is very difficult'

(21) jènè-y kur káŋ ni kurá ɗé
stay:VN-3M place DEM:P LOC good NEG
'his position at the location here is not good'

(22) yàá dí na jènè kè-y dà
say 3M HYP stay:VN GEN-3M PREP
màrùá èsì sìɗé
Maroua difficult very
'he$_1$ said that his$_{1/2}$ stay in Maroua is very difficult'

(23) yàá dí na jènè-y dà màrùá
say 3M HYP stay:VN-3M PREP Maroua
èsì sìɗé
difficult very
'he said that the place he lives in Maroua is very difficult'

5 Conclusions

The existence of two possessive constructions allows the language to have two types of nominalizations: one from the point of view of the subject of the verb and the other from the point of view of the object of the verb. The inalienable possessive construction is deployed to code nominalization from the point of view of the object of the transitive verb. The alienable possessive construction is deployed to code nominalization from the point of view of the subject of the clause, whether transitive or intransitive.

22

Adjunct clauses

1 Introduction

The term *adjunct clauses* refers to clauses whose presence within a sentence is not required by any of its elements. The clausal adjuncts behave thus in the same way as prepositional adjuncts. The following clausal adjuncts are described: purpose, reason, and time.

2 Purpose

In purpose clauses the subject of the embedded clause is expected to be the agent of the event. The purpose clause follows the matrix clause. The subordinator of purpose is the form **kolo** 'reason, because', whose other, and perhaps historically primary, meaning is 'word'. The form **kolo** may be preceded by the dative marker **bé**. One of the more interesting features of purpose clauses in Lele is that they can be coded for several epistemic modalities. The modality markers follow the subordinator (**bé**) **kolo**.

3 The realis modality of the reason clause

The realis modality of the purpose clause is coded by the apposition of the purpose clause immediately after the subordinator, i.e. without any additional modality markers. The verb of the adjunct clause is in the future form:

(1)

ɓòdu	kò-nòng,	ng	nè	ile	kolo
monkey	GEN-1SG	1SG	IMPF	cry	reason

ge	jè	éè	wálè-ng	kolo
HUM	IMPF	go:FUT	cut:FUT-1SG	reason

dèrè	kormo	go	dà	kùlè-nìng	ni,
extract:VN	child	REF	PREP	belly-1SG	LOC

'My monkey, I am crying because soon they will cut me in order to extract the child from my belly.' (G-C &W 1981: 2-3)

(2)

tòrò	yó-ró	è	jè	gé	ná
hen	mother-3F	go	VENT	3PL	ASSC

karan-do	kolo	dé	gé	kasa-ŋ
children-3F	reason	eat:FUT	3PL	corn-DEF

'the old hen went with her children to eat the corn'

(3)

kamda	sèn	gé	go	sé	tamá
women	know	3PL	REF	put:FUT	woman

kolo	wè	ɗé.
reason	give birth	NEG

'. . . women did not know how to position a woman for childbirth'

4 The hypothetical modality of the purpose clause

The hypothetical modality of the purpose clause is coded by the complementizer **na** following the subordinator (**bé**) **kolo**. The verb in the purpose clause has the future tense form. Because of the presence of the complementizer **na**, the third-person pronouns follow the complementizer and precede the verb:

(4)

ŋ	gìl-gì	gùyé	bé	kolo	na	gi
1SG	show-2M	work	DAT	reason	HYP	2M

hábe	ná	cà-m
find:FUT	ASSC	head-2M

'I have shown you the work so that you can succeed'

(5)

se	è	jè	gé	dà	tálwá	ni
INCEPT	go	VENT	3PL	PREP	pond	LOC

bé	kolo	na	ge	sée	kam(a)
DAT	reason	HYP	3PL	drink:FUT	water

'then they came to a pond intending to drink water' (according to the ensuing text in the story, the drinking never took place)

The omission of the subject pronoun in the adjunct clause yields an ungrammatical sentence, even if the pronoun follows the main verb of the complement clause:

(6)

*se	è	jè	gé	dà	tálwá	nì
INCEPT	go	VENT	3PL	PREP	pond	LOC

bé	kolo	na	séè	gé	kam(a)
DAT	reason	HYP	drink:FUT	3PL	water

for 'then they came to a pond in order to drink water'

5 Unrealized purpose

The unrealized purpose is coded by the imperative form of the verb of the purpose clause. That coding system operates with the same and different subjects of the matrix and embedded clause. The purpose clause is still preceded by the complementizer **na**, which follows the subordinator (**bé**) **kolo**:

(7)

ŋ	gìl-gì	gùyé	bé	kolo	na	gi
1SG	show-2M	work	DAT	because	HYP	2M

hábá	ná	cà-m
find:IMP	ASSC	head-2M

'I have shown you the work so that you could succeed, but you did not'

With different subjects, the verb of the embedded clause cannot have the past tense form:

(8)

*ŋ	gìl-gì	gùyé	bé	kolo	na	gi
1SG	show-2M	work	DAT	because	HYP	2M

hab	ná	cà-m
find	ASSC	head-2M

for 'I have shown you the work so that you could succeed, but you did not'

The imperative form of the verb explicitly codes the fact that the subjects were not successful:

(9)

se	è	jè	gé	dà	tálwá	ni
INCEPT	go	VENT	3PL	PREP	pond	LOC

bé	kolo	na	ge	sà	kam(a)
DAT	because	HYP	3PL	drink:IMP	water

'then they came to a pond in order to drink water, but they did not drink'

6 Reason clauses

Reason clauses may be marked by the same subordinator as the purpose clause, viz. (**bé**) **kolo** 'reason' preceding the embedded clause. The embedded clause differs from the purpose clause in that it is not marked by the complementizer **na**, and more important, the verb of the reason clause may be in the past tense form:

(10)

ge	dìgr-ìy	ná	kolo	tumad-iy	na
HUM	kill-3M	ASSC	reason	death-3M	HYP

gárnį-íy	ɗé
anger-1SG	NEG

'he can be killed, because death does not worry him.'

(11)

Ná	ɗigle	ná	ɗigle	kamda	nè	mar-wi
ASSC	year	ASSC	year	women	IMPF	die-PL
gé	kolo	ge	nè	wàl-wì-gè.		
3PL	reason	HUM	IMPF	cut-PL-3PL		

'Year after year women were dying because they were cut.' (G-C & W 1981: 2-3)

Embedded-clause subject pronouns, whether identical with the matrix clause or not, with the exception of the third-person masculine, must be overtly marked:

(12)

time	nè	gònì	nèy	bé	kolo
hunger	make	hyena	very much	DAT	reason
dìgrì	dú	ìsán	ɗé		
kill	3F	nothing	NEG		

'Hyena is very hungry because it did not kill anything.'

(13)

gònì	sùm-rò	se	yí	cà-rò
hyena	be mad:VN-3F	INCEPT	put	head-3F

kama	te-y	ni	ná	dusi	kolo
water	bottom-3M	LOC	ASSC	sink	because
sèn	go	nàlè	kama	ɗé	
know	REF	swim:VN	water	NEG	

'Foolish Hyena put its head at the bottom of the water, and it sank because it did not know how to swim.'

(14)

ŋ	è	je	kolo	ŋ	ɗénglì	na	gi
1SG	go	VENT	reason	1SG	hear	HYP	2M

hòmyá
sick

'I came because I heard that you were sick'

(15) gi è jè kolo gi kújíŋgile kùb
2M go VENT reason 2M learn:FUT language
lèlé
Lele
'you came to learn the Lele language'

Cf.:

(16) *gi è jè kolo kújíŋgile kùb lèlé
1SG go VENT reason learn:FUT language Lele
for 'you came to learn the Lele language'

The embedded clause may have a subject different from that of the matrix clause:

(17) gònì dusi kolo tu óm cà-rò
hyena sink reason goat hold head-3F
'the hyena sank because the goat held its head'

7 Temporal adverb clause

Temporal adverb clauses are those that indicate the beginning or the end of an event. The end of the event is coded by the particle **gàk** 'until' or **hàn** 'until' borrowed from Arabic:

(18) gìr ná ín-dì hàn è-gé
run ASSC ASSC-3M till (Ar.) go-3PL
ná dà kama kùb-ìy ni
ASSC PREP river edge-3M LOC
'She ran with him till they arrived at the bank of the river.'

(19) gìr ná ín-dì gàk è-gé ná
run ASSC ASSC-3M till go-3PL ASSC
dà kama kùb-ìy ni
PREP river edge-3M LOC
'She ran with him till they arrived at the bank of the river.'

8 Conclusions

Purpose clauses are marked by the subordinator **kolo,** identical with the noun 'word'. The subordinator may be preceded by the dative marker **bé**. There is a distinction between the realis modality, marked by the verb in the future tense form, and the irrealis, hypothetical, modality marked by the complementizer **na** following the subordinator **kolo**. The unrealized modality of the purpose clause is marked by the imperative form of the verb. The reason clause is also marked by the subordinator **kolo**, but the verb is in the past form.

23

Temporal Sentences

1 Introduction

In all temporal sentences the protasis clause, establishing the time of the event, precedes the apodosis clause, i.e. the clause that states what happened at the time established by the protasis clause. Translating this into English system of coding, the 'when clause' precedes the 'then clause'.

There are several means of coding temporal clauses. The fundamental means of coding the temporal protasis is through the associative marker **ná** preceding or ending the protasis clause.

2 Temporal protasis

In the imperfective aspect the temporal protasis may be coded simply by the deployment of the auxiliary **jè** preceding the verb:

(1) tùwà tóŋ pìnà ná [pause] jè yì dú
Sun certain:F one ASSC IMPF pound 3F
kąnya tòrò yó-ró è jè gé ná
thing hen mother-3F go VENT 3PL ASSC
karan-do kolo dé gé kasa-ŋ
children-3F reason eat:FUT 3PL corn-DEF
'One day, when she$_1$ was pounding, the old hen$_2$ came with her children to eat the corn.'

Recall that the auxiliary **jè** marks events contemporaneous with certain other events.

Coding the clause as background information with the associative preposition **ná** may induce temporal interpretation. Whereas the protasis clause has a past tense form, the apodosis clause has the auxiliary **jè**:

(2) tamá-ŋ ɗeŋlí ná jè wèy
woman-DEF understand ASSC IMPF turn
ín-dí-gè pílá pílá
ASSC-GEN:PL-3PL at the same time
'When the woman understood, she was turning around [the mortar] at the same time [as they did].'

In the above sentence the woman's understanding did not occur at any specific time, but her turning around the mortar occurred only when she understood the intentions of the other protagonist in the story.

In the following sentence **jè** occurs in both the protasis and the apodosis clause to code mutual interrelationship and mutual dependence of the two clauses:

(3) bàyndí-ŋ jè è sègré ná tìgrí
man-DEF IMPF go hunt ASSC kill:PL:VN
kàrgé sò ɗéŋ sùbù kura kʅnyé
wild animals two or three rabbit COLL
bísí kʅnyé nasú kʅnyé ná [pause]
antelope COLL gnu antelope COLL ASSC
jè è jè kèsi jáy bé tamá
IMPF go VENT share part DAT wife
túg ni lay jay kóŋ
compound LOC also part certain:M
jè ǻy ná kasa lay gùnà lay
IMPF take ASSC corn also peanuts also
'Each time the man went for a hunt, he killed two or three wild animals, rabbits, small antelopes, gnu antelopes; he shared some with his wife at home, and some he bartered for corn and peanuts.'

The specific temporal protasis markers are various temporal words and phrases, such as the word **kur** 'place, time', **tùwà tóŋ** 'certain time', etc. followed by the relative marker **go**, by the complementizer **na**, or by apodosis marker at the end of the clause. The complementizer **na** and the referential marker **go** retain their functions when other temporal words are used:

(4) Kur go gìdìrè Bàn-sà an ɗè
time REF moon Ban-sa come out leave
'When the moon Ban-sa comes out . . .' (G-C & W 1982: 52-53)

The temporal protasis clause does not have to be marked if the apodosis clause is marked, as in the following sentences where the apodosis is marked by the sequence **ɗe ná**:

(5) pe bé-y kasire-ŋ ɗe ná
dig DAT-3M medicine-DEF THEN ASSC
bayndí-ŋ se háb gèylè
man-DEF INCEPT find health
'When he$_1$ dug up the medicine, then the man$_2$ recovered his health.'

3 Modality coding in temporal protasis

Temporal clauses also display the modal distinctions observed in other functional domains. When the time of a temporal protasis refers to a general time, it is coded by the complementizer **na** preceding the protasis clause:

(6) na è gé dàwù-gé ná kámdà sò
HYP go 3PL gather-3PL ASSC women two
'when they went, it was a group with two wives'

(7) Na gi gol gìdìrè ba wèlè-ì gì
HYP 2M see moon man day-3M remain
mira go ane ɗe ná, gi
approach REF leave:VN THEN ASSC 2M
è kùyrò ɗé.
go travel NEG
'When you see that the male moon is about to come out, do not undertake any travel' (G-C & W 1981: 22-23)

The time in the domain de re is coded through the use of a lexical expression designating time, such as **kur** 'place, time' or **tuwa** 'Sun, day', followed by a modifier that in turn is preceded by the de re complementizer **go**.

(8) Kur go gìdìrè dè gùjù an
time REF moon eat:VN millet come out
ɗè ná, kara go Gùná ba dì
THEN ASSC people REF Guna COM eat
gé gùjù tùmò
3PL millet first
'When "the moon of eating millet" comes out, it is the people of Guna who are first to eat the millet ' (G-C & W 1981: 22-23)

(9) tùmò go kara ínɗwé ɗeŋlí
once REF people humankind:PL understand
gé kùb kąnya ame kè-gè
3PL language thing domesticated GEN-3PL
ná tamá tóŋ ɗeŋlí kùb
ASSC woman certain understand language
kòrà kè-gè
chickens GEN-3PL
'At one time, when humankind understood the language of domestic animals, a certain woman understood the language of chickens.'

The protasis markers **ná** and **go** have different functions. The marker **go** codes specific time reference; the marker **ná** codes non-specific time reference:

(10) wèlè go sò go jè yì dú kąnya
day REF two REF IMPF pound 3F things
'on the second day, when she was pounding'

(11) *wèlè go sò na jè yì dú kąnya
day REF two ASSC IMPF pound 3F things
for 'on the second day, when she was pounding . . .'

With indefinite time reference, one can use the form **ná**, i.e. the form that is identical with the de dicto complementizer but has a high tone.

(12) tùwà tóŋ pìnà ná jè yì dú
Sun certain:F one ASSC IMPF pound 3F
kąnya
things
'one day when she was pounding'

The syntactic relationship between the form **go** and the rest of the sentence, and that between the form **ná** and the rest of the sentence, indicate that the forms **ná** and **go** are in complementary functional distribution. Thus the form **ná** may in fact be a prepausal variant of the form **na**. One cannot use the marker **go** with indefinite time reference:

(13) *tùwà tóŋ pìnà go jè yì dú
sun certain:F one REF IMPF pound 3F
kąnya
things
for 'one day when she was pounding'

But it is enough to delete markers of unspecified time reference to obtain a perfectly grammatical clause with **go**:

(14)

tùwà	go	jè	yì	dú	kąnya
sun	REF	IMPF	pound	3F	things

'the day when she was pounding'

Thus the functions of both markers are the same as in other constructions where they code the de dicto and de re distinctions.

4 Temporal apodosis clause

The apodosis clause does not have to be overtly marked if the protasis clause is marked. In the following sentence, the temporal protasis is marked by the expression **kur go** 'time when':

(15)

kur	go	gų́nyé	àg-ìy	jè	na-y
time	REF	spider	take-3M	VENT	HYP-3M

é	jé-y	dà	kama-ŋ	ni	dày
go:FUT	throw-3M	PREP	water-DEF	LOC	3M

kàyo-ŋ	se	an	ná	galmbo
squirrel-DEF	INCEPT	leave	ASSC	bag

kín-dì	ba	se	gír
eye-3M	COM	INCEPT	run

'When Spider took him to throw him into the water, Squirrel left through the hole in the bag and ran away.'

The apodosis clause may be overtly marked by several means. One is the use of the associative marker **ná** at the end of the protasis clause. The use of the associative marker **ná** is therefore identical to the coding of the background information. The important prosodic element in the coding of the apodosis clause is that marker **ná** belongs intonationally to the protasis rather than the apodosis clause. The pause between the two clauses comes after **ná** and cannot come before **ná**:

(16)

ge	è	jè	ná	gùyé	tumadu	go
HUM	go	VENT	ASSC	news	death	REF

làmndá	yé-y	kò-rò	ná [pause]	gų́yé
mother	elephant-3M	GEN-3F	ASSC	spider

ɗeŋlí	se	jìb	se	gìr	è	cáaní
hear	INCEPT	push	INCEPT	run	go	ALL

'When the news of the death of the mother of the elephant was brought in, Spider heard it, got up, and ran away.'

The marker **ɗe** (mid tone) followed by the associative **ná** indicates that the event of the apodosis clause took place after the event of the protasis clause. The marker **ɗe ná** may be used only if the subjects of the apodosis and protasis clause are different:

(17)

kur	go	gɥ̨́yé	ay	tu	lèé	ɗe	ná
time	REF	spider	take	goat	eat	THEN	ASSC
ne	wèlè	kab	ɗe	ná	làmndá	yé-y	
COP	day	later	then	ASSC	elephant	mother-3M	
se	ma						
INCEPT	die						

'After Spider took the goat and ate it, a few days later the mother of elephant died.'

All attempts to insert the form **ɗe ná** with an identical subject resulted in ungrammatical sentences.

The form **ɗe ná** indicates a specific time after the time of the preceding event. The marker **ná** alone codes just the background event, without any further narrowing. The evidence for the function of **ɗe ná** as indicating posteriority in time is provided by the fact that the replacement of **ɗe ná** by **ná** results in a different meaning:

(18)

pe	bé-y	kasire-ŋ	ɗe	ná
dig	DAT-3M	medicine-DEF	already	ASSC
bayndí-ŋ	se	háb	gèylè	
man-DEF	INCEPT	find	health	

'When he$_1$ was digging up the medicine, then the man$_2$ recovered his health.'

(19)

pe	bé-y	kasire-ŋ	ná	bayndí-ŋ
dig	DAT-3M	medicine-DEF	ASSC	man-DEF
se	háb	gèylè		
INCEPT	find	health		

'While he$_1$ dug up the medicine, the man$_2$ recovered his health.'

In agreement with the hypothesis regarding the function of **ɗe ná**, this marker cannot be replaced by the marker **ná** in the following sentence:

(20) kur go gų̀yé ay tu lèé ɗe
time REF spider take goat eat THEN
ná ne wèlè kab ɗe ná làmndá
ASSC COP day later then ASSC elephant
yé-y se ma
mother-3M INCEPT die
'After Spider took the goat and ate it, a few days later the mother of elephant died.'

The temporal protasis clause may occur after the temporal apodosis clause. When this is the case, the protasis clause is marked by one of the subordinators. In addition, the subordinator is followed by the comment-clause marker **ba**. The subordinator **ɓey** corresponds to 'before':

(21) gònì dà kìrbé kò-rò ni ná
hyena PREP thought GEN-3F LOC ASSC
gèy go léè tu-ŋ ɓey ba
want REF eat:FUT goat-DEF before COM
sée kama-ŋ
drink:FUT water-DEF
'Hyena in its thoughts wanted to devour Goat before drinking water.'

5 Conclusions

The temporal protasis clause distinguishes two semantic domains: indefinite, unspecified time, coded by the de dicto complementizer **na**. This is an interesting development whereby the de dicto marker became a temporal marker. It appears that the intermediate stage in this process must have been a conditional function of **na**.

Specific or definite time is coded by the referential marker **go**. The apodosis clauses make the distinction between simultaneity of the event of the protasis and the event of the apodosis clause, coded by the complementizer **na**, and the posteriority of the event of the apodosis clause with respect to the event of the protasis clause, coded by the form **ɗe ná**.

5 Conclusions

24

Conditional Sentences

1 Introduction

The term *conditional sentences* includes several types of relationships. One of them is captured by the logical expression 'if-then'. But Lele presents several means of coding, which indicates that there are several types of semantic relationships that should be discovered and analyzed. Given the fact that English does not code the same number and types of distinctions, the translations should not be taken as descriptions of the functions involved.

The components of conditional sentences are referred to as the conditional protasis and the conditional apodosis, regardless of the narrower semantic function encoded by each component. The common characteristic of all conditional sentences is that the protasis precedes the apodosis clause. The differences between various conditional sentences pertain to the way the protasis and apodosis clauses are coded. Behind the formal differences in the coding lie important functional distinctions.

The conditional protasis and the conditional apodosis differ from the temporal protasis and the temporal apodosis in the coding means deployed.

2 The conditional protasis

The overt markers of conditional protasis are: **mábaná**, **na**, **gìna**. All three of these means include the marker **na**, identical with the de dicto complementizer and with the hypothetical marker. The process of grammaticalization led from the de dicto complementizer to the hypothetical to the conditional marker. Thus the conditional protasis clause is coded simply as being in the hypothetical modality.

The protasis marker **na** follows a nominal subject but precedes a pronominal subject:

(1) Na gi gol gìdìrè ba wèlè-ì gì
HYP 2M see moon man day-3M remain
mira go ane ɗè ná, gi
approach REF get out:VN leave ASSC 2M
è kùyrò ɗé.
go travel NEG
'If you see that the male moon is about to come out, do not go on a trip.' (G-C & W 1981: 22-23)

If the conditional protasis is not followed by the apodosis clause, it does not have the background marker. This is the case when several conditions are listed. The background marker occurs only after the final condition:

(2) dày háŋ ba na ge bé-y
3M DEM COM HYP HUM give-3M
kùrmbàlò tamą́-y ba na-y wèl ná
chief wife-3M COM HYP-3M sleep ASSC
un-do hą́ kur na wèl na ge
ASSC-3F until place HYP day HYP INDEF
dìgr-iy ná kolo tumad-iy na gárnį́-íy
kill-3M COM reason death-3M HYP anger-1SG
ɗé
NEG
'The first one said that if he is given the chief's wife to sleep with until daybreak, then he can be killed, because death does not worry him.'

The verb following the hypothetical marker may be in the future tense form. The future codes an event that may actually happen, one that the subject expects to happen:

(3) na me léè yé dí-nì
HYP 2F eat:FUT mother GEN-1PL.EXCL
ná me jè má lay
ASSC 2F IMPF die:FUT also
'If you eat our mother, you will also die'

(4) yàá bé-y na bé-y tamá pìnà
tell DAT-3M HYP give-3M wife one
dà dùrè dì-gè ni na-y bóre
PREP center GEN.PL-3PL LOC HYP-3M cut
bé-y kur na jènè ná
DAT-3M place HYP settle:VN ASSC
'He$_1$ told him$_2$ that if he$_2$ gave him$_1$ one wife from among those [three], he$_1$ would give him$_2$ instead a portion of land to settle in.'

The form **gìna** occurs in clause-initial position. The apodosis marker is the associative **ná** following the protasis clause. In the natural discourse data the verb follows the marker **gìna** in the past tense form. The past tense form does not code specific events but rather potential events:

(5) Gìna bè kanya kara go kila Lábí
COND give thing people REF spirit Labi
ɗé ná hòmnyá né-ì gàg
NEG ASSC sickness make:FUT-3M until
máre-ná.
die:FUT-ASSC
'If he does not offer the animals to the spirit of Labi, he will become ill until he dies.' (G-C & W 1981: 39-39)

(6) Gìna gi ày è ná túgú ná,
COND 2M take go ASSC village ASSC
túgú kò-m lóre pet.
village GEN-2M burn:FUT all
'If you take [it] and bring it home, your home will burn.' (G-C & W 1981: 32-34)

The past tense of the verb in the conditional protasis with the hypothetical marker **na** at the beginning of the clause also marks the potential event.

(7) Gìdìrè ba na an gi túgú kara
moon man HYP come out 2M village people
kè-gè ná kúrá ɗé
GEN-3PL ASSC good NEG
'If the male moon comes out while you are in the village of strangers, that is not good.' (G-C & W 1981: 22-23)

The form **gìna** can cooccur with the hypothetical marker **na**. When this is the case, the hypothetical marker follows the subject and precedes the verb of the protasis clause:

(8) Gìna kumno na ongi tom-gi cáaní\
like God HYP rain hit-2M bush
ná cà-m ángle.
ASSC head-2M fever
'If the rain hits you in the bush, you will get a fever.' (G-C & W 1981: 52-53)

The conditional protasis marker **gìna** is identical with the marker of comparison 'as, like'. This grammaticalization from comparative to hypothetical is reminiscent of what happened in contemporary colloquial American English where the form 'like' codes hypothetical, counterfactual modality.

The form **mábaná** 'if, since' can be the marker of both the protasis and the apodosis clause. Subject pronouns after **mábaná** behave as they do after the complementizer **na**, i.e., the third-person singular is suffixed to **mábaná**, and other pronouns follow **mábaná** as well. The complementizer **na** can be replaced by the marker **mábaná** in protasis clauses, but the complementizer **na** marking hypothetical non-conditional clauses cannot be replaced by **mábaná**:

(9) dày kóŋ na mábaná-y kálè
3M certain HYP COND-3M climb:FUT
jénè dà jaŋla kùrmbàlò kè-y
sit:FUT PREP bench chief GEN-3M
ni mábaná-y bórè sàríyà mábaná
LOC COND-3M cut judgment (Ar.) COND
ge dìgr-ìy na/*mábaná ùs-ìy ɗé
HUM kill-3M HYP/*COND concern-3M NEG
'The other said that if he could climb on the chief's bench and pronounce judgments, they could kill him; that would not concern him.'

In all clauses in which marker **mábaná** was given as the first choice for a conditional protasis, it could be replaced by **na** alone. The marker **mábaná** cannot occur as a conditional apodosis marker:

(10) mábaná/na ná-di ná luŋba
COND/HYP ASSC-3M ASSC horse
na/*mábaná nè ɓálè-dí go
HYP/COND IMPF be able:FUT-3M REF
é gòlé
go:FUT hunt
'if he had a horse, he would be able to go for a hunt'

3 The counterfactual condition

The unreal condition can be marked in the protasis clause. It is marked by the complementizer **na** followed by the imperative rather than the indicative form of the verb. Here is an illustration of the rule in elicited examples:

(11) na gi sìnà go yáge ná
HYP 2M know:IMP REF plant:FUT ASSC
gi jè hábe kàsà néyè
2M IMPF find:FUT corn be a lot:FUT
'if you knew how to plant, you would have a lot of corn'

Cf.:

(12) na gi sèn go yáge ná gi
HYP 2M know REF plant:FUT ASSC 2M
jè hábe kàsà néyè
IMPF find:FUT corn be a lot:FUT
'if you know how to plant, you will have a lot of corn'

(13) na gi wìlà kùnà na gi jè
HYP 2M sleep:IMP sleep HYP 2M IMPF
gílàlé ɗé
tire:FUT NEG
'if you had slept, you would not have tired'

Cf.:

(14) na gi wèl kùnà na gi jè
HYP 2M sleep sleep HYP 2M IMPF
gílàlé ɗé
tire:FUT NEG
'if you sleep, you will not tire'

Here is a natural discourse illustration and the evidence for the existence of the rule:

(15) kàyo se yàá na na-y
squirrel INCEPT say HYP HYP-3M
sìnà máàní na-y ɗe gų́yé
know:IMP ANAPH HYP-3M leave spider
na ge ímè-y ná làmndá
HYP HUM bury:FUT-3M ASSC elephant
yè-y
mother-3M
'Squirrel said that if he had known that, he would have left Spider to be buried together with the mother of elephant.' (**sèn** 'know', imperative **sìnà**)

Cf.:

(16) kàyo se yàá na na-y sèn
squirrel INCEPT say HYP HYP-3M know
máàní na-y ɗe gų́yé na ge
ANAPH HYP-3M leave spider HYP HUM
ímè-y ná làmndá yè-y
bury:FUT-3M ASSC elephant mother-3M
'Squirrel said that if he knows that, he will leave Spider to be buried together with the mother of elephant.'

4 The conditional apodosis

The conditional apodosis clause is marked by the associative marker **ná** that ends the protasis clause. The obligatory pause between the two clauses occurs after, rather than before, the apodosis marker. Thus, the conditional protasis is treated as background for the conditional apodosis. The temporal apodosis clause marker **ɗe ná** 'then, after' cannot be used to mark the conditional apodosis. The evidence that **ná** is the marker ending the background information is provided by the following sentence, which is comprised of three conditional protasis clauses and one apodosis clause. All four clauses are marked by the same complementizer **na**, but the background marker **ná** occurs only after the last conditional protasis clause:

(17) dày kóŋ na-y kále jénè
3M certain HYP-3M climb:FUT sit:FUT
dà jaŋla kùrmbàlò kè-y ni na-y
PREP bench chief GEN-3M LOC HYP-3M
bórè sàríyà na ge dìgr-ìy
cut judgment (Ar.) HYP HUM kill-3M
na ùs-ìy ɗé
HYP concern-3M NEG
'The other said that if he could climb on the chief's bench and pronounce judgments, they could kill him; that would not concern him.'

(18)

Gìna	bayndí	ma	dà	gìdìrè	kolòng		
if	person	die	PREP	moon	DEM:R		
kùlèn-dì	ni		ná	ge	yàá	na	bayndí
belly-3M	LOC		ASSC	HUM	tell	HYP	man
na	ma	nè	làbù	kolo	hab		
HYP	die	COP	hunger	reason	find		
kanya	go	lèé	géylè-ná		ɗé.		
thing	REF	eat	save:FUT-ASSC		NEG		

'If a man dies during that moon, people say he died of hunger because he could not find any food to save him.' (G-C & W 1982: 52-53)

5 Conclusions

Conditional clauses provide a three-way distinction between an event that may actually happen, coded by the future form of the verb; an event that may potentially happen, coded by the past tense form of the verb; and a counterfactual condition, coded by the imperative form of the verb. The apodosis clauses for all three types of protasis clauses are the same. The protasis clauses are treated as background information for the apodosis clauses.

25

Comparative Constructions

1 Introduction

Some comparative constructions in Lele are typical of what one can find in other Chadic and African languages, especially with respect to unequal comparisons. But other comparative constructions, for both equal and unequal comparisons, are quite atypical, which makes these constructions especially interesting.

2 Non-predicative comparisons

Non-predicative comparisons are those where the properties of a member of one category are compared to those of another member. Such a type of comparison is coded by the form **gìna** 'like' occurring between the object of comparison and the standard:

(1) kara go kila Lábí gìna kara go
people REF spirit Labi like people REF
Dèbrèng
Debreng
'Labi spirit people, like those of Debreng' (G-C & W 1981: 36-37)

3 Equal predicates

The equivalence of predicates is coded by a construction consisting of the preposition **gìna** 'as, like' and the anaphor **máàní**, both obligatory components of equal predicate comparison. The structure of the construction is Object of comparison **gìna** Standard **máàní**. In equational predicates there is no verb and no copula, and there is no distinction between human and non-human nouns:

(2) kiya gìna ságlè máàní
Kiya like Sagle ANAPH
'Kiya is like Sagle'

(3) tù gìna dùbàngú máàní
goat like sheep ANAPH
'a goat is like a sheep'

Pronouns in comparative constructions are drawn from the independent set:

(4) dày gìna dàŋ máàní
3M like 1SG ANAPH
'he is like me'

(5) dày gìna dìgì máàní
3M like 2M ANAPH
'he is like you'

If the predicate is verbal, the form **gìna** follows the object of comparison and precedes the standard clause. The anaphor **máàní** follows the standard:

(6) gi yàá kolo gìna nè gúùgdí
2M speak word like make pigeon
máàní;
ANAPH
'you speak [with a voice] like a pigeon makes' (G-C & W 1981: 32-33)

(7) ge yàá kolo gìna nè gúùgdí ile-rò
HUM say word like make pigeon cry-3F
máàní.
ANAPH
'one speaks with a voice like a pigeon makes' (G-C & W 1981: 32-33)

The standard, even if having a clause as its scope, may be reduced to a single noun if the predicate is the same as in the object of comparison:

(8) gìlkíníŋ hin dú gìna kìyà máàní
Gilkinin grow 3F like Kiya ANAPH
'Gilkinin is as tall as Kiya'

(9) hin gìna dàŋ máàní
tall like 1SG ANAPH
'he is as tall as I am'

(10) ɗàŋgá kán wìlé gìna dày kán
calabash DEM:P red like 3M DEM
máàní
ANAPH
'this calabash is as red as that one'

Adverbs of time may occur with the object of comparison or the standard depending on which one is marked for temporal characteristics:

(11) tùmò ɗàŋgá kán wìlé gìna dày
once calabash DEM:P red like 3M
kán máàní
DEM ANAPH
'this calabash was once as red as that one'

If one adds temporal or aspectual markers with the standard of comparison, the predicate is repeated in the standard clause. The repeated predicate occurs before the anaphor:

(12) ɗàŋgá kán wìlé gìná dày kán
calabash DEM:P red like 3M DEM
wìlé tùmò máàní
red once ANAPH
'this calabash is as red as that one was once'

If the predicate is not followed by an adverb, the scope of comparison is the predicate in general:

(13) jè nè gùyé gìná dàŋ máàní
IMPF do work as 1SG ANAPH
'he works in the field as I do'

If the predicate of the object clause has an adverbial expression, the scope of comparison is the adverbial expression:

(14) jè nè gùyé kurà gìna dàŋ máàní
IMPF do work well like 2M ANAPH
'he works in the field as well as you do'

(15) ŋ wèl gíná gìna nè kude-re
1SG sleep well like do husband-2F
máàní
ANAPH
'I am as well as your husband'[19]

(16) jè nè gùyé kurà gìna dàŋ
IMPF do work well in like 2M
máàní
ANAPH
'he works in the field like you do'

(17) nè dí gùyé móglì gìna dìgì máàní
do 3M work fast like 2M ANAPH
'he works as fast as you do'

The predicate in the object clause may be preceded by an intensifier **pɨ́yà** 'even':

(18) kiya pɨ́yà esì gìna sàglé máàní
Kiya even be strong like Sagle ANAPH
lày
also
'Kiya is as strong as Sagle'

If one compares different objects, the standard is preceded by the associative preposition **ná**:

(19) óm dí kùsá ɓàl ná gàn-ìŋ
catch 3M fish suffice ASSC leg-1SG
máàní cé
like that
'he caught a fish that is equal to my leg'

---

19 This is an answer by a man to a morning greeting. The greeting has the form: **gɨ́ wèl wángà**, lit 'did you sleep at all?'

4 Unequal comparison

There are several means of coding unequal comparison. One involves the deployment of **gìna** 'like' and the anaphor **máànì́**, i.e. the same markers that are used in unequal comparisons. The only instance of this type of unequal comparison in the data collected involved the expression for 'less than'. The construction has the form: Subject do a lot **gìna** Standard **máànì́** NEG.

(20)

Kara	nè-gé	gùyé	dà	gìdìrè	kàǹg	ni
people	do-3PL	work	PREP	month	DEM	LOC

nèǹy	gìna	nè	go	tùmò	máànì́	ɗé
be a lot	like	do	REF	past	ANAPH	NEG

'People work less than in the preceding month.' (G-C & W 1981: 32-33)

The second means of coding unequal predicates is the deployment of the verb **dèl** 'surpass' following the predicate of the clause, a construction commonly found in languages of Africa. The form of the comparative sentence with unequal predicates is Subject Predicate **dèl** Standard:

(21)

kiya	gùmyá	dèl	gìlkíníŋ
become	large	surpass	Gilkinin

'Kiya is larger than Gilkinin'

(22)

mìsèú	kè-y	dèl	cà-y
arousal	GEN-3M	surpass	head-3M

'he is too horny', lit. 'his excitement surpasses him'

The evidence for the meaning 'surpass' for the verb **dèl** is provided by the following sentence, where it is the only predicate in the first clause:

(23)

ísaŋ	pìnà	dèl-dù	kul	kùlen-di
nothing	one	surpass-3F	home	belly-3M

ni	ɗé	hàb	dú	kạnya	ɓàl	cé
LOC	NEG	find	3F	thing	suffice	like that

'She did not lack anything inside the house; she had everything in sufficient quantity.'

If the form **dèl** is followed by a pronoun, two options are available: The pronoun chosen may be an independent form or an object pronoun. The predicate in the following examples is **gùmyá** 'to become large':

(24)

gùmyá	dí
become large	3M

'he became large'

The standard as an independent pronoun:

(25) gùmyá dí dèl dìgì
become large 3M surpass 2M
'he is larger than you'

(26) gùmyá dí dèl dàŋ
become large 3M surpass 1SG
'he is larger than me'

The standard as an object pronoun:

(27) gùmyá dí dèl-gì
become large 3M surpass-2M
'he is larger than you'

(28) gùmyá dí dèl-íŋ
become large 3M surpass-1SG
'he is larger than me'

The option of having the pronoun following **dèl** in either the object form or the independent form indicates that the verb **dèl** is in the process of grammaticalization from a verb into a grammatical morpheme whose function is to code comparison. Verbs that have not grammaticalized into grammatical morphemes cannot be followed by independent pronouns:

(29 gol-íŋ dí
see-1SG 3M
'he saw me'

(30) *gol dí dàŋ
see 3M 1SG
for 'he saw me'

The comparative construction is used for logical notions 'greater than' and 'smaller than'. For the function 'larger than' and similar superlative comparisons, a superlative predicate is used followed by **dèl** and the standard of comparison:

(31) dày hin dí dèl-gì
3M grow 3M surpass-2M
'he is taller than you'

(32) màrgà dí dèl dìgì
short 3M surpass 2M
'he is shorter than you'

If the predicate is verbal, the comparison involves the adverbial modifiers of the verb, and the same principles apply, with the adverb following the predicate of the target clause, and the form **dèl** and the standard following it:

(33) dày jè nè dí gùyé hòdéì dèl-gì
3M IMPF do 3M work better surpass-2M
'he works better than you'

For a comparison of the type 'smaller than' the appropriate predicate, such as 'small', 'short', is also followed by the form **dèl** and the standard of comparison:

(34) dìgì gi màrgà dèl-ìy
2M 2M short surpass-3M
'it is you who are shorter than he'

(35) nè dí gùyé sị̀yá dèl-gì
do 3M work bad surpass 2M
'he works more poorly than you'

(36) dìgì gi nè gùyé sị̀yá dèl dày
2M 2M do work bad surpass 3M
'you work more poorly than he does'

(37) dìgì gi nè gùyé sị̀yá dèl-ìy
2M 2M do work bad surpass-3M
'you work more poorly than he does'

5 Conclusions

The most outstanding feature of the comparative constructions in Lele is the deployment of anaphor **máànı́** following the standard of comparison. This means of coding is deployed in both equal and unequal comparisons. Whenever **máànı́** is deployed, the standard must be preceded by the form **gìna** 'like'.

26

Relative Clauses

1 Introduction

Lele has only postnominal relative clauses. The maximal structure of the relative clause is as follows: Head Referential marker Relative clause-(DEF). The role of the head of the relative clause is coded by a number of means, chief among which are the presence of other arguments and anaphoric coding in the relative clause. The role of the head is that of the argument missing in the relative clause.

The presence or absence of the definite marker follows the same rules as the deployment of the definite marker in the simple clause. If the object has been previously mentioned in discourse, it is always coded as such by the definite marker following the clause. If the subject has been mentioned in discourse, it is coded by the definite marker only if it is the topic of the clause. If the subject is the topic but has not been mentioned in discourse, the relative clause is not followed by the definite marker. The word order in the relative clause is the same as in the main clause, viz. (Subject) Verb Object. The definite article comes after the last element of the relative clause, including the markers of propositional relations, such as the associative marker **ná**.

2 The forms and functions of referential markers

There are two relative markers: **go** 'masculine' and 'plural' and **do** 'feminine singular':

(1)

kormo	go	dà	kùlè-nìng	ni
child	REF	PREP	belly-1SG	LOC

'the child who is in my belly' (G-C & W 1981: 2-3)

(2)

tamá	do	nè	kere-ǹg se	è	
woman	REL:F	make	beer-DEF	INCEPT	go
túgú,					
village					

'the woman who makes beer goes to the village' (G-C & W 1981: 52-53)

Although the system as illustrated above could be considered a straightforward case of agreement whereby the choice of referential marker is determined by the features gender and number of the head noun, the facts of the language point to a much more complex picture. More specifically, in natural data there are many examples where a singular feminine head of a relative clause is followed by the masculine relative marker **go** rather than the feminine relative marker **do**. The hypothesis that accounts for this apparent anomaly is as follows: if the feminine noun is hypothetical, potential, in the domain de dicto, then the referential marker is **do**. It is an inherent property of the noun that dictates the choice of the relative marker. All the examples where the feminine noun is followed by the referential marker **do** do not involve a specific feminine noun, but rather a potential feminine. If a feminine noun is known, having been mentioned in the preceding discourse or being otherwise specific, it is marked by the referential marker **go**:

(3)

Wèlè	go	tamá	do	ná	kùlòngò
time	REF	woman	REL:F	ASSC	belly

'At that time, a woman who was pregnant . . . ' (G-C & W 1981: 2-3)

(4)

tamá	do	tòb go	gàrè	kanya
woman	REL:F	want	REF	form:VN	thing

'a woman who wants to be a potter' (G-C & W 1981: 20-21)

(5)

kamda	go	tèy-gé	kur	go	yage
women	REF	trace-3PL	place	REF	work
màybùlò					
sesame					

'a women who marked the place to plant sesame . . .' (G-C & W 1981: 52-53)

The following examples from natural discourse are particularly interesting because they contain a head that is a third-person feminine singular pronoun, hence unambiguously feminine in all possible interpretations. And yet, as a pronoun, it is specific, referential; hence the relative marker chosen is **go** and not **do**:

(6) kolo dàdù go tùmò
because 3F REF first
'Because the first one, . . . '

(7) dàdù go sò . . .
3F REF two
'The second one, . . . '

(8) dàdù go sùbù
3F REF three
'The third one, . . .'

Thus the patterning is as follows: The referential head has a relative marker **go** regardless of the number and gender of the head. If the head is non-referential, inherently feminine nouns have the relative marker **do**, masculine and plural nouns have the relative marker **go**.

The relative clause, in addition to having the marker **go**, also has the definite marker at the end. The definite marker may be attached to the verb, and the ventive marker follows the verb:

(9) tamá go è jé-ŋ nè kuryò
woman REF go VENT-DEF COP stranger
'the woman who came is a stranger'

(10) bayndí go è jé-ŋ nè kuryò
man REF go VENT-DEF COP stranger
'the man who came is a stranger'

(11) kara go èjé-ŋ nè kárye̱
people REF come-DEF COP stranger:PL
'people who came are strangers'

(12) tamá go è jé-ŋ nè tím-níŋ
woman REF go VENT-DEF COP sister-1SG
'the woman who came is my sister'

The definite marker may be attached to the object pronoun following the verb:

(13) tamá go è gol-gi-ŋ nè tím-níŋ
woman REF go see-2M-DEF COP sister-1SG
'the woman who came to see you is my sister'

The definite marker does not occur with relative clauses following non-specific heads, providing more evidence that the marker **do** codes a potential feminine noun as the head:

(14) tamá do hábè kanya àɣ
woman REL:F have thing take
kudò-rò ndóji ɗé
husband-3F difficulty NEG
'a woman who is rich marries without difficulty'

3 The relativized subject

The role of the relative head as subject is simply marked by the absence of a noun preceding the verb, and for transitive verbs by the presence of an object following the verb. If the head noun is masculine and indefinite, non-specific, the referential marker is **go** and the relative clause does not end in the definite marker:

(15) kasa go an dà cáaní
corn REF grow PREP field
'corn that grows in the field'

(16) bayndi go na ày kùná-y gų́yé . . .
person REF HYP take uncle-3M spider
'the person who would take his uncle Spider . . . '

The relativized subject cannot be coded by a pronoun following the verb:

(17) bayndí go na ąýn-*dí tu káŋ
person REF HYP take-3M goat DEM
na lèé
HYP eat
'A person who takes this goat and eats it . . . '

The relative clause does not have to have a verb. The following example illustrates the relativization of the subject of a locative clause:

(18) ge jè éè wálè-ng kolo
HUM IMPF go:FUT cut:FUT-1SG reason
dèrè kormo go dà kùlènì-ng ni,
take out child REF PREP belly-1SG LOC
'they will cut me in order to take out the child which is my belly'
(G-C & W 1981: 2-3)

If the relativized nominal subject is plural, the verb has to have the plural subject pronoun. Third-person plural subjects must always be overtly marked by a subject pronoun, regardless of whether there is a nominal subject:

(19) Kara go ngem-gé lòngmè kè-gè kúní
people REF keep-3PL horse:PL GEN-3PL home
ná
ASSC
'People who keep horses at home . . .' (G-C & W 1981: 18-19)

(20) Kara go yagi-gé mònò,
people REF plant-3PL eleusine
'People who planted eleusine . . .' (G-C & W 1981: 18-19)

The subject of a possessive construction can be relativized like the subject of any verbal clause. The verb, however, does not have a pronominal plural subject, because there is no morpheme to which the pronominal subject could be cliticized:

(21) kàrà go ná kolbé
people REF ASSC cows
'people who have cows'

(22) dàgè go ná sìbì go pore mònò
3PL REF ASSC knife REF cut eleusine
ɗé
NEG
'those who do not have a knife to cut eleusine' (G-C & W 1981: 18-19)

4 The relativized object

The role of the head of the noun phrase as the object is determined from the overt coding of the subject and other grammatical relations. In addition, definite or specific objects are coded by a system of resumptive pronouns. If the object is definite human, a resumptive pronoun coding the gender, number, and person of the head of the relative clause must occur after the verb:

(23) dàì go sùbù [go] ge dígre-y è go
3M REF three REF HUM kill:FUT-3M go
wèl ná kùrmbàlò tamą́-y
sleep ASSC chief wife-3M
'The third one, who was going to be killed, went to sleep with the chief's wife.'

(24) dà do sùbù go ge dígre-du
3M REL:F three REF HUM kill:FUT-3F
'The third one (F), who was going to be killed . . . '

(25) jàw dí-ngà go ngá
enemies GEN:PL-1DU:INCL REF 1DU.INCL
gol-ge
see-3PL
'our enemies that we were going to see'

If the subject is not overtly coded in the clause, as is often the case with the third-person singular masculine, the resumptive pronoun coding the object must be present, even if the object is indefinite:

(26) tamá go tey-du yí gùrbàlò go
woman REF call-3F wear cloth REF
kurà
nice
'a woman whom he invited wore nice clothes'

If the subject is overtly coded, the resumptive pronoun cannot occur if the object is indefinite:

(27) tamá go tey dí yí gùrbàlò
woman REF call 3M wear cloth
go kurà
REF nice
'a woman whom he invited wore nice clothes'

The deployment of the marker **go** with a resumptive pronoun and with overt subject coding yields an ungrammatical sentence:

(28) *tamá go tey-du dí yí gùrbàlò
woman REF call-3F 3M wear cloth
go kurà
REF nice
for 'a woman whom he invited wore nice clothes'

The resumptive pronoun must be used if the de re referential marker is deployed. If the subject of the relative clause is the third-person masculine pronoun, the subject is not overtly coded:

(29) tamá do tey-du yí gùrbàlò
woman REL:F call-3F wear cloth
go kurà
REF nice
'the woman whom he invited wore nice clothes'

If the subject of the relative clause is other than the third-person masculine pronoun, it must be overtly marked, regardless of whether it is referential:

(30) tamá do tey-du dú yí gùrbàlò
woman REF:F call 3F wear cloth
go kurà
REF nice
'the woman whom she invited wore nice clothes'

If the object is third-person plural, definiteness is coded by different means in the future and in the past tense. Even if the object is human, the definiteness of the object is coded by the definite marker **ŋ** following the verb:

(31) kamda go ge jè tégé-ŋ
women REF 3PL IMPF call:FUT-DEF
yé gé gùrbàlò go kurà
wear:FUT 3PL cloth REF nice
'the women whom they are going to invite will wear nice clothes'

(32) bámwé go ge jè tégé yé
men REF 3PL IMPF call:FUT wear:FUT
gé gùrbàlò go kurà
3PL cloth REF nice
'the men whom they are going to invite will wear nice clothes'

(33) bámwé go ge jè tégé-ŋ
men REF 3PL IMPF call:FUT-DEF
yé gé gùrbàlò go kurà
wear:FUT 3PL cloth REF nice
'the men whom they are going to invite will wear nice clothes'

(34)

*kamda	go	ge	jè	tégé-gè
women	REF	3PL	IMPF	call:FUT-3PL
yé	gé	gùrbàlò	go	kurà
wear:FUT	3PL	cloth	REF	nice

for 'the women whom they are going to invite will wear nice clothes'

Note that the definiteness of the singular human object in the future is coded by the resumptive pronoun and cannot be coded by the definite marker:

(35)

dà	do	sùbù	go	ge
3M	REL:F	three	REF	HUM
tége-dù/*ŋ				
call:FUT-3F/DEF				

'The third one (F), who was going to be called . . . '

The coding of the definiteness of the non-human object in the future tense is the same as the coding of the definiteness of non-human objects in all tenses. It can only be done through the definite marker **ŋ**:

(36)

dà	do	sùbù	go	ge
3M	REL:F	three	REF	HUM
tége-ŋ/*dù				
call:FUT-3F/DEF				

'The third one (F), who was going to be called . . . ' (about a female dog)

In the past tense, the definiteness of the plural human object is coded by the object pronoun **gè**:

(37)

kamda	go	tey-gè	yí	gé	gùrbàlò
women	REF	call-3PL	wear	3PL	cloth
go	kurà				
REF	nice				

'the women whom he invited wore nice clothes'

If the human object is indefinite, there is no resumptive pronoun:

(38)

kamda	go	ge	tey	yí	gé	gùrbàlò
women	REF	3PL	call	wear	3PL	cloth
go	kurà					
REF	nice					

'the women whom they invited wore nice clothes'

(39) bámwé go ge tey-gè yí gé
men REF 3PL call-3PL wear 3PL
gùrbàlò go kurà
cloth REF nice
'the men whom they invited wore nice clothes'

If the object is inanimate, it is not coded by resumptive pronouns:

(40) dàdù hàm kanya go ɓòdu yàá
3F find thing REF monkey say
bù-dù
DAT-3F
'she brought the things that monkey told her [about]' (G-C & W 1981: 4-5)

(41) gi ày sòlu go gi hìb sí
2M take fine flour REF 2M pour
kúsìnyo
put ground
'you take the fine flour that you have kept on the side' (G-C & W 1981: 16-17)

If the object was mentioned before in discourse, its definiteness is coded by the definite marker following the relative clause:

(42) kàjé kè-y go bòy cáaní-ŋ
throwing knife:PL GEN-3M REF throw ALL-DEF
hàb hábe ɗé tùm lay
find find:FUT NEG together also
'his throwing knives that he threw away, he also did not find'

For verbs that can take two objects, the role of the head noun as the object of the relative clause is determined from the fact that the subject and object position of the verb of the relative clause are occupied by other nouns:

(43) bàyndi go gi gìl-iŋ nò go
man REF 2M show-1SG COP REF
lelé ɗé
Lele NEG
'the man you have shown me is not Lele'

(44) tamá do gi gìl-iŋ nò do
man REF:F 2M show-1SG COP HYP:F
lelé ɗé
Lele NEG
'the woman you have shown me is not Lele'

(45) kara go gi gìl-iŋ nò go
man REF 2M show-1SG COP REF
lelé gé ɗé
Lele 3PL NEG
'the men you have shown me are not Lele'

If the head of the relative clause is non-human and indefinite, no resumptive pronoun is used:

(46) nàsú go na-y jè
gnu antelope REF HYP-3M IMPF
dígre na jè gúmyà
kill:FUT HYP IMPF fat
'The gnu antelope that he says he will kill should be fat'

(47) wó go jè wę̀y dú na kùrá
food REF IMPF cook 3F HYP good
'the food that she prepares is supposed to be good'

If the non-human object is definite or specific, the resumptive pronoun is the definite marker **ŋ**, regardless of the gender and number of the object. Consider the following example, where the subject **dà** is a reduced form of the feminine independent pronoun **dàdù**. The subject is being made definite by the ordinal numeral modifier that follows it. The verb of the relative clause is followed by the definite marker **ŋ**:

(48) dà do sùbù-ŋ do ge
3F REL:F three-DEF REL:F HUM
dígré-ŋ gìr káy
kill:FUT-DEF run get lost
'The third one [female animal], which was going to be killed, ran away.'

Similarly with the plural object:

(49) óré go sùbù go ge
goat:PL REF:M three REF HUM
tígré-ŋ kìr:nyí gé káy
kill:FUT-DEF run:PL get lost 3PL
'The three goats, which were going to be killed, ran away.'

If the verb is followed by the subject pronoun, the definite marker comes after the subject pronoun:

(50) wó go wę̀y dú-ŋ na kùrá
food REF cook 3F-DEF HYP good
'the food that she prepared is good'

(51) kanya kùsùbá go ngà gol ùngú-ŋ
animal bush REF 1DU INCL see-1PL-DEF
nè kùmrá
COP rat
'the animal that we saw is a rat'

5 The relativized indirect object

If the dative argument is relativized, a resumptive pronoun must be preceded by the dative marker **bè**, regardless of whether the head of the relative clause is specific. The definiteness or specificity of the head of the relative clause is coded either though the definite marker following the head noun phrase or through the referential marker. The requirement of the resumptive pronouns to occur in the relative clause provides the necessary evidence that the object of the verb **bè** 'give' is in fact dative and not a direct object. It must occur whenever the head of the relative clause is a nominal:

(52) bàyndi go ŋ bè-y kòjò ko-noŋ
man REF 1SG give-3M hoe GEN-1SG
è jè dí
go VENT 3M
'a man to whom I gave my hoe came'

(53) bayndí-ŋ go ŋ bè-y kòjò ko-noŋ
man-DEF REF 1SG give-3M hoe GEN-1SG
è jè dí
go VENT 3M
'the man to whom I gave my hoe came'

If the head of the relative clause is an indefinite human female, this is coded by the marker **do**:

(54) tamá do ŋ bù-dù kòjò ko-noŋ
man REL:F 1SG give-3F hoe GEN-1SG
è jè dú
go VENT 3F
'the woman to whom I gave my hoe came'

The definite marker **ŋ** cannot be used with the relative marker **do**:

(55) *tamá-ŋ do ŋ bù-dù kòjò
man-DEF REL:F 1SG give-3F hoe
ko-noŋ è jè-dú
GEN-1SG go VENT-3F
for 'the woman to whom I gave my hoe came'

Compare the definite head representing the relativized dative:

(56) tamá go ŋ bù-dù kòjò kò-noŋ
woman REF 1SG give-3F hoe GEN-1SG
è jè dú
go VENT 3F
'the woman to whom I gave my hoe came'

6 The relativized locative

When a locative argument is relativized, a locative anaphor **màní** occurs in the position of the locative argument in the matrix clause. The interesting thing about **màní** is that since it is a specialized locative anaphor, it is not preceded by a preposition in the relative clause. It can occur in both stative and directional locatives:

(57) kur go ŋ ír màní ày
place REF 1SG stay ANAPH clean
'the place where I stayed was clean'

(58) kur go ŋ è màní ègè-ŋ
place REF 1SG go ANAPH please-1SG
ɗé
NEG
'the place where I went did not please me'

As in other relative heads, there is a means in Lele of distinguishing between the known, specific, de re location and to the unknown, non-specific, de dicto location. The coding of a specific location is realized through the addition of the definite marker **ŋ** to the locative anaphor. In the example below, the locative head of the relative clause has been specifically identified before in the conversation:

(59) na ìrà gùl-gè kur go
HYP go:IMP show:IMP-3PL place REF
jé tumadu kòyè kè-y màní-ŋ
throw corpse thief GEN-3M there-DEF
'He should show them the place where he has thrown the corpse of the thief.'

The omission of the definite marker from the locative anaphor means that the place is unknown to the speaker:

(60) na ìrà gùl-gè kur go
HYP go:IMP show:IMP-3PL place REF
jé tumadu kòyè kè-y màní
throw corpse thief GEN-3M there
'he should show them where he has thrown the corpse of the thief'

The directionality of movement, the distinctions between source and goal, do not have to be overtly coded. The hearer can figure out the directionality from the lexical meaning of the verb and the nature of the arguments:

(61) kùlmà go ngà cìl kama màní
well REF 1DU.INCL fetch water ANAPH
dùglì ɗé
deep NEG
'the well from which we took the water is not deep'

The locative preposition may be used, however, to indicate the direction toward, in, and so on:

(62) kùlmà go jé dí gùjùlù (dà)
well REF throw 3M pebbles PREP
màní dùglì ɗé
ANAPH deep NEG
'the well into which he threw pebbles is not deep'

7 Relativized time adverbials

Relativized time adverbials are coded in the relative clause by the associative preposition **ná** following the verb:

(63) Kur go ng è-je-ná túgú ko-noǹg,
time REF 1SG go-VENT home GEN-1SG
'When I come home . . .' (G-C & W 1981: 14-15)

8 Relativized associative arguments

If the head of the relative clause is one of the adjuncts that in matrix clauses is marked by the associative marker **ná**, the relative clause has the associative preposition **ná** following the verb. The associative preposition and the following noun do not constitute a prepositional phrase. The associative preposition does not mark the role of the noun following it:

(64) kàlì go ŋ sìr ná hìdá géy
ax REF 1SG chop ASSC tree want
màglé
repair:VN
'an ax with which I chopped down the tree needs repairing'

(65) gi kíle kàlì go gi síre ná
2M buy:FUT ax REF 2M chop ASSC
hìdá
tree
'you will buy an ax with which you will chop a tree'

(66) póì kúsíge sèn ísàŋ pìnà
'Poi Kusige know nothing one
go na-y né go na-y
REL COMP-3M make:FUT REL COMP-3M
lámdè ná dòlò bé karan-di
cook gruel ASSC gruel DAT children-3M
ɗé
NEG
'Poi Kusige does not know with what he is going to cook gruel for his children.'

The definiteness of the head of the relativized associative is coded by the definite marker following the head noun phrase; it is not in the relative clause:

(67) kàlì-ŋ go ŋ sìr ná hìdá géy
ax-DEF REF 1SG chop ASSC tree want
màglé
repair:VN
'the ax with which I chopped down the tree needs repairing'

If the associative argument is human, a resumptive pronoun must follow the verb. Since the head is an associative argument, the pronoun must have the associative form, viz. the form with the prefix **ín**-:

(68) bayndí go ŋ è ná ín-dì
man REF 1SG go ASSC ASSC-3M
kòy gálmbò kò-nòŋ
steal bag GEN-1SG
'a man with whom I went stole my sack'

The specificity of the relativized associative masculine or plural argument is coded by the definite marker following the head noun:

(69) bayndí-ŋ go ŋ è ná ín-dì
man-DEF REF 1SG go ASSC ASSC-3M
kòy gálmbò kò-nòŋ
steal bag GEN-1SG
'the man with whom I went stole my sack'

(70) bàmwé-(ŋ) go ŋ è ná ín-dí-gè
men-(DEF) REF 1SG go ASSC ASSC:PL-3PL
kòy gálmbò kò-nòŋ
steal bag GEN-1SG
'the men with whom I went stole my sack'

The specificity of the relativized feminine associative argument is coded by the referential marker **do**. The definite marker **ŋ** cannot be used for this purpose. This constraint indicates functional complementarity between the de re complementizer **do** and the definite marker **ŋ**:

(71) tamá go ŋ è ná ún-do kòy
woman REF 1SG go ASSC ASSC-3F steal
gálmbò kò-nòŋ
bag GEN-1SG
'a woman with whom I went stole my sack'

(72) tamá do ŋ è ná ún-do
woman REL:F 1SG go ASSC ASSC-3F
kòy gálmbò kò-nòŋ
steal bag GEN-1SG
'the woman with whom I went stole my sack'

If the subject of a sentence is part of the relativized associative argument, the associative preposition **ná** follows the verb:

(73) dàngá go ngà sì ná
calabash REF 1DU.INCL drink ASSC
dòlò [pause] kùlèn-dì ɗą́y
hot gruel interior-3M bitter
'the interior of calabash with which we drank the gruel is bitter'

(74) *kùlèn-dì ɗą́y dàngá go ngà
interior-3M bitter calabash REF 1DU.INCL
sì na dòlò
drink ASSC hot gruel
for 'the interior of calabash with which we drank the gruel is bitter'

9 The relativized reason

The form **kolo**, or 'reason', is followed by the referential marker **go**. The verb is followed by the associative marker serving as an anaphor for the reason clause. If the head has been mentioned before in discourse or is otherwise known, the relative clause is followed by the definite marker **ŋ**. Note that the definite marker occurs after the associative preposition **ná**, which marks the backgrounded information:

(75) Tamá se jè ày kolo go
woman INCEPT IMPF take reason REF
nè ile ná-ǹg yàá bè
IMPF cry:VN ASSC-DEF tell DAT
ɓòdu.
monkey
'The woman explains to the monkey the reason for her crying', lit. 'took the reason for her crying told monkey.' (G-C & W 1981: 2-3)

10 Conclusions

All relative clauses follow the heads they modify. Relative clauses have a distinction between referential and non-referential heads. Within the domain of the non-referential head, there is a distinction between the feminine head, marked by the relative marker **do**, and the masculine and plural heads, marked by the referential marker **go**. In the referential domain there is no distinction between the masculine, feminine, and plural head of the relative clause.

The coding of the grammatical roles of heads of the relative clause is achieved through the configuration of the role of subject. The human object is coded through the resumptive pronoun following the verb. The non-human definite object is coded by the definite marker following the relative clause. The remaining grammatical roles are coded by prepositions occurring within the relative clause, rather than before the head of the relative clause.

27

Elements of Discourse Structure in Lele

1 Introduction

The aim of this chapter is to describe the grammaticalized means that function within a fragment of speech larger than a sentence. More specifically, I describe those elements of the discourse structure in Lele to which the speakers of this language must attend. I do not deal with presumably universal properties of narratives and conversations, such as presentation of setting and participants, development, or ending.

2 Coding of a new event

Lele has grammaticalized a marker whose function is to code a switch to a new event. This function is coded by the verb **se** 'get up' preceding the verb of the clause. Partial evidence for the proposed function of this marker is the fact that it never occurs at the beginning of narratives, because there is never a preceding event; hence, there is no environment necessary for the switch of events:

(1)

ná	ɗigle	tóŋ	pìnà	làmndá	yé-y
ASSC	year	certain:F	one	elephant	mother-3M

nè	hòmnyá	go	ma
COP	sick	REF	die

'One year, the mother of elephant was sick, close to her death.'
(ɗigle 'year' is feminine)

But inside the narrative, every new event that represents non-backgrounded information is preceded by the inceptive marker **se**:

(2) ɗe ná nòju-ro kínyé se
THEN ASSC relative-3F COLL INCEPT
óm gé tu go bàl nè
catch 3PL goat REF geld COP
òb ná kara
invite for work ASSC people
'Then, her relatives caught a large gelded goat and used it to invite people for the purpose of common work:'

The subject of the clause marked by the inceptive marker does not have be overtly coded if it has been mentioned in a previous clause, even in a function other than subject:

(3) bayndí-ŋ terèn-dì yá na húm-ge
man-DEF daughter-3M say HYP take:IMP-3PL
se hím-ge bòr ná kama
get up take-3PL skim ASSC water
'The daughter of the man told him to take them. He took them and crossed the river with them.'

If the information is provided as background, the marker **se** cannot occur:

(4) gìna gùyé kè-gè kày na se è
like work GEN-3PL finish HYP INCEPT go
gé tùgù
3PL home
'since their work finished, they returned home'

(5) *gìna gùyé se kè-ge kày na
like work INCEPT GEN-3PL finish HYP
se è-gé tùgù
INCEPT go-3PL home
for 'since their work finished, they returned home'

An event may consist of several predicates. In the following three sentences there are four events described: (1) catching and slaughtering a sheep, (2) background information: skinning the sheep, (3) cutting the sheep into various pieces, reassembling it for the purpose of disguise, and throwing it into a granary, and (4) waking up the wife. The backgrounded information is not marked by the verb **se**, but everything that follows it is:

(6) càg dí kùbàrò kúsíyòŋ è ná gàg
spread 3M blood ground go ASSC until
sùgyá go kul kàrgà-y ni
grass REF house behind-3M LOC
'he spread the blood on the ground [and] went with it up to the grass behind the house'

(7) wel dí dùbàngú kólí se
skin 3M sheep completely INCEPT
gày kùlòn-dò wàl-wì cà-rò ná gàn-dò
open belly-3F cut-PL head-3F ASSC leg-3F
dàw ná sí-ró tum saar
put together ASSC meat-3F together attach
ná kùyò jé dà mbóló ni
ASSC mat throw PREP granary LOC
'He skinned the sheep, cut its head and limbs, reunited them with its meat, rolled it in a mat, and threw the whole thing into the granary.'

(8) ná se è jè hìndì tamą́-y
ASSC INCEPT go VENT wake up wife-3M
kuná ni
sleep LOC
'And then he came and woke up his wife.'

One could assume that **se** is just an aspectual marker, coding the inceptive aspect. There is, however, considerable evidence against this interpretation. If inside the narrative there is a quoted speech, and even if the verbs in the quoted speech can be interpreted as being perfective, such verbs are not preceded by the marker **se**:

(9) bayndí go na aý tu káŋ na
person REF HYP take goat DEM HYP
lèé na làmndá yé-y na ma
eat HYP elephant mother-3M HYP die
ɗéená na-gé ágè-y ímmè-y ná
then HYP-3PL take:FUT-3M bury:FUT ASSC
làmndá yé-ì
elephant mother-3M
'If anybody takes this goat and eats it, and if the mother of elephant dies, then they will bury him together with the mother of elephant'

The inceptive marker cannot be introduced before any of the verbs of the preceding sentence. When the narrative returns to main line, i.e. after the quoted speech has ended, any new predicate is preceded by the inceptive marker **se**:

(10) gúyé ɗeŋlí se jìb se gìr è
spider hear INCEPT push INCEPT run go
cáaní
bush
'Spider heard it, got up, and ran away.'

(11) àlá se hab jè kùná-y kàyo
COM INCEPT find VENT uncle-3M squirrel
dà kìrè ni
PREP road LOC
'Unexpectedly he encountered his uncle Squirrel on the road.'

(12) kùnà-y kàyo se tòn-ìy na
uncle-3M squirrel INCEPT ask-3M HYP
gi jè gìrè mína mánì gà
2M IMPF run:VN where like that Q
'His uncle Squirrel asked him, where are you running like that?'

The inceptive marker cannot be deployed, even before perfective verbs, in complements of verbs of saying:

(13) dày se ày kolo yàá bé-y
3M INCEPT take word speak DAT-3M
na-y ày tu go na ge è
HYP-3M take goat REF HYP HUM go
jè ná go ímè ná làmndá
VENT ASSC REF bury:FUT ASSC elephant
yé-y
mother-3M
'He started telling him that he took the goat that was brought to be put in the grave together with the mother of elephant.'

(14) kàyo se om-iy jè se è
squirrel INCEPT catch-3M VENT INCEPT go
ná ín-dí dà kur go tumadu-ŋ
ASSC ASSC-3M PREP place REL death-DEF
ni
LOC
'Squirrel caught him [and] brought him to the place of the burial.'

The inceptive marker can be followed by the auxiliary **jè** occurring only in the imperfective aspect and in the future tense, which provides the evidence that **se** is not a purely aspectual category. The marker **se** occurs in the first clause with the imperfective aspect, but does not occur in complement clauses, even though the verbs in these clauses are in the perfective aspect:

(15) kàyo se jè àlé
squirrel INCEPT IMPF announce
dà kùnà-y gų́yé cà-y
PREP (concerning) uncle-3M spider head-3M
ni yàá na bayndi go na ày
LOC say HYP person REF HYP take
kùná-y gų́yé ba na ím ná
uncle-3M spider COM HYP bury ASSC
làmndá yè-y na dày ná na
elephant mother-3M HYP 3M ASSC HYP
nè tìibrè mayna
COP ashes ceiba tree
'Squirrel makes an announcement concerning his uncle Spider: The person who takes his uncle Spider and buries him together with the mother of elephant, this person will be considered like the ashes of the ceiba tree.'

(16) ge se ɗe gų́yé ba dày gų́yé
HUM INCEPT leave spider COM 3M spider
se yàá bè kàyo na máàní
INCEPT say DAT squirrel HYP like that
na à jè na írà tùu-ŋ
HYP go:IMP VENT HYP go:IMP home-DEF
ni na-y néè-y kùryò
LOC HYP-3M make:FUT-3M stranger
'Spider was left alone. Spider said to Squirrel: if this is like that, he should come and they will go to his [spider's] home, and he will make him a stranger' (i.e., he will make him welcome)

If the verb is a consequence of what has been said before, the inceptive marker cannot be used as in the first clause of the following sentence. Note, however, that the second clause has the inceptive marker **se** because it represents a new event:

(17) kur go gúnyé è ná kàyo tu-ŋ
time REF spider go ASSC squirrel home-DEF
ni ná se yàá bé tamą́-y
LOC ASSC INCEPT tell DAT wife-3M
na sú kama go lèr wá tùwà
HYP put:IMP water REF hot very fire
ni
LOC
'When Spider came home with him, he told his wife to put some water on the fire.'

The marker **se** does have an aspectual function as well when it codes the beginning of the event. In such a case it can be used with background information and with a verb that has been mentioned in a preceding sentence. Evidence that a new event is involved is provided by the fact that the clause has a new subject, the wife:

(18) kur go tamą́-y se sí kama
time REF wife-3M INCEPT put:VN water
go lerwa tùwà ni dàì kàyo
REF hot fire LOC 3M squirrel
se ɗéŋ-di se yìr galmbo
INCEPT hear-3M INCEPT bite bag
kíin-dì
hole-3M
'When the wife put water on the fire, Squirrel heard it, and he chewed a hole in the bag [in which he was held].'

Certain verbs, even if they are new in the narrative, do not allow the deployment of the inceptive **se** in front of them. One of these verbs is a **yàá** 'tell, say'. The reason it is not preceded by the inceptive marker is its discourse role in the narrative. The verb of saying is usually followed by a relative clause. The verb of saying is merely representing the background for the complement clause. Compare the following sentences:

(19) bayndí-ŋ terèn-dì yá na húm-ge
man-DEF daughter-3M say HYP take:IMP-3PL
se hím-ge bòr ná kama
INCEPT take-3PL skim ASSC water
'The daughter of the man told him to take them. He took them and crossed the river with them.'

One cannot omit the inceptive marker **se** from the second clause of this sentence. And one cannot insert **se** in the first clause of this sentence:

(20)

*bayndí-ŋ	terèn-dì	se	yá	na
man-DEF	daughter-3M	INCEPT	say	HYP

húm-gé	se	hím-gé	bòr	ná
take:IMP-3PL	INCEPT	take-3PL	skim	ASSC

kama
water

for 'The daughter of the man told him to take them. He took them and crossed the river with them.'

(21)

*bayndí-ŋ	terèn-dì	yá	na	húm-ge
man-DEF	daughter-3M	say	HYP	take:IMP-3PL

hím-ge	bòr	ná	kama
take-3PL	skim	ASSC	water

for 'The daughter of the man told him to take them. He took them and crossed the river with them.'

If the verb of saying has been omitted, the inceptive marker cannot be inserted either:

(22)

tormo	na	du	ódè	ná	ba-ro
daughter	HYP	3F	leave:FUT	ASSC	father-3F

ɗé	se	è	ná	bayndí-ŋ
NEG	INCEPT	go	ASSC	man-DEF

'The girl refused to go with her father and instead went with the man.'

The inceptive marker can occur at the end of narrative, which points to its role of the coding the new predicate rather than the beginning of a larger portion of discourse. The following sentence is the last in a narrative:

(23)

kùrmbàlò	se	bòr	bé-y	kur	ba
chief	get up	cut	DAT-3M	parcel	COM

se	jèn	màní	ná	kamda-y	go
INCEPT	settle	ANAPH	COM	wives-3M	REF

sùbù
three

'The chief cut him a parcel of land, and the man settled there with his three wives.'

3 Coding the (il)logical consequence of events

The logical connection between two events is coded by a sequence consisting of the negative marker **ɗé** followed by the marker **ba**. Such a sequence may indicate either the logical consequence or the logical inconsequence of events. The sequence **ɗé ba** occurs between the two sentences. There are no clear reasons to assign this sequence to the clause that precedes or follows the sequence. The clause following the sequence **ɗé ba** must be preceded by the complementizer **na:**

(24)

kàyo	se	yàá	na	na-y		
squirrel	INCEPT	say	HYP	HYP-3M		
sìnà	máàní	na-y	ɗe			
know:IMP	ANAPH	HYP-3M	leave			
gúnyé	na	ge	ímè-y	ná	làmndá	
spider	HYP	HUM	bury-3M	ASSC	elephant	
yé-y	ɗé	ba	na-y	bòr		
mother-3M	NEG	COM	HYP-3M	save		
gúnyé	gèyl-ìy	ba	gúnyé	na	è	jè
spider	health-3M	COM	spider	HYP	go	VENT
tòb	go	dígrè-y	gà			
want	REF	kill:FUT-3M	Q			

'Squirrel said that if he had known that, he would have left Spider to be buried together with the mother of elephant. Here he saved Spider, and Spider wants to kill him'

One cannot replace the marker **ba** with the complementizer **na**, the marker that occurs in the temporal sequence of events.

28

A Sample of Lele Texts

A story of three wives

Narrated by Mathias Mupin, 1993

The narrator heard this story from his schoolteacher, a Lele man. The division into sentences is the one suggested by the narrator, except for sentences 7 and 8, which the narrator considered to be one sentence. The text illustrates several interesting features of the Lele grammatical system, such as subject-less sentences with transitive and intransitive verbs, which would have been judged ungrammatical when produced in isolation. Another feature is the occurrence of the complementizer, not after the verb of saying, but preceding a complement clause; it precedes a portion of narration that reports statements by several speakers (sentence 2).

(1) dà túgú tóŋ ni kara kóndrè[20]
PREP village certain:F LOC people young men
kusi-ge sùbù
body-3PL three
'In a village there were three young men.'

(2) yàá gé na
say 3PL HYP
'They said:

[20] W & P 1982 have **kòndìrè**.

(3) dàì haŋ ba na gé bé-y
3M DEM COM HYP HUM give-3M
kùrmbàlò tamą́-y ba na-y wèl ná
chief wife-3M COM HYP-3M sleep ASSC
un-do hà kur na wèl na ge
ASSC-3F till place HYP day HYP HUM
dìgr-ìy na kolo tumadu-y ná ɗárí-níŋ
kill-3M COM reason death-3M ASSC shock-1SG
ɗè
NEG
'The first one said that if he were given the chief's wife to sleep with till daybreak, he could be killed, because death did not worry him.'

(4) dày kóŋ na-y kále jénè
3M certain HYP-3M climb:FUT sit:FUT
dà jaŋla kùrmbàlò kè-y ni na-y
PREP bench chief GEN-3M LOC HYP-3M
bórè sàríyà na ge dìgr-ìy
cut judgment (Ar.) HYP HUM kill-3M
na ùs-ìy ɗé
HYP concern-3M NEG
'The other said that if he could climb on the chief's bench and pronounce judgments, they could kill him, he did not care.'

(5) dày kóŋ na-y kálè jénè
3M certain HYP-3M climb:FUT sit:FUT
dà luŋba kùrmbàlò kè-y ni na-y
PREP horse chief GEN-3M LOC HYP-3M
bórè sàríyà na ùs-ìy ɗé
cut:FUT verdict HYP concern-3M NEG
'The other said that if he could climb on the chief's horse and pronounce judgments, [they could kill him], he did not care.'

(6) ge yàá bé kùrmbàlò
INDEF tell DAT chief
'The chief was informed.'

(7) kùrmbàlò nè bé-ge kanya mánì
chief make DAT-3PL thing ANAPH
tù
all (Fr.)
'The chief did all those things'

(8) ge dìgrì-gè sò
HUM kill-3PL two
'Two were killed.'

(9) dày go sùbù ge dígrè-y è wèl
3M REF three HUM kill:FUT-3M go sleep
ná kùrmbàlò tamą́-y
COM chief wife-3M
'The third one, who was going to be killed, went to sleep with the chief's wife.'

(10) kùrmbàlò tamą́-y àn ná wáyngulú
chief wife-3M leave ASSC morning
àgi-y saar-iy dà kàrgà-ro ni
take-3M attach-3M PREP back-3F LOC
'The chief's wife left in the morning, took the fellow, attached him to her back.'

(11) gìr ná ín-dì hàn è-gé ná
run ASSC ASSC-3M till go-3PL ASSC
dà kama kùb-ìy ni
PREP river edge-3M LOC
'She ran with him till they arrived at the bank of the river.'

(12) bayndí è jè ná kòbró bayndí-ŋ tòb
man go VENT ASSC boat man-DEF want
go na hímé-gé ɗé
REF HYP take:FUT-3PL NEG
'A man came with a boat but he refused to take them.'
Variant:
bayndí-ŋ tòb na-y hímé-gé ɗé
man-DEF want HYP-3M take:FUT-3PL NEG

(13) bayndí-ŋ teren-di yàá na húm-gé
man-DEF daughter-3M say HYP take:IMP-3PL
se hím-gé bòr ná kama
INCEPT take-3PL skim ASSC water
'The daughter of the man told him to take them. He took them and they skimmed across the river.'

(14) tormo na du ódè ná ba-ro
daughter HYP 3F leave:FUT ASSC father-3F
ɗé se è ná bayndí-ŋ
NEG INCEPT go ASSC man-DEF
'The girl refused to go with her father and instead went with the man.'

(15) hą́ è gé dàwù ge ná kamda sò
till go 3PL gather 3PL ASSC women two
'until they went and joined the two wives'

(16) è gé cáanì bayndí-ŋ kalo se
go 3PL bush man-DEF snake INCEPT
yír-íy ɗe ná bayndí go segre
bite-3M THEN ASSC man REF hunter
è jè ná teren-ɗì máànı́
go VENT ASSC daughter-3M there
'When they went into the bush, a snake bit the man. Then a hunter with his daughter came to the place.'

(17) tòn-ìy na pa bé-y kasire
ask-3M HYP dig:IMP DAT-3M medicine
bayndí-ŋ na-y pe kasiré-ŋ ɗè
man-DEF HYP-3M dig medicine-DEF NEG
'He told him to dig medicine for him, but the man refused.'

(18) ɗe ná bayndí-ŋ teren-dì se yàá
THEN ASSC man-DEF daughter-3M INCEPT tell
na pa bé-y kasire-ŋ
HYP dig:IMP DAT-3M medicine-DEF
'Then the hunter's daughter told her father to dig up the medicine for the man.'

(19) pe bé-y kasire-ŋ ɗe ná
dig DAT-3M medicine-DEF THEN ASSC
bayndí-ŋ se hab gèylè
man-DEF INCEPT find health
'After he dug up the medicine, the man recovered his health.'

(20)

[bayndí-ŋ]	tormo-ŋ	na	du
[man-DEF, wrong start]	girl-DEF	HYP	3F

ódè	ná	ba-ro	ɗé
leave:FUT	ASSC	father-3F	NEG

se	kal	è	gé	ná	kamda	sùbù
INCEPT	pass	go	3PL	ASSC	wives	three

'The girl said that she would not go with her father; she passed [from the father to the man] and he went with three wives.'

(21)

è	gé	dà	túgú	kóŋ	ni	àlá
go	3PL	PREP	village	certain	LOC	then

kùrmbàlò	gol	kamda-y	sùbù	nè	go
chief	see	wives-3M	three	COP	REF

láy	wa	tú
pretty	very	all (Fr)

'They arrived at a certain village, [and] the chief saw that the three wives of the man were all beautiful.'

(22)

yàá	bé-y	na	bè-y	tama
tell	DAT-3M	HYP	give:IMPER-3M	wife

pìnà	dà	dùrè	dì-gè	ni	na-y
one	PREP	among	GEN-3PL	LOC	HYP-3M

bóre	bé-y	kur	na	jénè
cut:FUT	DAT-3M	place	HYP	settle:FUT

ná
ASSC

'He told him that if he gave him one wife among those [three], he would give him instead a portion of land to settle in.'

(23)

dày	le	gol	kamda-y	sùbù	tu
3M	himself (Ar.)	see	wives-3M	three	all

nè	go	láy-wa	na-y	bé-y
COP	REF	pretty-REF	HYP-3M	give:FUT-3M

tama	mànì́	pínà	ɗé
wife	ANAPH	one	NEG

'He himself saw that all his three wives were pretty, and he said that he would not give one of them to him.'

(24)

kòlò	dàdù	go	tùmò	dàdù	ba
because	3F	REF	first	3F	COM

bor-iy	gèylè
save-3M	health

'Because the first one, it was she who saved his life.'

(25) dàdù go sò dàdù ba è jè
3F REF two 3F COM go VENT
bor-iy gèylè dà kama kìb-ìy ni
save-3M health PREP river mouth-3M LOC
'The second one, it was she who came and saved his life at the shore of the river.'

(26) dàdù go sùbù dàdù ba bor-iy gèylè
3F REF three 3F COM save-3M health
tą go màgàyndí yír-íy
time (Fr.) REF viper bite-3M
'The third one, it was she who saved his life when the viper bit him.'

(27) donc na-y béè kùrmbàlò tama
therefore (Fr.) HYP-3M give chief wife
ɗé
NEG
'Therefore, he would not give a wife to the chief. '

(28) na-y jénè ná kamda-y go sùbù
HYP-3M stay:FUT ASSC wives-3M REF three
bas (Ar.)
only
'he said that he would remain with his three wives.'

(29) kùrmbàlò se bòr bé-y kur ba
chief INCEPT cut DAT-3M parcel COM
se jèn màní ná kamda-y go
INCEPT settle ANAPH ASSC wives-3M REF
sùbù
three
'The chief cut him a parcel of land and the man settled there with his three wives.'

Spider and Squirrel

Narrated by Mathias Mupin, 1993

This is an abbreviated version of a story the narrator heard from his mother. The narrator considers it part of family lore, transmitted from generation to generation.

(1) ná ɗigle tóŋ pìnà làmndá yé-y
ASSC year certain:F one elephant mother-3M
ne hòmnyá go ma
COP sick REF die
'One year, the mother of elephant was sick, close to her death.'

(2) ɗe ná nòju-ro kínyé se
THEN ASSC relative-3F COLL INCEPT
óm gé tu go bàl nè
catch 3PL goat REF geld COP
òb ná kara
invite for work ASSC people
'Then, her relatives caught a large gelded goat and used it to invite people for the purpose of common work:'

(3) bayndí go na ay tu káŋ na
person REF HYP take goat DEM HYP
lèé ná làmndá yé-y na ma
eat ASSC elephant mother-3M HYP die
ɗe ná na ge ágè-y
THEN ASSC HYP HUM take:FUT-3M
ímè-y ná làmndá yé-y
bury:FUT-3M ASSC elephant mother-3M
'If anybody takes this goat and eats it, and if the mother of elephant dies, then they will bury him together with the mother of elephant'

(4) kur koloŋ ba dày gų̀yé se yàá
time DEM:R COM 3M spider INCEPT say
bé-gè na na-y jè nè hòmyá
DAT-3PL HYP HYP-3M IMPF make sick
go ma nò go tég lay na
REF die COP REF long time also HYP
bé-y gé na-y lèé
give-3M 3PL HYP-3M eat
'At that time Spider said that since was sick for a long time, close to dying, they should give [it] to him to eat.'

(5) kur go gų̀yé ay tu lèé ɗe
time REF spider take goat eat THEN
ná ne wèlè kab ɗe ná làmndá
ASSC COP day later then ASSC elephant
yé-y se ma
mother-3M INCEPT die
'After Spider took the goat and ate it, a few days later the mother of elephant died.'

(6) ge è jè ná gùyé tumadu go
HUM go VENT ASSC news death REF
làmndá yé-y kò-rò ná [pause] gų́yé
elephant-3M mother GEN-3F ASSC spider
ɗeŋlí se jìb se gìr è cáaní
hear INCEPT push INCEPT run go ALL
'When the news of the death of the mother of elephant was brought in, Spider heard it, got up, and ran away.'

(7) àlá se hab jè kùná-y kàyo
COM INCEPT find VENT uncle-3M squirrel
dà kìrè ni
PREP road LOC
'Unexpectedly he encountered his uncle Squirrel on the road.'

(8) kùnà-y kàyo se tòn-ìy na
uncle-3M squirrel INCEPT ask-3M HYP
gi jè gìrè mína mánì gà
2M IMPF run:VN where like that Q
'His uncle Squirrel asked him, where are you running like that?'

(9) dày se ày kolo yàá bé-y
3M INCEPT take word tell DAT-3M
na-y áy tu go na ge è
HYP-3M take goat REF HYP HUM go
jè ná go ímè ná làmndá
VENT ASSC REF bury:FUT ASSC elephant
yé-y
mother-3M
'He told him that he took the goat that was brought to be buried together with the mother of elephant.'

(10) na-y áy na-y lèé ge yàá ɗe
HYP-3M take HYP-3M eat INDEF say leave
na bayndí go na lèé tu na
THEN person REF HYP eat goat HYP
ge ímè-y ná làmndá yé-y
HUM bury:FUT-3M ASSC elephant mother-3M
ba na-y nè gìr
COM HYP-3M COP run
'[He said] that he took the goat and ate it, and it was said that if a person were to eat the goat, he would be buried together with the mother of elephant, and that is why he was running.'

(11) kàyo yàá bé-y na mánì ná [pause]
squirrel say DAT-3M HYP ANAPH ASSC
na à jè na ge é
HYP go:IMPER VENT HYP INDEF go:FUT
'Squirrel said, if it is like that, then come, let us go.'

(12) kàyo se om-iy jè se è
squirrel INCEPT catch-3M VENT INCEPT go
ná ín-dí dà kur go tumadu-ŋ
ASSC ASSC-3M PREP place REL death-DEF
ni
LOC
'Squirrel caught him [and] brought him to the place of the burial.'

(13) kàyo se jè àlé dà
squirrel INCEPT IMPF announce PREP
kùnà-y gṵ́yé cà-y ni yàá na
uncle-3M spider head-3M LOC say HYP
bayndi go na ày kùná-y gṵ́yé
person REF HYP take uncle-3M spider
ba na ím ná làmndá yé-y
COM HYP bury ASSC elephant mother-3M
na dày ná na nè tìibrè mayna
HYP 3M ASSC HYP COP ashes ceiba tree
'Squirrel makes an announcement concerning his uncle Spider: The person who takes his uncle Spider and buries him together with the mother of elephant, this person will be considered like the ashes of the ceiba tree.'

(14) ge se ɗe gṵ́yé ba dày gṵ́yé
HUM INCEPT leave spider COM 3M spider
se yàá bè kàyo na máàní
INCEPT say DAT squirrel HYP like that
na à jè na írà tùu-ŋ
HYP go:IMP VENT HYP go:IMP home-DEF
ni na-y néè-y kùryò
LOC HYP-3M make:FUT-3M stranger
'Spider was left alone. Spider said to Squirrel: If this is like that, he should come and they will go to his [Spider's] home, and he will make him a stranger.' (i.e., he will make him welcome)

(15) kur go gúnyé è ná kàyo tu-ŋ
time REF spider go ASSC squirrel home-DEF
ni ná se yàá bé tamą́-y
LOC ASSC INCEPT tell DAT wife-3M
na sú kama go lèr wá tùwà
HYP put:IMP water REF hot very fire
ni
LOC
'When Spider came home with him, he told his wife to put some water on the fire.'

(16) kur go tamą́-y se sí kama
time REF wife-3M INCEPT put water
go ler-wá tùwà ni dày kàyo
REF hot-REF fire LOC 3M squirrel
se ɗeŋlí se yír galmbo
INCEPT hear INCEPT bite bag
eyes-3M
kin-di
'When his wife put water on the fire, Squirrel heard it, and chewed a hole in the bag [in which he was held].' (One speaker proposed instead of **yír** plural **yír-wì** 'to chew'.)

(17) kur go gų́nyé àg-ìy jè na-y
time REF spider take-3M VENT HYP-3M
é jé-y dà kama-ŋ ni dày
go:FUT throw-3M PREP water-DEF LOC 3M
kàyo-ŋ se an ná galmbo
squirrel-DEF INCEPT leave ASSC bag
kín-dì ba se gír
eye-3M COM INCEPT run
'When Spider took him to throw him into the water, Squirrel left through the hole in the bag and ran away.'

(18) kàyo se yàá na na-y
squirrel INCEPT say HYP HYP-3M
sìnà máànì na-y ɗe gúnyé
know:IMP ANAPH HYP-3M leave spider
na ge ímè-y ná làmndá yé-y
HYP HUM bury-3M ASSC elephant mother-3M
ɗé ba na-y bòr gúnyé gèyl-ìy
NEG COM HYP-3M save spider health-3M
ba gúnyé na è jè tòb go
COM spider HYP go VENT want REF
dígrè-y gà
kill:FUT-3M Q
'Squirrel said that if he had known that, he would have left Spider to be buried together with the mother of elephant. Here he saved Spider, and Spider wants to kill him?'

The woman and the chicken

Narrated by Mr. Houmina Pinabeye, 1998

(1) tùmò go kara índwé ɗeŋlí gé
once REF people humankind:PL understand 3PL
kùb kạnya ame kè-gè ná tamá
language thing domestic GEN-3PL ASSC woman
tóŋ ɗeŋlí kùb kòrà kè-gè
certain understand language chickens GEN-3PL
'At one time, when humankind understood the language of domestic animals, a certain woman understood the language of chickens.'

(2) tamá-ŋ jé tòrò túg ni ná
woman-DEF throw chicken home LOC ASSC
tòrò-ŋ tèy karma yùg yùg
chicken-DEF peck children many (Ideophone)
'The woman raised a chicken at home and the chicken produced many chicks..'

(3) wèlè go jè yì kạnya tòrò
day REF IMPF pound thing hen
yó-ró-ŋ dèr kàràn-dò è ná
mother-3F-DEF carry children-3F go ASSC
tìnɗí to-ro ni jè dì-gé kasa
mortar bottom-3F LOC IMPF peck-3PL corn
'Each time she$_1$ was pounding, the old hen$_1$ carried her children under the mortar and they pecked corn.

(4)

tamá-ŋ	jè	tè-gè	hire
woman-DEF	IMPF	chase away-3PL	often

'The woman often chased them away.'

(5)

tùwà	tóŋ	pìnà	ná [pause]	jè	yì	dú
Sun	certain:F	one	ASSC	IMPF	pound	3F

kąnya	tòrò	yó-ró	è	jè	gé	ná
thing	hen	mother-3F	go	VENT	3PL	ASSC

karan-do	kolo	dé	gé	kasa-ŋ
children-3F	reason	eat:FUT	3PL	corn-DEF

'One day, when she$_1$ was pounding, the old hen$_2$ came with her chicks to eat the corn.'

(6)

ná	yàá	bé	kàràn-dò	na	ngu	gol
ASSC	tell	DAT	children-3F	HYP	2PL	see

gaw	go	kun-do	pìnà	tésí	ɗé-ŋ
well	REF	eye-3F	one	break	already-DEF

ná	da	ngù	kasa	ná	já	koloŋ
ASSC	eat:IMP	2PL	corn	ASSC	side	DEM:R

'So she said to her chicks: you see well that she is blind in one eye, so go and peck at the other side [that she does not see]'

(7)

tamá-ŋ	ɗeŋlí	ná	jè	wèy
woman-DEF	understand	ASSC	IMPF	turn

ín-dí-gè	pílá pílá
ASSC-GEN:PL-3PL	at the same time

'When the woman understood, she was turning around [the mortar] at the same time [as they did].'

(8)

tòrò	yó-ró	yà	bé-gé	na
hen	mother-3F	tell	DAT-3PL	ASSC

tamá-ŋ	nò	go	sìyą́	bùg	ìrà
woman-DEF	make	REF	bad	by nature	go:IMP

nga	dà	gùbù	cà-y	ni
1PL.INCL	PREP	trash area	head-3M	LOC

'The old hen told them: this woman is by nature nasty; let us go on top of the trash pile.'

(9)

tamá	dèr	tíndí	ná	mųndu	se
woman	raise	pestle	ASSC	silence	INCEPT

wàdì	ná	tòrò-ŋ	dìgrì
hit	ASSC	then-DEF	kill

'The woman quietly raised the pestle and beat the hen with it to death.'

(10) àlá sé yàá bé kàràn-dò na
then INCEPT tell DAT children-3F HYP
'Then she$_1$ told her$_2$ chicks . . . '

(11) yé dú-ngù posí-ŋ ɗe
mother GEN:PL-2PL insult-1SG THEN
ná ŋ jè lée-dú ná kasa
ASSC 1SG IMPF eat:FUT-3F ASSC corn
go ŋ yì háŋ
ASSC 1SG pound DEM:P
'Your mother has insulted me; therefore I am going to eat her with this corn I pounded.'

(12) tòrò kàràn-dò jé gé dú máàní na
hen children-3F throw 3PL 3F ANAPH HYP
'The chicks answered her thus'
(high tone on object **dú** because it follows high tone **gé**)

(13) na me léè yé
HYP 2F eat:FUT mother
dí-nì ná me jè má
GEN:PL-1PL.EXCL ASSC 2F IMPF die:FUT
lay
also
'If you eat our mother, you will also die.'

(14) tamá-ŋ sòndrí ná se ày tòrò è
woman-DEF fear ASSC INCEPT take hen go
ìm
bury
'The woman became scared, took the hen, and buried her.'

(15) nè máàní ba kamda go tùmó lèè
COP ANAPH COM women REF before eat
gé tòrò ɗé-ŋ
3PL hen NEG-DEF
'That is why women in the old times did not eat chickens.'

Hyena and Goat

Narrated by Mr. Houmina Pinabeye, 1998

(1) gònì dàgè ná tu
hyena 3PL ASSC goat
'Hyena and goat'

(2)

kur	wèlè-y	pìnà	gònì	dàgè	ná
place	lie:VN-3M	one	hyena	3PL	ASSC
tu	è gé	sègré	dà	cáaní	
goat	go 3PL	hunt	PREP	bush	

'One day Hyena and Goat went hunting in the bush.'

(3)

kàw	gé	gàg	tùwà	dùgì-gè	gílalé
walk	3PL	till	sun	drown-3PL	tiredness
pínyà	nè-gè				
also	make-3PL				

'They walked till the sun had drowned them and tiredness overwhelmed them.'

(4)

kìb	di-gè	hay	lay
mouth	GEN:PL-3PL	dry	also

'their mouths are also dry'

(5)

time	nè	gònì	nȩ̀y	bé	kolo
hunger	make	hyena	very much	DAT	reason
dìgrì	dú ìsą́n	ɗé			
kill	3F nothing	NEG			

'Hyena is very hungry because it did not kill anything.'

(6)

dàdù	tu-ŋ	lèé	kàsùma	ɓàl-dù
3F	goat-DEF	eat	feed	satisfy-3F

'As for Goat, it ate feed to its satisfaction.'

(7)

se	è	jè	gé	dà	tálwá	ni
INCEPT	go	VENT	3PL	PREP	pond	LOC
bé	kolo	na	ge	sà		kam(a)
DAT	because	HYP	3PL	drink:IMP		water

'then they came to a pond in order to drink water'

(8)

gònì	dà	kìrbé	kò-rò	ni	ná
hyena	PREP	thought	GEN-3F	LOC	ASSC
gèy	go	léè	tu-ŋ	ɓey	ba
want	REF	eat:FUT	goat-DEF	before	COM
sée	kama-ŋ				
drink:FUT	water-DEF				

'Hyena in its thoughts wanted to devour Goat before drinking water.'

(9) tu-ŋ gol go gonì kún-do jèn
goat-DEF see REF hyena eye-3F remain
téŋ
different
'Goat noticed that Hyena had different intentions . . .'

(10) ìrà-ngà dà kama dùrè-y ni
go:IMP-1DU.INCL PREP water inside-3M LOC
ba nga séè dày go
COM 1DU.INCL drink:FUT 3M REF
ɗínglé lay me ágè ísì go bòré
clear also 2F take:FUT bone REF white
koloŋ
there
'Let us go inside this water; we will drink the one that is clear, and you will take the white bone there'

(11) goni cál ba kama ni ná ɓàdì
hyena jump fall water LOC ASSC go after
nè ísì-ŋ càr
COP bone-DEF immediately
'Hyena jumped into the water and went immediately after the bone.'

(12) tu yàá bú-dù na
goat tell DAT-3F HYP
'Goat told her:'

(13) yú cà-rè dà kama te-y ni
put:IMP head-2M PREP water bottom-3M LOC
ba me ágè ísí-ŋ
COM 2F take:FUT bone-DEF
'plunge to the bottom of the water and you will get the bone'

(14) gònì sùm-rò se yí cà-rò
hyena be mad:VN-3F INCEPT put head-3F
kama te-y ni ná dusi kolo
water bottom-3M LOC ASSC sink because
sèn go nàlè kama ɗé
know REF swim:VN water NEG
'Foolish Hyena put its head at the bottom of the water and it sank because it did not know how to swim.'

(15) tu se yàá bú-dù na
goat INCEPT tell DAT-3F HYP
'Then Goat told her:'

(16) ŋ sèn toto go mé
1SG know completely REF 2F
gèy léè-ŋ àlá mé hábe
want eat:FUT-1SG but 2F find:FUT
kìrè-níŋ ɗé
way-DEF NEG
'I know very well that you want to devour me, but you will not be able to.'

(17) láà gìdìrè go dà kama te-y
eat:IMP moon REF PREP water bottom-3M
ni ɓàlà-mè dàŋ ŋ jè òdì
LOC suffice:IMP-2F 1SG 1SG IMPF go
'Eat the moon that is at the bottom of the water; it should satisfy you; as for me, I am going away.'

(18) nè máàní ba goni jè ɗe ná
COP ANAPH COM hyena IMPF leave ASSC
tu ɗé-ŋ
goat NEG-DEF
'That is why Hyena does not leave Goat alone.'

Story of a theft

Narrated by Mr. Houmina Pinabeye, 1991

(1) wàyŋgùlú táŋ pìnà
morning DEM:F one
'One morning'

(2) kumno se mìl, mìl, míl
cloud raise thick, dark (about the clouds)'
'there were thick clouds'

(3) pói kúsíge dàgè ná tamą́-y ná
Poi Kusige 3PL ASSC wife-3M ASSC
gé ná ísàn go lèé túŋ
3PL ASSC nothing REF eat:VN home
ni ɗé
LOC NEG
'Poi Kusige and his wife had nothing to eat at home'

(4) kasa kín-dí pìna pínyà túŋ ni ɗé
corn eye-3M one even home LOC NEG
'there wasn't even one grain of corn at home'

(5) kumno se bá ongi
God INCEPT fall rain
'It started to rain' (God has pushed something from her belly, folk etymology)

(6) póì kúsíge sèn ísàŋ pìnà
'Poi Kusige know nothing one
go na-y né go na-y
REL COMP-3M make:FUT REF COMP-3M
lámdè ná dòlò bé karan-di
cook gruel ASSC gruel DAT children-3M
ɗé
NEG
'Poi Kusige did not know with what he was going to cook gruel for his children.'

(7) ày bùgú kàb-ìy ni an ná kumno
take bag hand-3M LOC leave ASSC God
kam-dì
water-3M
'he took a [50kg] bag in his hands [and] he left with the rain'

(8) ba se è dà kúso bayndí kè-y
COM INCEPT go PREP field man GEN-3M
ni da kàrgà túgú ni
LOC PREP behind compound LOC
è póì jè tèmlé wén bùgú
go break:PL VENT corn fill bag
'there he went into somebody's field behind the compound, broke off corn, filled his bag'

(9) njárnjár go na-y è je túŋ ni
when REF HYP-3M go VENT home LOC
ná kumno-ŋ se bà̦y
ASSC rain-DEF INCEPT cease
'Just as he came home, the rain stopped'

(10)

dày	bay	go	kúsó-ŋ	è	na-y	gólè
3M	man	REF	field-DEF	go	HYP-3M	see:FUT

tèmlé	kè-y	ná	gol	bayndí	gàŋ-dì	dà
corn	GEN-3M	ASSC	see	man	foot-3M	PREP

kúso	ni
field	LOC

'When the owner of the field went to see his corn, he saw foot tracks in his field'

(11)

tab	jè	gàrma-ŋ	gàgàk	è	jè	ná
follow	VENT	traces-DEF	until	go	VENT	ASSC

dà	túgú	pói	kúsígè	kè-y
PREP	house	Poi	Kusige	GEN-3M

'He followed the footsteps until he arrived at the compound of Poi Kusige.'

(12)

tey	pói	kúsíge-ŋ	tòn-ìy	na
call	Poi	Kusige-DEF	asked-3M	HYP

'He called Poi Kusige and asked him:'

(13)

gàrmà	háŋ	nè	kò-m	ɗé	ba
footsteps	DEM	COP	GEN-2M	NEG	COM

ne	wèy	kè-y	ba	è	jè
COP	who	GEN-3M	COM	go	VENT

pói	tèmle	kò-nòŋ	háŋ	gà
break:PL	corn	GEN-1SG	DEM:P	Q

'If those footsteps aren't yours, whose are they, then? who came to break off my corn like that?'

(14)

pói	kúsíge-ŋ	se	mąy	na-y
Poi	Kusige-DEF	INCEPT	deny	HYP-3M

sèn	go	na-y	àn	kwáni	ná
know	REF	HYP-3M	leave	outside	ASSC

kúmno	kam-di	háŋ	ɗé
God	water-3M	DEM	NEG

'Poi Kusige denied that he knew, that [he] had not left in this rain'

(15)

gí	àn	kwáni	ná	kúmno	kam-di
2M	leave	outside	ASSC	God	water-3M

háŋ	ɗé	lay	tèmle	màyfò-y	dà
DEM	NEG	also	corn	hair-3M	PREP

mbùlúm	ni	háŋ	gà
chin	LOC	DEM:P	Q

'If you did not leave in this rain, is that not a hair of corn on your chin?'

(16)

dìgì	ba	gí	poy	jè	tèmlè
2M	COM	2M	break:PL	VENT	corn

kò-nòŋ
GEN-1SG

'It is you who broke my corn.'

(17)

nè	dàŋ	ɗé	na	gí	gèy	pìyạ̀	ná
COP	1SG	NEG	HYP	2SG	want	even	ASSC

ŋ	je	wále	kus-iŋ
1SG	IMPF	swear:FUT	body-1SG

'It is not me, if you want, I will swear.'

(18)

ɗá	wala	kusu-m	bàb	ɗé
leave:IMP	swear:IMP	body-2M	all	NEG

'Do not swear for nothing'

(19)

nga	é	ná	kùrmbàlò	tìmè-y
1DU.INCL	go:FUT	ASSC	chief	front-3M

ni
LOC

'we will go with it before the chief'

(20)

se	è	gé	da	kùrmbàló-ŋ	tìmè-y
INCEPT	go	3PL	PREP	chief-DEF	front-3M

ni
LOC

'They went in front of the chief.'

(21)

kùrmbàlò	tòn	pói	kúsíge	na
chief	ask	Poi	Kusige	HYP

'The chief asked Poi Kusige:'

(22)

dìgì	gí	kòy	tèmlé-ŋ	gèsé
2M	2M	steal	corn-DEF	or

gí	kòy	ɗé	gà
2M	steal	NEG	Q

'Was it you who stole the corn, or was it not?'

(23)

pói	kúsíge-ŋ	se	mąy	na-y	kòy
Poi	Kusige-DEF	INCEPT	deny	HYP-3M	steal

tèmlé-ŋ	ɗé	na-y	àn	kwáni	ná
corn-DEF	NEG	HYP-3M	leave	outside	ASSC

kúmno	kam-di	na	ɗé
God	water-3M	HYP	NEG

'Poi Kusige denied that he stole the corn. He claimed that he did not leave in the rain.'

(24)

à	bayŋdí-ŋ	yàá	dí	na	na-y	gol
but	man-DEF	tell	3M	HYP	HYP-3M	see

tèmlè	màyfò-y	na	mbùlù-m	ní-ŋ
corn	hair-3M	HYP	chin-2M	LOC-DEF

'but the man said that he apparently saw corn hair on your chin'

(25)

kà[w]	ngà	túg	kò-m	ni	gólè
go:IMP	1DU.INCL	home	GEN-2SG	LOC	see:FUT

kùní	kùlè-ndì
home	interior-3M

'let's go to your home [and] we will see the interior of the house'

(26)

se	è	gé	da	túgú	pói
INCEPT	go	3PL	PREP	home	Poi

kúsíge-ŋ	kè-y
Kusige-DEF	GEN-3M

'They went to the house of Poi Kusige.'

(27)

dòb	gé	kùní	kùlè-ndì	ni	ná
enter	3PL	house	interior-3M	LOC	ASSC

'They entered the house and'

(28)

hàb	gé	tèmlè	wén	bùgú	lay
find	3PL	corn	fill	sack	also

'they found corn filling the sack'

(29)

gàrbá	pói	kúsíge	kè-y
shoes	Poi	Kusige	GEN-3M

'and the shoes of Poi Kusige'

(30)

ná	kama	njòbnjòb	lay
ASSC	water	dripping	also

'with water dripping also'

(31) ne mánì ba kàra túgú
COP ANAPH COM people village
sèn gé go na pɓ́ì kúsíge
know 3PL REF HYP Poi Kusige
na jè kóy tèmlè kè-gè
HYP IMPF steal corn GEN-3PL
'And that is how people of the village know that it is Poi Kusige who steals their corn.'

Story of a hunt

Narrated by Mr. Houmina Pinabeye, 1998

(1) kíya dàgè ná ólkusíŋ è gé dà
Kiya 3PL ASSC Olkusin go 3PL PREP
segré
hunt
'Kiya and Olkusin went on a hunt.'

(2) è kè-gè go se géŋ ná
go GEN-3PL REF INCEPT change? ASSC
kíya hím kàjé so lay
Kiya gather throwing knife:PL two also
ìlú pìnà lay
stick one also
'When they went, Kiya gathered up two knives and one stick'

(3) dày ólkùsiŋ áy tàbál lay ná
3M Olkusin took lance also ASSC
kàjé poriŋ
throwing knife:PL four
'Olkusin took one lance and four throwing knives'

(4) è gé segré-ŋ hàb gé bisí
go 3PL hunt-DEF find 3PL antelope'
'they went for the hunt [and] they found an antelope.'

(5) dày kíya way-wi bisí-ŋ in
3M Kiya launch-PL antelope-DEF xxx
mbàtmbàt kàb-ìy án jé dí bisí
miss:PL hand-3M leave throw 3M antelope
kàb-ìy om-du gàrmà tóòmé
hand-3M catch-3F times many
'Kiya threw at the antelope many times, but missed.'

(6) ólkúsìŋ jé bisí-ŋ jé-dú dòŋlo-ro
Olkusin throw antelope-DEF throw-3F thigh-3F
ni
LOC
'Olkusin threw at the antelope; he threw at her thigh'

(7) bìsí-ŋ gír è da kámá tálúa kíbì ni
antelope-DEF run go PREP water pond mouth LOC
ná bá mànì
ASSC fall there
'The antelope ran away, went to the edge of a pond, and collapsed there.'

(8) ólkùsìŋ tab kàrgà-rò ké è hab-du kúsíoŋ
Olkusin follow back-3F till go find-3F ground
tòprí-dú ná tàbàl kè-y
kill-3F ASSC lance GEN-3M
'Olkusin followed behind her till he found her on the ground [and] killed her with his lance.'

(9) dày kíyà se e jé
3M Kiya INCEPT go VENT
è jé na ge kíse írà
go VENT HYP 3PL share:FUT EXCL
'Kiya started to come; he came in order to share.'

(10) dày ólkùsiŋ se ya bé-y na
3M Olkusin INCEPT say DAT-3M HYP
dìgì gí nò mbúlo
2M 2M COP clumsy
'Olkusin told him: you are clumsy'

(11) ladá bìsí kò-nòŋ ná
touch:IMP antelope GEN-1SG ASSC
kà-m ɗé
hand-2M NEG
'Do not touch my antelope with your hands.'

(12) kíya sé jé í màní na
Kiya INCEPT throw ASSC:3M ANAPH HYP
'Kiya replied to him like that:'

(13) nga e jé túm ba
1DU:INCL go come together COM
gi dìgrì bìsà-ŋ ba
2M kill game-DEF COM
ŋ kése únù-m ɗé gà
1SG share:FUT ASSC-2M NEG Q
'we came together, and you killed the game, but am I not to share it with you?'

(14) gi kése ná kà-m ɗé
2M share:FUT ASSC hand:2M NEG
'you will not share'

(15) gi láde ná kà-m ɗé
2M touch:FUT ASSC hand:2M NEG
'you will not touch it'

(16) òlkúsíŋ yá bè-y mánì
Olkusin tell DAT-3M ANAPH
'Olkusin told him like that'

(17) kíyá-ŋ se dèr te-y ír
Kiya-DEF INCEPT retrieve buttock-3M stand
kàrgà-nì
back-3M
'Kiya went back and remained behind'

(18) òlkùsíŋ wél bìsí-ŋ ná kóli
Olkusin skin antelope-DEF ASSC everything
sáar dí je ndám kàb-ìy
attach 3M VENT well-packed (Ideoph) hand-3M
ni òdì je ná túgù
LOC leave VENT ASSC home
'Olkusin skinned the antelope, packed it well, and brought it home.'

(19) dày kíyá-ŋ ír tè-y bándà
3M Kiya-DEF stand buttock-3M here and there
dà cáaní-ŋ kolóŋ gàgàgàgà
PREP bush-DEF there long time
'Kiya remained there in the bush for a long time'

(20)	túwa	nóm	dóbe	í	(índì)	màní
	sun	appear	set down	with	him	there
	kín	jé	ɗé	kásyá	né-y	í [ndì]
	return	VENT	NEG	shame	make-3M	ASSC:3M

'The sun set with him there, he didn't return, he was ashamed'

(21)	ne	ɗálàŋ	kùlòŋ-dò				
	COP	night	belly-3F				
	ɓèí	ba	áy	je	kìb-ìy	e	je
	still	COM	take	VENT	mouth-3M	go	VENT

'It was only in the middle of the night that he took his courage and returned'

(22)	kàjé	kè-y	go
	throwing knife:PL	GEN-3M	REF

'His throwing knives that

(23)	bòy	cánì-ŋ	hàb[p]	hábe	ɗé	tùm
	throw	bush-DEF	find	find:FUT	NEG	together
	lay					
	also					

'he had thrown in the bush he did not find.'

(24)	me	pyą	e	jè	ná	ɗé
	what	small	go	VENT	ASSC	NEG

'He didn't bring even a small thing'

(25)	tùm	lay	bìsà	pína	pią́
	together	also	dead game	one	small

'Not even one animal killed'

(26)	kàb-íy	ni	ɗé	tùm	lay
	hand-3M	LOC	NEG	together	also'

'There was nothing in his hands.'

(27)	kára	aswí-y	tú	kúlón-dó
	people	laugh-3M	village	belly-3F

'People laughed at him in the village'

The woman who betrayed her husband

Narrated by Mr. Houmina Pinabeye, 1998

(1)

tàmá	jé	kudo-ro	te-y
woman	throw	husband-3F	buttocks-3M

'a wife betrayed her husband', lit. 'woman threw away her husband's buttocks'

(2)

dà	túgú	tóŋ	ni	ná [pause]	gáw
PREP	village	INDEF:F	LOC	ASSC	hunter
kóŋ	ná	tamą́-y	tòb	gé	kusi-gè
certain:M	ASSC	wife-3M	like	3PL	body-3PL
néỳ					
very much					

'In a village a certain hunter sorcerer and his wife loved each other very much.'

(3)

bàyndí-ŋ	jè	è	sègré	ná	tìgrí	
man-DEF	IMPF	go	hunt	ASSC	kill:PL:VN	
kàrgé	sò	ɗéŋ	sùbù	kura	kį́nyé	
wild animals	two	or	three	rabbit	COLL	
bísí	kį́nyé	nasú	bísí	kį́nyé	ná [pause]	
antelope	COLL	gnu	antelope	COLL	ASSC	
jè	è	jè	kèsì	jáy	bé	tamá
IMPF	go	VENT	share	part	DAT	wife
túg	ni	lay	jay	kóŋ		
compound	LOC	also	part	certain:M		
jè	ą́y	ná	kasa	lay	gùnà	lay
IMPF	take	ASSC	corn	also	peanuts	also

'Each time the man went for a hunt, he killed two or three wild animals, rabbits, small antelopes, gnu antelopes; he shared some with his wife at home, and some he bartered for corn and peanuts.'

(4)

ísaŋ	pìnà	dèl-dù		kul	kùlen-di	
nothing	one	surpass-3F		home	belly-3M	
ni	ɗé	hàb	dú	kąnya	ɓàl	cé
LOC	NEG	find	3F	thing	suffice	like that

'She did not lack anything inside the house; she had everything in sufficient quantity.'

(5)

tamą́-ŋ	ba	kùb-rò	hamli	síɗé
wife-DEF	COM	mouth-3F	light	too much

'The wife had too light a mouth.'

(6) kaŋya pet go jè kàl túg
thing all REF IMPF pass compound
ni ná [pause] jè yàá kwánì bé
LOC ASSC IMPF tell outside DAT
karan-do kamda
friends-3F women
'Everything that was going on at home she would tell to her women friends'

(7) kudo-ro-ŋ jè ɗeŋlí kolo ką́nyé
husband-3F-DEF IMPF hear word certain:PL
kwáni ná [pause] yàá ísaŋ ɗé
outside ASSC tell nothing NEG
'Despite the fact that her husband heard certain things outside, he did not say anything.'

(8) wèlè pìnà ná gèy na-y
day one ASSC want (Ng.) HYP-3M
gísè-dù
try:FUT-3F
'One day he wished to test her.'

(9) ɗe-du jaŋ jè wèl dú kuná ná
leave-3F quietly IMPF sleep 3F sleep ASSC
an dí è om dùbàngú yó-ró
leave 3M go catch sheep mother-3F
ná mundu wàl
ASSC silence slaughter
'He left her quietly while she was asleep, left the room, [and] caught an old sheep in silence and slaughtered it.'

(10) càg dí kùbàrò kúsíyòŋ è ná gàg
spread 3M blood ground go ASSC until
sùgyá go kul kàrgà-y ni
grass REF house behind-3M LOC
'He spread the blood on the ground [and] went with it up to the grass behind the house.'

(11)

wel	dí	dùbàngú	kólí	se	gày
skin	3M	sheep	completely	INCEPT	open

kùlòn-dò	wàl-wì	cà-rò	ná	gàn-dò
belly-3F	cut-PL	head-3F	ASSC	leg-3F

dàw	ná	sí-ró	tum	saar	ná
put together	ASSC	flesh-3F	together	attach	ASSC

kùyò	jé	dà	mbóló	ni
mat	throw	PREP	granary	LOC

'He skinned the sheep, opened its belly, cut its head and limbs, reunited them with its meat, rolled it in a mat, and threw the whole thing into the granary.'

(12)

ná	se	è	jè	hìndì	tamą́-y
ASSC	INCEPT	go	VENT	wake up	wife-3M

kuná	ni
sleep	LOC

'And then he came and woke up his wife.'

(13)

yàá	bú-dú	na	ŋ	án	kwánì
tell	DAT-3F	HYP	1SG	leave	outside

ba	ŋ	jìb	cà-nìŋ	ná	kòyè	ba
COM	1SG	bump	head-1SG	ASSC	thief	COM

ŋ	dìgr-ìy
1SG	kill-3M

'He told her: leaving the house I bumped against a thief and killed him.'

(14)

à	jè	gulá	kùbàrò	go	bòy
go:IMP	VENT	look:IMP	blood	REF	pour

dà	kúsìnyoŋ	ba	ŋ	sáde	cáaní
PREP	ground	COM	1SG	clean:FUT	ALL

ɓéy
still/yet

'Come and see the blood spread on the ground before I clean it.'

(15)

se	yàá	na-y	jé-y	dà	tòmbòsò
INCEPT	say	HYP-3M	throw-3M	PREP	grass spc.

dùré-y	ni	dà	sóyó	te-y	ni
inside-3M	LOC	PREP	tamarind	bottom-3M	LOC

'He said he threw him in the grass under the tamarind tree.'

(16) cib-du kàbú nę́y ná yàá bé
pierce:PL-3F hand very much ASSC tell DAT
bayndí ɗé
man NEG
'He prohibited her from telling anybody'

(17) è gé kùl ni wèl gé kùná [kùni]
go 3PL room LOC sleep 3PL sleep
'They went into the room and slept.'

(18) kur wèl kay ɗé ɓey ná tamá
place pass finish NEG still ASSC woman
na du è sógú ni
HYP 3F go toilet LOC
'Before the day ended [while it was still dark], the wife pretended that she was going to the toilet.'

(19) àlá gìr è yàá kolo-ŋ bé kùrmbàlo
lo run go tell word-DEF DAT chief
'But instead she ran and informed the chief.'

(20) kùrmbàlò se bòg [bòy] kara kè-y
chief INCEPT send people GEN-3M
ná wáyngulu na ìrà gé hàbà
ASSC morning HYP go:IMP 3PL find:IMP
gáw-ŋ́
hunter-DEF
'The chief sent his people in the morning to go and find the hunter.'

(21) na ìrà gùl-gè kur go
HYP go:IMP show:IMP-3PL place REF
jé tumadu kòyè kè-y màní-ŋ
throw corpse thief GEN-3M there-DEF
'He should show them the place where he had thrown the corpse of the thief.'

(22) bayndí-ŋ an è kàl mbóló ày jé
man-DEF leave go climb granary take VENT
sìí-ŋ gìl-gè
meat-DEF show-3PL
'The man left and went into the granary, took the meat, and showed it to them.'

(23)

se	tey	tamą́-y	dà	kara	kùrmbàlò
INCEPT	call	wife-3M	PREP	men	chief
kè-y	tìme	dì-gè	ni	ná	yàá
GEN-3M	front	GEN:PL-3PL	LOC	ASSC	tell
bùdù	na				
DAT-3F	HYP				

'Then he called his wife in front of the chief's men and told her:'

(24)

ge	yàá	bé-ŋ	na	kìb-rè	hamli
HUM	tell	DAT-1SG	HYP	mouth-2F	light
nę́y	ba	ŋ	gìsì-mè	gùdá	káŋ
very much	COM	1SG	test-2F	today	DEM

'I was told that you do not keep secrets, so I have tested you today'

(25)

me ɓàl	go	wesé	cà-nìŋ	ɗé
2F able	REF	hide:VN	head-1SG	NEG
ná ìrá	túgú	ka-re	kè-gè	
ASSC go:IMP	home	parents	GEN-3PL	

'You cannot cover up for me, so go to your parents.'

(26)

kàsìyà	nè	tamá-ŋ	néy	ná	
shame	make	woman-DEF	very much	ASSC	
se	sar-wí	kąya	kò-rò	òdì	è
INCEPT	attach-PL	thing	GEN-3F	leave	go
túgú	ka-ro				
home	parents-3F				

'Since the woman was very much ashamed, she tied up her stuff, left, and went to her parents.'

References

Bright, William, ed. 1992. *Encyclopedia of linguistics*. Oxford: Oxford University Press.

Frajzyngier, Zygmunt. 1965. An analysis of intensive forms in Hausa verbs. *Rocznik Orientalistyczny* 29.2.31-51.

Frajzyngier, Zygmunt. 1977. The plural in Chadic. In *Papers in Chadic Linguistics*. Ed. by Paul Newman and Roxanna Ma Newman. Leiden: Afrika-Studiecentrum, 37-56.

Frajzyngier, Zygmunt. 1985. Truth and the indicative sentence. *Studies in Language* 9.2.243-254.

Frajzyngier, Zygmunt. 1987. Ventive and centrifugal in Chadic. *Afrika und Übersee* 70.1.31-47.

Frajzyngier, Zygmunt. 1989a. *A Grammar of Pero*. Berlin: Reimer.

Frajzyngier, Zygmunt (ed). 1989b. *Current progress in Chadic linguistics*. Amsterdam: Benjamins.

Frajzyngier, Zygmunt. 1991. The de dicto domain in language. In *Approaches to Grammaticalization*. Ed. by Elizabeth C. Traugott & Bernd Heine. Volume I. Amsterdam & Philadelphia: Benjamins. 219-251.

Frajzyngier, Zygmunt. 1995. Two complementizers of Lele. In *Studia Chadica et Hamitosemitica*, Akten des Internationalen Symposions zur Tschadsprachenforschung, Johann Wolfgang Goethe-Universität, Frankfurt am Main, 6-8 Mai 1991 Ed. by Dymitr Ibriszimow & Rudolf Leger, with Gerald Schmitt. Cologne: Rüdiger Koeppe, 163-170.

Frajzyngier, Zygmunt. 1996. On sources of demonstratives and anaphors. In *Studies in Anaphora*. Ed. by Barbara Fox. Amsterdam & Philadelphia: John Benjamins, 169-203.

Frajzyngier, Zygmunt. 1997a. Grammaticalization of number: From demonstratives to nominal and verbal plural. *Linguistic Typology* 1: 193-242.

Frajzyngier, Zygmunt. 1997b. Bidirectionality of grammaticalization. In *African Linguistics at the Crossroads.* Papers from Kwaluseni. Ed. by Robert K. Herbert. Cologne: Rüdiger Köpe, 17-38.

Frajzyngier, Zygmunt, & Jan Mycielski. 1998. On some fundamental problems of mathematical linguistics. In *Mathematical and computational analysis of natural language.* Ed. by Carlos Martin-Vide. Amsterdam & Philadelphia: Benjamins, 295-310.

Garrigues, Martine. 1974. Kaselem mabaymu. Etude d'un village lélé (Tchad). Thèse présentée pour le doctorat d'ethnologie. Paris: Université René Descartes.

Garrigues-Cresswell, Martine, avec la participation de Christophe Weibegué. 1981. *Livre de lecture lélé.* Sarh: Centre d'études linguistiques.

Giono, Jean. 1929. *Colline.* Paris: Grasset.

Hoffmann, Carl. 1971. Provisional Check List of Chadic Languages. *Chadic Newsletter.* Special issue. January 1971.

Leben, William. 1989. Intonation in Chadic: An overview. In Frajzyngier 1989b, 199-217.

Matthews, Peter. 1997. *The Concise Oxford Dictionary of Linguistics.* Oxford: Oxford University Press.

Newman, Paul. 1977. Chadic Classification and Reconstruction. *Afroasiatic Linguistics* 5/1.

Newman, Paul. 1990. *Nominal and verbal plurality in Chadic.* Dordrecht: Foris.

Newman, Paul. 1992. Biu-Mandara Languages. Chadic languages. East Chadic languages. In Bright 1992.

Palmer, Frank. 1987. Truth Indicative? *Studies in Language* 11.1-2, 206-210.

Simons, Pamela C. N.d. Lele-French Dictionary. Unpublished.

Simons, Pamela C. 1982. ne . . . ba marking in Lele. *Studies in African Linguistics* 13.3, 217-229.

Simons, Pamela C., & Donald A. Burquest. 1986. Some comments on nasalization in Lele. *Journal of West African Languages* 16.2, 34-38.

Weibegué, Christophe. N.d. *Sagesse lélé.* Sarh: Centre d'études linguistiques.

Weibegué, Christophe. N.d. *Syllabaire lélé.* Sarh: Centre d'études linguistiques.

Weibegué, Christophe. 1982. *Conversations et textes lele. Complément au syllabaire lélé.* Sarh: Centre d'études linguistiques.

Weibegué, Christophe. 1992. *Système phonologique du Lélé.* Mémoire en vue de l'obtention de la Licence ès Lettres, Université du Tchad.

Weibegué, Christophe, & Pierre Palayer. 1982. Lexique lele-français. Sarh: Centre d'études linguistiques.